Political Power
in Pre-Colonial Buganda

Eastern African Studies

Revealing Prophets
Edited by David M.
Anderson & Douglas H.
Johnson

*East African Expressions
of Christianity*
Edited by Thomas Spear &
Isaria N. Kimambo

The Poor Are Not Us
Edited by
David M. Anderson &
Vigdis Broch-Due

Potent Brews
Justin Willis

Swahili Origins
James de Vere Allen

Being Maasai
Edited by Thomas Spear &
Richard Waller

Jua Kali Kenya
Kenneth King

*Control & Crisis in Colonial
Kenya*
Bruce Berman

Unhappy Valley
Book One: State & Class
Book Two: Violence &
Ethnicity
Bruce Berman &
John Lonsdale

Mau Mau from Below
Greet Kershaw

*The Mau Mau War
in Perspective*
Frank Furedi

*Squatters & the Roots
of Mau Mau
1905–63*
Tabitha Kanogo

*Economic & Social Origins
of Mau Mau 1945–53*
David W. Throup

Multi-Party Politics in Kenya
David W. Throup
& Charles Hornsby

Empire State-Building
Joanna Lewis

*Decolonization & Independence
in Kenya 1940–93*
Edited by B.A. Ogot
& William R. Ochieng'

Eroding the Commons
David Anderson

*Penetration & Protest in
Tanzania*
Isaria N. Kimambo

Custodians of the Land
Edited by Gregory Maddox,
James L. Giblin &
Isaria N. Kimambo

*Education in the Development
of Tanzania 1919–1990*
Lene Buchert

The Second Economy in Tanzania
T.L. Maliyamkono
& M.S.D. Bagachwa

*Ecology Control &
Economic Development in
East African History*
Helge Kjekshus

Siaya
David William Cohen
& E.S. Atieno Odhiambo

*Uganda Now
Changing Uganda
Developing Uganda
From Chaos to Order
Religion & Politics in East Africa*
Edited by Holger Bernt
Hansen & Michael Twaddle

*Kakungulu & the Creation
of Uganda 1868–1928*
Michael Twaddle

Controlling Anger
Suzette Heald

Kampala Women Getting By
Sandra Wallman

*Political Power in Pre-Colonial
Buganda*
Richard J. Reid

Alice Lakwena & the Holy Spirits
Heike Behrend

*Slaves, Spices & Ivory in
Zanzibar*
Abdul Sheriff

Zanzibar Under Colonial Rule
Edited by Abdul Sheriff &
Ed Ferguson

*The History & Conservation of
Zanzibar Stone Town*
Edited by Abdul Sheriff

Pastimes & Politics
Laura Fair

*Ethnicity & Conflict
in the Horn of Africa*
Edited by Katsuyoshi Fukui
& John Markakis

*Conflict, Age & Power
in North East Africa*
Edited by Eisei Kurimoto
& Simon Simonse

*Property Rights & Political
Development in Ethiopia & Eritrea*
Sandra Fullerton Joireman

*Revolution & Religion
in Ethiopia*
Øyvind M. Eide

Brothers at War
Tekeste Negash &
Kjetil Tronvoll

From Guerrillas to Government
David Pool

*A History of Modern Ethiopia
1855–1991*
Second edition
Bahru Zewde

*Pioneers of Change
in Ethiopia*
Bahru Zewde

Remapping Ethiopia
Edited by W. James, D.
Donham,
E. Kurimoto & A. Triulzi

*Southern Marches
of Imperial Ethiopia*
Edited by Donald L.
Donham & Wendy James

*A Modern History
of the Somali*
Fourth edition
I.M. Lewis

* forthcoming

Political Power in Pre-Colonial Buganda

Economy, Society & Warfare in the Nineteenth Century

RICHARD J. REID
Asmara University

James Currey
OXFORD

Fountain Publishers
KAMPALA

Ohio University Press
ATHENS

James Currey Ltd
73 Botley Road
Oxford
OX2 0BS

Fountain Publishers
PO Box 488
Kampala

Ohio University Press
Scott Quadrangle
Athens, Ohio 45701, USA

1 2 3 4 5 06 05 04 03 02

British Library Cataloguing in Publication Data
Reid, Richard, J.
Political power in pre-colonial Buganda : economy, society
& warfare in the nineteenth century. - (Eastern African
studies)
1. Uganda - History - To 1890
I. Title
967.6'1'01

ISBN 0-85255-451-6 (James Currey Cloth)
0-85255-450-8 (James Currey Paper)
99-02-297-0 (Fountain Publishers Paper)

Library of Congress Cataloging-in-Publication Data
available on request

ISBN 0-8214-1477-1 (Ohio University Press Cloth)
0-8214-1478-X (Ohio University Press Paper)

Typeset in 10/10½ pt Baskerville
by Long House Publishing Services, Cumbria, UK
Printed and bound in Britain
by Woolnough, Irthlingborough

Contents

Acknowledgements	ix
Maps	xi-xiv

One
Introduction

Introduction	1
The political & territorial kingdom	3
The 'wars of religion' & the establishment of colonial rule	5
The secondary literature	7
The aims & structure of the book	13

Part One   17

Land & Livelihood
A survey
of the Ganda economy

Two
Land & Cultivation   19

Introduction	19
The kingdom of the banana	22
Crops & plantations in the nineteenth century	25
The historical & cultural environment	31
'Queer foods' & famine in the nineteenth century	32
Political turmoil & agricultural collapse in the 1880s & 1890s	36

Three
Herdsmen & Hunters   40

Pastoralism in pre-colonial Buganda	40
Herds & herdsmen in politics & society	45
The consumption & utilization of livestock	50
Livestock disease in the late nineteenth century	52
The economics & culture of hunting in pre-colonial Buganda	55

The hunt for ivory 60
Hunters of river & lake: the political economy of fishing 64
The waters of Ganda history 68

Four
Crafts & Craftsmen 70
Barkcloth production 70
The expansion of the barkcloth economy 72
Iron & the state 76
Pre-colonial pottery culture 86

Summary of Part One 89

Part Two 93

Labour & Liberty
The state
& its human resources

Five
Labour & Taxation 95
Taxation in the nineteenth century 98
Working for the state: the organization of public labour 103
The highways of Buganda 107
Mwanga's reign: an abuse of the system 111

Six
Slavery 113
Acquisition of slaves 116
Women & slavery 119
Slave hierarchies 124

Summary of Part Two 131

Part Three

133

Buyers & Sellers
Developments in commerce

Seven
Domestic & Regional Trade
Local commerce & commodities
Pre-colonial currencies

135
136
144

Eight
The Growth of Long-Distance Trade
Beginnings
Coastal merchants in Buganda
Commercial change in the late nineteenth century

149
149
151
160

Summary of Part Three
171

Part Four

175

War & Peace

Nine
The Rise & Decline
of Ganda Military Power
Ethos & motivation
Military growth before the nineteenth century
'Restless warfare': conquest & consolidation under Kamanya
Stability & decline in the nineteenth century, 1:
the reign of Suna
Stability & decline in the nineteenth century, 2:
the reign of Mutesa

177
179
185
190

194

198

Ten
Developments in Organization, Tactics & Weaponry

Developments in Organization,
Tactics & Weaponry   206
    Structures & hierarchy   206
    Structures & tactics   210
    The new elite: from bodyguard to vanguard 214
    The tools of war: weaponry & the role of firearms 218

Eleven
Lake Victoria, the Final Frontier

Lake Victoria,
the Final Frontier   227
    Canoe construction   228
    Naval developments c. 1700 – c. 1840   231
    The growth of naval power from c. 1840   234
    'The helots of Uganda': the Sesse & Ganda naval expansion 237
    The expansion of ports   240
    The organization of the fleet   243

Summary of Part Four   249

Twelve
Conclusions

Conclusions   251

Sources & Bibliography   259
Index   267

Acknowledgements

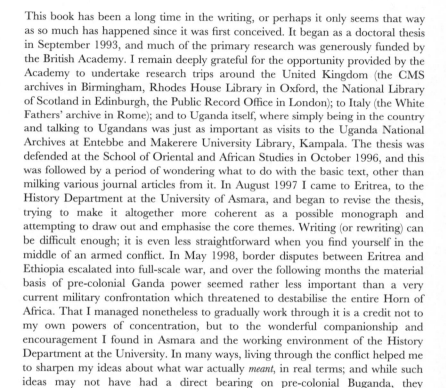

This book has been a long time in the writing, or perhaps it only seems that way as so much has happened since it was first conceived. It began as a doctoral thesis in September 1993, and much of the primary research was generously funded by the British Academy. I remain deeply grateful for the opportunity provided by the Academy to undertake research trips around the United Kingdom (the CMS archives in Birmingham, Rhodes House Library in Oxford, the National Library of Scotland in Edinburgh, the Public Record Office in London); to Italy (the White Fathers' archive in Rome); and to Uganda itself, where simply being in the country and talking to Ugandans was just as important as visits to the Uganda National Archives at Entebbe and Makerere University Library, Kampala. The thesis was defended at the School of Oriental and African Studies in October 1996, and this was followed by a period of wondering what to do with the basic text, other than milking various journal articles from it. In August 1997 I came to Eritrea, to the History Department at the University of Asmara, and began to revise the thesis, trying to make it altogether more coherent as a possible monograph and attempting to draw out and emphasise the core themes. Writing (or rewriting) can be difficult enough; it is even less straightforward when you find yourself in the middle of an armed conflict. In May 1998, border disputes between Eritrea and Ethiopia escalated into full-scale war, and over the following months the material basis of pre-colonial Ganda power seemed rather less important than a very current military confrontation which threatened to destabilise the entire Horn of Africa. That I managed nonetheless to gradually work through it is a credit not to my own powers of concentration, but to the wonderful companionship and encouragement I found in Asmara and the working environment of the History Department at the University. In many ways, living through the conflict helped me to sharpen my ideas about what war actually *meant*, in real terms; and while such ideas may not have had a direct bearing on pre-colonial Buganda, they nevertheless allowed me to approach an understanding of reality, rather than simply studying the abstract. At any rate, perhaps I can use the excuse of 'war stress' to explain away the book's remaining flaws.

Over the last few years many people have contributed, directly or indirectly, wittingly or otherwise, to the writing of this book. My doctoral supervisor at SOAS, Professor Andrew Roberts, did more than anyone to create something readable. His penetrating advice, the often staggering breadth of his knowledge, his attention to detail, as well as his appreciation of the broader picture, both emboldened and, at times, overwhelmed me; he took someone with little more than raw enthusiasm and attempted to transform him into a 'scholar'. I am deeply indebted to him. Also at SOAS, Dr Dave Anderson was always on hand with crucial and friendly advice. I should also like to record my thanks to Professor Robin Law at the University of Stirling. Robin has had little direct involvement in the writing of this book, but as my undergraduate tutor at Stirling, it was he who introduced me to Africa and its history. Robin's own high scholarly standards, moreover, have been the model against which I have measured my own efforts, however unwise this may be. Dr John McCracken, also at Stirling, offered invaluable advice to an ambitious and somewhat clueless undergraduate when the project was in its infancy. My heartfelt thanks also go to Professor John Rowe.

Friendships outside the too-often cosseted world of academia are as important as those inside it in the preparation of a work of this kind, and thus I mention the following, in no particular order, by way of gratitude. First, I must mention Claire Brittain and her father Ronnie, for only they know how much they have contributed to the successful completion of this book, and much more besides. Numerous people in Uganda did more than they will ever know to enhance my appreciation of their country and to assist in the research: in particular I should like to mention Richard Ssewakiryanga, Adolf Mwesige and Ephraim Kamuhangire. Many others, too numerous to mention individually, in Kampala, Jinja and Kabarole (Toro) district, made my stay in Uganda such an enlightening and enjoyable experience. Other friendships straddled both Africa and Europe, and special mention must go to Henri and Valerie Medard, Torbjorn Engdahl, Grace Carswell and Cato Lund. In London, Neil Elder was a constant and invaluable friend and companion, while his family offered boundless hospitality; I also enjoyed the company of Andrew Burton at SOAS. I must also mention Vina Bartholomew, my grandmother, who was never in London or Uganda but did not need to be; she gave me much valued support nevertheless, as did both David and Tory.

In Eritrea, I have made many good friends who have had little or nothing to do with the writing of this book but who did more than they might ever realise to help keep the author sane, an important prerequisite to its completion. Alex Last and I have spent many – perhaps too many – evenings together in Asmara chewing the historical fat and many other kinds of the stuff; if such companionship is sometimes taken for granted, it is perhaps because its value is ineffable. There are many others of whom the same can be said, and I should mention Boris Sartori, the warmest and most generous friend one could hope to have. Into the same category must come Tracey Hopps, John Weakliam, James Racicot and Sergey Kotelnikov. Friends such as Tsegezeab, Petros and Ibrahim only come along once in a while, but I have enjoyed their company immensely while we have all been here together. Iyob Abraha has also been a good friend. In the History Department itself, I have been privileged to work with Drs Uoldelul Chelati and John Distefano, and with Tekeste Melake, Tekeste Habtu and Habtai Zerai. 'Lul' and John in particular have been good friends as well as colleagues; both have stimulated many of my ideas and encouraged me directly and indirectly through countless conversations over the last 3 or more years. My deep and eternal gratitude goes, penultimately, to Hannah Petros.

I would like to dedicate this book to my parents, Anne and Victor Reid.

RJR
Asmara

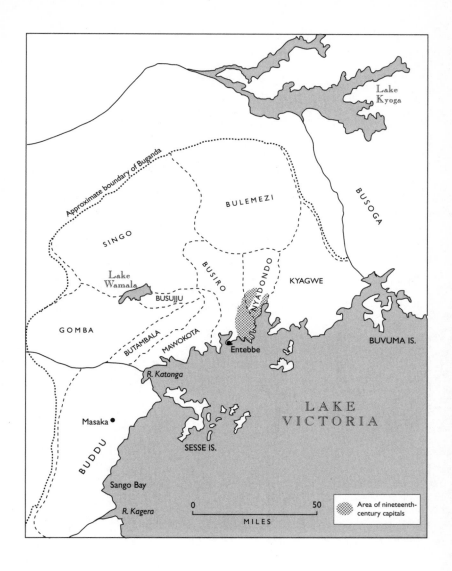

Map 1 Buganda on the Eve of Colonial Rule

xi

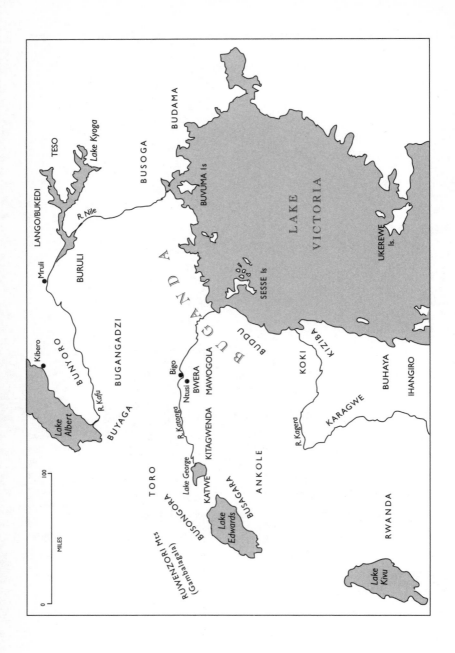

Map 2 The Northern Lake Region

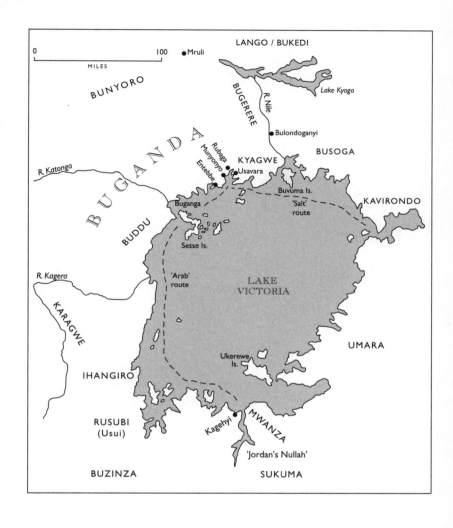

Map 3 Buganda & Lake Victoria in the Nineteenth Century

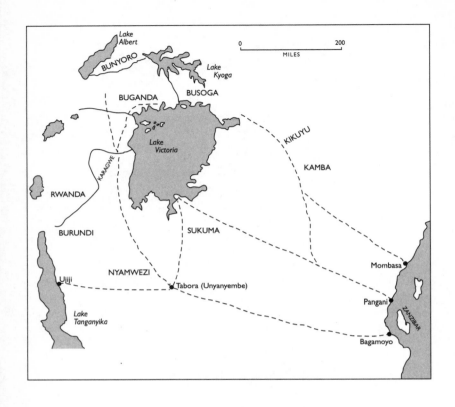

Map 4 Land Trade Routes in the Late Nineteenth Century

One

Introduction

Buganda was situated on the northern shore of Lake Victoria. By the beginning of the nineteenth century it stretched between two major rivers: the Nile to the east, on the far bank of which were the people known loosely as the Soga, and the Kagera to the southwest, beyond which lay the kingdoms of Karagwe and Kiziba. As such Buganda possessed an extensive shoreline, and by the nineteenth century the kingdom had incorporated numerous islands in the northern waters of the lake, notably the Sesse group. The kingdom's lacustrine position was a key factor in its historical development. To the north was Bunyoro: as a result of the Uganda Agreement of 1900,[1] the northern boundary of Buganda was considered to be the Kafu river, which flows between lakes Albert and Kyoga. The pre-colonial Ganda boundary probably lay some 20 or 30 miles to the south of the Kafu.[2] One other significant river ran through the kingdom, namely the Katonga, while numerous smaller rivers and streams, many of them slow-moving swamps at various times of the year, made up the Ganda drainage system. They are indicative of the moisture with which the area has been blessed. The southern part of Uganda enjoys quite high rainfall, particularly during the two major wet seasons, which are between February and June and between October and December. In the nineteenth century, as now, Buganda was markedly greener than many of its neighbours, even in the more pastoral areas in the north and west. The areas bordering the lake are particularly rich in vegetation. The landscape is characterized by regular and evenly spaced hills, between which often lie the sluggish streams mentioned above. Further north and west, the land becomes slightly less hilly, and this terrain facilitates the keeping of livestock in greater numbers than is possible closer to the lake. Throughout nineteenth-century Buganda,

---

[1] See the section below outlining the religious wars and the establishment of colonial rule.
[2] This gave rise to the controversy of the 'lost counties', lost, that is, by Bunyoro at the hands of the British and the Ganda at the end of the nineteenth century.

1

agriculture was combined with the keeping of livestock. Broadly speaking, however, agriculture was predominant in the east and south, and cattle in the north and west. Although the Ganda were not unfamiliar with crop failures and drought, the region is in general characterized by fertile and well-watered soil, capable of supporting a fairly dense population. Recognition of this crucial fact is the first, and perhaps the most important, step towards understanding the material basis of Ganda power and the growth of the kingdom.

The aim of this book is to examine the material basis of Ganda political power, in both internal and external terms, in the pre-colonial period, with particular reference to the nineteenth century. It is our purpose to trace the changes wrought upon the kingdom's economic base and to survey the kingdom's material state on the eve of colonial rule. Fundamentally, therefore, the book is an examination of economic and military change in pre-colonial Buganda, and as such it is not a political study. Rather, it represents an attempt to place the political kingdom, which as we shall see is well documented, in its economic and material context, and to examine what lay behind it in economic, social and military terms. As will be clear from our survey of the secondary literature, some understanding of these dimensions of the pre-colonial Ganda state is essential, as otherwise our appreciation of this most complex of African polities remains one-dimensional. The history of Buganda has been interpreted almost wholly in terms of its political organization, from a centrist and elitist approach. Important aspects of Buganda's past have been ignored, while early analyses have remained largely unchallenged. It is hoped that this book, while acknowledging and building on the efforts of previous scholarship, will contribute to our understanding of what Ganda power meant in real terms, how the kingdom used the resources at its disposal and met the challenges which confronted it, and, ultimately, the limitations to its dominance of the East African lake region.

Before we move into the substance of the argument, however, it is necessary to provide a brief outline of Ganda political structures and the changes brought to bear on them, for two main reasons. Firstly, and perhaps most obviously, many of the developments and organizational changes which the book examines cannot be understood without some knowledge of political Buganda, as examined by numerous scholars over the past 40 years. Secondly, one of the core arguments of the book is that the political history of the pre-colonial state should be read in a new light as a result of the examination of social, economic and military developments. It is precisely because of the earlier concentration on Ganda political history that the book focuses on issues which, while not overtly concerned with politics or chieftainship, are critical to a clearer comprehension of the political state. It is hoped, therefore, that the well-documented political changes of the nineteenth century might be placed alongside those spheres of Ganda history examined here and that a new synthesis may emerge.

2

The political & territorial kingdom

Buganda is believed to have emerged in its modern sense around the fifteenth century, its appearance probably in some way connected to the migration of western Nilotic Luo-speakers into the lacustrine region. It remained a comparatively small and insignificant kingdom for the first 200 years of its discernible history, prone to attack from its much stronger northerly neighbour Bunyoro, although this period was clearly crucial in the formation of identity as well as of the means of self-defence. During the seventeenth century, the kingdom embarked on a journey of territorial expansion, developing a centralized political system and a powerful military ethos and organization; it also took advantage of the internal problems of Bunyoro. This expansion continued steadily until the early nineteenth century, as we will see in a later chapter. During this period the Ganda pushed their frontiers north towards the Kafu river, east towards the Nile, and south and west towards the Kagera river and the plains approaching the Ruwenzori mountains. We will see in detail in the ensuing analysis how particular areas of expansion were critical to the growth of the Ganda state. Here it is sufficient to mention that the incorporation of Kyagwe in the early eighteenth century and that of Buddu a few decades later were among the most significant, in terms of the resources which were thus acquired and the strategic positions thus gained, in the kingdom's development. By the early nineteenth century, the kingdom had reached its greatest territorial extent.

Buganda was originally composed of a number of clans – by the nineteenth century there were around 50 – at the head of which was the *kabaka*, king or 'head of the clan heads'. The single most important theme of Ganda political history over the 300 years before the nineteenth century began was the gradual shift of political and territorial power from the *bataka* or clan heads to the *kabaka*. The latter was able, by eroding the freehold estates (*butaka*) of the hereditary clans, to control more directly land and thus political appointments. The *batongole*, the chiefs appointed directly by the *kabaka*, became the main agents of government in Buganda, while the *bataka* were increasingly marginalized from the political process. The position of the *kabaka* thus grew more powerful, so that by the end of the eighteenth century he had power of appointment and dismissal over all the major chieftainships in the kingdom. Importantly, non-clan land was in the gift of the *kabaka*, as it were, and could not be inherited; thus the Ganda political system was founded to a large extent on competition, between ambitious chiefs seeking the favour of the *kabaka*. Life at the royal court – which was, superficially at least, the political hub of the kingdom – was characterized by jostling for position and marked, dangerous and often fatal intrigue.

The *kabaka* himself was the holder of a secular office. The position of *kabaka* did not belong to any one clan; rather, the *kabaka* took the clan of his mother. By the nineteenth century, Buganda appeared to outsiders to be an autocracy dominated at all levels of social, political and economic life by the *kabaka*. His power over chieftainship appeared to demonstrate this, as did the unconditional loyalty and constant displays of affection demanded from his ministers. While the *kabaka* was without question an important and potent figure in many spheres of Ganda life, however, his authority should not be exaggerated; as was the case in a number of other African societies at this time, much of the personal authority of the ruler was more apparent than real. It is clear that at various points during the nineteenth century, one or two of the *kabaka*'s chiefs had as much political power as the *kabaka* himself. To some extent, as we shall see, a situation of this kind had developed by the late 1880s, and indeed the overthrow of Mwanga in 1888 had many precedents.

Most of the principal royally appointed chiefs were provincial governors. By the second half of the nineteenth century, Buganda was divided into a number of *ssaza*s (usually translated as 'counties'), which are listed below along with the title of governing chief.

Busiro – the *mugema*
Busujju – the *kasujju*
Butambala – the *katambala*
Gomba – the *kitunzi*
Mawokota – the *kaima*
Kyadondo – the *kago*
Kyagwe – the *sekibobo*
Bulemezi – the *kangawo*
Buddu – the *pokino*
Singo – the *mukwenda*

Several other important chieftainships, notably the *kimbugwe* and the *katikiro*, were not territorial titles; it was possible, however, for one man to hold more than one position. Thus the *katikiro* might also hold the title of *pokino*, as was the case for some time during the reign of Mutesa. In general, the *katikiro* was noted as being the second most powerful position in the kingdom after the *kabaka* himself. The title was usually described by contemporary Europeans as being that of a prime minister or supreme judge. In theory, all of these powerful posts might be filled by lowly sub-chiefs or even ordinary peasants (*bakopi*) who had come to the notice of the *kabaka* through economic, military or political endeavour (or intrigue). This will be demonstrated throughout the ensuing analysis, and it will be seen that military achievements and particular branches of economic activity were lauded by such a process. The *kabaka* was thus seen to have absolute control over the careers of the *bakungu* or high-ranking territorial chiefs.[3]

The Ganda are noted for having compiled a substantial kinglist by the end of the nineteenth century, and particular rulers are regarded in both the indigenous sources as well as European accounts from the late nineteenth century as having been instrumental in the process of the kingdom's expansion. The mythical Kintu and his no less improbable successor Chwa I are viewed as the founding fathers of the kingdom, and can

---

[3] There has been some debate among historians concerning the definition of such terms as *batongole* and *bakungu*; the discussion here represents an attempt at neutrality. See for example Southwold 1961; Twaddle 1969, 1974b; Low 1971: 15–17.

probably be associated with the migration mentioned above. As we shall see throughout the following chapters, Kintu in particular was by the nineteenth century associated with almost everything 'good' concerning the kingdom of Buganda and may be viewed as the most potent symbol of Ganda identity. In the early to mid-sixteenth century, Nakibinge appears as the leader who heroically battled against vastly superior Nyoro forces during an invasion which almost resulted in the destruction of the small Ganda kingdom. Out of the ashes of Nakibinge's defeat arose a wiser and stronger people, and the lessons learnt during this period served to elevate Nakibinge himself to almost divine status; certainly his reign seems to have been something of a watershed, as we shall see below. In the eighteenth century, several rulers stand out as successful expansionists and state-builders, including Mawanda, who probably presided over the advance of the eastern frontier to the Nile, and Junju, who annexed Buddu and established the southern frontier along the Kagera. In the nineteenth century, Buganda was governed successively by Kamanya, perhaps the last great soldier-statesman in the kingdom's history, Suna, who presided over the beginnings of dramatic commercial and military change, and Mutesa, who struggled with the burdens of a glorious past to maintain the kingdom's position in an increasingly hostile world. It is the reign of Mwanga in which much of our story culminates, for he was the last ruler of pre-colonial Buganda and proved singularly unequal to the tasks which faced him, although the crises of the period also went some way towards ensuring a harsh historical judgement, again as we shall see.

It is of course impossible to date with any certainty the reigns of Mutesa's predecessors, and the problems of the existing kinglist have been highlighted by David Henige.[4] The basic chronology used in this book does not differ greatly from that tentatively constructed by M.S.M. Kiwanuka, which was in turn based on Apolo Kagwa's kinglist,[5] as indeed most subsequent scholarship has been. Kiwanuka's dynastic chronology was calculated at 30 years per generation, which is probably as accurate as we can expect. None the less, the criticisms recently made by Christopher Wrigley are sound.[6] In particular, this book takes note of Wrigley's estimates for the reigns of nineteenth-century rulers. Thus, it is likely that Suna became *kabaka* around 1830, and died in c. 1857; Semakokiro and Kamanya probably reigned between the late 1790s and c. 1830.[7]

The 'wars of religion'
& the establishment of colonial rule

The political history of Buganda in the second half of the nineteenth century is intertwined with the introduction of foreign religions. A brief

[4] Henige 1980.
[5] See Kagwa 1971: Appendix 3. Kagwa was the *katikiro* of Buganda from 1889 to 1926; much of his work was based on oral history, as well as his own experiences at the centre of Ganda politics.
[6] Wrigley 1996: see Chapter 2 in particular.
[7] Ibid.: 229.

outline of these developments is required here as they form the backdrop to much of the ensuing analysis; the politico-religious history of Buganda in the late 1800s has received some excellent coverage in recent years, and the works mentioned below in the review of the secondary literature provide much greater detail than is offered here. Kabaka Suna, who probably reigned between c. 1830 and 1857, first became acquainted with Islam in the mid-1840s, with the arrival in Buganda of the first merchants from the East African coast. In 1862, the first Europeans to reach the kingdom, John Speke and James Grant, made Kabaka Mutesa aware of Christianity. Between this time and the establishment of the British Protectorate in 1894, politics in Buganda, at least in the capital, were increasingly influenced by allegiance to either Islam or Christianity, and even within the latter, to either Protestantism or Roman Catholicism. At the same time, indigenous belief systems, the worship of *balubaale* or deities and spirits, remained influential. Mutesa declared himself to be Muslim for much of the 1860s and 1870s, but the situation became more volatile with the arrival of the first Anglican missionaries, members of the Church Missionary Society, in 1877. French Catholics, members of the White Fathers, reached Buganda in 1879, much to the dismay of the Anglicans, and henceforward matters were complicated by the presence of two competing Christian denominations. Moreover, the growing Egyptian and Sudanese presence to the north was a source of concern. Visitors from the province known as 'Equatoria', governed in succession by Sir Samuel Baker, General Gordon and Emin Pasha, reminded Mutesa in the late 1870s of the potential military threat from this direction.

In his last years, Mutesa attempted to play the different groups off against one another, and for a period at least was able to remain more or less in control of the powerful new influences entering his kingdom. To Mutesa, who until his twilight years was above all a pragmatic ruler, each group represented something which Buganda could utilize to its advantage. The coastal traders were agents of the vital international trade system, connected ultimately to Zanzibar, which carried to Buganda cloth and guns among other commodities. The *kabaka* was thus keen to curry favour with those whom he saw as the representatives of the Zanzibari sultan. The European missionaries were similarly ambassadors of a powerful technological culture whose presence in Buganda could only lead to the kingdom's advancement. It may be argued that recognition of these potential material gains was the sole reason behind Mutesa's tolerance of such disruptive influences.[8]

In the meantime, however, Islam, Catholicism and Protestantism were all claiming converts from among the chiefs in the Ganda capital. This was especially true among the young and militant chiefs and pages of the royal court with whom Mutesa and, after the latter's death, Mwanga were increasingly surrounding themselves. In the mid-1880s, Mwanga, whose handling of state matters was even less assured than that of his ailing father, attempted to violently crush allegiance to foreign religions and indulged in a ferocious persecution of Christians in particular. By 1888,

[8] See also Reid 1999a.

however, political camps identifying themselves with one or other of the new religions had developed in the capital. Ostensibly at least, one of the justifications for the coup which removed Mwanga in 1888 was his intolerance of foreign religions. Although he was reinstated in 1889, following the brief reigns of the puppet-rulers Kiwewa and Kalema, these politico-religious camps remained in conflict with one another until the British imposed a settlement, using a mixture of military force and negotiation, in the mid-1890s. The British presence in the area was at first represented by the Imperial British East Africa Company (IBEAC), to which a royal charter had been granted in 1888. The IBEAC, headed in Buganda by Frederick Lugard, signed a treaty with Mwanga in December 1890, five months after an Anglo-German treaty had confirmed that 'Uganda' was within the British sphere. Financial difficulties led to the withdrawal of the IBEAC in 1893; it was replaced by a provisional protectorate under Sir Gerald Portal. A little over a year later, the Liberal government of Lord Rosebery formally assumed the protectorate over Buganda; this was extended in 1896 to include Bunyoro and the kingdoms to the west. The culmination of this process was the Uganda Agreement of 1900, which established the pattern of relations between the British and the native council, and dealt with the questions of law, taxation and land tenure. Overall, Buganda's role in assisting the British to establish hegemony throughout the region of modern Uganda sowed the seeds of resentment among the surrounding peoples, and indeed distorted a clear understanding of nineteenth-century Ganda history for many years.

The secondary literature

Buganda is well known to historians of Africa, even though the kingdom came to the attention of literate society comparatively late in the pre-colonial period. But the manner in which the early observations were made seems to have had an enduring influence over the historiography of Buganda. The explorers Speke and Grant arrived in the kingdom just as Mutesa's reign was beginning, and their admiration of the complex and highly bureaucratic socio-political structure was echoed by the escalating numbers of Europeans who passed through Buganda in various capacities in the 1870s and 1880s. Adventurers, missionaries and, eventually, colonial administrators were struck by Buganda's hierarchical organization, the like of which, it was frequently suggested, did not exist anywhere else in eastern Africa. After the obligatory caveat concerning the kingdom's essential savagery, it was widely held that the Ganda possessed an intelligence and a capacity for self-improvement which held out great potential. This was demonstrated by the alacrity with which so many Ganda embraced Christianity in the 1870s and 1880s. Indeed, the basic framework of Buganda's political structure was used as the model of government for the whole Uganda Protectorate from 1900.

This fascination with political Buganda has continued to shape scholarship on the kingdom throughout the twentieth century, and especially as the study of African history expanded. In spite of the enormous volume of material produced by historians relating to Buganda over the last few decades, it is possible to identify certain strands of thought and established patterns of approach. It will be seen, thus, that quantity does not necessarily mean variety and, while certain aspects have attracted the attention of writers over the years, critical spheres of Ganda history have been neglected. Buganda, which undoubtedly ranks alongside other states with large historiographies, such as Asante, Dahomey and the Zulu, has been overtaken by studies of these. Political history, and in particular that of the last quarter of the nineteenth century, has been made the primary focus of study among the analysts of Buganda's past, the implication being that social or economic change could not be studied either because there was none, or because the evidence for it was irretrievably lost. It is hoped that the current work demonstrates that its sources, none of which represents a new find and all of which have been used by other historians, do contain an enormous amount of data germane to studies of this kind.

The distinction between primary and secondary sources is often blurred, particularly in the period of the late nineteenth and early twentieth centuries. The definition depends on the purpose for which the source is used. Thus, much early historiography may be described as 'primary source material' as it includes work written by those who observed or directly participated in many of the events and developments they purported to describe. The same can be said of those early writers who based their work on recorded oral history and data provided by a wide range of informants. The historiography of Buganda, therefore, really begins with Robert Ashe, a CMS missionary who observed at first hand the events of the late 1880s and early 1890s, and his work represented the earliest attempt to place these events in a historical context.[9] In the years following the establishment of the protectorate, another CMS missionary, John Roscoe, and the *katikiro* of Buganda, Kagwa, likewise sought to compile both historical and ethnographic surveys of Buganda, using oral traditions and a number of informants.[10] These are also, therefore, among the most valuable primary sources. Others followed during the 1930s, by which time the *Uganda Journal* offered a new outlet for historical debate. Ham Mukasa and John Gray had important articles published,[11] and B.M. Zimbe and J. Miti also wrote books based on oral history and on their own experiences during the last years of the nineteenth century.[12]

---

[9] Ashe 1889, 1894. Earlier travellers had made limited investigations into Buganda's past, but Ashe's work constituted a more serious exploration: see also Speke 1863b, especially Chapter 9; and Stanley 1878: I, especially Chapter 14.

[10] I have used translations of Kagwa's three main works: [tr. E.B. Kalibala, ed. M.M. Edel], *Customs of the Baganda* (New York, 1934); [tr. J.Wamala], 'A Book of Clans of Buganda' (MS in Makerere University Library, Kampala, c. 1972); and *Kings* (see bibliography for a full citation. This is a translation of the first half of Kagwa's book only, but it covers the era relevant to the present study). Roscoe's most important works are: *The Baganda: an Account of their Native Customs and Beliefs* (London, 1911); and *Twenty-five Years in East Africa* (Cambridge, 1921).

[11] Gray 1934, 1935; Mukasa 1934, 1935.

[12] Again, translations have been used: J. Miti, 'A History of Buganda' (MS in the School of Oriental and African Studies Library, London, 1938); B.M. Zimbe [tr. F. Kamoga], 'Buganda ne Kabaka' (MS in Makerere University Library, Kampala, 1939). Miti,

After the Second World War, there was a considerable surge in interest in Ganda history, and much research was undertaken at Makerere University and the East African Institute of Social Research. Pre-colonial Buganda attracted the attention of a number of writers in the 1950s, including A.H. Cox, Abu Mayanja, R. Oliver, D.A. Low and Wrigley,[13] who shared an interest in late nineteenth-century political developments. Wrigley and C. Ehrlich alone began to research the kingdom's economic past, albeit the impact of colonial rule on what was perceived to be a static indigenous economy.[14] They were basically concerned to show that the pre-colonial economy was almost completely lacking in dynamism, and that only with the establishment of the protectorate did conditions permit any kind of economic change or growth. I shall challenge this long-standing view in due course. In the late 1950s and the 1960s, Martin Southwold, A.I. Richards, L.A. Fallers and P.C.W. Gutkind also undertook research into socio-political Buganda, often from a historical-anthropological standpoint.[15] The work done during this time was critical in establishing a professional approach to the Ganda past; it also established the major themes of study with regard to nineteenth-century Buganda, namely the role of kingship, political office and the religious wars of the late 1880s and early 1890s.

During the 1960s and early 1970s, further ground-breaking work on pre-colonial Buganda – and in particular on the politics of the late nineteenth century – was undertaken, notably by J.A. Rowe, Kiwanuka and Michael Wright.[16] Rowe and Kiwanuka especially pushed Ganda historiography forward in their analyses of Luganda source materials and the kind of pre-colonial past which could be reconstructed using such sources. The immense potential for historians of nineteenth-century Buganda was made clear through their efforts. At the same time, on a wider regional level, a number of scholars were turning their attention away from a purely political interpretation of the past and towards the development of the nineteenth-century economy and the role of commerce. In so doing they were building on the earlier efforts of Wrigley and Ehrlich. Thus, B.W. Langlands published work on Ganda crops;[17] J. Tosh, G.W. Hartwig and M. Kenny on the growth of trade;[18] and G.N. Uzoigwe and C.P. Kottak

---

[12] (cont.) according to Kiwanuka, was a 'Muganda historian, a contemporary of Kaggwa and a product of the royal court in the 1880s and 1890s': see Kiwanuka's 'Introduction' to Kagwa 1971: xlvi. Zimbe was also a junior court page during the 1880s; he later joined the CMS mission and became a clergyman.

[13] These writers came from varying backgrounds: Oliver, Low and Wrigley were trained scholars, Cox was a colonial government official and Mayanja was a political activist, the first secretary-general of the Uganda National Congress. See: Cox 1950; Mayanja 1952; Oliver 1959; Wrigley 1959a; Low 1957; Low & Pratt 1960. Low also published a number of essays, which later appeared together in Low 1971.

[14] Wrigley 1957; Ehrlich 1956.

[15] Southwold 1961, 1966, 1968; Richards 1964, 1966. L.A. Fallers produced a number of essays: see Fallers 1959, 1964. For P.C.W. Gutkind see 1960, 1963.

[16] Rowe 1964b, 1966, 1969; Kiwanuka 1966, 1967, 1971; Wright 1971.

[17] See two articles in particular: Langlands 1966a, 1966b.

[18] See Tosh 1970. Gerald Hartwig's interests lay primarily with Ukerewe, but his examination of lake commerce raised a number of questions pertinent to the Ganda position: see Hartwig 1970, 1976; Kenny 1974, 1979. See also Austen 1971 and Holmes 1971. The work of R.W. Beachey should also be mentioned in this context, although his analysis is often weakened by over-generalization and factual error: see Beachey 1962, 1967, 1976.

on the role of markets and the material basis of state power.[19] R.D. Waller's MA dissertation on the pre-colonial Ganda economy[20] also opened up a wide range of critical issues which earlier scholars had either overlooked or considered unimportant; his analysis of commercial changes in the late nineteenth century has to some extent acted as a signpost for the relevant parts of the current work. During the 1970s, too, a number of works on Buganda's immediate neighbours emerged, such as Uzoigwe, C. Buchanan and E.I. Steinhart on Bunyoro, S.R. Karugire on Ankole, I.K. Katoke on Karagwe and D.W. Cohen on Busoga.[21]

Above all, however, the most popular topics of examination in Ganda historiography have been the lives of Mutesa and Mwanga, and more especially the political and religious factions at their courts, culminating in the religious civil wars of that period. Critical as such themes are, they have tended to overshadow equally significant spheres of the Ganda past to the detriment of our appreciation of this complex society. To some extent this imbalance was offset with the appearance in 1971 of Kiwanuka's major monograph on pre-colonial Buganda. Indeed, in many ways the scope of his *History of Buganda* has yet to be rivalled. But, while it is the best we have had to date, it is one of the aims of the current work to address certain key questions overlooked by Kiwanuka. He repeatedly reminds us of Buganda's power and prestige, which the book in some ways aims to underpin, and of how the neighbouring peoples regarded the Ganda with awe and terror, but we are scarcely told why. We need to analyse the structure and motivation of the army and fleet which so terrorized the region. It is also necessary to examine long-term trends and the policy objectives of successive rulers in the nineteenth century, as well as the economic and material bases of Ganda expansion and the critical role played by expanding commerce. The main strength of *A History of Buganda* is in its treatment of political history, and in this Kiwanuka offers often exemplary analysis; still, in a monograph covering seven centuries, more than a third is taken up with the last 20 years of the nineteenth century. In any case, after Kiwanuka's contribution, from around 1970 onward, research on pre-colonial Buganda suffered, largely because of political turmoil within Uganda itself, which only in recent years has subsided sufficiently to permit the renewal of academic enquiry within the country. Indeed, the study of Uganda's modern traumas has tended to take precedence over any pre-1900 investigation. The period between Amin's seizure of power in 1971 and Museveni's capture of Kampala in 1986 saw a suspension of research in Uganda itself, although certain scholars continued to publish work on Buganda, for example Michael Twaddle, W. Rusch, R.R. Atkinson, A.B.K. Kasozi, Henige and B. Ray.[22] Even here, for example, Ray and Twaddle had been to Uganda to undertake important research before the country became effectively closed to scholars. In general, the interests of these writers lay in analysing Ganda

[19] Uzoigwe 1972; Kottak 1972.
[20] Waller 1971.
[21] Uzoigwe 1973; Buchanan 1978; Steinhart 1981; Karugire 1971; Katoke 1975; Cohen 1972, 1977.
[22] Twaddle 1972; Rusch 1975; Atkinson 1975; Kasozi 1975; Henige 1980; Ray 1972.

kingship, the structure and ritual of royal authority, and the political and religious events of the late nineteenth century. With the exception of Rusch, whose work was based in large part on secondary sources, there was during the 1970s no further study of the pre-colonial material basis of power. Rusch's work, while thematically structured and thorough in its coverage of certain key issues, sought to offer a Marxist interpretation of the Ganda economy, notably, that the Ganda peasantry were trapped within an exploitative system operated by an indolent aristocracy. In the light of earlier work, for example that of Tosh and Hartwig, Rusch's approach was somewhat regressive.

Since the mid-1980s, comparative stability in Uganda has encouraged scholars such as Schiller,[23] Ray[24] and in particular Twaddle and Wrigley to renew academic study. Twaddle's work has established him, deservedly, as the leading scholar of late nineteenth-century Ganda political developments,[25] while Wrigley's most recent work is the culmination of four decades' enquiry into the pre-colonial past and the usefulness to the historian of 'traditional' Ganda accounts.[26] It is not the intention of the present work to supplant this scholarship, but rather to build upon it, correct some wrongly held assumptions, and offer alternative perspectives on the Ganda past to the conventional political histories. For example, most of the works already mentioned have something to say about military organization, but, as with the economic and commercial past, this is dealt with cursorily. This central topic of debate has become swamped by clichés, and few have seriously tried to analyse what Ganda military power actually amounted to. One exception is Twaddle, who has offered some insights into the organization of the army and the role of firearms;[27] moreover, as we shall see, he alone has attempted to explore the complexities of slavery and the slave trade.[28] But otherwise these areas of Ganda history have remained untouched, except by the most uncritical of analyses. Indeed, there seems to have been an assumption that, if Speke found Buganda a powerful state in 1862, then the kingdom must have been at the height of its power. Little attempt has been made to place the Ganda of 1862 in their historical or indeed geographical context, and Kiwanuka's account has remained the closest there is to such an approach for a quarter of a century, and his concern appears to have been to depict Buganda as undisputed master of all it surveyed and Mutesa as an unqualified success in everything he did.[29]

The omissions of the secondary literature are further highlighted when work on other parts of sub-Saharan Africa is considered. Inspiration can be drawn from the commitment and energy so evident in S. Feierman's study of the Shambaa,[30] and from the fine detail and detached analysis of R.C.C. Law's work on the Yoruba empire of Oyo in the seventeenth and

---

[23] Schiller 1990.
[24] Ray 1991.
[25] In particular, see Twaddle 1988a, 1988c, 1993.
[26] Wrigley 1996. Also see Wrigley 1974, 1989.
[27] In particular, Twaddle 1993: *passim.*
[28] Twaddle 1988b; see also Twaddle 1988a.
[29] For an earlier response to this, see Reid 1999a.
[30] Feierman 1974.

eighteenth centuries, a period and subject area for which the sources are hardly profuse.[31] Law's study on the 'slave coast' of West Africa is also exemplary in its treatment of domestic economies and the social and military dimensions of commerce.[32] I. Wilks's study of the Asante, primarily a work of political history, also offers much to historians of other parts of Africa in its treatment of commercial developments and communication networks.[33] Again in a West African context, mention should be made of A.G. Hopkins's work:[34] while the current book is not a study of economic history in this sense, it has drawn inspiration from Hopkins's considerable achievement. Work on social, commercial and military change in nineteenth-century Tanzania and Kenya should also be mentioned: although more than 30 years old, the collection of essays on Tanzania edited by A.D. Roberts, for example, is important as it explores historical themes either ignored or taken for granted in the context of Buganda.[35] This is also true of work on nineteenth-century Kenya, and on the Kamba in particular.[36] More recently, C.H. Ambler's study of central Kenya has taken this kind of study forward through its examination of the interaction between trade and the domestic economy.[37] In the context of long-distance trade and, in particular, the development of canoe transport, R. Harms on pre-colonial Congo provides a useful and instructive reference point.[38] The material basis of power and the organization of resources to meet external challenges are also themes which have been pursued in a southern African context, most recently in a fine study of Lesotho by E. Eldredge.[39]

Again, studies of armies, warfare and the background to military expansion in other parts of Africa have served as models or inspiration for the current work. Jeff Guy's work, for example, examines Zulu military expansion in remarkable depth,[40] while Kagame produced an admirably thorough study of the regiments, as well as the campaigns in which they were involved, of pre-colonial Rwanda.[41] In central Africa, Roberts's essay on the introduction and impact of firearms in Zambia raises issues and problems germane to much of sub-Saharan Africa in the nineteenth century.[42] But it is once again on West Africa that some of the best scholarship has been focused. Robert Smith in particular, in his excellent study of armies, tactics, weaponry and the ethos of warfare, was the pioneer of an approach to pre-colonial history which should surely be taken much further;[43] indeed, a number of other West Africanists have shown themselves willing to explore these subject areas.[44]

---

[31] Law 1977.
[32] Law 1991.
[33] Wilks 1975.
[34] Hopkins 1973.
[35] Roberts 1968. Roberts's own work on Mirambo and the Nyamwezi remains relevant.
[36] For example, Kimambo 1970; Jackson 1976.
[37] Ambler 1988.
[38] Harms 1981.
[39] Eldredge 1993; see also Beinart 1980.
[40] In particular, see Guy 1979, 1980.
[41] Kagame 1963.
[42] Roberts 1971.
[43] Smith 1989; Smith & Ade Ajayi 1971.
[44] See Falola & Law 1992; also Whitehead & Ferguson 1992.

The aims & structure of the book

In the present work I have attempted to fill in the gaps of the historiography, and to expand on a number of themes dealt with briefly by earlier scholars.[45] The fundamental rationale of the book is the ways in which Buganda organized its material and human resources in the pursuit of three central objectives: profit and the generation of wealth through both commerce and homestead production; internal cohesion; and external security. Each chapter is therefore concerned with both private enterprise and public life, and the book is not so much a study of the state in itself, but of the relationship between the state and its subjects, and between the state and its resources.

The book systematically examines the following topics, each concerned, in different ways, with these relationships and objectives. Part I deals with land and livelihood, in other words with production, a broad term I have used to include agriculture and animal husbandry, hunting and fishing, and the fabrics and metal industries. These activities were, collectively, the very basis of the growth of the Buganda kingdom, and I have attempted to develop the analyses ventured by a number of earlier scholars, notably Langlands, Wrigley and Richards. In general the importance placed on Ganda agriculture by earlier authors was implicit, rather than fully explained, and as such I attempt to make explicit the vitality of farming in pre-colonial Buganda; the kind of crops produced and in this connection regional variation; and the extent to which the productivity of the land was frequently offset by drought and subsequent crop failure. Alongside this, it is clearly essential to examine the roles played by fishing, hunting and livestock-keeping; these activities, like food production, had socio-political and commercial, as well as nutritional, dimensions. I endeavour to show that, in the 1870s and 1880s, Buganda's productive base was being undermined by cattle disease, drought and crop failure; I argue that these calamities were in fact more powerful determinants of the course of political and military events at this time than earlier authors have suggested. A similar approach is employed when examining the main industries of the Ganda: metal-working, fabrics and pottery. The importance of these occupations – and the ways in which they changed in the course of the nineteenth century – has been overlooked in the secondary literature. It is clear that the search for sources of iron influenced the nature and direction of Ganda expansion, but I also aim to demonstrate how this influence worked in practice. I examine the cultural, economic and social dimensions of activities such as iron-working, and attempt to show how iron was both a means and an end in the context of territorial expansion. I also seek to demonstrate how so seemingly mundane a material as barkcloth should be seen as one of the keys to Buganda's economic and indeed political strength in the lake region.

Part II sees a continuation of the general theme of the state's utilization of its resources. Here I focus on the organization of public labour in the construction of roads and buildings, the development of state taxation, and

[45] I have also attempted this in Reid 1997, 1998a, 1998b, 1999a.

the relationship between particular professional and social groups within the labour system. I argue that the organization of public labour was critical to the maintenance of the political establishment; it demonstrated the pursuit of internal cohesion, which was achieved by balancing individual commercial and productive freedom with an ethos of collectivity in certain spheres of public life. While the first part of this section considers the nature of 'free' labour, the second part deals with the institution of slavery and its importance to the economic and political life of Buganda. Here I develop themes which have been considered in detail by few historians, Twaddle being an exception. In addition, the critical issues of what slavery meant in its many manifestations, who was enslaved and the functions performed by slaves are examined.

We then move on in Part III to trade, both regional and long-distance, and here I develop some of the themes first examined by scholars such as Tosh and Waller a quarter of a century ago. We examine the growth and operation of commerce in greater detail than has previously been the case, and our study includes the range of goods traded, the development of pre-colonial currencies and the growth of the slave trade in the second half of the nineteenth century. I suggest that the Ganda were relatively un-restricted by centralized political control, and that participation in long-distance trade was not confined to chiefs and the powerful men of the kingdom. Perhaps the most important contribution which this section makes to our understanding of pre-colonial Buganda is in its examination of the role of commerce in the growth of the state. The Ganda were vigorous traders, and the kingdom to some extent owed its regional dominance in the nineteenth century to its commercial strength.

Yet commercial advantage often had to be protected and promoted through military action, and in Part IV we turn to military organization. I pursue in depth a number of themes which have been either taken for granted or simply ignored in the secondary literature, including the constitution of the army, the development of weaponry and the impact of firearms. I also analyse the role of militarism and war in Ganda history; the motivation behind war, for example, is a subject for too long ignored or treated uncritically by scholars. The army was critical to internal cohesion and the stability of the political system. Above all, I challenge the view that in the nineteenth century Buganda was all-powerful and that its neighbours regarded the kingdom with awe and dread. On the contrary, I argue that Buganda was in military decline after c. 1850, for a number of reasons, not least of which were internal political developments and, later on, the detrimental effects of what might be called the firearm cult. Finally, I draw together the themes of commercial expansion, military aspirations and, of course, the state utilization of resources to examine the Ganda on Lake Victoria, which may be termed the last frontier for the pre-colonial kingdom. As outlined above, a number of scholars have highlighted the importance of the lake as a trade route, notably Hartwig and Kenny. I take this theme further by examining the history of the canoe in Ganda military and economic history. I argue that the canoe fleet as developed in the nineteenth century had its origins in Buganda's ancient fishing communities, but was created in order to stem military decline on land

and to control the long-distance trade which had become so vital to the kingdom.

We have already noted how political turmoil in Uganda in the 1970s and 1980s is partly responsible for the failure to develop the research themes discussed above. This said, interest in pre-colonial history has diminished over the last 20 years or so, as will have been evident from the age of some of the scholarship cited above. That this is the case is due to a number of factors. Prominent among them is the renewed interest in the colonial period, engendered by the availability of archives and other source materials relating to this era since the 1970s. Conversely, confidence in the sources for the pre-colonial period has waned somewhat, with optimism about the possibilities of using recorded oral histories in the reconstruction of the pre-colonial past fading after the 1960s and being replaced by scepticism about the genuine historical value of such sources. In the case of Buganda, this scepticism is perhaps best and indeed most eloquently expressed in Wrigley's latest work.[46] It is, however, clear from my own use of such sources that outright pessimism at the end of the 1990s is as unwarranted as was, perhaps, the optimism of the 1960s. Unpublished archival material still yields many new data, in part because different questions are now being asked. Recorded oral 'traditions' and indigenous histories may demand greater scepticism in the reconstruction of political events, but they can be extraordinarily rich in the information they often inadvertently yield regarding broader social and economic patterns. If a recorded oral account is compared with an old photograph – a dubious comparison, admittedly, although old photographs may also be 'touched up' from time to time – then it is the background scene, rather than the foreground in closer focus, which can offer some of the richest data on the period it describes.

When dealing with European sources, Western contextualizations are clearly visible, especially in the earlier accounts describing political customs and institutions. Perhaps the most obvious example is the manner in which Mutesa was perceived as omnipotent, an absolute despot with whom no one dared disagree. Europe had only recently cast aside the notion of divine kingship, and European observers, imbued with the values associated with science and reason, assumed that Africa must still belong to that dark and savage era. They witnessed the highest chiefs in the land grovel in the dust before the *kabaka*; the court rang with cries of loyalty to the *kabaka* and reverent proclamations concerning the time-honoured authority vested therein. Only in the late 1870s a few recently arrived missionaries began to wonder if all of this was not some elaborate but meaningless court performance. Similar contextualizations occurred when Europeans observed the Ganda economy. Most travellers commented upon the apparent prosperity of the country: the abundance of luxuriant vegetation, the fertility of the soil and the seeming ease with which the Ganda won their livelihood from a freely giving environment. But these observations led Europeans to conclude that the Ganda economy was static; sometimes depicted as a soporific idyll, the economic system of the

---

[46] Wrigley 1996, especially Chapters 2 and 3.

15

kingdom was inherently unprogressive, while the people themselves were lazy and unwilling to aspire to anything greater than a regular supply of bananas. This was a one-dimensional view of a tropical production system. Representatives of the workshop of the world imposed, and their modern counterparts continue to impose, their own notions of economic progress on Buganda and tropical Africa more generally.

I find myself in the position, then, of disagreeing on a fundamental level with the views expressed by contemporary Europeans while relying on their evidence to reconstruct the past which they have witnessed. As we shall see, it is usually possible to pinpoint comments and observations which in fact contradict the overall conclusions of the witness. In the economic context, such evidence supports the thesis that the Ganda economy was in many aspects dynamic, that it exhibited signs of both change and continuity, and that it was certainly more complex than might initially be supposed. Unfortunately, as we have seen, extant scholarship has tended to overlook this,[47] assuming that only with the establishment of European administration and the development of large-scale export crops did the Ganda economy begin to 'expand' and 'progress'. Despite the wealth of economic and social data, 'however, the preoccupation of nineteenth-century observers with political organization is clear, and modern scholars have tended the follow the line of their gaze. In general, Europeans were more interested in Ganda political structures and the rationalization of kingship than in exchange or production; they were more likely to convey a sense of bloody and mindless violence when describing military activity, than to attempt to understand the complexity of military organization and the motives behind the waging of war. But the evidence to support an alternative history does exist, if one looks hard enough. Of course work of this kind is a gamble, as was suggested to the present writer by one senior scholar; the source material is not as straightforward as it is for a later period and on more overtly political developments. But, in the realm of historical enquiry, to remain stationary is eventually to go backwards.

It can be seen that selected areas of Buganda's past – crudely summarized, centralized political society – have received ample attention over the past 40 years. However, many critical themes have been ignored, or only partly and uncritically examined. Despite the decline in the study of the pre-colonial past, investigation in other parts of Africa – particularly West Africa – has indicated what still needs to be done and what can be done. Buganda still has much to offer the interested historian. The phenomena of Ganda organization, expansion and decline have needed further examination for some time. These themes – Ganda military structure and ethos, the role of commerce, economic development, the material basis of power – surely represent that which is special about Buganda in the nineteenth century.

---

[47] See Waller 1971, for a partial exception to this rule.

Part One

Land & Livelihood

A survey
of the Ganda economy

Two

Land & Cultivation

Introduction

Historians wishing to analyse changes in Buganda's pre-colonial domestic economy are to some degree frustrated by a lack of adequate source materials. There is some cold comfort to be taken from the fact that this is not an uncommon affliction. Studies of other regions of East Africa and indeed of West Africa, for which more detailed sources of greater antiquity are often to be found, have encountered similar difficulties.[1] Indeed, the danger lies in the very attempt to depict local socio-economic conditions and the changes brought to bear upon these: before we know it, we find ourselves inadvertently portraying a static environment which has remained so for as long as anyone cares to remember, and which is only wrenched from its slumber by the infiltration of sudden, external (usually European) influences. This study follows a long and illustrious line of scholars of other parts of Africa in wishing it was able to describe Buganda's local economy before the nineteenth century, but is unable to offer anything more than tentative observations based on late nineteenth-century conditions. Thus, the charge may be levelled that no discernible changes took place, and in any case we can only look in detail at one relatively short period – that immediately preceding the establishment of colonial rule – and therefore any such study hardly belongs in the sphere of history. Wrigley, the eminent historian of Buganda, seems to gloomily summarize these arguments, suggesting after more than 40 years of research that 'there was no new kind of industrial production' in pre-colonial Buganda, while 'agricultural methods were basically unchanged'.[2]

Yet courage and comfort may be drawn from Wilks's suggestion that 'there is a time when the historian must be prepared to risk being wrong in the effort to develop a synthesis of the materials in terms of which new

[1] To name but two examples, see Alpers 1975: 1 and Law 1991: 33.
[2] Wrigley 1996: 252.

19

issues may be posed – though not necessarily resolved even to the satis-
faction of the author himself'.[3] On the face of it, Wrigley's conclusions are
sound, although there is something gratuitously pessimistic in such a blatant
comparison between an African society and industrial western Europe.[4]
None the less, some attempt, however unsatisfactory, should be made to
examine in detail the workings of Buganda's domestic economic base, and
there are two main justifications for this. Firstly, some degree of change and
innovation can be discerned from the available sources, and wherever
possible, and however tentative, I have attempted to identify these. The
recognition that these developments occurred makes the survey below
worth undertaking. Secondly, a survey of the kingdom's main areas of production seems an integral part of any study of the material basis of power.
It is intended to form the foundation of this book, just as the spheres of
activity discussed below constituted Buganda's socio-economic backbone
and facilitated adventures and enterprises in commerce and warfare in the
pre-colonial era. The outline presented below, therefore, should be seen as
an overview of domestic economic conditions in late nineteenth-century
Buganda, with historicization attempted wherever possible.

The aim of this and the following two chapters, therefore, is to examine
the key areas of production, a term which is used with a certain flexibility.
Thus there are included in the present chapter outlines of farming and the
organization of the homestead of the *mukopi* (pl. *bakopi*, peasant or
commoner), the basic unit of production in nineteenth-century Buganda,
and in the next we look at pastoralism, hunting and fishing. Following this,
we survey what were in general more specialized enterprises, namely
barkcloth production, metal-working and pottery. All of these are germane
to the broader appreciation of the ways in which land was used and energy
expended. Certain occupations were clearly more important than others
by the second half of the nineteenth century, but all had a significant
impact on the economic, social and material development of the kingdom.

At first glance Buganda appears uniform, if scenic, in relief, soil cover
and vegetation, and there is little doubt that the landscape is less variable
than that of other East African societies. Upon closer inspection of the
sources, however, it is clear that nineteenth-century agricultural and
husbandry systems varied according to region more widely than might be
assumed. There was a broad distinction between the lake shorelands and
the slightly drier hinterland, with agriculture being more intensive close to
the lake, particularly around the sites of the royal capitals in Busiro,
Mawokota and Kyadondo *ssazas*, and in the districts of Buddu and
Kyagwe. Indeed, the Busiro–Mawokota–Kyadondo heartlands were the
cradle of the kingdom, where good rainfall and the successful application
of agricultural skills originally encouraged relatively dense settlements,
making land a valuable asset worth fighting for.[5] In late 1877 Emin Pasha

---

[3] Wilks 1975: xiii.
[4] For example, in Goody 1971, these fundamental differences are analysed and accepted,
    but this surely does not preclude studies of African societies in their own right, and the
    analysis of economic conditions, innovation and industrial development from within these
    societies.
[5] Wrigley 1996: 234–5.

observed as he approached the lake that 'here there is one cultivated stretch of land after another, and houses in great number'. He captured the essence of economic life on the shorelands thus: 'On all the hills which we subsequently passed people were industriously employed, new fields and plantations were springing into existence, and bonfires of plucked-up grass sent forth clouds of smoke and the smell of burning. The women were busy digging in the fields, planting sweet potatoes or plucking up the grass.'[6] Further north and west, for example in the areas of Singo and Bulemezi, the soil was less arable and large tracts of land were more suited to the keeping of cattle than to cultivation. Travelling outwards from the centre into these regions, *bakopi* plantations became less common, largely because of the lower level of rainfall than in the south and east.[7] Plantations never disappeared from view entirely, however: by the late nineteenth century, there were few uncultivated areas in Buganda. Even in the frontier regions between Singo and Bunyoro, or between western Buddu and Ankole, which were characterized by rolling pastureland, bananas were grown, as were maize, sorghum and sweet potatoes.

But, if a balance between cultivation and herding was the chief characteristic (and the driving force) of the domestic economic infrastructure, each *ssaza* had, by the late nineteenth century, a reputation for certain agricultural produce and for preferring either agriculture or pastoralism. These reputations were undoubtedly based to some extent on local stereotypes; moreover, the agricultural and pastoral economies of the *ssazas* themselves were probably not static but underwent perpetual change, especially during the nineteenth century, when new crops were introduced, commercial priorities altered and natural blights affected cultivation and grazing patterns. Nor should the *ssaza* be seen as a complete and autonomous economic unit in this context. *Ssazas* had their own markets and *ssaza* chiefs drew revenue from these (see Chapter 7 below), while the *ssaza* might itself be subject to taxation, thus implicitly recognizing it as a separate unit of production (see Chapter 5). But, in terms of actual production, no *ssaza* was rigidly fixed within its political and administrative boundaries.[8]

Still, Kagwa was able to offer a snapshot of *ssaza* economic systems in the second half of the nineteenth century. Kyadondo, for example, was actually considered to have a relatively low plantain yield, and depended more on sweet potatoes. As already alluded to, Singo was noted more for its pastureland than its cultivation, although it is striking that famine and food shortages were said by Kagwa to have been absent from Singo's history. Although parts of Kyagwe were devoted to the raising of livestock, this fertile *ssaza* was also rich in bananas, particularly near the lake. The Kyagwe districts of Kasai and Mpoma were renowned for producing plentiful and much favoured coffee crops by the late nineteenth century. Bulemezi was

---

[6] Schweinfurth *et al.* 1888: 39.

[7] A near-contemporary report is provided in Roscoe 1911: 4.

[8] By way of a qualification of this statement, the socio-political infrastructure of Buganda was such that homesteads on the border of two *ssazas* would have known very well to which chief they owed allegiance. It is therefore true to say that in theory the exact production levels of any *ssaza* could have been known. The Ganda, however, would have had little use for this information, and such precision was probably only approached in the collection of tax.

not considered to have been agriculturally prosperous (as we shall see below, the goddess of drought had her shrine in Bulemezi), but Busiro at the centre of the nineteenth-century kingdom enjoyed a high yield of sweet potatoes, yams, sugar-cane and a number of fruits, if not (in relative terms) of bananas: again, however, Kagwa tells us that famine 'was never felt here as severely as in other parts of the country'. Mawokota was wealthy in bananas and potatoes, while cattle-keeping was predominant in Busujju and Gomba, although the former also encompassed extensive tracts of arable land. Buddu, as we shall see throughout the present work, was considered rich in just about everything, although in indigenous accounts cultivation is to some extent overshadowed by the famed local industries and material culture, particularly iron-working and barkcloth production.[9] Alongside bananas and sweet potatoes, sesame was common in most districts.[10]

Two further points are of interest regarding this survey. Firstly, although Kagwa had a sense of how each *ssaza* had its own distinctive features and individual histories – for example, he makes the rather contentious claim that the people of Kyadondo were the most intelligent in the kingdom[11] – *ssaza* economies are in another sense understood in terms of what they contributed to a national economy. They were essential components of a nineteenth-century whole, and this is critical to an understanding of how the Ganda had come to perceive the creation of wealth by the second half of the nineteenth century. The fundamental idea had developed of 'individual' enterprise on whatever level – county, district, village, personal – but always within the concept of national cohesion, the economic strength of the whole and the benefits of communal effort. This theme recurs throughout the present study. Secondly, it is remarkable that for all the demonstrable ubiquity of the banana, the staple crop in Buganda by the nineteenth century as in many areas of East Africa, Kagwa states that certain regions did not produce as freely as others. This is, perhaps, hardly surprising, but it does suggest that the agricultural economy was rather more complex than might be assumed. Plantain cultivation was not uniform throughout the kingdom, while knowledge of particularly productive areas and, by the same token, those regions which were more prone to shortage was essential to maintaining economic stability. As we shall see, the Ganda were not always successful in so doing; none the less, the fundamental importance of the banana in the kingdom's historical development is clearly underlined.

The kingdom of the banana

Anyone who has ever written on Buganda has acknowledged the role played by the plantain.[12] As we have noted, it was the high rainfall on the

---

[9] Kagwa 1934: 162–6.
[10] For example, Stanley 1878: I, 383; Thomas & Scott 1935: 113, 153.
[11] Kagwa 1934: 162. This, of course, is Kalibala's translation. Kagwa may have meant that they were more sophisticated and knowledgeable on account of being close to the urban environment of the capital.
[12] To mention just a few writings: Wainwright 1952; Langlands 1966a; Wrigley 1957, 1989.

northern shore of Lake Victoria which encouraged original settlement and, thereafter, dense population and the growth of chieftaincy. It was, however, the introduction of the banana which facilitated the production of surplus, a permanent community and the growth of the state which came into the view of the wider world in the mid-nineteenth century. Exactly when the plant was introduced remains a matter of some speculation.[13] Most recently, Wrigley has put forward the idea that 'the full development of the banana economy [in Buganda] may have been as recent as the sixteenth or seventeenth century', which would help to explain the growth of the modern Ganda state at that time. He stresses, however, that this is (as yet) an unproven hypothesis.[14] Most scholars have certainly considered the banana tree to have been crucial in the early Bantu-speakers' colonization of the forest environment. Ganda society developed around the banana plant: to use Feierman's neat summary, 'Buganda's banana and plantain gardens were the key to the economic, and therefore political, value of land.'[15] The relative stability of the crop facilitated the stability of settlement, as Richards has argued: 'Ganda villages certainly had fixed names and, since bananas can be cultivated many years on the same spot, many such settlements may well have been in existence for 200 to 300 years.'[16]

The banana tree transcended divisions of class and clan. It was an investment for life, as once fully grown it can produce fruit for many years. It was a multidimensional economic asset. A staple food, it was also used to make various kinds of beverage; the fronds of the plant served as thatch for huts, and were also used for wrapping and covering, as commercial packaging in the market-place and for convenient carriage of items on long journeys; the stems were used to build fences and defensive enclosures, and served as rollers for the movement of heavy objects, for example canoes; the fibres of the stalk made cord, while the stalk itself could be used in the manufacture of an inferior shield. For H.M. Stanley, who exaggerated but clearly understood its importance, the banana was 'almost everything but meat and iron'.[17] For the Ganda, the plant was closely associated with the foundation of their kingdom and was perhaps seen to possess viviparous qualities,[18] which would not have been too far from the truth. According to one tradition told to Stanley, Buganda's mythical founding father Kintu brought to the kingdom the first banana

---

[13] Just two suggestions serve to demonstrate the uncertainty surrounding this question. In 1968, John Sutton suggested that bananas 'began to reach Africa about two thousand years ago along the trade and migration routes of the Indian Ocean': Sutton 1968: 72. Vansina placed their introduction considerably earlier, possibly in the first millennium BC. He pointed out that after the banana tree was brought to Buganda, it produced there 'twenty-one original somatic mutants – mutations in the body cell, not from cross-fertilisation'. This process in itself may have taken 2,000 years. In Curtin *et al.* 1978:18.

[14] Wrigley 1996: 235; see also Wrigley 1989.

[15] Feierman in Curtin *et al.* 1978: 170.

[16] Richards 1966: 19.

[17] Stanley 1878: 411–14.

[18] This may be set in interesting contrast with the perception of the banana in eastern religion. For Buddha, the banana plant symbolized the futility of earthly possessions, because its 'flowers' were sterile and no fertilization thus occurred: Toussaint-Samat 1994: 678.

plant (and, notably, sweet potato).[19] Indeed the *ngo* clan were keen to claim that they were in possession of the first plantain under Kintu, an assertion which underlines the perceived sacredness of the plant.[20]

There may be a case to be made for research into the history of words relating to bananas and their cultivation in Buganda and the surrounding region, a project which in a much wider sense Jan Vansina impressively undertook for equatorial Africa.[21] Certainly, by the nineteenth century, there was a wide variety of bananas as well as words to distinguish subtle differences in type, methods of cultivation and purpose: if their etymological past could be traced, a great many clues would emerge relating to the development of the banana economy itself. In 1877, the German scientist and khedival envoy Emin Pasha observed that certain types were used in the making of beer, and others only for cooking.[22] A number come under the generic term *gonja*, which is a large sweet plantain eaten either baked or boiled, while the most common type consumed was and remains *matooke*. *Kitembe* refers to a wild plantain, although it is unclear whether this was put to any use, while *kiwata* was the plantain peel, which was often fed to domestic animals as supplementary food. Some regional names also existed for bananas grown in particular *ssaza*s: *nnakabululu* and *nnakinnyika*, for example, were the commonest types cultivated in Buddu, the region annexed by the Ganda in the second half of the eighteenth century,[23] and these would presumably have become widely available to the Ganda after this time. Similarly, *nnakyetengu* refers to a short plantain tree common in Kyagwe. As we have already noted, production was not uniform, and certain plantations had reputations for particularly high-quality yields. Again, Emin Pasha mentioned the area of 'Debatu', just north of the Ganda capital, which in the late 1870s was 'celebrated throughout Uganda on account of the quality and excellence of its bananas'.[24]

Such differentiation is further evidence that the agricultural economy was both more complex and more fragile than might be assumed at first glance. Writers such as Wrigley, who considered cultivation of bananas simple and food preparation even simpler, and Low, for whom food production was equally straightforward and undemanding,[25] have suggested that the banana virtually cultivated itself. This meant that women could thus take charge of production, leaving the men to indulge in their preferred pursuits of war and politics. The implied argument is that, because cultivation was largely (but by no means wholly) a female occupation, it was therefore a less significant activity in Ganda life: this is surely gratuitous. Indeed, one must challenge the sharp distinction thus made between cultivation on the one hand, and war and politics on the other, as though they were not perpetually changing and intermingling within the

[19] Stanley 1878: I, 345–6.
[20] Roscoe 1911: 141.
[21] Vansina 1990: see particularly the appendix, Comparative Lexical Data. It is true, however, that Vansina had many more sources from which to work.
[22] Schweinfurth *et al.* 1888: 38–9.
[23] See Chapter 10 below.
[24] Schweinfurth *et al.* 1888: 48.
[25] Wrigley 1996: 60; Low 1971: 13.

overall make-up of Ganda society. It is certainly not clear that bananas were as easily produced as has been suggested. One missionary regarded the process as 'quite an art', involving constant pruning, the laying of fertilizer (using dead leaves and outer layers of fibre from the stems) and, above all, the struggle to ensure successive crops.[26] It was, in sum, a formidable responsibility. It is no easy task to reconcile the evidence of skilled agriculture with earlier ideas concerning tropical soil fertility. Exponents of the latter seem simply to have inherited a form of the nineteenth-century European notion that such natural abundance made Africans inherently lazy, or at least unwilling to progress, and prevented the development of a work ethic. In its more modern form, it may be that such all-giving fertility was used to explain – the assumption being that this needed to be explained – why even a relatively 'advanced' society like that of Buganda was unable to attain the level of economic progress of Europe. The Ganda, it seems, simply did not have to work hard enough, thus limiting their capacity to progress according to the standards held by the West. It is nevertheless the case, as we shall see below, that Buganda's food supply was not always as assured as has been assumed; certainly, the Ganda did not take their environment for granted in the way that some commentators have.

Crops & plantations in the nineteenth century

Plantations or homesteads were, by the middle of the nineteenth century, the basic units of Ganda economic society. They varied enormously in size, and in terms of what they produced. Save for the larger estates, many of which were described in glowing terms by contemporary Europeans, they are impossible to quantify.[27] It will be clear, however, from the discussion below and the later analysis of exchange that what may be called the average plantation of the *mukopi* was the basic cell in the body economic, and the *bakopi* the engineers of the production system which placed the kingdom at the economic heart of the lacustrine region. The plantation was the source of labour, on both a local and national scale; of production and reproduction; of the surplus which drove the exchange economy and rendered Buganda so receptive to the infiltration of longer-distance commercial impulses; and of the loyalty and energy critical to the kingdom's outward expansion and internal cohesion. Their owners were overlooked or treated at best as shadowy, insignificant and wretched creatures in much of the contemporary literature, and so there are few hard data on

---

[26] Roscoe 1911: 429–31; Schweinfurth *et al.* 1888: 38; Ashe 1889: 49. During the dry season, banana trees were left largely to themselves, although fruit was removed as it ripened. The bulk of the work was performed during the wet season. Banana trees have the great advantage of producing food all year round (although less so during the dry season), but the price of this is intensive labour. Moreover, a banana plant produces only one bunch or hand in its life, although that bunch may consist of anything up to 400 bananas. After this it dies, and a banana plantation is perpetuated by the planting of rhizomes or cuttings of spontaneous shoots: Toussaint-Samat 1994: 678–9.

[27] Stanley mentions being given a hut in the middle of a plantain garden 'about 100 feet square', which seems a little on the small side: Stanley 1878: I, 200.

their existences; but it can certainly be assumed that they led infinitely more complicated lives than the history of 'big men' has allowed for.

Much of the agricultural work was performed by women, although – as with the assertion that war was a male activity – this statement requires qualification. Most of the nineteenth-century accounts of the maintenance of plantations describe the female struggle to keep the family supplied with food. Emin Pasha noted women 'digging in the fields, planting sweet potatoes or plucking up the grass'.[28] There were specialisms which appear to have been divided along lines of gender. Kagwa tells us that millet, for example, had to be harvested by women. None the less, men also had important roles to play in agriculture: it was they who constructed racks for the storing of sesame and, while the women winnowed it, the men beat the grain.[29] Moreover, it was the men who undertook the initial clearing of land for a homestead plantation, removing grass and bush so that the women could begin their digging.[30] Still, there seems little doubting the essential truth of Roscoe's assertion that '[g]irls were taught to cook and to cultivate as soon as they could hoe; to be a successful manager of the plantain grove and to be an expert cook were regarded as a woman's best accomplishments'.[31]

Banana trees usually took pride of place in any homestead, but plantations were never devoted solely to this crop and indeed diversity was one of the great strengths of Buganda's agricultural economy in the nineteenth century. When a family or what might be termed a 'peasant unit'[32] acquired land and sought to establish a plantation, banana tree shoots would be provided by the extended family, or perhaps by friends and neighbours; yet the first crop of bananas would not appear for at least 12 months. In the meantime, other foods were used to supplement the diet, again often provided by relatives. Most prominent among these alternative crops, by the nineteenth century, was the sweet potato.[33] From the outset, then, bananas necessarily formed only part of a farmer's produce. The sweet potato was probably of more recent introduction than the banana, but by the middle of the nineteenth century it was well established.[34] It may have been planted first in new plots of land, to prepare the soil for banana trees. Even so, it seems to have acquired a symbolic foreignness in popular tradition. Stanley was told that Kabaka Nakibinge 'fought and subjected the Wanyoro, who, from their predilection for sweet potatoes, may have deemed themselves long ago a separate people from the Waganda'.[35] If Wrigley's hypothesis concerning the

---

[28] Schweinfurth *et al.* 1888: 124.
[29] Kagwa 1934: 108.
[30] Ibid.: 79.
[31] Ibid.: 427.
[32] For our purposes, the definition given by Thomas and Scott seems adequate, not to mention uncomplicated: 'It may be explained that the term "family" ... should be understood in its restricted sense, as describing a number of persons living together, and forming one household': Thomas & Scott 1935: 277.
[33] Ibid.: 429–30.
[34] In 1858 Richard Burton reported that 'sweet potatoes, and the highly nutritious plantain ... are the chief articles of diet': Burton 1995: 405.
[35] Stanley 1878: I, 349–50.

introduction of the banana has any basis in truth, this 'tradition' may be a distorted reflection of a historical process, whereby the growth of Buganda at the expense of Bunyoro coincided with the supplanting of the sweet potato by the banana as the staple crop of the lake shorelands.

Plantations tended to be laid out on the sides of the hills which characterize much of central Buganda's landscape. The Ganda, it seems, rarely cultivated in the valleys, although an exception may have been made at times of low rainfall, when they were forced to seek moisture for their crops. Nor did they cultivate too close to the lake shore or on the edges of major rivers, where flooding was a danger at certain times of the year.[36] Plantations of bananas might cover considerable areas of land, the larger estates reflecting the wealth and importance of their owners; many encompassed several hills, being criss-crossed by streams and swamps.[37] In 1875 Stanley observed that the 'average plantation' was divided into numerous plots in which were planted:

> large sweet potatoes, yams, green peas, kidney beans, some crawling over the ground, others clinging to supporters, field beans, vetches, and tomatoes. The garden is bordered by castor-oil, manioc, coffee, and tobacco plants. On either side are small patches of millets, sesamum, and sugar-cane. Behind the house and courts, and enfolding them, are the more extensive banana and plantain plantations and grain crops, which furnish [the peasant's] principal food ...[38]

This is probably a somewhat idealized picture, but it does seem likely that most Ganda cultivated a wide variety of crops within their enclosures, and that such crops were carefully chosen. Roots such as sweet potatoes and yams, for example, were rich in starch, sugars, mineral salts and various vitamins, and the underground parts of root vegetable plants prospered in the kind of climate present in Buganda.

Moreover, food production was undoubtedly further diversified with the development of long-distance trade with the East African coast. Stanley's description above mentions tomatoes and kidney beans, for example, which may have been introduced by coastal traders. It is clear that such merchants had an impact on local agriculture, although it is not easy to assess the strength of this impact beyond the vicinity of the capital. Our appraisal depends to a large degree on how long we consider the coastal traders to have been growing their own crops in Buganda, and on our understanding of the interaction between the traders and the local populace. Arab merchants had probably begun their own cultivation after 1860, from which time there was a permanent Arab settlement at or near the Ganda capital, and it is clear that within a few years their produce had begun to permeate indigenous husbandry. The precise nature of the relations between the Arab community and the autochthones at the capital is more closely examined in the chapter on commerce below; it is clear,

---

[36] Speke 1863a: 326, 329.
[37] Roscoe 1911: 4. Again, Burton heard that bananas grew in 'groves a whole day's march long', which may be assumed to have been the property of chiefs rather than ordinary farmers: Burton 1995: 405.
[38] Stanley 1878: I, 383.

however, that there was close, if not always officially sanctioned, local interaction. A useful comparison can be made with Tabora in Unyanyembe
from the 1850s onward. The obvious differences between Buganda and
Unyanyembe include the distance from the coast (coastmen at Tabora had
much firmer links with Zanzibar) and political structure (the merchants
were able to take advantage of less centralized and weaker government at
Unyanyembe). But, as in the Ganda capital, traders lived some distance
away from the majority of Africans at Tabora; they too brought many of
their own foodstuffs with them, although they were certainly more self-
sufficient than their fellows in Buganda. But such foodstuffs spread among
Africans in both Buganda and Unyanyembe; merchants in both countries
still relied on local producers for certain basic produce; and both sets of
traders depended to some degree on locally recruited porters and carriers,
which drew them inextricably into the local economy.[39]

Roscoe suggested that the coastal merchants had introduced a number
of fruits which the Ganda had begun to grow themselves.[40] At the end of
the 1870s, it was reported that wheat and rice were grown solely by the
Arab community: the production of these crops was still in the hands of
the traders and the Ganda remained untutored in their cultivation. Yet it
is likely that the produce itself was stored and consumed by local Ganda at
least in the environs of the capital.[41] In 1875 Stanley was offered a 'basket
of rice' alongside bananas and sweet potatoes upon his arrival in Buganda,
and rice seems to have been common enough by this time.[42] In 1880
wheat was sold to the French mission by a coastal trader who had brought
it from Tabora, and around the same time Mutesa himself sent a present
of rice to the mission.[43] The missionary Mackay assumed that cotton was
indigenous to Buganda:[44] there is very little other evidence for this, and
certainly no direct evidence to suggest that the Ganda made use of it.[45]
Notably, however, Roscoe also suggested that Nubian, not coastal,
influence had led to the introduction of cotton: Ganda envoys, returning
from a mission to Khartoum, 'brought back cotton seed and started the
growth of an inferior kind of cotton tree'.[46] Roscoe does not date the
introduction (although we know that Ganda emissaries were in Khartoum
in 1879–80) and says nothing of the extent of cultivation. It is possible that
the cotton thus identified was in fact being grown by the coastal traders at
the capital, although (perhaps more likely) Mackay may have mistaken a
similar plant for cotton.

Maize, like the sweet potato, was introduced from the New World.[47] It
was apparently grown by Semakokiro, before he became *kabaka*, in the
second half of the eighteenth century.[48] Through much of the nineteenth

[39] Burton 1995: 229–30, 232; Waller 1874: II, 192; Bennett 1970: 26.
[40] Roscoe 1911: 5.
[41] Mackay 1890: 108.
[42] Stanley 1878: I, 190.
[43] White Fathers: Rubaga Diary I/18 May 1880, 28 May 1880.
[44] Mackay 1890: 107–8.
[45] See for example Thomas & Scott 1935: 125–6.
[46] Roscoe 1921: 79.
[47] Sutton 1968: 72.
[48] Kagwa 1971: 91.

century, however, maize was probably not grown in particularly large quantities, being viewed as a relish or supplementary food, although this may have been changing by the 1870s. The modern term *pposo* describes corn or maize meal, which is today widely eaten: it is in fact a Swahili word, and may well have been introduced by Swahili traders and porters – the 'Wangwana' of the explorers' accounts – in the second half of the nineteenth century. The ingredients already existed: the methods of preparation and cooking were imported. Maize was noted by Speke in 1862,[49] while in 1877 a missionary noted that a variety of corn grew 'luxuriantly' on higher ground around the capital.[50] By the mid-1890s, maize or 'Indian corn' was being grown in northern Bulemezi, and appears to have been almost as common as bananas, sweet potatoes and beans.[51] Beans, peas, yams and sesame were common, while marrows, groundnuts and tomatoes were probably introduced by coastal merchants, perhaps after 1860. Onions, which had been introduced by the mid-1870s, also belong to the latter group, although it is unclear to what extent, if at all, they were grown outside the capital.[52] One missionary noted in the late 1880s that onions were 'not largely cultivated'.[53]

Among Buganda's other indigenous staples, sugar-cane seems to have been reasonably common, and was chewed in a raw state.[54] Millet was used primarily in the brewing of beer.[55] Other drinks, of variable alcoholic content, were (and still are) brewed from bananas and plantains. *Kabula*, *lujjukira* and *mufuka* are all types of banana used solely for brewing; beer in general was an important part of the Ganda diet, and its consumption was an integral part of social interaction during the nineteenth century. Another crop of great social importance was coffee, although its commonness is difficult to assess. Buddu was certainly a major coffee-producer. Arriving at Masaka, the district capital of Buddu, Speke observed that coffee grew 'in great profusion all over this land in large bushy trees, the berries sticking on the branches like clusters of holly-berries'.[56] Indigenous coffee had probably been grown in the region for several centuries. The berry was known locally as *mmwanyi* and was classified as *robusta* in 1898.[57] The antiquity of the crop is hinted at, if not with any great accuracy, by the 'tradition' that it was a member of the *ennyonyi* clan who originally 'came with Kintu' to be the latter's 'coffee cook'.[58] It was rarely, if ever,

[49] Speke 1863b: 266.
[50] CMS CA6/025/11 Wilson to Wright 21 November 1877.
[51] UNA A2/2 Gibb's 'Diary of Mruli Expedition' 7 May 1894.
[52] CMS CA6/025/11 Wilson to Wright 21 November 1877.
[53] Ashe 1889: 302ff.
[54] For example, Thomas & Scott, 1935: 151: 'The indigenous types [of sugar] found in Buganda are not suitable for economic cultivation, but are largely grown by natives on their own plots for chewing.' Contemporary accounts are replete with references to this ruminative activity.
[55] Roscoe 1911: 432–4.
[56] Speke 1863b: 275. Emin Pasha also believed 'Southern Uganda' to be rich in coffee: Schweinfurth *et al.* 1888: 118.
[57] Thomas & Scott 1935: 143–4. *Robusta* was distinct from *arabica*, the seeds of which were distributed by the Protectorate Government from 1904, and which became the more important export coffee from Uganda.
[58] Kagwa 1934: 11.

made into a drink, but was normally chewed after being dried and baked in the sun. Throughout the lake region, coffee berries played an important ceremonial role, being offered to guests as part of an elaborate diplomatic process indigenous to Buganda, Toro, Ankole and Bunyoro. Buddu was probably Buganda's most coffee-rich *ssaza*,[59] suggesting, as with certain types of plantain, that coffee became even more widely available in the second half of the eighteenth century. Lugard also tells us that coffee grew 'with little cultivation and care' in Buddu.[60] It was also cultivated on several islands by the nineteenth century,[61] and indeed the story of the crop, if it were known, would tell us much about the history of diplomatic relations between the islands and the mainland.

In the same category of crops which by the nineteenth century were considered part of the kingdom's agricultural heritage was tobacco. This was grown in a number of districts, in general those closer to the lake, although the American adventurer C. Chaillé-Long was given tobacco almost as soon as he entered Buganda from Bunyoro.[62] According to Emin Pasha, tobacco grown on higher-lying ground was considered the best.[63] It was both smoked and chewed.[64] In either southern Singo or northern Busiro, a white-flowering and rose-tinted variety was widely cultivated; in addition to the tobacco itself, the leaves of the plant were apparently eaten as a vegetable.[65] The Ganda were also importing tobacco from Ankole by the nineteenth century.[66] This crop also seems to have been of considerable age: as with other venerated foodstuffs, it was supposedly brought to Buganda by Kintu,[67] and by the 1800s the *kabaka* himself had an attendant, from the *ennonge* clan, in charge of the royal tobacco.[68]

The tools and implements used to manage the plantation and the crops produced were subject to great regional variation. Again, as with the banana, the history of words for particular tools would enhance enormously our understanding of changing agricultural methods and practices. The hoe, of course, was the basic tool in use throughout the region in the nineteenth century, but that of the Ganda, with its flattened shoulders, was distinct from that of surrounding peoples. The Ganda bill-hook, however – used for clearing bush and pruning banana trees – was basically very similar to that of the Soga and the Nyoro.[69]

---

[59] Schweinfurth *et al.* 1888: 118. Upon reaching Bunyoro, James Grant discovered that Buddu coffee was greatly prized: Grant 1864: 294.

[60] UNA A26/4 Lugard to Admin.-Gen., IBEAC 13 August 1891.

[61] Roscoe 1911: 5.

[62] Chaillé-Long 1876: 92. The problem with contemporary reports describing how their authors were offered particular foodstuffs is that it is not always clear if the produce was grown on the spot, as it were, or brought in from elsewhere.

[63] Schweinfurth *et al.* 1888: 78.

[64] Ibid.: 32.

[65] Ibid.: 40.

[66] Ibid.: 78.

[67] Macdonald 1897: 135.

[68] Roscoe 1911: 143.

[69] See Trowell & Wachsmann 1953: 27, 102. This work painstakingly documents dozens of tools used throughout the region and contains an enormous number of detailed drawings. As we shall see in a later chapter, however, hoes were traded throughout the region, and the Ganda in particular imported iron implements from both Busoga and Bunyoro.

The historical & cultural environment

The usage of conventional fertilizer in the form of vegetable debris has already been noted, but the enhancement of fecundity was also attended by a range of deities and taboos. A discussion of these may seem somewhat out of place in the context of material culture, but they are mentioned here not for their religious significance but for what they tell us about Ganda perceptions of their environment; such facets of human life emphasize, like all religion, the perceived fragility of existence and the delicacy which must attend certain critical spheres of human endeavour. For example, the Ganda made use of amulets in the form of 'half-charred pieces of human skulls', according to Emin Pasha; these, scattered around plantations, were thought to increase the fertility of the soil.[70] This practice seems a less violent version of the human sacrifices – sometimes known as the watering of the graves – performed in eighteenth-century Dahomey, where such killings were in part designed to perpetuate royal life;[71] in Buganda, the symbols and regalia of mortality were clearly used to enrich the earth of ancestors with a view to perpetuating the life-giving properties of the plantation.

The greatest ancestor of them all, of course, was Kintu: the historical and cultural honour attached to the mythical founding father in an economic sense is clearly demonstrated, as we have seen, by his association with a number of crops of national importance. He was, in the nineteenth century, commonly presumed to have brought to Buganda the first banana root and sweet potato (despite, according to one tradition, the association of the latter with Bunyoro), as well as various types of livestock and, perhaps the most valuable socio-economic asset of all, in masculine tradition at least, a wife. Kintu's reign is synonymous with agricultural affluence; late nineteenth-century Ganda tradition (if not that of an earlier era) clearly wished to pinpoint some historical figure to whom thanks could be offered for Buganda's vivifying environment. From Kintu's arrival in the area – which, according to most versions, was conveniently deserted – Buganda's economic strength can be dated: livestock multiplied, crops spread with miraculous speed. Wrigley, drawing on Claude Levi-Strauss, suggests that this was part of the 'humanizing' process of myth-making: in other words, the preparation of food is associated with the foundation of civilized culture.[72] Like Oduduwa, the founder of the Oyo dynasty in West Africa, Kintu was seen, either implicitly or explicitly, as having supernatural gifts. Oduduwa did not create the world, but created dry land in the midst of the endless ocean which covered the world's surface;[73] in Buganda, there existed a creator god, Katonda, but his role in most aspects of nineteenth-century Ganda life was restricted. In this context, Katonda is virtually ignored in favour of Kintu, who did not create the earth but who brought life and economic wealth to it. For nineteenth-century Buganda, a relatively secular society at least at its urban centre, this was a more impressive

---

[70] Schweinfurth *et al.* 1888: 36.
[71] Law 1991: 108, 274.
[72] Wrigley 1996: 91.
[73] Law 1977: 27.

achievement, suggesting as it did the creation of civilization rather than nature.

None the less, a number of deities were also in attendance by the nine-teenth century, covering a range of occasions and eventualities. Mukasa, the apparently omnipotent god of the lake, was seen as the god of plenty, and was thus closely associated with fertility.[74] In addition, there existed Kitaka, the earth god, who 'was consulted by women when they wished to secure good results from a newly-made garden; offerings and requests were also made to him in order that the land might yield abundant crops'.[75] The goddess Nagawonyi (or Nnagawonye) is supposed to have possessed the ability to end periods of drought or hunger, an ability derived from her acquaintance with the gods of the elements. During such periods of hard-ship, people approached her shrine, which was in Bulemezi, with enquiries as to when they might expect rain to fall.[76] Another goddess, Nagadya, was also propitiated when lack of rain had caused a shortage of food.[77] Katonda, the creator god, was rarely mentioned in any of these contexts, although during the dearth of 1880 (see below) he was brought to the attention of the French missionary Livinhac, who wrote: 'There are still complaints of hunger. The people say that the banana trees do not give fruit. When asked why, they say that it is Katonda who makes it this way.'[78]

'Queer foods' & famine in the nineteenth century

One of the most fundamental misjudgements made by many nineteenth-century observers was that the Ganda were the dumb recipients of their country's natural wealth: foodstuffs grew in abundance and apparently without assistance, and all the Ganda had to do was consume them. The Ganda may have been, as Wrigley has argued, 'as well secured against famine as any [people] in Africa',[79] but they were not immune from severe shortages. The existence of famine foods suggests that there was a greater struggle to procure food from the land than has hitherto been suggested.[80] This is also evident from the existence of deities associated with the breakdown of the food supply, and also from the importance in the Ganda diet of roots and other back-up provisions.[81] Less nutritious roots – for

---

[74] Roscoe 1911: 290.

[75] Ibid.: 313.

[76] Ibid.: 315; see also Murphy 1972: 428.

[77] Roscoe 1911: 318.

[78] White Fathers: Rubaga Diary 1/25 June 1880.

[79] Wrigley 1996: 61.

[80] This was clearly recognized by commentators in the mid-1930s: 'Rainfall seasons through-out the country are, in fact, subject to considerable fluctuations and, since irrigation is for all practical purposes unknown, a deficiency or delay of the seasonal rainfall, upon which agriculture in Uganda relies, may create famine conditions even in those areas of Buganda where additional rainfall is produced by evaporation from Lake Victoria.' The writers went on to describe how the colonial authorities had encouraged the growth of 'drought-resisting food crops', including cassava: Thomas & Scott 1935: 50. Yet Stanley mentions the existence of cassava in the mid-1870s, as does Ashe in the late 1880s: Stanley 1878: I, 207; Ashe 1889: 302ff.

[81] Schweinfurth *et al.* 1888: 37.

example, *bikoso*, the edible root of a water plant – were mostly used as emergency food, and were not normally preferred. Many roots were only eaten in times of famine or at least of food shortage. The roots of plantain trees, for example, were eaten during such periods.[82] In 1880, one missionary wrote that at the *kabaka*'s court 'many people have told me that a good number of Baganda were reduced to eating the roots of banana trees'.[83] The root of the water lily, *nsakwa*, was probably eaten only at times of dearth. In 1890, during the political and religious upheavals, Simeon Lourdel noted that large numbers of Ganda had retreated to forested areas, where they were able to live on roots.[84] A British official wrote from Buddu in 1906: 'I have been through each country and have seen for myself that there is scarcity of food but no real famine … I have seen no case of "living skeletons", for the natives always procure roots and herbs which, though coarse, are nourishing enough.'[85]

The existence of a number of Luganda terms for famine foods suggests that the Ganda made allowances for the failure of staple crops. *Kaama*, for example, is a small yam, seemingly growing wild, eaten during shortage. The preparation of *kigomba* is evidence of local foresight: it consisted of a mash made from dried plantain, being stored away and consumed during periods of dearth. Likewise, *mutere* was food chopped into small pieces and dried for future use. Other emergency foods were *mpambo* (gourd seed) and *mpengere* (dry sorghum millet). Although strangers and travellers were entitled to help themselves to local reserves of food and to arrive uninvited to meals, Kagwa stipulates that this occurred only in times of plenty.[86] Indeed, the custom – if it can be so called – probably says more about social behaviour and ideas of community than it does about agricultural productivity. Moreover, certainly as far as the *kabaka*'s guests were concerned, such local generosity could have devastating results. In 1862, a short distance outside Mutesa's capital, Speke found that a foreign diplomatic mission had been waiting a month for permission to proceed. The European observed that '[n]ot a villager was to be seen for miles round; not a plantain remained on the trees, nor was there even a sweet potato to be found in the ground. The whole of the provisions of this beautiful place had been devoured by the king's guests.'[87]

It is clear, moreover, that in nineteenth-century Buganda food was not taken for granted, and indeed had great political and cultural importance. Grand ceremonies involving the distribution of food were often held at the royal enclosure. Chiefs of varying rank were brought together for impressive feasts in what amounted to conspicuous culinary consumption: the *kabaka*'s power-base may have been strengthened by these displays of his substantial food resources, the implication being that much of the food was produced from his own plantations in or near the capital.[88] None the

---

[82] Roscoe 1911: 439.
[83] White Fathers: Rubaga Diary 1/24 August 1880.
[84] White Fathers: C14/192 Lourdel to Superior-General 25 January 1890.
[85] UNA A8/7 Isemonger to Sub. Comm. 31 January 1906.
[86] Kagwa 1934: 130.
[87] Speke 1863b: 280.
[88] Kagwa 1934: 88.

less, as we shall see below, large amounts of food were also brought into the capital from various provinces, a relationship which, as far as the urban environment was concerned, had grim consequences in the last years of the nineteenth century. It is also worth pointing out that, in terms of distribution, the royal food reserves affected a comparatively tiny proportion of the total urban population, albeit politically the most significant. This meant that, although famines and shortages could affect all echelons of society equally, it was still possible for the *kabaka* to eat well while the rest of the townspeople went hungry. The capital was not bereft of cultivators – a great deal of cultivation was undertaken at the capital by *bakopi* – but it was an environment which was more prone to shortage than many parts of the kingdom. This was because a much higher proportion than usual of the people who lived there were engaged in activities other than agriculture.[89] This in turn meant that, as is shown below, there were unique pressures in the system of feeding the urban environment; it also meant that shortages at the capital very often reflected crop shortfalls in the supplying provinces.

None the less, the *kabaka* had, by the 1870s and 1880s, a formidable army of cultivators and cooks who belonged to a personalized production system. The precise origins of such a system are unclear, although in the late seventeenth century Kabaka Ndawula 'gave the village of Kikaaya to his mother's relatives, where they could cultivate food for him'.[90] It seems logical to suppose that the royal plantation system developed in step with the growth of the *kabaka*'s own authority and importance; moreover, it probably expanded considerably from the middle of the nineteenth century onward, as the procession through his capital of important guests requiring sustenance and (from the *kabaka*'s point of view) displays of wealth increased. Certainly, it was critical that the *kabaka* was seen to be able to adequately feed the large number of people attached to his enclosure, a number which had itself grown enormously by the late nineteenth century. In a sense this made food shortage a matter of grave concern as regards the *kabaka*'s authority in the capital: it is likely, therefore, that the failure of crops both in the area of the capital and, later, further afield in the late nineteenth century served to undermine his position.

Famines are periodically noted, before the emergence of contemporary reports, in the indigenous sources: for example, a 'disastrous famine' is noted during the reign of Kamanya in the early nineteenth century, when people 'ate queer foods', while a famine, resulting from drought, was apparently raging at the time of Suna's accession, perhaps around 1830.[91] It is difficult to know to what degree the proliferation of contemporary evidence from the 1860s onward distorts the picture, but it does seem as though the encroachment of coastal commerce and European imperialism coincided with more frequent food shortages and crop failures in Buganda. European missionaries in the early 1880s often complained about a shortage of food at the capital, as did, more significantly, those Ganda

---

[89] Reid 1998c: 4–18; see also Reid & Medard 2000.
[90] Kagwa 1971: 59.
[91] Kagwa 1934: 142–3.

attached to them, who would have been better judges of what was typical. In early April 1880, in the middle of the wet season, Livinhac wrote: 'For the past several weeks, bananas have been scarce because of the drought during the months of October, November, December and January.'[92] Although Livinhac was indeed describing the hot and dry season, rainfall seems to have been low even by normal standards. The effects of this were evident in the middle of 1880, when the missionary Pearson noted a scarcity of food around the capital and indeed described it, possibly with some exaggeration, as a 'veritable famine'. Even bananas were sparse.[93] Livinhac also wrote that the Ganda 'are always complaining of hunger. It is not without a lot of trouble that we procure the necessary provisions for ourselves.' A little later he reported that one of the *katikiro*'s men had died of hunger, having been sent some distance from the capital in search of food; in the capital itself, 'provisions are very rare'.[94]

Two years later, in October 1882, the missionary O'Flaherty reported that for the past month there had been 'a dearth in the land', and that food prices had increased considerably.[95] This 'famine' continued to bite through November.[96] Nor was it confined to the lower echelons of society: in August of that year, Lourdel recorded a visit to the mission by the young Mwanga, who 'suffers from hunger like the others'.[97] In mid-1884 Mutesa abandoned a proposed military campaign in view of the smallpox, cattle disease and famine then present in Buganda. Notably, however, the 'famine' did not prevent O'Flaherty from enjoying a 'royal dinner' of beef, mutton, venison, edible rat, fowls, fish, various fruits and plantain wine.[98] This was indeed a veritable feast, but it should not necessarily disprove the existence of a more widespread dearth. Nineteenth-century Buganda, as in other parts of the world in the twentieth century, may be an example of how shortages were sometimes caused by a decline not in the volume of food but in the availability of existing food resources, and by the ways in which these were distributed. This argument is particularly germane to the organization of production and distribution in the capital.[99] In October 1884, O'Flaherty was once again complaining about the want in Buganda,[100] and in late 1886 Mackay reported a 'severe time of drought', resulting in equally severe food shortages.[101]

This situation was aggravated by the persistence and indeed spread of various recently introduced diseases, notably strains of smallpox and syphilis, which had been increasingly common in Buganda since the arrival of coastal merchants in the 1840s. One Ganda writer expressed ill-disguised contempt for the 'diseased immigrants' who permeated Ganda

---

[92] White Fathers: Rubaga Diary 1/1 April 1880.
[93] CMS G3 A6/0 1881/22 Pearson to Mackay 29 July 1880.
[94] White Fathers: Rubaga Diary 1/16 April 1880, 1 May 1880.
[95] CMS G3 A6/0 1883/55 O'Flaherty to Wigram 1 October 1882.
[96] CMS G3 A6/0 1883/56 O'Flaherty to Wigram 10 November 1882.
[97] White Fathers: Rubaga Diary 2/16 August 1882.
[98] CMS G3 A6/0 1884/115 O'Flaherty to Wigram ? July 1884.
[99] This theory of famine causation has been forwarded in Sen 1982; see also Arnold 1988: 43.
[100] CMS G3 A6/0 1885/24 O'Flaherty to Wigram 6 October 1884.
[101] CMS G3 A5/0 1887/162 Mackay to Lang 27 December 1886.

society in the second half of the nineteenth century.[102] The White Fathers also noted the prevalence of *kawumpuli*, a term which today means bubonic plague or, more generally, a serious epidemic, and which doubtless meant something similar 100 years ago.[103] The proliferation of disease in Buganda at this time is of undoubted importance in understanding the history of the kingdom in the late nineteenth century, especially when set in conjunction with other environmental factors. Unfortunately, little detail is known. It is, however, worth noting Wrigley's arresting hypothesis that AIDS may have been 'present in a muted form for generations' in Buganda,[104] which might at least partially explain the toll taken by recognizable diseases in the 1880s. Wrigley suggests that such a hypothesis might also elucidate the historical problem of how Buganda remained, in spite of its relative ecological advantages, underpopulated and generally prone to labour scarcity.[105] I may in turn suggest that this could explain, even more than periodic lack of rainfall, the recurrence of food shortages, especially in the increasingly diseased era of the late nineteenth century. None the less, it is important to echo Wrigley's caution that this is purely speculative.

Political turmoil & agricultural collapse in the 1880s & 1890s

Conditions in Buganda continued to fluctuate through the late 1880s: in April 1888, for example, the missionary Walker observed that food was cheap and by implication relatively abundant.[106] Significantly, however, by that year the army's long-standing licence to plunder within the kingdom had been curtailed. While moving across country, soldiers were no longer permitted to seize livestock, but only bananas and certain other common crops.[107] The reason for this is not made explicit, but it was probably connected to the fact that Buganda's agricultural and pastoral base was increasingly unstable, ravaged in recent years by drought and disease: we shall turn our attention to livestock in the following chapter.

Roscoe asserted that the *bakopi* preferred not to live in the capital because of the perpetual shortage of food there.[108] There is a major qualification to be made to this statement, namely that a great many *bakopi* did in fact live in the capital, and were engaged in this very activity, that is, producing food. Nevertheless, it is indeed likely that there were major logistical difficulties in keeping the urban population adequately fed, and that these difficulties were exacerbated during times of social and political upheaval. As we shall see, the late 1880s and early 1890s represented one

[102] Miti 1938: I, 130–1.
[103] White Fathers, C13/101 Livinhac to Lavigerie 10 June 1888. For a discussion of human disease in Buganda during this period, see Medard 1996.
[104] Wrigley 1996: 238.
[105] Ibid.
[106] CMS G3 A5/0 1888/325 Walker to Lang 25 April 1888.
[107] CMS G3 A5/0 1888/389 Walker to Lang 18 June 1888.
[108] Roscoe 1911: 246.

such period. Although the *kabaka* had his own plantations near the royal enclosure and in the environs of the capital (as did a number of prominent chiefs) , a great deal of food was carried in from outside the capital both for exchange and to supply chiefs and the *kabaka*. The capitals in the second half of the nineteenth century were unable to produce the food – either in volume or in variety – to feed their inhabitants. *Ssaza* chiefs, while in residence at the capital, probably had food brought in from their provincial estates on a regular basis.[109]

This urban dependency on rural production was probably even more pronounced once the capital was in the grip of political upheaval, upheaval which, initially at least, affected the provinces less directly. In September 1888 Mwanga was removed by a Christian–Muslim coalition in a comparatively bloodless coup. However, following the defeat of the Christian chiefs and the removal of Kabaka Kiwewa in October 1888, tension spread from capital to *ssaza*, and during 1889 scattered fighting broke out throughout the kingdom as far as the borders of Bunyoro. Thus a missionary wrote in 1889 that 'the people of the capital only live on that which is brought to them from the countryside'.[110] As the 'religious wars' began to spread beyond metropolitan Buganda, the fertility of the Sesse islands proved essential. Many of these islands – noted for their fine bananas, sweet potatoes, yams and coffee – fed a great many mainland Ganda afflicted by the collapse of the agricultural economy.[111] Even so, not all the Sesse were noted as being cultivators, and the fertile soil may not have been used to the full because of the emphasis placed on fishing.[112] Moreover, the islands were also affected by the concatenation of natural and man-made disasters at this time. In late 1890 the banana crop on Sesse failed, and the islanders were reduced to eating the roots of banana trees.[113]

Food shortages, resulting from the widespread abandonment of plantations, became both chronic and frequent in the last years before colonial rule, with heightened social and political insecurity. Agricultural production was deeply undermined from the late 1880s; large tracts of land both around the lake and further inland – notably in Singo and Bulemezi, which were badly affected by war – were laid waste of people and, thus, cultivation. At the beginning of 1890, a missionary reported that there had been 'little cultivation in Buganda for some two years past'.[114] Towards the end of the year, Walker wrote:

> The whole country of Buganda on the borders of Bunyoro is a desert. The houses have been burnt, the gardens destroyed, & the people carried away into Bunyoro as slaves ... The whole country of Singo ... has been depopulated and destroyed. Just about the capital here the land is cultivated, & the people are numerous, but in all other parts the country is desolated. From plague, war, & famine thousands have died.[115]

[109] Roscoe 1921: 193.
[110] White Fathers: quoted in *Les Missions Catholiques* 21 (1889) p.155.
[111] Kagwa 1934: 157.
[112] Ibid.: 158.
[113] White Fathers: Rubaga Diary 4/1–6 September 1890.
[114] CMS G3 A5/0 1891/66 Gordon to Lang 20 January 1890.
[115] CMS G3 A5/0 1891/77 Letters from Walker 1–4 November 1890.

The imagery of destruction is characteristic of late nineteenth-century writings – particularly those of missionaries – on East Africa, and there is undoubtedly a degree of exaggeration here. This said, the description can be taken to be essentially accurate. It seems that, ironically, the capital was recovering somewhat while the rest of the kingdom was increasingly desolated. Indeed, by 1895, the capital around Mengo was described by a British officer as a centre of prosperity and industry, numbering about 70,000 inhabitants, most of whom had their own plots on which to cultivate.[116] In the context of a wider civil war, the capital was doubtless deemed a safer, more protected place than the more scattered settlements characteristic of most of the kingdom; the idea of urban security was probably further encouraged by the presence of the British, who had helped impose political stability there.

None the less, the extent to which the capital was dependent on the provinces for much of its food is clear, and the situation in the early 1890s would have amounted to a crisis of supply for urban dwellers. In 1892 a missionary noted that chiefs in the capital were dependent on produce brought in 'from distant gardens'.[117] Moreover, the gravity of the economic situation was almost certainly a factor in the ease with which the IBEAC established itself in Buganda.[118] Many of Mwanga's most prosperous food-producing areas had been devastated, and it is clear that the embattled *kabaka* was attracted by the company's promises of material assistance. Certainly, Buganda's economic weakness cannot be seen in isolation from the political decisions taken by the *kabaka* and chiefs at the capital. In the early 1890s, Colonel Colvile casually observed that Buganda was, 'owing to an insufficient population, sparsely cultivated'. Few observers visiting the kingdom for the first time had described the country in these terms before. Gone were the images of verdant, indeed idyllic, prosperity of the 1860s and 1870s. Colvile went on to describe how '[o]n the outskirts of nearly each village, banana plants may be seen carrying on an unequal struggle for life with the overpowering grass, and testifying to the comparatively recent desertion of a shamba [= plantation]'.[119]

In Buddu in 1891, the missionary Baskerville noted the apparent prosperity of that *ssaza*: Buddu was 'full of resources to draw upon' and food was abundant. However, Baskerville observed that 'the poor eat sweet potatoes without salt or relish of any kind generally, [and] to them plantains are a great treat'.[120] Baskerville was a recent arrival to the kingdom and had not known Buddu in its prime: clearly even this *ssaza*'s famously ample resources were stretched. Iliffe has taken Baskerville's testimony to suggest a growing poor stratum in Buganda, which is a trenchant observation;[121] it is, however, misleading to argue that such poverty can be seen in terms of an enslaved class, and also in terms of a gulf between the capital and rural districts. We have seen not only how

---

[116] Ternan 1930: 156–7.
[117] CMS Acc.84 F3/1 Book 3, p. 3.
[118] See Chapter 1 for a brief summary of this process.
[119] Colvile 1895: 32, 41.
[120] CMS G3 A5/0 1892/50 Baskerville to Stock 13 August 1891.
[121] Iliffe 1987: 59.

food shortage could strike the capital as well as the outlying districts, but also how the capital was often directly affected by agricultural breakdown in the provinces. Moreover, as we shall see in a later chapter, slavery did not necessarily mean poverty.

The establishment of colonial rule did not immediately reverse the effects of war, disease and agricultural breakdown engendered by ecological adversity. Later, depopulation and the attendant outbreak of sleeping sickness would destroy formerly prosperous areas in the late nineteenth and early twentieth centuries. A report from Buddu in 1897, for example, suggests that many settlements and plantations had recently been abandoned and left to the mercies of the bush.[122] Around the same time, another official in Buddu wrote: 'All the food brought by the Waganda today to feed the troops & c. consisted of about a dozen small packets of potatoes which would probably make about one load in weight ... There is quite a famine in this part of Buddu.'[123] The situation was little improved by the following year, Wilson observing that the plantations 'have been sadly neglected, and one of the richest of the provinces is, for the moment, in a somewhat desolate state'.[124] It is worth noting that all of these observations were made after Mwanga's rebellion in the area in 1897; this uprising may be seen as the latest in a series of local calamities which weakened the province's economic base. As we shall see in the study of local commerce below, however, many such regions had recovered sufficiently within a few years to permit some reconstruction of the pre-colonial exchange economy. None the less, in using these reports as sources for an earlier era, one must always keep in mind the degree of devastation which fundamentally, and in some cases permanently, altered pre-colonial domestic economies and weakened the Ganda state as it faced its greatest challenges: political transformation and the loss of sovereignty.

As many areas did begin to recover, European observers – now the masters of the country – once again marvelled at the potential prosperity of the land. Milk and honey returned to their rightful places in the imagery flashed to a distant audience mostly interested in picturesque inanity. It is deeply ironic, however, that one colonial officer should return so blithely to the 'ease of production' idea, especially in light of what had been witnessed since the late 1880s. Around the turn of the century, Kitching opined that 'a minimum of labour is required to keep a household in food, when once a garden has begun to yield its regular crop of bananas'.[125] This particular affront – that the Ganda did little to cultivate their own food and really had it pretty easy – was to haunt the country for many decades to come.

[122] UNA A4/9 Pordage to Wilson 4 September 1897.
[123] UNA A4/9 Grant to Wilson 12 September 1897.
[124] UNA A4/12 Wilson to Berkeley 4 September 1898.
[125] Kitching 1912: 148.

Three

Herdsmen & Hunters

Pastoralism in pre-colonial Buganda

Compared with Ankole, Busongora and Toro to the west, Buganda was not ideal pastoral country, a point noted most recently by Wrigley.[1] Yet, while rolling hills and dense foliage could not support large concentrations of cattle, this kind of landscape did not cover the whole of the nineteenth-century kingdom; and where it did exist, it did not prevent the keeping of a large number of small herds (small, that is, by the standards of those to the west). Many contemporary Europeans believed that the Ganda were snobbish about the keeping of cattle, even though it was clear that the Ganda had no qualms about keeping goats and other livestock. This notion was largely based on a socio-economic stereotype, the provenance of which is unclear. Something similar, though in reverse, can be seen in Bunyoro, where, as J. Beattie has shown, the people were supposed to have been traditionally pastoral, but where even in the nineteenth century the possession of cattle was seemingly restricted to a select few. Having said this, the pastoral existence was clearly the economic and cultural ideal in Bunyoro, reflected through language as well as socio-political institutions, just as the plantain garden was in Buganda.[2]

Nineteenth-century sources repeatedly suggested that the Ganda regarded pastoral communities as inferior. There is little real evidence for this, although there are scattered indications that Hima herdsmen were sometimes regarded as essentially alien and not to be trusted.[3] There was

---

[1] 'Cattle do not greatly thrive in the over-lush vegetation of Buganda, and one of the main themes of the country's history is their acquisition from the drier grasslands to the west and their subsequent distribution to a population hungry for meat and milk': Wrigley 1996: 61.

[2] Beattie 1971: 14, 248.

[3] Kagwa, for example, describes a plot against Kayira, the *katikiro*, during the reign of Mutesa. The plot was designed to have Kayira dismissed from office. He was accused of being 'a Munyoro and a Muhima'; he replied that his mother was Hima, but this was not deemed sufficient reason for dismissal: Kagwa 1971: 148-9.

no linguistic, let alone racial, distinction between professional cultivators and pastoralists in nineteenth-century Buganda.[4] Contemporary Europeans perceived the Hima as the keepers of the herds; one missionary described them as 'the great cattle tribe',[5] a portrayal which was reasonably accurate. At the end of the 1870s, a missionary estimated the Hima population in Buganda as standing at 40,000–50,000, inhabiting numerous settlements scattered throughout the kingdom.[6] They belonged to the large and widely dispersed pastoral people, known as Tutsi in the southern lake region, who straddled several kingdoms in the area. In some of these, most notably Rwanda and Burundi, they constituted the governing class, for whom cattle, rather than the products of the soil, were the objects of political and cultural power. As such they were economically and socially distinct from the Iru (or Hutu in the south), for whom cultivation was the primary pursuit. That there were important social and economic distinctions between cultivators and herdsmen, therefore, is clear: most of the cattle in Buganda were probably tended by the Hima, and in so doing they appear to have been, in general, politically subordinate, although even this is by no means demonstrable in every scenario. It is certainly not clear, as Waller suggests, that 'herding was done by Hima war-captives'.[7] The Hima were not, as far as they can be identified as a class, enslaved. It is true, however, that Hima women, considered highly attractive by Ganda men, were extremely popular as wives. Many Hima women found their way into the harems of chiefs and the *kabaka*.[8] More generally, relations were usually defined in terms of exchange of services: this normally involved cattle-keeping in return for land.

Emin Pasha described the following scene a short distance from the capital in 1877:

> we passed a neat zeriba, and shortly afterwards a village inhabited by dark-coloured Wahuma herdsmen. Six or seven houses for cattle, and two or three for herds, encircled by high, thick, thorn hedges, formed the dirty

[4] It is universally accepted that such racial notions were perpetuated by contemporary Europeans to explain the existence of 'advanced' African civilizations. One French missionary was fairly typical in setting the Hima apart from the predominantly agricultural Ganda, suggesting that the pastoralists were 'an aristocratic class' and that they 'retained a dignity and a kind of independence of which the Negro is incapable': White Fathers: Rubaga Diary 1/18 January 1980. The Hamitic myth was applied to Buganda by Speke (1863b: Chapter IX), who was convinced that anything remotely civilized encountered in sub-Saharan Africa must have its origins in a more northerly, and lighter-skinned, people. Ideas of this nature continued to be bandied about well into the twentieth century, notably by C.G. Seligman, whose *Races of Africa*, first published in 1930, was reprinted several times. Seligman, considering the supposed arrival from the north of a 'white' or Hamitic aristocracy, wrote: 'No doubt it is at least in part due to this "European" influence that we find the curious mixture of primitive and advanced elements in the social institutions of the interlacustrine communities' (1966: 138). For a brief but informative criticism of the argument, see Wrigley 1996: 72–3.

[5] CMS Acc.84 F3/1 Book 5, p. 23.

[6] Robert Felkin, in Schweinfurth *et al.* 1888: 517. Caution should be exercised here, however: the same missionary estimated the total population of 'Uganda', by which he must assume he meant Buganda, at 5 million people, which now seems an extraordinary exaggeration: Felkin 1885–6: 700, 702. See also footnote 23 below.

[7] Waller 1971: 20. The evidence he cites does not warrant such a statement.

[8] Schweinfurth *et al.* 1888: 517.

and neglected compounds ... On account of the character of the Wahuma, who live almost entirely on milk, cultivation worth naming was not to be seen. A small, newly planted field of sweet potatoes and a few gourd plants ... and that was all.[9]

Their mode of living, distinctive in relation to the agriculturists among whom they lived, was characterized by a heavy reliance on livestock. Lourdel also stated that they depended 'almost entirely on milk'.[10] Theirs was a critical contribution to Ganda economic life in the nineteenth century. Kagwa offers an example of this, as well as of the curious mixture of autonomy and servility which characterized the pastoral life: 'When Suna became king there was a famine. The Bahima people worked very hard to supply their masters with milk. Those who were suffering from hunger saw these people with milk and thought they were not suffering.'[11] It is clear that the Hima, not cultivating extensively themselves, exchanged such goods as milk and butter in local markets and villages for agricultural produce.[12] Ghee had become a particularly important product of pastoral communities by the late nineteenth century, being both consumed by them and also sold locally.[13] It seems likely, therefore, that in the nineteenth century the Hima owned cattle, as well as tending those of chiefs; taking a share of produce for either trade or consumption may have been part payment for the task of herding for chiefs. Farmers probably tended their own herds, which would have been small in comparison, in some cases perhaps consisting of as few as a couple of head of cattle. Often women had the role of tending livestock in smaller homesteads, even though, in theory, women were forbidden to eat sheep, chicken and the eggs of certain fowls.[14] The *kabaka* and the chiefs sustained their own herds partly through war booty, and partly through the imposition of a livestock tax, or *kikungo*, which according to Kagwa involved the payment of one in every 20 cattle, and the same for goats.[15] Doubtless the poorer echelons of society paid their *kikungo* in the latter; the tax ratio mentioned by Kagwa, who was fond of notional figures, should probably be treated sceptically, as the state tribute system in Buganda was nothing if not flexible.

Some time later, Emin Pasha noted another Hima settlement, this time

---

[9] Ibid.: 43. The essentially negative imagery of this depiction – 'dirty and neglected compounds' and lack of cultivation – suggests that Emin himself regarded the pastoralists as inferior to their agricultural compatriots, who were, after all, often praised by foreign observers for their tidiness and cleanliness. This stands in contrast to the standard view, outlined in footnote 4 above, that the pastoralists were a little higher in the league of civilization than the cultivators.

[10] White Fathers: Rubaga Diary 2/15 January 1881.

[11] Kagwa 1934: 143.

[12] Schweinfurth *et al.* 1888: 131.

[13] UNA A9/2 Comm.'s office to Sub. Comm. 10 August 1903. Ghee is, of course, usually associated with Indian cuisine and its antiquity in the lake region is unclear.

[14] Kagwa 1934: 104–5.

[15] Ibid.: 94. As I shall suggest in Chapter 5, there is every reason to suppose that the Ganda paid tax in livestock, considering the value placed on cattle in particular. However, Kagwa's use of the term *kikungo* is of interest as it can also mean a raid or round-up. Perhaps Kagwa was being circumspect; it is possible that the term had a double meaning in the nineteenth century. See Murphy 1972: 193.

much further north, which had charge of a portion of the *kabaka*'s cattle.[16] It is clear that both *kabaka* and *bakungu* (royally appointed high-ranking territorial chiefs) had herds scattered throughout the kingdom, in areas more suited to grazing. In 1862, Speke mentioned 'Kari', probably in Bulemezi, as being one of Mutesa's 'most extensive pasture grounds'.[17] Near Bulondoganyi in the northeast corner of Kyagwe, Speke also observed 'the exclusive ill-natured Wahuma, who were here in great numbers tending their king's cattle'.[18] the wording of which again suggests both exclusivity and subservience. In 1879, the missionary Robert Felkin noted a large herd in northern Singo tended by 'the King's herdsman',[19] a post (or one of several, to be exact) more closely examined below. Lugard reported from northern Buddu in 1891: 'Here I saw a few cattle of the King's, the first cattle I have seen in Uganda, and the fact of their being sent here proves that the place is considered richer in pasture, or healthier, than the majority of Uganda.'[20] These herds were jealously guarded: in 1885, according to Mackay, Mwanga dispatched a force of soldiers 'far off to the borders of Bunyoro to plunder a chief who had been arrested for appropriating some of the king's cattle'.[21] This was indeed a rash act on the part of the offending chief: however, he may have been compelled into such knavery as a result of the cattle diseases which had been taking toll of the kingdom's herds since the late 1870s, as we shall see below.

As has already been noted, particular areas were good for grazing, and the larger herds of cattle were accordingly widely distributed. In more densely populated districts, clearly, space was a problem (not to mention the fact that densely populated areas tended to be those less suited to extensive grazing). The spacing of homesteads in the more open country to the north would have been less problematic, although, ironically, these were the areas more vulnerable to cattle-grabbing foreign invaders. Nearer the lake, land had to be used with greater efficiency by the middle of the nineteenth century. Vegetable plantations were usually divided by small tracts of land set aside for grazing, and these may have been shared by the owners of adjoining cultivated plots.[22] This ran the risk of over-grazing, however, and the lack of good grazing land in the more populated areas would have compounded (if not, indeed, initiated) the problems of cattle disease in the last two decades of the nineteenth century, as is examined below. There is no way of knowing whether Buganda's population was growing during the nineteenth century,[23] in spite of the numerous and extremely variable estimates forwarded in the 20 years before colonial rule began,[24] so it would be unwise to suggest that this phenomenon caused a

---

[16] Schweinfurth *et al.* 1888: 131.
[17] Speke 1863b: 454.
[18] Ibid.: 459.
[19] CMS CA6/010/48 Felkin's Journal 9 February 1879.
[20] UNA A26/4 Lugard to Admin.-Gen., IBEAC 13 August 1891. As will be shown below, Buganda's herds had been ravaged by disease by this time, in particular rinderpest.
[21] CMS G3 A6/0 1885/98 Mackay to Wigram ? May 1885.
[22] Stanley1878: I, 383; Roscoe 1911: 4.
[23] Wrigley 1996: 145–6.
[24] See for example Fallers 1964: 115 n. 53, 116 n. 70; Hailey 1957: 120.

shrinkage of land formerly used for grazing. However, it is possible to argue that the capital itself had been expanding rapidly since around the 1830s,[25] and this would have had this very effect in a part of the kingdom which did not enjoy large areas of pastureland in the first place. In the second half of the nineteenth century, good pastures became increasingly rare in the neighbourhood of the growing urban environment.

It is clear, however, that the *kabaka* at least possessed extensive herds in the vicinity of the capital, which he used to feed his enclosure and his guests, and to distribute as largesse.[26] Lourdel suggests that the *kabaka* and the more prominent chiefs regularly moved their herds between their estates and the better pastures. A herd would be kept close to the capital for no longer than a month or two, when it would be replaced by another.[27] The purpose behind this system of circulation was clearly to ensure that all the major herds were given the better pastures in which to graze for a certain period. Perhaps, too, certain superior pastures were left unoccupied for a time to allow them to rejuvenate, through a system of pastoral rotation.

Better grazing was to be found in parts of Gomba, Singo and Bulemezi. Emin Pasha noted a large area in either northern Busiro or southern Bulemezi which had many cattle.[28] Singo was noted for its fine grazing land, particularly, Kagwa tells us, in the districts of Kitesa and Kyana-mugera.[29] This was not, however, the case in the southern part of the *ssaza*, to the east and north of Lake Wamala. From here a British official wrote in 1901: 'None of the part referred to being a cattle country, the grass is not burnt with the object of getting good grazing.'[30] It is not clear whether the method of grass-burning to induce better pastureland was widely applied. Kyagwe also supported large numbers of livestock, boasting a wealth of cattle and goats; the districts of Busubika and Matembe in Bulemezi also contained good grazing land. Further south, cattle-keeping was important in the economic life of Busiro, particularly in the district of Bulam; most of Busiro's pastureland was located in the north of the *ssaza*, although, as we have, seen herds of cattle – as well as goats, which were ubiquitous – were kept around the capital. Mawokota had a thriving pastoral economy, and Busujju contained several noted grazing lands. Buddu, lying close to the cattle-rich country of Ankole, boasted a wide variety of cattle, as well as goats and sheep.[31] Western Buddu in particular afforded substantial grazing areas.[32] To the northwest, Gomba was largely a cattle *ssaza*: Kagwa recorded that the districts of Ekitabuza and Kaku-bansiri were 'the healthiest and most fattening pastures'.[33]

The growth of Buganda's pastoral economy can thus be tentatively and roughly traced with regard to the kingdom's territorial expansion. There is no doubt that, as Buganda expanded west and north, it incorporated

[25] Reid 1998c: *passim*; Reid & Medard: 2000, *passim*.
[26] CMS CA6/016/35 Mackay to Wright 17 November 1878.
[27] White Fathers: Rubaga Diary 2/15 January 1881.
[28] Schweinfurth *et al.* 1888: 133.
[29] Kagwa 1934: 162ff.
[30] UNA A8/1 Tomkins to Comm. 5 September 1901.
[31] Kagwa 1934: 162ff.
[32] Lugard 1892: 832.
[33] Kagwa 1934: 166.

much excellent pastureland; the same can be said of its enlargement east to the Nile, encompassing Kyagwe. This took place largely during the reign of Mawanda in the first half of the eighteenth century (see Chapters 9 and 11), which allows us to consider that Ganda livestock resources increased markedly between 1700 and 1750. An even sharper increase probably occurred in the century between 1750 and 1850, during which time Buganda annexed Buddu and spread to the borders of Ankole, renowned for both its cattle and its pastureland, while also expanding Singo and Bulemezi *ssaza*s at the expense of Bunyoro. Even as this expansion was taking place, however, the security of the newly captured pastures was frequently in doubt, lying as they did on Buganda's borderlands. The renowned pastures of Kitesa in Singo, for example, were successfully raided by a Nyoro force under the command of the renegade Ganda prince Kakungulu, during the reign of Kamanya in the early nineteenth century.[34] The district was not retaken by Bunyoro, but its vulnerability – and that of its cattle – to predation was clearly demonstrated. Even in the early 1870s, Kyanamugera district was borderland territory, with Mutesa apparently leading an expedition there as part of a general campaign to the west.[35] Clearly, then, although the Ganda did maintain some livestock in the core areas (Busiro, Mawokota and Busujju), the kingdom was able to access much more pastureland between the seventeenth and nineteenth centuries; the irony lay in the fact that the superior pastures were difficult to defend against foreign incursion. This meant that the Ganda continued to have recourse to both trade and war to keep their herds supplied throughout the nineteenth century,[36] and there seems little doubt that both these activities were in part driven by the need for livestock. Abroad, the Ganda reputation as agriculturists, whether wholly accurate or not, remained: according to Zimbe, pastoralists in late nineteenth-century Ankole looked down upon the Ganda 'and wanted no Muganda to own cattle because they considered us Baganda to be "Ugly-Rustic-Slaves"'.[37]

Herds & herdsmen in politics & society

Like most critical components of pre-colonial Ganda life, cattle are mentioned in the context of Kintu, who, according to one version, arrived in Buganda with a man of the *ngabi* clan: the latter was the *kabaka*'s personal herdsman and, by implication, the head of all other herdsmen.[38] Another indigenous account appears to suggest that Kintu found cattle already being tended in the area, and that the local ruler himself had a chief herdsman named Kajongoro. This would seem to have a kernel of historicity, in so far as cattle-keeping certainly predates the kingdom itself.

---

[34] Kagwa 1971: 105.
[35] Ibid.: 160.
[36] Buganda was certainly not unique in using war to accumulate cattle: in the second half of the nineteenth century, Rwanda frequently attacked neighbours in order to supplement its own herds: see Bourgeois 1957: 146, 149.
[37] Zimbe 1939: 219.
[38] Kagwa 1934: 11.

Indeed, Zimbe tellingly observes that 'cattle, then, were regarded as important as banana gardens are these days'. The pasturelands referred to here were probably in the area of southern Singo, possibly near Lake Wamala.[39] Zimbe was careful to make a distinction between Kintu's people and those who, in this account, were there already: the latter smeared their bodies with earth and kept cattle. Zimbe attempted to explain how their distinctiveness was respected within the new social and political order established by Kintu and his successors:

> Some of the customs which the people of Kabaka Wamala [the indigenous ruler] had are even now still existing: for instance, Basekabaka of Buganda wore bracelets around their ankles. And Basekabaka of Buganda were jealous people that they did not like to see peasants wearing the things they themselves wore, [but despite this] the herdsmen were allowed to wear bracelets around their legs and could come in front of the Kabaka ... almost nude, having on only a goat skin.[40]

Significantly, too, they 'had permanent places for their abode, such as flat places and plains'.[41] Somewhere in this uncomplicated version of events is, in all probability, an account of the origins and growth of the nineteenth-century economy, balanced between livestock and cultivation, and the fluid relations between herdsman and farmer.[42]

Whatever the precise origins of the position or positions, the role of the *kabaka*'s chief herdsman remained a significant one until the end of the nineteenth century. Kanyambo, the official royal herdsman in the mid-1880s, was a great favourite of Mwanga, who took pleasure in giving him the best of the royal herds to tend. Kanyambo's cattle enclosure was at Kisubi, a few miles south of the capital. The Hima under Kanyambo's charge regularly brought cows to fill the enclosures of Mwanga's favourite chiefs at the capital. Kanyambo was not alone, however: another royal herdsman, Kamutasa, had his enclosure within the grounds of the palace, where he apparently tended at least 300 cattle. He was responsible for supplying the *kabaka* with milk.[43]

As in other spheres of the economic past, many such posts were regarded as belonging to particular clans, and the award of such honours was enshrined in clan histories. For example, Kawuka, of the *ngeye* clan, was the title of the *kabaka*'s chief goatherd.[44] The *nsenene* clan was closely associated with pastoralism: one tradition has it that, significantly, the clan

---

[39] Zimbe 1939: 10.
[40] Ibid.: 11–12. Wamala or Wamara has been identified as being the last of the Chwezi rulers in the region: see Were 1968: 179. A discussion of the Chwezi, who are still shrouded in some mystery, is outside the scope of the present work, but, for the findings of the most recent archaeological research, see Sutton 1993. See also Wrigley 1996: 75, who suggests that Nilotic immigrants 'may well have helped to develop the mixed agro-pastoral economy that took shape on the central grasslands and the social relations that went with it'.
[41] Zimbe 1939: 12.
[42] See Wrigley 1996.
[43] Zimbe 1939: 161.
[44] Kagwa 1972: 4. This edition appears to have been produced in c. 1972, and would seem to be different from that which was commissioned by the East African Institute of Social Research in the late 1950s or early 1960s.

originally migrated from the west – Busongora, to be exact – and that one of the founding fathers of the clan was himself a Hima shepherd. Kagwa, who belonged to this clan, wrote:

> They came to Buganda with their cows and on their arrival in Buddu, they settled at Bwera and they dug a pond which they called Balibowa Mpungu. This still exists in Buddu today. It was from this pond that their cattle drank. From Bwera, they settled ... in Gomba and they were staying at Nakanoni village where they grazed their cattle. From this place, they went to Kisozi in the same county and they established themselves and had a lot of cattle. Kalibbala separated from the others and befriended Chwa Nabaka [= Chwa I, Kintu's supposed successor] and settled at Nsisi [in Gomba], where he is up to now.[45]

Elsewhere, Kagwa is more explicit concerning the political benefits that might result from pastoral connections. In this version, Mugalula, the father of the *nsenene* clan, entered the service of Kabaka Chwa and handed over his brother, Kalibbala, to the royal court. 'Originally', Kagwa tells us, 'Kalibbala was Chwa's herdsman. Because of this, he became a favourite of the king and he was subsequently promoted to the chieftainship of *kayima*.'[46] The *kayima* was the governor of Mawokota *ssaza*, which, as we have seen, comprised much of the best grazing land in the kingdom: the post was, in sum, politically significant.

Despite the myth and muddle, the messages emanating from these traditions seem clear enough. Firstly, cattle-keeping and pastoral culture were, in general, highly esteemed in pre-colonial Buganda and were important enough in the nineteenth century to be woven into the kingdom's foundation myths; the importance of livestock in Kintu's world could not be disguised even by those nineteenth-century Ganda narrators who sought to promote the plantain as Buganda's primary economic icon. Indeed, it may be possible to speculate that, during the nineteenth century, the 'contempt' for pastoralists supposedly expressed by cultivators was less to do with cattle-keeping per se and more to do with the Ganda state's relations with its western and northerly neighbours. It was, perhaps, a kind of propaganda exercise, even an unconscious one: we do not have to accept that these international relations were consistently awful (they were not) to accept that Buganda (or its rulers and chroniclers) used the fact that it was a predominantly agricultural society to assert a national identity. This was the case in the nineteenth century in particular because after c.1850 it was clear that Buganda had reached the limit of its westward, and indeed northward, expansion. By way of consolidation, the plantain became the symbol for all that made the Ganda different and, of course, superior. This does not, of course, explain Buganda's relations with the Soga, for whom the basic unit of economic life was also the banana plantation; but it does not need to. In any case, Ganda–Soga relations were played out within an entirely different context and set of imperatives. Secondly, it is clear that pastoral chiefs occupied a central position in the early political growth of the kingdom; the form of political economy

[45] Ibid.: 13.
[46] Kagwa 1971: 14.

which emerged over several centuries was facilitated by the intertwining of cattle and cultivation and the social arrangements such a balance required. Powerful pastoral chiefs could expect political promotion and authority within a system of governance which was as flexible as it was pragmatic; for the system to succeed, it was essential that the diverse socio-economic elements of the region were, however slowly, allied to a central authority represented by the *kabaka*. This, it would seem, is indeed what happened.

Considering their pastoral origins, it should come as no surprise that many *bansenene* (members of the *nsenene* clan) should see their main role in nineteenth-century Buganda as that of cattle-keepers, although it is always dangerous to make block generalizations concerning clans and their socio-economic make-up. Kagwa, however, records that Mugalula Buyonga, the 'parent' of the clan, 'is a "Muhima" up to now'. Precisely what he means by this is unclear, but Muhima may well be as much an expression of a way of life as of ethnic differentiation. What is more certain is that the *nsenene* clan provides a good example of how social and cultural interaction might gradually dilute a purely pastoral way of life, if such a state ever existed. Members of the *nsenene* clan who had given up pastoralism in favour of cultivation were known as *abaima abatasunda*, which literally means 'the Bahima who did not churn milk'.[47] This fascinating turn of phrase implies something of an erosion of pastoral living in favour of the relatively new economics of plantation cultivation. By 1800, the Hima population may have been much lower than a century before, although by the early nineteenth century Buganda had expanded to incorporate more pastureland. The missionary Ashe suggested that by the late 1880s many Hima had begun to eat sweet potatoes and other vegetables, which he saw as evidence of a gradual shift from the pastoral to the agricultural life.[48] During the 1880s, however, this process was hastened as a result of live-stock disease, as we shall see below.

The *njovu* clan also claims to have arrived with Kintu and to have become his official cattle herdsmen. Kimera supposedly appointed a *njovu* sub-chief, Sensalire, his official herdsman, a post which remained hereditary over the following centuries. According to Kagwa's history of the clan,

> Sensalire had many herdsmen under him. Each month they used to bring bulls from which the Kabaka had his meat. Each day the herdsman brought six cows, sometimes four, which would yield enough meat for the whole month. Sensalire's turn would come first. After him the next month was provided for by Namenyeka of the Mamba clan. After him it was the turn of Sebalijja the chief cowherd.[49]

The importance of the *njovu* clan is underlined by the fact that, according to Roscoe, it was responsible for instructing new kings in 'the arts of herding';[50] the significance of the pastoral economy is further emphasized by

47 Kagwa 1972: 19. Kagwa himself presumably belonged in this category.
48 Ashe 1889: 339.
49 Kagwa 1972:.26–7.
50 Roscoe 1911: 147.

the fact that the new *kabaka* had at least to be seen to know how to herd cattle. Namenyeka was a sub-chief of the *mamba* clan based in Busiro, although oddly, in the section dealing specifically with this clan in his 'Clans', Kagwa does not mention this duty. Kamenyamiggo, a sub-chief of the *lugave* clan, also based in Busiro, was noted as being 'the king's chief herdsman';[51] according to a different text, this appears to date from the reign of Kabaka Mutebi in the mid-seventeenth century, when 'Kasoma of the Pangolin clan ... presented Kamenyamiggo and he was left in charge of the royal cattle.'[52] It seems likely that this position was purely honorific by the nineteenth century.

Sebalijja is noted in a number of late nineteenth-century sources as being the chief herdsman, although his history – in the context of clan or anything else – is unclear. Perhaps the title was the property of no one clan. Kagwa describes him as being an 'officer of the royal household' in the middle of the eighteenth century, when he was important enough to be executed by the short-lived Kabaka Mwanga I.[53] In 1880, Lourdel mentioned 'the Savaridja', the 'great keeper of the king's herds', as being stationed near the capital. The missionary reported that 'the guard of the herds is given by preference to the Bahimas who have a particular talent for this profession, having reliable remedies for the illnesses of their animals'; unsurprisingly, therefore, Sebalijja 'has all the traits of the Muhima'.[54] It is not clear whether this last remark refers to ethnic or economic distinctions, or both; interestingly, however, Lourdel mentioned the fact that Sebalijja was actually the brother of a Musoga named Namutwa,[55] which would seem to suggest a reference to socio-economic rather than ethnic Hima. Sebalijja is also mentioned as being in charge of the *kabaka*'s cattle in 1906,[56] which is at least suggestive of the longevity of the post, although the author of a Luganda dictionary published in 1972 places 'formerly' in front of the entry for *Ssebalijja*.[57] There seems little doubt that such posts dwindled as did the real power of the monarchy itself.

Finally, the *nyonyi* clan claims that one of their chiefs, Kabengwa, was made the grazier of the *kabaka*'s cow (singular) at some indefinite date.[58] Roscoe, however, tells us that the clan was 'deprived of that privilege' at some equally indefinite date:[59] their transgression must have been significant. These various duties, as well as the repeated appearance of cattle in symbolic terms, are important. Nakibinge, *kabaka* in the sixteenth century, having approached Wanema of the Sesse islands for military assistance, was given by the latter the symbolic gifts of a coffee tree, a plantain tree and a cow. The *nvuma* clan was entrusted with the care of this cow, which, apparently, provided Nakibinge with milk on the way to his

---

[51] Kagwa 1972: 45.
[52] Kagwa 1971: 45. *Lugave* means an ant-eating mammal.
[53] Ibid.: 77.
[54] White Fathers: Rubaga Diary 2/15 January 1881.
[55] Ibid.
[56] UNA A8/7 Sturrock to Sub. Comm. 9 April 1906.
[57] Murphy 1972: 514.
[58] Kagwa 1972: 101.
[59] Roscoe 1911: 159.

great battle with the Nyoro.[60] That this event should be mentioned at all in the clan 'traditions' – regardless of whatever historicity might or might not be attached to it – underlines the extent to which it was perceived as a great honour.

The consumption & utilization of livestock

In the nineteenth-century kingdom, goats were less important socially than cattle, but more numerous. Goats were a much more immediate and practical source of income for the majority of Ganda. They were regularly bought and sold at market and they often formed part of a dowry; as such they were, like most livestock, standards of wealth. Perhaps most importantly, they were more readily eaten than cattle among the bulk of the population. The flesh of goats may have been the only meat eaten by *bakopi* on a regular basis, although even at the palace Speke described a meal of 'the usual sweet potatoes and goat's flesh'.[61] Cattle, much more than goats, were standards of wealth in themselves, and were probably eaten regularly only by chiefs. The missionary Fisher, for example, mentions the *kabaka*'s uncle, Ndalika (usually known as the *sabaganzi*, the eldest brother of the *kabaka*'s mother), who 'was reputed very rich, maintaining a big establishment of nearly 100 wives with flocks and herds'. His possession of extensive herds suggests his considerable wealth; indeed, he 'gave himself the airs of a king and was looked upon by the whole country as the stronghold of the heathen & slave regime'. His main enclosure was in Gomba, one of Buganda's prime grazing regions.[62]

For *bakopi* cattle were symbols of wealth and, often, influence, and any they possessed were probably usually eaten in the event of the animal dying naturally, although beef might be purchased in markets. The missionary Girault wrote that 'the Wagandas eat little meat; however, they like it very much; when a cow dies, they eat it … Today, one of the cows which we have at Savaganzi's died; Savaganzi sold it for two goats.'[63] It is striking that on this occasion the *sabaganzi* (who in 1879 was clearly different from the holder of that office mentioned above) sold the meat for more livestock. During the 1860s and 1870s, the consumption of all meats at the capital was probably periodically influenced by the coastal traders, who described themselves as practising Muslims. In 1862 Grant was told that Speke 'was a favourite with the king, because he was not, like the Arabs, particular about having the cattle or goats killed according to Mohammedan rites'.[64] It is not clear how seriously Islamic practice was taken by the Ganda in this respect; however, it almost certainly did not spread beyond urban chiefs and their entourages.

[60] Kagwa 1972: 58.
[61] Speke 1863b: 370.
[62] CMS Acc.84 F3/1 Book 5, pp. 2, 7, 8. This was in 1894. Ten years earlier, this powerful chief may have been involved in the fateful military expedition against Bukedi, which was riddled with dissension and disease. Kagwa refers in this instance to 'Ndaalike': Kagwa 1971: 180. See Chapter 9 below.
[63] White Fathers: Rubaga Diary 1/2 October 1879.
[64] Grant 1864: 217.

Kagwa tells us that '[o]riginally, the Baganda did not eat meat', and that it was Kintu's son Mulanga who converted the Ganda to carnivorousness.[65] Exactly why this assertion should be made is unclear, but it may be related to the elevation of the plantain as national icon, as we have noted above; it may be also be connected to the fact that the regular consumption of beef was the preserve of chiefs. Certainly, the rate at which the *kabaka* killed cattle for food would have seemed wildly extravagant to the vast majority of Ganda and was not representative of the norm. By 1906, one cow was slaughtered per week from the royal herds to feed a much-reduced household.[66] Although probably still above average, this was a fraction of the numbers killed weekly on the *kabaka*'s orders during much of the nineteenth century. In the early 1860s, Mutesa ordered cattle to be killed regularly, and often shot them himself for sport.[67] Kagwa records that Mutesa would order his Hima herdsmen 'to bring about one hundred or two hundred head of cattle every day' in order to spear them.[68] This is clearly exaggerated, markedly so when compared with Kagwa's other assertion, noted above, that between four and six cattle were brought to the royal enclosure every month. But Mutesa was indeed notably – and necessarily – wealthy in cattle. This was not, however, a constant: indeed, the overall impression conveyed by Speke is that cattle were remarkably abundant in 1862, and from later evidence were much more so than in the late 1870s.

Cows were also bought and sold at market (see Chapter 7), and in the late nineteenth century were usually exchanged for substantial goods such as slaves. Indeed, it may be, although it is impossible to go beyond speculation, that cattle became a more common exchange good for slaves in the internal market as the external demand for slaves escalated, and as Ganda became ever more desperate to find slaves either for export or to supplement their domestic establishments. Moreover, as we shall see below, livestock itself probably acquired new trade values with the spread of cattle disease during the 1880s. Healthy cattle would have been highly valued, whereas in infected areas the exchange value of cattle may well have plummeted. By the early 1890s, according to Lugard, beef was widely available at markets in the capital:[69] again, this may have been quite a recent phenomenon, linked to the death of large numbers of cattle from disease. Their social and economic significance and the impact which a change in livestock fortunes had on the wider community are always clear enough. A colonial official in Kampala wrote in 1901: 'During the early part of this month ... the natives got an idea into their heads that Government intended taking all their cattle, sheep and goats, with the result that they were killing them off wholesale ... [A]pparently [the rumour] was started by some Baganda traders who wanted to buy up goats etc. at a

---

[65] Kagwa 1971: 6. Even so, in theory at least women were forbidden to eat mutton, chicken and hog, as well as certain types of fish, although royal women were exempt from some of these prohibitions: Kagwa 1934: 105.
[66] UNA A8/7 Sturrock to Sub. Comm. 9 April 1906.
[67] Speke 1863b: 370, 380.
[68] Kagwa 1971: 140.
[69] Lugard 1892: 831.

cheap rate.'[70] This was a cunning ploy indeed: there is no evidence for such artfulness in the nineteenth century, although one suspects that an impending *kikungo* may have had the same results.

Livestock was also traded between Buganda and its neighbours. In the early 1900s, at the important Ganda–Soga market in what was to become modern Jinja, bulls, cows, sheep, goats and fowls were regularly exchanged.[71] In Ankole, barkcloth was given in exchange for cattle,[72] a line of commerce which was probably of immeasurable importance in the nineteenth century. As is examined in Chapter 9 below, the Ganda derived substantial numbers of cattle and goats through warfare in the nineteenth century and earlier, but tribute was also an important source, if only for the *kabaka*, a number of prominent chiefs and the environs of the capital. Busoga in particular continued to supply Buganda with livestock until the 1890s.[73] Mwanga was especially keen to have access to Soga animals, and instances of tribute from Busoga in the form of cattle and goats seem to become more numerous after 1884. Some cattle may also have been acquired in this way from Karagwe.[74] The increasing incidence of disease among Ganda cattle at this time may account for the heightened demand for imported livestock.

Livestock disease in the late nineteenth century

The Ganda may not have been as heavily reliant on cattle as many surrounding peoples, but the role of cattle was critical enough for the diseases of the late nineteenth century to have a devastating impact on many districts and in many spheres of life. Livestock suffered heavily during the droughts and food shortages of the early 1880s. As early as 1879, Lourdel's attention was drawn to the unhealthy state of local livestock: 'cows and goats scarcely give any milk. All the animals seem to be suffering from a disease of the intestines which is due to the bad water which they drink.'[75] Two years later, Lourdel noted that herds in the vicinity of the capital (which was of course the only district the missionaries could observe closely) were diminishing, while the cattle that remained were unusually thin; again, he considered that this was due to bad water and poor pastures.[76] In 1882, the missionary O'Flaherty complained that cows and goats were becoming expensive, suggesting their relative scarcity, and a month later he recorded that a number of cattle at the mission had recently died.[77] At the same time, Mackay reported that cattle disease was rampant, stating that 'we have lost nearly all our cows and goats'.[78] In mid-

---

[70] UNA A8/1 Tomkins to Comm. 8 November 1901.
[71] UNA A8/1 Grant to Jackson 16 March 1902.
[72] UNA A8/4 Anderson to Sub. Comm. 6 January 1904.
[73] UNA A2/1 Arthur to Berkeley 12 April 1893; A2/2 Grant to Colvile 6 August 1894.
[74] UNA A26/4 Lugard to Admin.-Gen., IBEAC 24 December 1890.
[75] White Fathers: C14/123 Lourdel to his parents 20 July 1879.
[76] White Fathers: Rubaga Diary 2/15 January 1881.
[77] CMS G3 A6/0 1883/55 O'Flaherty to Wigram 1 October 1882; G3 A6/0 1883/56 O'Flaherty to Wigram 10 November 1882.
[78] CMS Acc.72 F1/6 Mackay to his father 6 July 1882.

1883, this state of affairs persisted, O'Flaherty writing that '[o]ne can get a goat or a cow to buy only very seldom'.[79] The situation was doubtless exacerbated by recent military defeats, the army failing to bring cattle from Bunyoro.[80]

By mid-1884, cattle disease seems to have been prevalent throughout Buganda; this, in addition to human illness such as smallpox and severe food shortages, prompted Mutesa to abandon a planned military expedition to the north.[81] As noted in the previous chapter, by 1888 armies on the move across country had been prohibited from seizing livestock, formerly a common practice.[82] This decree reflects the deep concern felt regarding the kingdom's increasingly weak pastoral base. Nor was it simply a matter of economics, critical though this was; the societal role of cattle and the abstract value placed on them in the nineteenth century meant that any breakdown in the system of distribution and reproduction could have grave social and political consequences.[83] As with crop failures in the 1880s, the decline in cattle stocks during the same period probably weakened the *bwakabaka* or kingship as the focal point of a complex and potentially fragile network of patronage and redistribution. One of the *kabaka*'s cardinal functions – to bestow – had been impaired. Ambitious chiefs, keen to take advantage of perceived weaknesses at the centre, dissatisfied with the failure of the redistributive process or simply anxious to protect their economic security, would have been similarly motivated to act in their own interests, to the detriment of royal authority. This situation cannot be viewed in isolation from the wider political and religious events of the late 1880s and 1890s. By the end of the 1880s, levels of livestock in Buganda appear to have been extremely low. Unable to wage war in a weakened and divided state following the deposition of Mwanga in September 1888, the Ganda were compelled to rely on tribute. A missionary observed in early 1890 that a number of tributary societies, among them Busoga and Kiziba, had been supplying Buganda with livestock 'on the understanding that help from the Company [= IBEAC] is near'.[84] In 1891, as we have already noted, the situation was so grim that the first cattle which Lugard encountered, having entered Buganda from the east, were in Buddu;[85] by this time, of course, rinderpest had arrived in the kingdom to compound and exacerbate existing problems.

The chronology of these events is striking. The great African rinderpest pandemic did not erupt until 1889–90 and yet a local livestock disease had broken out in Buganda (and perhaps some neighbouring states) several years earlier, a sequence of circumstances overlooked by the major works

[79] CMS G3 A6/0 1883/103 O'Flaherty to Wigram 1 June 1883.
[80] CMS G3 A6/0 1883/104 O'Flaherty to Wigram 19 June 1883. It was reported the following month that 'tens of thousands' of cattle were due to arrive after a successful campaign in Ihangiro: the figure is surely grossly exaggerated, and it is not clear if any ever did arrive: CMS G3 A6/0 1883/120 Mackay's Journal 4 July 1883.
[81] CMS G3 A6/0 1884/115 O'Flaherty to Wigram ? July 1884.
[82] CMS G3 A5/0 1888/389 Walker to Lang 18 June 1888.
[83] Similar crises developed in the pastoral societies to the west, for example Ankole: see Steinhart 1977: 134.
[84] CMS G3 A5/0 1891/66 Gordon to Lang 20 January 1890.
[85] See footnote 20 above.

on the subject.[86] It is, however, difficult to identify the disease (or diseases) alluded to by missionaries from the late 1870s onward. There are two main local terms describing livestock maladies, *kyeyago* and *makebe*. *Kyeyago* provides few clues regarding cause or condition, although it may be significant that the word takes as its stem *kyeya*, which itself can mean drought. As we have seen, Buganda was suffering from a marked lack of rainfall by the early 1880s, and this may well explain, at least partially, the death of cattle and goats during this period, as well as the emaciated appearance of those that remained. Lourdel may have been right to point towards 'bad water' as the cause of disease, as livestock were compelled to drink from less salubrious sources as a result of the prolonged and severe dry season. *Makebe*, most prevalent in calves, was the local term for the affliction elsewhere known as east coast fever, a parasitic disease transmitted by ticks. In Buganda in 1903, for example, a colonial official noted the prevalence of *makebe*, reporting that '[t]he best known cure among the "Wahima" appears to be to slightly incise the growth and to blister with the raw juice of the Euphorbia tree'. He estimated that this cured around a third of infected cattle.[87] Research undertaken during the early colonial period revealed that east coast fever was indeed widespread throughout the region, as was anthrax – particularly in Buddu – and bovine tuberculosis.[88] It is also likely that in some areas the rejuvenation of bush, caused by the disappearance of elephants as natural destroyers of the latter (see below), led to an increase in tsetse flies and thus trypanosomiasis. This perhaps seems the most plausible explanation. Even so, it may reasonably be supposed that any of these conditions and perhaps a combination of several were responsible for the depletion of herds from the late 1870s onward; they were mostly enzootic,[89] which explains the absence of a sudden widespread outbreak on the scale of rinderpest in the 1890s. Overgrazing and the unsustainability of concentrated herds in areas such as the capital where human settlement was expanding rapidly may also have contributed to the unhealthiness of livestock.

By 1890, however, rinderpest had arrived in Buganda, and the kingdom was struck by a second, more destructive wave of disease, which had swept from the direction of the Horn, following the Italian occupation of Eritrea. It was a wholly new virus against which no acquired immunity existed. By 1891, the plague had decimated herds in both Buganda and Bunyoro.[90] Bulemezi was among those districts worst affected.[91] In many

---

[86] In his important work on trypanosomiasis in Africa, John Ford has markedly little to say on pre-colonial outbreaks of the disease, while Buganda itself is scarcely mentioned: Ford 1971. See also MacKenzie 1988: 134ff; Musere 1990: 106ff.

[87] UNA A6/12 Campbell & Co. to Dep. Comm. ? January 1903. See also Thomas & Scott 1935: 201.

[88] Hailey 1957: 881–2.

[89] Thomas & Scott 1935: 206.

[90] UNA A26/4 Lugard to Admin.-Gen., IBEAC 13 August 1891. At the same time, Baskerville was rather more sanguine about livestock in Buddu. He wrote that 'when the country has recovered from the late troubles cows, sheep & goats will again be plentiful. Even now it is easy to keep a supply of meat. Fowls and eggs too can be procured': CMS G3 A5/0 1892/50 Baskerville to Stock 13 August 1891. This tallies to some degree with the fact that the *kabaka*'s herds were sent to Buddu, as reported by Lugard.

[91] Kagwa records of Bulemezi that 'for the most part the cattle perished by some introduced

areas, bush and certain wildlife had encroached on human settlement as a result of depopulation, which in turn would have contributed to the later outbreaks of sleeping sickness.[92] The social and economic consequences of the epidemic for the Hima must have been catastrophic, although the fate of many pastoral communities is unclear. Lugard observed that 'prior to the death of the cattle [the Hima] were the herdsmen of the Waganda; but now they have gone I know not whither, and one sees few of them'.[93] They may have been compelled to take up agriculture, as happened in other parts of East Africa at this time.[94] The Marxist historian Walter Rusch is partially correct when he states that the Hima 'were more and more included and integrated into the Baganda economy as professional herdsmen':[95] they were undoubtedly 'integrated' (although this term implies formerly a measure of 'exclusion', which is misleading) but not necessarily as herdsmen, and it took the devastation of cattle in the last years of the nineteenth century to effect this process. It is now a commonplace to state that the great pastoral peoples of East Africa such as the Maasai were ravaged by the rinderpest of the late nineteenth century; although clearly not to the same degree, the economic and political foundations of the Ganda state were also violently shaken.

The economics & culture of hunting in pre-colonial Buganda

By the nineteenth century, the main aim of hunting was the provision of ivory, and this is more closely examined in the following section. It is clearly important to distinguish between hunting for commercial purposes on the one hand, and for protection, food and even sport on the other, and these distinctions remained significant in the nineteenth-century kingdom. The hunting of wild animals – large cats, antelopes, buffalo and elephants – recurs throughout Buganda's traditional history, with reference to either the heroism and masculinity of great men, or the need for food. It also represented part of the idea of civilization versus nature dominant, as noted in the previous chapter, in nineteenth-century Buganda's self-image: the taming, control and efficient utilization of the environment was prevalent in the Ganda ideology of statehood and society. One tradition has it that herein lay the origins of the clan system of Buganda: having arrived in a barren and foodless part of the country, Kintu and his followers were forced to kill and eat any beast which crossed their path. This threatened with extinction the already fragile meat reserves, so Kintu decreed that in the event of anyone being made ill by the meat of a certain

---

[91] (cont.) disease', which is somewhat vague but most probably refers to rinderpest: Kagwa 1934: 163.
[92] See for example Thomas & Scott 1935: 299; CMS G3 A5/0 1892/89 Baskerville's Journal 18 November 1891.
[93] Lugard 1892: 823.
[94] For example, see Kjekshus 1996: Chapter 7.
[95] Rusch 1975: see English summary, p. 374.

animal, neither he nor his descendants were to touch that meat again. These aversions became clan totems.[96] Namugazi, for example, the 'father' of the *mpologoma* (lion) clan, supposedly went hunting with Kintu and became ill after eating the meat of the lion he had tracked and killed.[97] Thus was social and political organization carved from the hostile wilderness.

Speke considered that, when the *kabaka* retired from his court, he adopted a rather odd gait: it was, Speke tells us, 'the traditional walk of his race, founded on the step of the lion'. The 'outward sweep of the legs' was 'intended to represent the stride of the noble beast'.[98] There is no other evidence of this royal swagger, nor indeed is the provenance of Speke's theory very clear: perhaps he made it up. It is, however, an interesting idea which, if proven, would allow us to rationalize the relationship between the Ganda and their natural environment: the *kabaka*, the embodiment of the civilized state, himself adopts the characteristics of the deposed ruler of the former wilderness, the lion, a process which in a sense legitimizes the new reign of man over nature. Strikingly, indeed, Burton reported that among Suna's praise-names was the title 'Purgoma, a lion',[99] which is clearly a corruption of *mpologoma*. All this may seem a little over the top, but there is, thankfully, more sensible evidence to suggest a similar idea, namely the royal menagerie. The history of this institution is unclear, but in the 1850s Burton heard that Suna 'had a large menagerie of lions, elephants, leopards, and similar beasts of disport, to whom he would sometimes give a criminal as a "curee"'.[100] This collection of animals was kept, it seems, purely for amusement or pleasure: it might be argued that the menagerie was, explicitly or otherwise, a monument to the control of humankind (that is, Buganda) over its environment, a celebration of the game-hunting tradition which itself belonged to the elaborate pantheon of Ganda creation myths. The effort to demonstrate the triumph of civilization over nature in this way must have been considerable, and is, at the very least, evidence that Buganda's mud and cane fences were rather more solid than might be assumed.

Mutesa inherited his father's zoo upon becoming *kabaka* in 1857; by the time Speke arrived five years later, however, it had all but disappeared. Speke asked to see the menagerie, 'said to be full of wonderful animals', but Mutesa replied that 'although he once kept a large number of animals, he killed them all in practising with his guns'.[101] But Mutesa retained, for a time at least, another royal hunting symbol in the form of a dog. Burton, again, repeated what he had presumably heard from the coastal merchants that Suna 'presented himself sitting before his gate, with a spear in the right hand, and holding in the left the leash of a large and favourite dog

---

[96] Kagwa 1972: 1.
[97] Ibid.: 2.
[98] Speke 1863b: 292.
[99] Burton 1859: 401.
[100] Ibid., and Kagwa 1971: 122. Stanley also recorded that Suna 'kept a lion and a leopard, and another animal which, from its description, I take to have been either a species of wolf or lynx; the two former became quite tame, but the latter was so incorrigibly fierce that he finally ordered it to be destroyed': Stanley 1878: I, 363. The allegorical 'wolf or lynx' (nature) could not be tamed by Suna (civilization), but Suna had in the final analysis the power to destroy it.
[101] Speke 1863b: 327.

resembling an Arab suluki or greyhound. The master of the hounds was an important personage.'[102] Little is known concerning the position of 'master of the hounds', but Stanley also heard that Suna was 'exceedingly fond of dogs. For the sustenance of one of his pets he caused an entire district to be cultivated and planted with the sweet potato, which was its favourite diet; and when it died, he caused each chief to contribute bark-cloths for its burial.'[103] Doubtless Stanley is, as usual, exaggerating somewhat, but Suna's partiality to the animal is clear enough. When Speke was in Buganda Mutesa was often to be seen with a dog by his side,[104] although in 1875 Colonel de Bellefonds suggested that 'the dog which Speke mentions has been done away with'.[105]

The keeping of dogs by the *kabaka* was undoubtedly connected to hunting, dogs being brought on hunting expeditions up to the late nineteenth century. It is surely no coincidence that Suna was himself a keen hunter, both for sport and for more tangible objectives; but there is little evidence that Mutesa, under whom the court dog seems to have disappeared, was a serious hunter, and although he enjoyed shooting birds, hippopotamuses and the occasional buffalo this seems to have been more closely linked to his enthusiasm for guns. Suna, however, regularly led hunting expeditions, including one to Singo, where, according to Kagwa, he killed twenty buffalo which 'used to terrorise the whole of the country'.[106] Burton reported that Suna 'would accompany his army to a battue of game, when the warriors were expected to distinguish themselves by attacking the most ferocious beasts without weapons: even the elephant, borne down by numbers, yielded to the grasp of man'.[107] Far-fetched as this may seem, Burton may well have been referring here to the regiments of professional hunters which had come into being by the nineteenth century (see below), but it is equally plausible that soldiers were expected to perform such feats of bravery as part of their preparation to face the kingdom's human enemies. It may be that Mutesa's lack of reputation as a hunter (despite being, in Kiwanuka's words, a 'keen sportsman')[108] was linked to the demise of game in the kingdom, particularly the royal quarry of lions and leopards.[109]

The importance of game-hunting is underlined by the fact that a newly appointed *kabaka* was expected to undertake a symbolic 'first hunt',[110] just as he had to be initiated into the arts of herding, as we have seen. The ritual and cultural importance of the hunt was evident by the middle of the nineteenth century. The great economic reviews, which were probably also elaborate tribute collections, held by Mutesa involved hunters: Speke described how '[t]he master of the hunt exposes his spoils – such as antelopes, cats, porcupines, curious rats, & c., all caught in nets, and

[102] Burton 1859: 401.
[103] Stanley 1878: I, 363.
[104] Speke 1863b: 257, 291.
[105] Quoted in Stanley 1878: I, 204.
[106] Kagwa 1971: 122, also 117, 124.
[107] Burton 1859: 401.
[108] In Kagwa 1971: 140.
[109] For example, Stanley 1878: I, 421.
[110] Kagwa 1972: 14.

placed in baskets – zebra, lion, and buffalo skins being added'.[111] Speke also referred to the presence at the royal court of the *kabaka's* game-keepers,[112] who probably belonged to one of the kingdom's professional and comparatively elite hunting societies, alluded to above. The explorer observed 'a party of the king's gamekeepers' only a few miles west of the capital, placing their nets on the side of a hill 'hoping to catch antelopes by driving the covers with dogs and men'.[113] By the second half of the nine-teenth century, however, these hunters were preoccupied with hunting elephants rather than those animals which were formerly highly valued for their skins. Ivory had a more tangible economic value by the 1850s and 1860s. This remained the case until the 1880s, even though the hunters themselves were increasingly redundant as Buganda's elephant population all but disappeared. Mwanga is known to have gone elephant-hunting in 1886,[114] while in 1887 one missionary noted that Mwanga 'has killed a dozen elephants in his hunts'.[115]

Other game hunted included buffalo, possibly for meat and certainly for skins, at least up to the early nineteenth century. While buffalo may have been disappearing from the core areas of Buganda by the second half of the nineteenth century, like many species of game they were once again on the increase by the 1890s, after the initial devastation wrought by rinderpest.[116] During the nineteenth century, eland, antelope, zebra and bush buck were also hunted for their skins, horns and flesh.[117] The skins of smaller, non-royal cats were also highly prized. The missionary Livinhac described a hunt for wild cats in 1880:

The hunt usually takes place with a great collection of people, dogs, sticks, and, when the chief is in the party, some guns. Each man has in one hand a dog and in the other a stick and advances in this way towards the place where he hopes to find the animal. I refer here to the hunt for cats which are rarely dangerous. For the [Ganda] are not a people to go with a simple stick to face the lion, the panther, or the elephant. When the hunters are fortunate enough to kill the animal, they carry it back to the sound of the horn, shouting loudly.[118]

Before skins began to be supplanted by barkcloth in the second half of the eighteenth century,[119] they were widely worn, and during the nine-

[111] Speke 1863b: 258–9.
[112] Ibid.: 297.
[113] Ibid.: 279.
[114] White Fathers: Rubaga Diary 3/4 March 1886.
[115] White Fathers: Rubaga Diary 3/6 October 1887.
[116] UNA A8/7 Notes on Games and Reserves by Tomkins 25 July 1905; see also MacKenzie 1988: 214. Speke, however, observed that 'buffaloes were very numerous in the tall grasses that lined the sides and bottoms of the hills' in what appears to have been Mawokota. Further north, at Bulondoganyi near Bugerere region, he noted that buffalo were 'as numerous as cows': Speke 1863b: 278, 459.
[117] See Thomas & Scott 1935: Chapter XXVI.
[118] White Fathers: Rubaga Diary 1/2 September 1880.
[119] Barkcloth was an indigenous fabric of some antiquity, but its production seems to have escalated dramatically in the late eighteenth century. Even so, in the 1850s, according to Burton, 'plantain fibre' was more commonly worn than barkcloth among the *bakopi*: we should be cautious about accepting this unreservedly: Burton 1859: 401. See Chapter 5 below.

teenth century they continued to have great commercial value, particularly as exports,[120] and also had cultural and ceremonial importance. As noted above, the skins of lions, zebras and buffalo were regularly presented at the royal court. Leopard skin was associated with royalty or at least considerable authority. In 1862 Speke observed how a young Ganda male aroused great indignation in a south Buddu village when it was noticed that he was wearing 'a leopard-cat ... tied round his neck – a badge which royal personages only were entitled to wear'. The young man was forced to trace his ancestry before an improvised court, whereupon it was demonstrated that 'he did not branch in any way from royal stock'. The leopard skin was removed and a hefty fine imposed.[121] Only the *kabaka* could possess the skin of a zebra,[122] and Roscoe suggests that there was also a royal monopoly on lion skins.[123] Fittingly, indeed, hides of lions, zebras and leopards were among the gifts sent by Mutesa to Queen Victoria in 1879.[124] Antelope (the 'Uganda kob') skins appear to have been more commonly worn by the *bakopi*,[125] as were the skins of goats, which also seem to have transcended social rank. Speke observed in 1862 that the *kangawo*, on the occasion of a military campaign, was splendidly attired in 'long white-haired goat-skins'.[126] Indeed, the wearing of skins was closely associated with military activity, much more so than barkcloth. 'Sandals' of sorts were also made from hide and probably had been since long before 1800. By the early sixteenth century, cowhide shoes were associated with the fortune-telling profession, according to the history of the *ngonge* clan.[127] This suggests a certain elitism, and indeed sandals seem to have normally been made for use among the rich and powerful. One version has it that the wearing of hide shoes among chiefs dates to the reign of Kabaka Kimbugwe in the early seventeenth century.[128] A missionary purchased shoes as worn by a chief in 1879; these were made of buffalo hide,[129] and at this time, considering the increasing scarcity of buffalo themselves, were probably highly valuable. Mats, probably made from the hides of more prevalent animals, were also common in the late nineteenth century.[130]

If hunters, as the gatherers of these raw materials, were highly regarded, so were the tanners of nineteenth-century Buganda, who probably represented a specialized profession. In 1874, Chaillé-Long considered that tanning was an important *bakopi* industry, if no longer concerned exclusively (or at all) with clothing: tanners made large sheets from cow, leopard and rat skins 'beautifully tanned and sewed together'.[131] The

---

[120] For example, Schweinfurth *et al.* 1888: 120–1. See Chapter 6 below for a fuller examination of such commerce.
[121] Speke 1863b: 273.
[122] Ibid.: 458.
[123] Roscoe 1911: 408–9.
[124] Zimbe 1939: 53.
[125] Grant 1872: 273.
[126] Speke 1863b: 420.
[127] Kagwa 1972: 10.
[128] Roscoe 1911: 410.
[129] White Fathers: Rubaga Diary 1/22 November 1879.
[130] Roscoe 1911: 408–9.
[131] Chaillé-Long 1876: 134.

following year Stanley noted the importance of 'otter skins of a very fine quality'.[132] In 1879 Girault reported that '[w]e have purchased some tanned goat-skins; these skins, cut in the shape of a hat and sewn together, are coloured dark red, those which serve as hats being very strong and water-proof'.[133] In the late 1880s Ashe observed that working with the skins of cows, goats, antelopes, leopards and buffalo still represented a significant industry,[134] although it must be assumed that livestock disease and the disappearance of much game from within Buganda's borders had a detrimental effect on the profession. The *kabaka*, of course, had his own tanners, an honour associated with the *nkerebwe* clan. Suna is supposed to have established a village in Mawokota in which members of this clan could work with skins: according to Kagwa, the chief, Kiina, 'is even at the present day the owner and leader of those who are in charge of preparing the skins'.[135]

The hunt for ivory

Much of the game-hunting discussed above originally provided food, and as the agricultural and pastoral base became more stable skins became important, although they varied widely, as we have seen, in social significance. The hunting of smaller game often constituted sport, at least by the nineteenth century, and the protection of plantations was frequently a major consideration. Elephants could certainly represent a threat to crops, and this was sometimes a motivating factor in their being hunted; but the lure of ivory was more powerful even than this. We shall examine in more detail the commercial value of ivory in the chapter on trade below: here we look briefly at its actual acquisition by the Ganda.

There had been an external demand for ivory since the second half of the eighteenth century, but this reached dramatic proportions from the 1840s onward. During the half-century before colonial rule, the Ganda were both middlemen and producers. Much of the ivory traded by the Ganda originated outside the kingdom's borders, the Ganda themselves acquiring it through trade, tribute or warfare. By the second half of the nineteenth century, Buganda's own elephant population seems to have become somewhat depleted.[136] But Ganda elephant hunters, if ever fewer in number, remained active throughout this period, operating in the *bizigo* or hunting grounds at the fringes of the kingdom, in the areas bordering Bunyoro, Busoga and Ankole. Known as *batujju*, they were (possibly

---

[132] Bennett 1970: 227.

[133] White Fathers: Rubaga Diary 1/28 November 1879.

[134] Ashe 1889: 312–13.

[135] Confusingly, however, Kagwa elsewhere suggests that Kiina belonged to the *mamba* clan: Kagwa 1972: 46, 98.

[136] Jonathan Musere has suggested that the continued slaughter of elephants during this period aided the spread of the tsetse fly throughout the region, as elephants themselves were more natural hosts of the insect, as well as being 'natural destroyers of bush, hence instrumental barriers to the existence of tsetse habitat'. In other words, the disappearance of elephants led to a movement of the tsetse fly into bush-restored countryside: Musere 1990: 121. As noted above, this probably affected livestock by the 1870s and 1880s.

because of their dwindling numbers) highly favoured by chiefs and *kabaka* alike; they represented an increasingly specialized profession, and were often distinct from the hunters of smaller and less important game. A missionary described an attempt in 1886 by Mwanga's 'police' to arrest a group of ivory hunters who were suspected Christian readers (i.e. literate converts). The hunters, who were clearly of an independent mind, resisted arrest by opening fire on their would-be persecutors. Mwanga may have temporarily disregarded the honour normally bestowed on such men in his anti-Christian zeal; soon after the incident, however, he ordered that 'no-one is to touch my ivory hunters and those who have already been arrested are to be set free'.[137]

It is clear from this anecdotal evidence that elephant hunters were sometimes equipped with guns;[138] this was probably increasingly the case after the 1870s. In 1901, for example, a number of chiefs were sending parties of hunters to shoot elephants.[139] There is, however, no evidence to suggest that the Ganda made use of actual elephant guns, nor is it clear that guns replaced indigenous methods of hunting. As late as 1905, older devices were still widely used. An official wrote at this time that '[t]he gun is not the weapon we have to fear in our preserves; the net, spear and native snares are what do the mischief',[140] although this may be a reference to the hunting of small game rather than elephants. None the less it suggests that hunting, unlike soldiery, remained for the most part in the hands of professionals whose methods and surrounding culture were jealously guarded. A wide range of apparatus was in use by the late nineteenth century,[141] and permanent traps were also constructed. The explorer L. Decle noted the existence of elephant traps south of the Kafu river in 1900: these were 'long & very narrow ditches in the long grass so that elephants passing at night are bound to break their leg if they put a foot in one of these ditches'.[142] A British official recorded another method in 1904: 'four elephants were wounded by Mkwenda's hunters in Uganda, by means of spear heads concealed in the ground, in such a way that when an elephant crossed the path it trod on the spears so placed with the result that they penetrated the elephant's foot, and remained there'.

The Ganda then followed the injured beasts across the Kafu into Bunyoro 'in the hope of being able to shoot them in their disabled condition'.[143] By 1904, of course, the border between Buganda and Bunyoro was less significant than it had been; yet it seems likely that, as the nineteenth century progressed, it was increasingly common for Ganda

---

[137] White Fathers: Rubaga Diary 3/10 August 1886. Strikingly, hunters continued to be attracted to the mission: in late 1887, it was noted that, of recent converts, 'six or seven were ivory hunters who are four or five days' march from here': White Fathers: Rubaga Diary 3/2 December 1887.

[138] See for example Twaddle 1993: *passim*.

[139] UNA A8/1 Tomkins to Comm. 11 December 1901.

[140] UNA A8/7 Notes on Games and Reserves by Tomkins 25 July 1905. The bow and arrow, the established weapon of the hunter in most of the surrounding states, were used by the Ganda in neither hunting nor war: see Chapter 8 below.

[141] See Trowell & Wachsmann 1953: 262–9.

[142] UNA A6/9 Decle to Johnstone 30 October 1900.

[143] UNA A8/2 Grant to Fowler 28 June 1904.

hunters to operate in Nyoro territory in search of ivory. In large expeditions, the hunters may well have tracked their prey over many miles, and it is not inconceivable that they were often oblivious to passing from one territory to another.

Professional hunters were scattered throughout the kingdom, but were nowhere more concentrated than in the *ssaza* of Kyagwe. Kyagwe was noted for its large game population, and elephant-hunting remained important there until the late nineteenth century.[144] The most prominent clan of the *ssaza*, the *njaza* clan, had been renowned as hunters for several centuries, and indeed it is likely that hunting was one of the most deeply rooted and ancient economic activities in the Kyagwe region. The *njaza* apparently possessed a special spear used in the hunting of elephants, called 'Nakungu',[145] and Kagwa tells us that the *njaza* were made the 'chief elephant hunters for the king'. The fact that Kabaka Kimera 'found them already established in that office as they were hunters for Namuyonjo' suggests the antiquity of their profession and the fact that their reputation had been established long before Buganda had.[146] On this level, the professional hunters of Kyagwe can be compared with many of the pastoral communities in the west of the kingdom. Although over several centuries they were thoroughly incorporated into a political society driven in the first instance by the expansion of cultivation, they retained a clear sense of their own identity and origins. The centralized political state was perfectly at ease, as was the case with professional herdsmen, with the perceived or actual autonomy of these groups: the contribution made by hunters to the local economy was regarded as critical and more important than any idea of cultural or social conformity, while the making of the contribution itself was sufficient to loosely tie the hunters to the central authority of the Ganda state. It is significant that, according to Kagwa's history, the clan was originally from Bunyoro; by the beginning of Kimera's reign, some branches of the clan were to be found in the Mabira forest in southern Kyagwe.[147] The Bunyoro connection becomes even more interesting when one considers the traditions of the *mbogo* clan: the 'parent' of this clan had become 'Kimera's man' while Kimera was still in Bunyoro, before the latter returned south to become *kabaka* of Buganda. This man, Kayirra, later became Kimera's chief hunter.[148] It is clear that many hunting skills – as well as traditions and cultures – derived from the Nyoro, who were of course the dominant power in the region during the period in which Kimera was supposed to have lived.

It is, of course, impossible to gauge the extent of the elephant population within Buganda before the nineteenth century, or indeed during much of it; just as we cannot be certain whether the human population steadily grew, we cannot know whether the elephant frontier had been gradually pushed back, or if it remained fairly constant. But it does seem likely that the frontier did recede from the late eighteenth century onward

[144] Kagwa 1934: 163.
[145] Kagwa 1972: 92.
[146] Ibid.
[147] Ibid.
[148] Ibid.: 96.

as external demand grew and the market value of ivory sharply increased. Kabaka Semakokiro, who reigned sometime between around 1780 and 1810, was described by Kagwa as 'the one who saved the country from being devastated by elephants, as he used to organise hunting expeditions. He would sound the drum, and when the people assembled, they would start driving the elephants into Bunyoro.'[149] This at least suggests that elephant herds were reasonably common around the turn of the century; but it is odd that Semakokiro should want to drive these herds out of Buganda and into Bunyoro, of all places, at a time when the external demand for ivory was escalating. None the less, if this tradition is accurate, it seems reasonable to expect that ivory was indeed collected in the course of these expeditions, and Semakokiro's actions reflected the need, referred to above, to protect plantations and villages from the incursions of wildlife, particularly in more outlying districts.[150] This may also be an example of how hunting expeditions could actually straddle international frontiers, as already alluded to; in the case at hand, Semakokiro did not intend to chase the elephants into Bunyoro, but this was the result of a large-scale expedition for which national frontiers were not especially significant.

By the late nineteenth century, the Ganda were hunting primarily at the edges of the kingdom: in 1900, for example, elephant traps were observed in northern Singo and Bulemezi.[151] In the early 1890s Macdonald noted that in Bulemezi 'the great plains which form the northern part of that province [have been] abandoned to game'. The same was true of Singo, where isolated plantations were vulnerable to roaming herds of elephants, encroaching once more on previously peopled areas.[152] This indicates, by extrapolation, the degree to which the elephant frontier had indeed been pushed back in recent decades; the human depopulation caused by the civil war and political upheavals from 1888 onward meant that these outlying districts were the first to witness the rejuvenation of game, and represented renewed sources of quarry for the Ganda. In 1905, a colonial official noted that 'there are nearly always a few big herds to be found in Singo', as well as in Buwekula, Buruli and Mawogola.[153] Elephants could also be found in Buddu, although in 1905 a local officer observed that much of the larger game had been driven away by drought.[154] The droughts of the early 1880s undoubtedly had a similar effect. Moreover, a missionary claimed in 1890 that disease had carried off great numbers of wild animals, including elephants;[155] this is, however, uncorroborated.

[149] Kagwa 1971: 99.
[150] The idea of Semakokiro driving cattle into Bunyoro suggests that the hunts took place in Singo and Bulemezi.
[151] UNA A6/9 Decle to Johnstone 30 October 1900.
[152] Macdonald 1897: 194.
[153] UNA A8/7 Notes on Games and Reserves by Tomkins 25 July 1905.
[154] UNA A8/7 Isemonger to Comm. 11 August 1905.
[155] White Fathers: Rubaga Diary 4/5–11 October 1890. Rinderpest did affect certain species of game, although these tended to recover much more quickly than cattle.

Hunters of river & lake:
the political economy of fishing

By the end of the nineteenth century, big-game hunting had become a specialized profession accessible to few, and certainly not open to individuals: by definition it was a communal activity. Fishing, however, offered comparatively fewer obstacles, save the obvious one of geographical location, and was one of the key economic activities of precolonial Buganda. Even so, it was still subject to some internal differentiation and had become, by the nineteenth century, a highly specialized occupation in certain areas, with, like hunting and pastoralism, its own culture and socio-economic identity.[156] Although increasingly arduous demands were made on the labour of shoreline and island communities as the state extended its territorial reach on to the waters of Lake Victoria, the methods of fishing appear to have been basically unaffected by the expansion of long-distance lake travel. The enormous canoes which so impressed contemporary observers and made the Ganda the most potent 'maritime'[157] power in the region were rarely, if ever, used for fishing. Indeed, many long-established fishing communities may have looked somewhat askance at these huge vessels, which were intended to carry Ganda influence far beyond the home waters, in which they were usually cumbersome and overly labour-intensive for the requirements of fishing. Kagwa stressed the exclusivity of the fishing life, suggesting that 'in the old days' fishermen rarely travelled to the mainland, if they lived on the islands, or to the capital, if they lived on the mainland shore.[158] The highly active trade network which existed between fishing communities and the hinterland shows this to be exaggerated, but clearly cultural barriers were discernible.

Fishing was critical to regional diet and the local economy, and undoubtedly played an important role in the early growth of the state.[159] According to Roscoe, fish was 'one of the principal articles of diet among the poorer people', and the *kabaka* and a number of eminent chiefs had their own fishermen to supply them with fish in return for plots of land.[160] The Ganda hauled a wide variety of fish from Lake Victoria. Speke described a fish called by his men 'Samaki Kambari': the Luganda term is unclear.[161] Stanley mentioned the 'Sama-Moa', which he claimed was the local term, and, more importantly, the 'Ngogo fish'.[162] The *ngege*, resembling the carp, was perhaps the most important fish in Buganda, and is still

---

[156] For example, one fishing fraternity specialized in the capture of lungfish: Kagwa 1934: 150.
[157] It is not wholly inappropriate to use the term 'maritime' in this context. Lake Victoria is the third largest inland water mass in the world, after the Caspian Sea and Lake Superior. At around 69,500 sq. km, approaching the area of Scotland, it is more of an inland sea than a lake.
[158] Kagwa 1934: 148.
[159] Wrigley intriguingly asserts that '[t]he trade in dried fish made a major contribution to Buganda's diet and perhaps also to its political evolution': Wrigley 1996: 62.
[160] Roscoe 1911: 391.
[161] Speke 1863b: 306–7.
[162] Stanley 1899: I, 269, 325.

widely eaten today. Otherwise known as tilapia, it was noted for the quality of its flesh. Other widely eaten fish included lungfish, barbels, cat-fish and the type known to Europeans as Nile perch.[163] Further inland, supplies of dried fish from the lake were supplemented by river fishing.[164] By the 1890s, most chiefs of high rank owned land either bordering the lake on the mainland, or on one of the islands.[165] Lake and river fishermen may at one time have been socially and culturally affiliated, but by the nineteenth century they did not regard themselves as professionally related. Lake fishermen in particular had fostered an exclusive, even intro-verted, group consciousness. Roscoe remarked that '[i]t was a common practice for the Baganda, when travelling by canoe, to rob traps as they passed them; but the fishermen did not play such tricks upon one another; they feared the curses and imprecations of their robbed companions, and also the wrath of the god [Mukasa]'.[166]

To a considerable degree this collective consciousness stemmed from the cultural affinity of deference to Mukasa, the spirit of the lake and the most powerful deity in Buganda.[167] Mukasa was of course shared by all Ganda, but his influence and the significance attached to his veneration was especially profound at the water's edge; it might indeed be argued that the professional fishermen of Buganda had closer cultural ties with their colleagues in other lakeside societies than they did with their own com-patriots. Kagwa suggests that inland or river fishermen, known as *abasambazi*, did not share the taboos and observances of their lacustrine counterparts.[168] Even so, regular festivals were held in Mukasa's honour, in which the *kabaka* would offer the great *lubaale* slaves and livestock. This was reciprocated in a separate festival, during which Mukasa (through his priests) sent to the *kabaka* a wide range of edible fish. In what was a veritable cele-bration of Buganda's maritime culture, this fish-offering was conveyed to the *kabaka* by men singing songs and performing the motions of canoe travel.[169] This may have been the ceremony observed in 1862 by Speke, who drew attention to the regular celebrations of Buganda's natural produce at the royal court, during which fishermen brought samples of their catches before the *kabaka*.[170]

By the second half of the nineteenth century, a wide variety of traps and implements were in use among fishing communities, depending on environment and quarry. Drag-nets, floating lines hung with iron hooks and variously sized basket traps were among the most common tools.[171] Basket traps, mostly used on inland rivers, were made of cane, or else stiff reeds commonly found along the lake shore,[172] while ropes were made

---

[163] See for example Thomas & Scott 1935: 192–3.
[164] Roscoe 1911: 398.
[165] Ibid.: 391–2.
[166] Ibid.: 398.
[167] See for example Kenny 1977: 717–33.
[168] Kagwa 1934: 150.
[169] Roscoe 1911: 298–300. Many contemporary Europeans made reference to the choral abilities of oarsmen; the songs themselves were doubtless representative of a cultural bond.
[170] Speke 1863b: 259, 297.
[171] These are well documented in Roscoe 1911: 394–7.
[172] Ibid.: 412.

from *buyanja*, a type of grass which grew near the water.[173] The waters off Kyagwe were noted as being a particularly rich fishing area, and by the early eighteenth century the markets along the Kyagwe shore were renowned throughout the kingdom.[174] The Mawokota shoreline economy was also heavily reliant on fishing.[175] Fishing was at the economic heart of the Sesse islands, and the Sesse themselves were experts in the use of a line and hook. By the 1880s, many Sesse were employing their fishing skills on long-distance canoe journeys. This was partly because long-distance crews were often required to provide their own food and provisions throughout the voyage; it may also have been an attempt to compensate for the fact that they were compelled to spend months at a time on such journeys, unable to fish in their home waters. Some of the fish they caught while *en route* may have been brought back to their own communities. The missionary Giraud recorded in 1885: 'When we arrived at the place of encampment, the Wasese took their vicious lines hung with iron hooks in the shape of fish-hooks and returned with ample provisions.' The Sesse also hunted crocodiles, apparently for their flesh.[176] Giraud claimed that the Sesse steered clear of hippopotamuses, but other evidence suggests that these were hunted on the Sesse islands, by means of placing traps in forests near the water's edge.[177] Hippopotamuses were indeed probably avoided while actually on the water, as these huge and volatile beasts were the biggest non-human threat to the stability of canoes, but they were hunted for their flesh and their teeth, the latter having a market value akin to ivory. Ashe claimed that the Sesse ate both crocodile and hippopotamus meat, but that the Ganda would not touch either.[178] As we have noted, however, Mutesa himself was a keen hunter of hippopotamuses, apparently for sport.[179]

The historical growth of river fishing was impeded in many parts of Buganda by *kifuuyi* or sudd, a mass of floating vegetation obstructing the course of a stream or river. This was the case, for example, on stretches of the Kagera and Katonga rivers, and river fishing often involved wading into the water equipped with spears or nets, or standing on the bank. Kagwa tells us that Singo was the most important *ssaza* for river fishing, particularly on the Nabakazi, Bimbye and Kitumbi rivers,[180] which might go some way towards explaining Singo's supposed historic immunity to famine. These relatively minor rivers lie north and west of Lake Wamala. But it was on the Nile between modern-day Jinja and Bulondoganyi that both Ganda and Soga river fishing flourished during the nineteenth

---

[173] Kagwa 1934: 149.
[174] 'Ebye Buganda: Entabalo za Sekabaka Mawanda', *Munno* (1921) pp. 11–12.
[175] Kagwa 1934: 164.
[176] White Fathers: C14/167 Giraud to Bridoux 24 July 1985.
[177] White Fathers: Rubaga Diary 3/28 September 1886.
[178] Ashe 1889: 302.
[179] Speke 1863b: 394. Again, although Mutesa had little reputation as a hunter, it is possible that notions of 'sport', for which Mutesa was seemingly enthusiastic, became more prevalent with the arrival of firearms. Shooting for fun with guns was rather less demanding than stalking and attacking prey with indigenous weaponry; Mutesa's destruction of his own menagerie may be evidence of this idea.
[180] Kagwa 1934: 162.

century, and again the extension of Buganda's eastern limit to the Nile in the eighteenth century would have greatly enriched the kingdom's fishing economy. On reaching the 'Ripon Falls' in 1862, Speke observed that a number of the larger islets in the middle of the river were 'occupied by fishermen's huts'.[181] The drawing accompanying Speke's text depicts a number of fishermen squatting on the rocks in midstream or at the river's edge, or in canoes. Both spears and rods can be seen.[182] Moving north along the river bank toward Bulondoganyi, Speke discovered that dried fish was a common commodity and undoubtedly one of the mainstays of the local economy.[183] The explorer described 'the thousands of passenger-fish, leaping at the falls with all their might, the Wasoga and Waganda fishermen coming out in boats and taking post on all the rocks with rod and hook'.[184] He later wrote:

> In addition to the rod-and-line fishing, a number of men, armed with long heavy poles with two iron spikes, tied prong fashion to one end, rushed to a place over a break in the falls, which tired fish seemed to use as a baiting-room, dashed in their forks, holding on by the shaft, and sent men down to disengage the pinned fish and relieve their spears. The shot they make in this manner is a blind one – only on the chance of fish being there – and therefore always doubtful in its result.[185]

There was almost certainly more skill in this operation than Speke appreciated. Inland fishermen also used herbs, *muluku*, which they sprinkled in the water in order to poison the fish, which were then picked off the surface of the water.[186]

By the nineteenth century, it is likely that many Ganda practised river fishing from time to time, unlike the shoreline communities, for whom fishing was a way of life. It is rather flimsy evidence, but Stanley noted that iron hooks were common in the 'average Muganda's hut':[187] these may have been used for occasional fishing trips to local streams. In northern Buganda, Grant observed that fishing was an important feature of the local economy and that basket traps 'were constantly found in the houses of the people'. Here, trenches were dug into swamps in order to create a network of artificial streams, and at various intersections 'the baskets were laid on their sides, and the fish driven into them'. There was, however, something of a dearth when Grant was passing through in mid-1862: he complained that there were no fish to be had in the area.[188] Roscoe suggests that river fishermen made extensive use of basket traps, 'which they fastened in the running streams, or in places where the streams had overflowed the banks

[181] Speke 1863b: 459.
[182] Ibid.: opposite 466.
[183] Ibid.: 464, 472; also Chaillé-Long 1876: pp. 160ff. On one occasion Mutesa sent to Speke 'a load of sun-dried fish strung on a stick in the shape of a shield'. This may have been the usual mode of transportation from the shore inland: Speke 1863b: 302.
[184] Speke 1863b: 467.
[185] Ibid.: 470.
[186] Kagwa 1934: 150.
[187] Stanley 1878: I, 384. In 1862 Grant described the interior of a 'typical' homestead in Buddu, in which 'sacks of grain, dried flesh or fish' were strung from supporting poles: Grant 1864: 215.
[188] Grant 1864: 241.

and had spread over large tracts of country'; they were also strategically placed during the breeding season 'so that the fish might swim into them'.[189] This suggests that fishing, at least inland, was nearly as much a seasonal activity as cultivation and herding, and could also be affected by periods of low rainfall.

The waters of Ganda history

There is something intrinsically compelling about a comparison between human history and the movement of water, however indulgent such a notion may seem within the confines of academic study. We have already examined the historical importance of environment in terms of cultivation, the maintenance of livestock and hunting in Buganda, and the great significance attached to these central activities in Ganda culture and in the various expressions of local tradition. The same can be said of the lake, rivers and streams, which formed the organs and veins of the country, supplying the fish which were so essential to diet and exchange (see Chapter 7), and watering the land from which plantations sprang and on which livestock were bred. In this sense, water was central to the Ganda story of survival and expansion, for none of the kingdom's nineteenth-century economic mainstays could have flourished without water, and all suffered when water was in short supply, as we have seen. The struggle with environment and climate can clearly be seen, for example, in the pastoral country to the north and west, and the paradox was caught by Grant while passing through what was probably northern Singo in 1862. This was, he wrote, 'low grazing country', occupied by 'almost 'prize' animals'.[190] Ironically, however, although the region contained some of the finest grazing land in the kingdom, it was also more prone than many areas to periodic water shortage, being drier than the hilly land closer to the lake. Grant observed that water was often scarce, and that wells had to be dug for cattle.[191] In this sense, it may be argued that Buganda's expansion into pastoral country to the north and west often meant the kingdom running to stand still: the search for more livestock to replenish existing stocks was in essence a metaphorical search for water.

Human life and, with it, social communities grew up along the rivers and streams of the region, and on the edges of the great lake from which so much was taken. As the water flowed, so did the progress of human society; political economy in Buganda was at origin born of proximity to water, be it for the sustenance of the plantation or for fishing. Rivers bound communities, districts and, ultimately, the kingdom together. The political and economic importance of rivers was reflected in Ganda culture by the nineteenth century. Each river had its own deity, to be appeased, thanked, entreated for the produce and prosperity so vital to the survival and growth of communities. On one level these were the blood cells of the

---

[189] Roscoe 1911: 396, 398.
[190] Grant 1864: 237–8.
[191] Grant 1872: 285.

nineteenth-century corpus: their continued flow and the rainfall drawn from the lake were a prerequisite for the economic growth of the kingdom. Failure, or even slowing down, threatened the very fabric of the social and political community, and surely contributed to the crises of the period from the late 1870s onwards. It was not unprecedented; but, in the late nineteenth century, it coincided with the arrival of a foreign power – Britain, whose strength overseas rested above all on its fleet – which had, by comparison, somewhat more complicated methods of utilizing water with rather more potent results.

Four

Crafts & Craftsmen

Barkcloth production

The manufacture of barkcloth was the first among what might be termed homestead or *bakopi* industries, a source of income (not to mention of clothing, sheeting, packaging and means of tribute) open to virtually anyone with a plot of land. During the nineteenth century, it came to be seen as a symbol of the kingdom itself, and it successfully competed with imported cloths and textiles for several decades. The barkcloth of the Ganda was renowned throughout the region: worn by just about everyone in Buganda itself, it was often the garb of royalty or at least of prosperity in neighbouring societies, being imported by the wealthier traders of Karagwe, Bunyoro and, to a lesser extent due to their own barkcloth industry, the Soga.[1] This commerce is more closely examined in a later chapter. By the 1870s, imported cotton and calico goods were becoming both more fashionable and more attainable, particularly in the capital, but barkcloth remained prevalent among the majority of Ganda and retained its cultural importance everywhere.

The cloth was derived from bark stripped from various kinds of fig trees, which were found throughout the kingdom. The bark was repeatedly beaten until thin and flexible, and then left to dry. The process generally took several days. Although, as we shall see, a number of different mallets were used throughout the operation, most shared the characteristic of being grooved, giving the cloth an appearance similar to fine corduroy. Quality was by no means uniform, but varied according to the type of tree stripped and the age of the tree itself. The superior kinds were greatly sought after, such as those from the Sesse islands and Buddu, and their producers must be considered to have had greater social standing. Occasionally, the cloth was dyed or patterned according to market

---

[1] One contemporary report suggests that Ganda barkcloth found its way as far as Rwanda, and it is also possible that it was traded on the eastern shore of the lake: Schweinfurth *et al.* 1888: 119–20.

demand, although this operation was not as widespread in Buganda as in, for example, Busoga.[2] One colonial official observed in 1895 that some cloths were stained using 'water taken from a certain spring near Mengo, which contained some chemical which left a permanent black mark'.[3] Trowell suggested that 'black stamp-patterns' were symbols of royalty or authority.[4] It is unclear how common dyeing was: barkcloths were often naturally coloured, such as *ndogo*, which was comparatively dark. With regard to dyeing generally, Roscoe states that red dye was produced from a crimson-coloured deposit found in streams where there were traces of iron in the clay; the deposit was mixed with ashes and water. Black dye was often obtained by boiling a herb which Roscoe calls *mzugizi*.[5]

Generally, it was the role of women to strip the bark from the trees, but the actual manufacture of the cloth was a male preserve.[6] Barkcloth was mainly used for clothing, but it also provided bedding and partitions within homesteads, and was commonly used to wrap up goods for transporting.[7] The trees were usually located within plantations. Emin Pasha wrote: 'There are no trees in the banana groves except several varieties of the fig, which are used for the manufacture of cloth ... The bark may be employed for this purpose until the tree is two and a half to three years old, but as a rule the same tree is only stripped twice. The first time it produces a thick coarse cloth, the second time a uniformly finer one.'[8]

Although this account seems to underestimate the lifespan of the tree, it indicates the complexity of the production process. According to Roscoe, it might take two years before a tree was sufficiently mature to produce a worthy bark.[9] As with banana plants, the planting of fig trees was essential to the prosperity of a homestead in most parts of nineteenth-century Buganda; and, again as with the banana, the barkcloth tree facilitated permanent settlement and political stability.

The list of trees from which barkcloth might be produced is a lengthy one indeed. There may have been up to 19 kinds in Buddu alone, although in Bulemezi, which was considered to have rather a poor barkcloth industry, there were perhaps eight. The first bark removed was generally of the poorest quality, as Emin Pasha observed: this was known as *kitentegere*, literally meaning the rough bark, and was used for burials and on other occasions when finery was unnecessary. Certain trees, known as *kkookoowe*, yielded this kind of bark continually. The first stripping of bark was beaten with the mallet *nsaasi*, which had particularly large grooves. The choice of mallet was critical in the process which actually produced the cloth. *Nsera* referred to a mallet with slightly smaller grooves, and towards the end of the process the mallet known as *nzituzo* was used for patterning and had very fine grooves. According to Roscoe,

[2] For example, Lugard 1892: 823, 831.
[3] Ternan 1930: 156–7.
[4] Trowell & Wachsmann 1953: 182.
[5] Roscoe 1911: 371.
[6] Schweinfurth *et al.* 1888: 517–18.
[7] Ibid.: 37.
[8] Ibid.: 39–40.
[9] Roscoe 1911: 405.

Barkcloths that were intended for use on beds were left much thicker than those intended for wear. Different trees yielded different textures and qualities and also different colours. The common barkcloth, when beaten and dried, was a light brown, but the better sorts, when exposed to the sun for drying, became a rich terracotta. Peasants commonly wore the light brown barkcloths, but they had darker cloths of finer quality for use when paying visits ... The best barkcloth trees did not grow freely in any district except Budu, and in that district the best trees were grown at Sango. For the King a species of tree was grown, which gave a white barkcloth; this was used at the coronation, but seldom at other times.[10]

Sango, in southern Buddu just north of the Kagera river, was renowned for barkcloth production. The missionary Girault mentioned the region on his way to Buganda by canoe in 1879: 'Around midday we passed the mouth of the river [Kagera] which marks the boundary between Ouganda and the country of Ohaia [= Buhaya]. Here there is the tree called mbougo, the bark of which the Waganda make into cloth.'[11] The area even gave its name to a particular type of cloth, *ssango*, a fine red-coloured textile. The acquisition of Buddu by Buganda in the late eighteenth century opened up access to this thriving industry, and indeed may well have been a motivating factor behind the expansion;[12] certainly, the incorporation of Buddu had a significant impact on production much more widely.

The expansion of the barkcloth economy

We cannot with any certainty date the introduction of barkcloth in Buganda's, or indeed the wider region's, economic history. Indigenous sources mention its use in royal burials but rarely is any indication given of its antiquity. One tradition states, entirely predictably, that the art of barkcloth-making was brought to Buganda by Kintu; Roscoe, however, pointed toward a more specific tradition suggesting that it was taught to the Ganda by the Nyoro. This is problematic in so far as Bunyoro, certainly by the nineteenth century, was wealthy in neither the skills nor the natural resources. According to the somewhat garbled version of the story reported by Speke, barkcloth was supplied by the lake shore peoples to their Nyoro masters when Buganda was little more than a tiny affiliation of descent groups.[13] Gideon Were has noted that the mysterious Chwezi are associated with the introduction of barkcloth to the region, which is to some extent consistent with Speke's findings.[14]

The *ngonge* clan trace the discovery of barkcloth to one of their sub-chiefs during the reign of Kimera, a form of dating which suggests an

[10] Ibid.: 406.
[11] White Fathers: Rubaga Diary 0/13 June 1879.
[12] Similar considerations doubtless lay behind the expansionist drive towards Busoga, a region which also had a thriving barkcloth industry; but the Nile was a rather greater obstacle than the Katonga, and the Ganda were unable to bring the area under direct or permanent control. This is demonstrated in Chapter 9 below.
[13] Speke 1863b: 251–2.
[14] Were 1968: 179.

impossibly distant point in time. The chief in question made his discovery quite by accident, hammering a piece of bark he found particularly attractive in order to break it up. He found that the bark, rather than cracking, simply expanded. The resultant material was fortuitously noticed by a daughter of Kimera, who was greatly taken with it; the rest, as they say, is history. Much of the story is clearly mythical, but barkcloth was worthy of such an elaborate myth: the telling of the story, undoubtedly a centrepiece in the history of the *ngonge* clan, was a way of honouring the perceived event and underlining the importance of the discovery. Such tales are monuments to the past, even though, as we shall see, this one was probably developed not much earlier than the late eighteenth century. Kagwa wrote: 'At the start, there were not many bark cloths but the amount increased very much especially during the reign of Semakokiro. This is the honour of the Ngonge clan; they are in charge of manufacturing the bark clothes of the Kabaka. This has been so since the reign of Kimera up to now, because they were the founder of the way to make bark clothes.'[15]

It is unlikely, however, that any one clan had a monopoly on royal barkcloth production. Kagwa also mentioned Kasumba of the *kasimba* clan, largely based in the *ssaza* of Mawokota, who was the *kabaka*'s barkcloth-maker. This particular post was created by Junju in the second half of the eighteenth century: Kasumba, originally from the Bujaju district of Buddu, came to Junju's notice following the capture of that barkcloth-rich region.[16] The *nnamunnoona* clan in Buddu (who claimed to have come with Kintu but moved south into Buddu) were also renowned for their manufacture of barkcloth: in the late eighteenth century, they saw many of their villages given over to members of Junju's family, whose descendants acquired their barkcloth from there up until the late 1890s.[17] The *mpindi* clan had a somewhat less glamorous claim: they were noted for making rough barkcloths for the *kabaka*'s women.[18]

The popularity of the fabric before 1800 is not altogether clear. It may have been the garb of royalty, as it was in many neighbouring societies in the nineteenth century. Certainly, by the end of the sixteenth century, the *kabaka* was probably being robed in barkcloth, possibly as part of the coronation rites.[19] There is, however, little doubt that the modern history of the cloth begins in the second half of the eighteenth century during the reign of Kabaka Semakokiro. The exact details of what seems to have amounted to a sartorial revolution are unknown, but the implication is that up until his reign barkcloth and the trees from which it was made were officially royal property. The commonest type of clothing in the kingdom had been skins, but Semakokiro decreed that the country at large should grow the trees in plantations and that everyone should wear barkcloth, apparently, Roscoe tells us, under the threat of death.[20]

---

[15] Kagwa 1972: 8–9.
[16] Ibid.: 63.
[17] Ibid.: 108.
[18] Ibid.: 103.
[19] Kagwa 1934: 17.
[20] Roscoe 1911: 403.

This may simply have been the whim of a fashion-conscious ruler, but even this simple explanation implies that the trees were not as common in the eighteenth century as they were in the nineteenth, suggesting in turn that there must have been the enormous operation of expanding their cultivation throughout the country. Alternatively, the trees may have been common enough but simply not used, and Semakokiro may have sought to compel his subjects to tap this underutilized source. But why at this juncture in particular, considering that the manufacture of the fabric had been known for several centuries? The answer must lie, at least partially, in the acquisition of Buddu. Buddu had come under Ganda control only a few years before, during the reign of Semakokiro's brother Junju. The consequent rise in Buganda's total barkcloth production may have opened up opportunities in other parts of the country: for example, if royalty favoured, as it did, the Sango cloths of southern Buddu, restrictions on tree plantations in other parts of the kingdom may have been lifted. It is not inconceivable, moreover, that the Buddu economy persuaded Semakokiro and a number of entrepreneurial chiefs that in barkcloth there were the seeds of a potentially lucrative industry both at home and abroad. As already noted, this may indeed have been a motivating factor in the entire expansionist operation, as important as control of iron deposits and, as we shall see, commerce. Perhaps, also, the relatively sudden infiltration of Buganda's internal market of often superior Buddu cloths served as a fillip for the kingdom's older centres of production. There is certainly no reason to doubt that eighteenth-century producers could respond to external economic stimuli in the way that their descendants did in the late nineteenth and early twentieth centuries with regard, for example, to cotton. The import of cotton and calico through Karagwe, which was probably under way by this time,[21] may also have influenced the popularization of barkcloth under Semakokiro. It might be argued that, as early as the 1780s, chiefs and royalty perceived these imports as greatly superior, if only in terms of prestige, to anything available locally, whether from Buddu or not. Restrictions on the widespread production of barkcloth were therefore eased, with the *kabaka* now having less interest in controlling production, and it became with some rapidity a nationwide industry, especially considering the demand for Ganda textiles throughout the surrounding region. Perhaps barkcloth production expanded markedly at the end of the eighteenth century in direct competition with imported cloths: this theory, however, exaggerates the volume of imported cloths at this time, as well as their direct impact on the bulk of the population. Clearly, the process of popularization did not exclude the political and social elite: as we have already noted, barkcloth was regularly worn by both royalty and chiefs through most of the nineteenth century. Yet an important shift had taken place in or around the 1780s and 1790s, a process culminating in the almost total abandonment of indigenous fabrics except as cultural relics by the early 1900s.

Even so, barkcloth was dominant for a century or more; in the early

---

[21] For example, see Kagwa 1971: 99, who states that coastal commodities had begun to arrive in the late eighteenth century.

1860s, bundles of barkcloth were still being presented regularly to the *kabaka* as tribute,[22] and in the early 1890s the fabric was still prevalent. At this time Lugard observed that '[e]very man and woman is dressed in an mbugu, or large piece of bark-cloth, except those big chiefs who can afford fine white linen'.[23] While there is no doubt that cotton had come to dominate the upper end of the market, and was the most visible and lucrative commodity in a thriving exchange economy, barkcloth was the bedrock upon which the latter was based. Ashe asserted in the late 1880s that barkcloth was made 'by slaves and the poorer class of peasants':[24] it is possible that by this time production was for the most part located in the lower strata of society, the value of the fabric having decreased against imported textiles, and that producers were largely on the periphery of the international exchange economy. But the value of the cloth was such that it remained a common medium of taxation.[25] As in most areas of the economy, however, the civil war of this period took its toll on production. In 1890, Lourdel observed the extent to which the barkcloths of the displaced population were 'nearly all worn out' because production had ceased;[26] this gives some idea of the regularity with which new cloths were normally made. Permanent decline set in after 1900. Lucy Mair, for example, wrote in the early 1930s that 'European stuffs are popular and barkcloths [are] made for sale by not more than three or four men in each village.'[27] Iliffe's assertion that 'imported cloth destroyed most of eastern Africa's textile production' is to some extent demonstrable in the case of Buganda,[28] although Mair's findings represent an important qualification.

The eventual demise of the barkcloth economy did not have a uniform impact throughout the kingdom: it is clear that certain regions were noted for their barkcloth production above others and, as with livestock and much else, the incorporation of these regions into the Ganda state repre-sented a continually evolving economic system. Bulemezi, for example, imported a sizeable proportion of its cloth from Busiro and Mawokota, as the trees themselves did not greatly prosper in the hotter, drier climate of that *ssaza*. Busiro, Mawokota and, in particular, Buddu were regarded as the best areas for barkcloth, and in Buddu, as we have seen, those cloths made at Sango and Bujaju were especially prized.[29] The Sesse islands were also home to several famous centres of production.[30] Any analysis of the origins and development of barkcloth production must, therefore, take account of these regional differences. We have already seen how the acquisition of Buddu represented a significant boost to the industry; similarly, parts of Mawokota which were gradually brought under Ganda control before 1800 must have led to an expansion in overall production.

---

[22] Speke 1863b: 297.
[23] Lugard 1892: 831.
[24] Ashe 1889: 300.
[25] Macdonald 1897: 139.
[26] White Fathers: C14/192 Lourdel to Superior-General, 25 January 1890.
[27] Mair 1934: 95.
[28] Iliffe 1995: 185.
[29] Kagwa 1934: 165.
[30] Speke 1863b: 399.

The Ganda would have to some extent exported their extant skills from the core area to these newly acquired provinces, but the population of Buddu, for example, was also already well acquainted with the manufacture of barkcloth. Buganda adopted something of a mercantilist approach in this sphere, as in many others, as we shall see; it is certainly no coincidence that by the nineteenth century the Ganda should be so renowned in the production of this valuable fabric among their neighbours. It is highly likely that Bunyoro actually lost its international share of the barkcloth economy once it lost control of parts of Mawokota and, more importantly, Buddu in the seventeenth and eighteenth centuries. In so doing, it would have lost a vital source of income and one of the mainstays of homestead production, and its control of regional commerce was noticeably weakened. By the same token, Buganda was by the early 1800s a fairly recent beneficiary of the barkcloth economy, its position as producer of the best cloths in the region to a large extent founded upon the territory it had managed to wrest from others. Barkcloth was undoubtedly one of the biggest prizes to be gained from regional hegemony, as perhaps other empires had discovered several centuries earlier.

Iron & the state

While barkcloth was peculiar to the region, iron was as important among the lakes of the Great Rift as it was elsewhere as human society flourished. Metal technology was critical to Buganda's economic and military growth, and the kingdom's relations with its neighbours, violent or otherwise, were regularly influenced by the need for iron. The desire for access to areas where both skills in iron-working and natural resources were located was certainly a key factor in expansion: once again, Buddu provides the best example. But, in contrast to the barkcloth tree, iron was not abundant within the kingdom's frontiers, and it seems likely that during the eighteenth and nineteenth centuries the bulk of Buganda's iron was imported. Where the kingdom was unable to directly control either production or producers, it often resorted to the system of informal empire, and it was such a system which for many decades guaranteed the supply of this prized metal: perhaps the best example is Koki, southwest of Buddu, which in a loosely tributary position regularly supplied the Ganda with iron hoes and implements such as knives from at least the second half of the eighteenth century. In the mid-1890s, iron was still being brought in bulk from Koki as tribute.[31] Blacksmiths may also have travelled from Koki to Buganda on a fairly regular basis, either to sell their implements or to teach the profession itself. Roscoe was left in no doubt that iron and iron-workers had existed in the vicinity of Koki since long before the reign of the mythical Kintu.[32] Certainly, as we shall see later, the regional

---

[31] UNA A4/1 Wilson to Jackson, 5 January 1895.
[32] Roscoe 1911: 379. The origins of iron-working in the Great Lakes region is unclear, although the Chwezi are thought to have been involved in the diffusion of knowledge. Koki expertise may have come from Katuruka on the southwest shore of Lake Victoria: Katuruka is one of the earliest known smelting sites, dating from the early first millennium

trade in iron was as vital as it was extensive.

It is not clear to what extent iron was actually mined within Buganda's nineteenth-century frontiers; the smelting and reworking of iron brought in from further afield, however, was quite widespread, and in this respect Buganda had much in common with many of its immediate neighbours. Iron which was mined in Kavirondo, for example, was carried west in an unworked form to Busoga and Buganda, where it was made into hoes.[33] Unworked iron was also increasingly important for the making of bullets: in 1879, Mutesa sent a quantity of iron for such a purpose to the White Fathers, an exercise which may be seen as something of a 'rite of passage' for newly arrived Europeans.[34] A contemporary report describes a market in Busoga where iron from Kavirondo was exchanged for bananas and fowls,[35] and Ganda traders undoubtedly travelled considerable distances to acquire those metals regarded as superior to anything produced locally: hoes of a harder and more resilient iron are described as having come from Busoga in 1894.[36] While many states in the region did rely on imported iron, Buganda's resource base was markedly inferior to that of other less celebrated societies around the Great Lakes. This source of potential weakness, the heavy reliance on imported metal, figured prominently in Buganda's foreign policy from the sixteenth century onward. At the same time, one of the key themes of Ganda history concerns the ability and readiness to absorb foreign ideas, skills and raw materials. The case for arguing that Buganda was materially or technologically inferior in the context of the iron industry could only be sustained if it was demonstrated that the Ganda economy was essentially insular. This it was assuredly not: a vibrant, dynamic and inclusive (if selective) society, Buganda drew on the wealth and skills of its neighbours and thus guaranteed not merely survival but rapid growth in industries such as iron-working.

This is not intended, however, to convey the impression that the Ganda mined no iron of their own. Much of the nineteenth-century kingdom was covered with lateritic ironstone, otherwise known as murram,[37] from which it is possible to extract iron ore. Iron was extracted from deposits in southern Kyagwe, some of which, apparently, were close to the main enclosure of the *sekibobo*, the governing chief of Kyagwe.[38] Emin Pasha considered that ore in Buganda was derived from two main sources: bog iron ore in low-lying ground and, more commonly, 'clay ironstone' found lying upon granite on higher ground.[39] Granite was certainly found in the western parts of Buddu and Singo,[40] which goes some way towards

---

[32] (cont.) BC: Schmidt 1978; Iliffe 1995: 34.
[33] UNA A2/1 Owen to Rhodes, 29 March 1993.
[34] White Fathers: Rubaga Diary 1/19 August 1979.
[35] Scott Elliot 1896: 38.
[36] UNA A2/3 Ansorge to Colvile, 5 October 1894.
[37] For example in Thomas & Scott 1935: 59. Lateritic ironstone was less common in Buganda than in Bunyoro and other societies to the west; nevertheless, Mackay, who knew something about iron-working himself, asserted that in Buganda 'every stone is iron': Mackay 1890: 107–8.
[38] Scott Elliot 1896: 39.
[39] Schweinfurth *et al.* 1888: 122.
[40] Thomas & Scott 1935: map between 44 & 45.

verifying Emin Pasha's remarks. Indeed, mining was a common activity in western Buganda, particularly in western Buddu, where the *ngabi* clan had a long history of ore extraction. Once again it is clear that Buganda's acquisition of Buddu in the late eighteenth century provided an enormous economic boost for the kingdom as a whole. More generally, mining on a small scale, based around the family unit or *bakopi* homestead,[41] probably existed throughout the kingdom. The availability of wood for charcoal, essential for both mining and smelting, provides some clues to the prevalence of the activity. In the late nineteenth century, Roscoe observed that '[t]he fuel for smelting was charcoal made from two kinds of wood'. He did not name them, but described them as 'dry papyrus stems' and, if these were unavailable, 'dry, strong, coarse grass'.[42] Specifically, *musasa* was a forest-edge tree producing a hard wood which was used for making charcoal, and was found in several districts, including central Buddu (in the Minziro forest), the Sesse islands, southern and central Kyagwe (in the Mabira forest) and parts of Singo.[43] Kagwa also mentions 'misese', as well as the Lutoro word for this type of wood, 'emizanvuma' or *masanvuma*, and *nongo* as the types of 'coal' used in mining and smelting.[44] The Toro linguistic influence is significant, suggesting the ancient influence of the western kingdoms on iron-working along the northern Lake Victoria shore. *Nongo* was found in many of the same districts as *musasa*: it is perhaps significant, however, that Thomas and Scott, in their wide-ranging survey, mentioned *nongo* only in the context of Bunyoro, which also points towards a profound influence originating outside Buganda's nineteenth-century borders.[45]

Foreign influence in the development of iron-working is evident in many other sources. Kagwa declared openly that 'the knowledge of smelting was acquired originally from the Banyoro and the Banabudu';[46] this is supported by the presence of northern and western vernacular within the industry, while, as we have seen, Buddu itself later became the most important iron-producing region in the nineteenth-century kingdom. These areas are also closely linked with the Chwezi, who, as in so many other spheres of economic activity, have been credited in the older literature with the introduction or at least the diffusion of iron-working to the region.[47] It is important to note, however, that more recent archaeological research has dated iron-working to around the middle of the first millennium BC.[48] Again, Bunyoro figures largely in the early growth of the industry, and traditions relating to Kimera point towards the significance of this influence. The early influx of iron implements and expertise in mining is to some extent personified in Kimera, who is supposed to have spent time before becoming *kabaka* in Bunyoro, whence he brought the

---

[41] Significantly, there is no evidence of iron-workers as magicians in Buganda, as was so often the case in other parts of Africa. This may be a strong indication of the pragmatism or instrumentalism of Ganda material culture.
[42] Roscoe 1911: 379.
[43] Eggeling 1940: 140; Thomas & Scott 1935: 534–5.
[44] Kagwa 1934: 160.
[45] Thomas & Scott 1935: 534–5; Eggeling 1940: 220, 222.
[46] Kagwa 1934: 160.
[47] Were 1968: 179.
[48] For example, Ambrose 1982: 134–5.

first tools and weapons and, by inference, knowledge of extraction. Roscoe wrote: 'When [Kimera] had fled from Wunyi's court in Bunyoro because of his undue familiarity with Wunyi's wife, he attached himself to a smith, and remained with him for some time, learning his work; after a time, when he had mastered the art of smithing, he sent hoes and weapons to Uganda.'[49]

Kagwa suggests that it was in fact Mulanga, a son of Kintu and supposedly living some time before Kimera, who 'learnt to work in iron',[50] while it was apparently under Chwa that iron spearheads were first made, as we shall see below. It is certainly the case that much of this tradition, while having been used almost exclusively in the reconstruction of the political past, also contains important messages concerning the region's economic history. The emphasis placed on such data may be a matter of debate: which should we regard as the more important, the great founders and rulers thus depicted, or the powerful economic and social forces for change which they appear to represent? Although it is now generally accepted that figures such as Kintu and Kimera are wholly mythical, the economic revolutions which facilitated their transmission into mythology were both real and dramatic, and it may be that the clues thus provided to the economic past should be regarded as being as important as those to political development. In any case, whatever the truth behind these tangled messages,[51] it is again significant that the commonest basic term for iron ore in Buganda is *matale*, which is Lunyoro.

Kabaka Kimera is supposed to have named his enclosure *Kanyakasasa*, which conveyed the striking imagery that 'just as the blacksmith's shop has coal burning all the time yet no ashes accumulate, so it is with the king who always kills people and yet they go to him'.[52] This clearly expresses rather more about the nature of Ganda kingship than about metal-working, but the early imagery of the forge is significant. The antiquity and importance of both mining and smelting are reflected in a number of clan histories, and it may reasonably be assumed that many of these early clansmen were either 'foreigners' themselves or itinerant craftsmen, learning new trades abroad and returning with their skills to the Ganda heartland. For example, Kisawo of the *ngeye* clan is supposed to have been an early metal-worker whose job it was to fit ornaments on the arms of *basekabaka* or deceased kings.[53] These ornaments, however, are likely to have been copper, which was of course imported (the Luganda *kikomo* means both copper and bracelet). Kisawo, therefore, probably had commercial connections, but the arrival of copper in Buganda is difficult to date. By the second half of the eighteenth century, copper wire was an increasingly common commodity, being carried by traders from the coast to the lake region, but it is possible that copper had arrived much earlier, from the Katanga region to the southwest, where it had been mined since the fifth century AD.[54] There is little concrete evidence for commerce of

[49] Roscoe 1911: 379.
[50] Kagwa 1971: 6.
[51] For example, see Wrigley 1996: 194–6.
[52] Kagwa 1934: 20.
[53] Kagwa 1972: 4.
[54] For example Connah 1987: 221.

this kind before 1800, although the Nyamwezi were trading with Katanga by the 1820s.[55]

Great social honour was attached to blacksmiths, particularly those in royal service or living within the compounds of prominent chiefs. Although precise details of Kisawo's occupation are not provided, the fact that he is mentioned at all in the *ngeye* clan history is a measure of his perceived importance. Similarly, Mubiru of the *mamba* clan was a renowned smith who gave his name to a popular nineteenth-century adage regarding toil and application in industry.[56] He was scarcely a member of the profession's rank and file: one of his ceremonial duties was to provide the ornaments for the *gabunga*, the head of the clan, an act which according to Kagwa 'installed [the *gabunga*] judge of the whole clan': in effect, Mubiru 'handed that clan over to [the *gabunga*]'.[57] Although his importance may have been partially derived from another unconnected position, his role as a worker of metals undoubtedly enhanced his standing.

The *kkobe* clan also claimed involvement in the early history of metal-working: one of the sub-chiefs of this clan, Lwabiriza, was a noted metal-worker in the Kintu story. Although, once again, the precise nature of his occupation is unclear, Lwabiriza was successful enough to be given several villages in Busiro by Kintu in recognition of his services, according to the clan traditions.[58] The fact that Kintu himself did not exist is, again, not particularly relevant: the story represents the idea that political favour might be granted to the economically successful and was not the preserve of court sycophants or what might be called today professional politicians. Iron-working was clearly one of many economic activities which were encouraged by the political establishment. Indeed, it might be argued that material or nominal rewards handed out on merit by the *kabaka* tended at one time to be responses to economic, rather than political, endeavour: in the fourteenth and fifteenth centuries, for example, the power of the *kabaka* was still curbed by the clan-heads, and *bataka* rather than *batongole* controlled the political make-up of the nascent kingdom. The *kabaka* had not yet been able to erode the authority of clan to the point where he might make political appointments with impunity. Certainly, the well-documented state of political patronage in late nineteenth-century Buganda, engineered by flattery and intrigue and to a considerable extent detached from life outside the royal court, did not necessarily prevail in an earlier age, when, at the risk of depicting a 'merrie Buganda', priorities were rather different and political power more evenly distributed.

Lwabiriza did not represent the *kkobe* clan's only prowess in iron-working. Magere was in charge of Kintu's spears, which, one tradition tells us, were originally made of wood. According to Kagwa's history of the clan, Magere held this position 'up to Kabaka Chwa Nabale and it was under him that iron spears were made. Magere's grandsons fixed their handles and sharpened them.'[59] There seems little doubt that this, though typically

[55] Waller 1874: II, 180; see also Roberts 1968: 125.
[56] Kagwa 1972: 37–8.
[57] Ibid.
[58] Ibid.: 78.
[59] Ibid.: 79.

understated by Kagwa, is meant to represent a revolution of the profoundest importance. The shift from wood to iron is symbolic of a gradual transformation which deeply affected the kingdom's military structures and strategies (see Chapters 9 and 10 below) as well as the metal-working economy itself. With the replacement of wooden spearheads by iron ones, the smithing industry took on a new and vital dimension. That this fundamental technological shift should be credited to the reign of Chwa, another mythical figure associated with Buganda in its political infancy, and perhaps representative of an era for the wider region, is clearly a fantastic telescoping of actual events. As noted above, such technology was probably being developed more than a millennium before. It would be several centuries before the Ganda were a significant force on the battlefields of the lacustrine region; but the superiority of the iron blade was clear to the peoples of the area much earlier, as was the need to search for new sources of iron, although wooden spears were never entirely obsolete even in the nineteenth century.

None the less, although these developments clearly predated Buganda itself, there is no doubting the importance of the reign of Nakibinge, probably in the early or mid-sixteenth century,[60] for the kingdom's ironworking economy. A macrocosmic reading of the relevant sources would seem to suggest that this was the first time that Buganda's recently acquired military technology was properly tested in an international conflict: one Ganda account tells us that Nakibinge greatly prized his blacksmiths 'because they made deadly arrows and spears which helped to conquer the enemies with which he was surrounded on all sides'.[61] Nakibinge may have been the first Ganda ruler to clearly identify the link between iron technology and warfare, and to recognize that the successful prosecution of military activity was heavily dependent upon economic conditions at home. Ultimately, Nakibinge himself was unsuccessful on the battlefield: Buganda was all but crushed by the Nyoro and the *kabaka* appears to have died in the fighting. But certain important lessons were driven home. A key factor behind the defeat of the Ganda army was the limited reserve of iron upon which it could draw for weaponry: 'all the iron for weapons', Kagwa records, 'was exhausted'.[62] Buganda's subsequent recovery, consolidation and gradual expansion was at least in part driven by the need to secure those raw materials, the most important being iron, which lay outside a heartland noted primarily for its agricultural potential.

The extent to which iron was regarded as fundamental to a successful war policy is conveyed by the story of Suna's war against Kiziba, as told to Stanley: '[Suna] commanded his Katekiro to make up 300 man-loads of hoes and old iron and to send them to Kytawa, and to say to him, "Suna sends these hoes and iron to you, for it may be that you are short of spears, arrow-heads, and hatchets. Make weapons for your people in abundance during three months, and prepare for war".'[63]

Unusual though it may seem for the aggressor to send war *matériel* to the enemy, this was a powerful piece of reverse psychology, even allowing for

[60] Reid 1997.
[61] Kagwa 1934: 160.
[62] Ibid.
[63] Stanley 1878: I, 376.

the injection of exaggeration somewhere along the line. Such self-confidence, indeed arrogance, is all the more fascinating as Buganda itself relied so much on imported iron, as we have noted. Yet the Ganda were never complacent about the search for iron as well as the skills necessary to utilize it effectively. In the early eighteenth century, Kabaka Mawanda employed a Nyoro smith Kongonge and provided him with an estate in Kyagwe, a *ssaza* in which, as we have seen, certain areas near the lake shore were ore-bearing. Some 30 or 40 years later, Junju, having completed the annexation of Buddu, brought to the capital and employed a number of blacksmiths from that region.[64] Foreign expertise was clearly still coveted and, as in many other spheres of social, economic and political life, the Ganda were prepared to accept anyone who could contribute to the common good through unusual talents, while at the same time the state did not shrink from offering individual rewards for such endeavour. The role of the *ngabi* clan in Buddu smithing has already been noted: they were based in the south and west of the *ssaza*, particularly in the areas bordering Koki,[65] and in the years following annexation they found themselves linked to a thriving and lucrative commercial metropolis to the north, which perhaps offered greater financial and political rewards than anything they had experienced previously. In addition, the *nte* clan in Buddu were known as prodigious iron-workers, and according to Kagwa 'became the best blacksmiths because they knew how to extract the iron from the ores'.[66] This suggests once again that, as far as Buganda as a whole was concerned, the knowledge of extraction was not as widespread as the actual working of the metal.

Perhaps the most famed clan in this connection was that of the *kisimba*, which contained within its number a certain Walukaga, regarded as the head of all blacksmiths in Buganda. The holder of this title stood at the apex of a 'guild' whose hierarchy straddled the nineteenth-century kingdom. Each *ssaza* also had a head smith, suggesting that, although certain districts stood above others in this regard, forges were located throughout the kingdom.[67] The difficulty with many of the indigenous sources, however, is that mention is usually only made of prominent blacksmiths: less important forge-workers or what we might call country smiths rarely appear in the great traditional pageantry of pre-colonial fame. When the missionary Mackay built the coffin in which Mutesa was to be buried in 1884, some 400 local smiths turned up to assist.[68] If it is assumed that even half this number came from the capital or its environs, some idea is conveyed concerning the prevalence of the profession, at least by the late nineteenth century. Indeed, it seems likely that the nineteenth century bore witness to an enormous expansion in iron-working, coinciding with the

---

[64] Kagwa 1934: 160.
[65] Roscoe 1911: 379.
[66] Kagwa 1934: 160.
[67] Ibid. Walukaga's main enclosure was in Butambala; examples of regional chief iron-workers include Serugoti of Busiro and Mutagubya of Buddu. The *kasimba* clan history states that 'Walukagga was the chief person in charge of making the king's spears and other implements': Kagwa 1972: 63.
[68] Zimbe 1939: 94.

increasing availability of the metal itself. At the height of its territorial power and regional influence, Buganda acquired iron from many sources, including Koki through tribute; moreover, by the 1870s and 1880s coastal merchants were bringing iron to Buganda in considerable quantities, and Livinhac observed in 1879 that axes, knives and hoes of coastal or European manufacture were greatly in demand among the Ganda.[69] The regional iron trade in the second half of the nineteenth century also guaranteed a constant movement of the material in various forms into the kingdom.

The expansion of the industry – which, by the very nature of the acquisition of the iron, consisted largely of melting down and reworking by the nineteenth century – seems not, however, to have led to an erosion of the professional hierarchy which had evolved, as one might have expected. Writing in the context of the 1880s, Zimbe mentions Walukaga, the 'chief of the smiths in the Kingdom, a very honoured man'.[70] The existence of such a figure underlines the disciplined, structured and deferential approach of the Ganda towards their key professions; the personage of Walukaga is a good example of that almost indefinable quality called by the Ganda *kitiibwa*, loosely translated as dignity, respect, authority or prestige, to which most Ganda aspired.[71] It was, moreover, an honour implicitly bestowed on every blacksmith in the country, being on one level an emblematic recognition of the significance of the industry to Buganda's development. We cannot know how provincial smiths viewed Walukaga, assuming of course most had heard of him, or precisely what role he was perceived to perform within the context of the profession as a whole; none the less, references to local forges themselves and iron-working more generally in both indigenous and European sources suggest a deep-rooted pride, perhaps to be expressed as *kitiibwa*, in the profession, and an implicit understanding on the worker's part of his importance in the history and culture of his own society.

Metal-working, then, was seen as a dignified and honourable profession. Blacksmiths would have been well aware of the esteem in which they were held (although, again, this was presumably subject to regional variation), not least because they were exempt from arbitrary arrest, hammers being carried as proof of status. Yet, according to Kagwa, it was not on the whole a particularly profitable profession, and smiths generally did not lead affluent lives: 'The trouble lay in the low rates received for the conversion of metal tools into others. The manufacture of some objects paid rather well, fifty cowry shells being the price of a hoe, axe, spear, or large knife, but a small knife or razor would bring only one or two cowry shells.'[72]

This might be treated somewhat sceptically, and as something of an over-generalization, especially in the context of the late nineteenth century, when the expanding profession must have been profitable enough. Still, there is little reason to doubt that a depressed end of the professional spectrum – hampered by geography, or lack of capital, or insufficient demand –

---

[69] White Fathers: C13/7 Livinhac to Deguerry, 6 November 1879.
[70] Zimbe 1939: 146.
[71] See for example Southwold 1964: 220, and the comments on expressing the concept in English in Murphy 1972: 210. This is also a key concept in Twaddle 1993.
[72] Kagwa 1934: 161.

did indeed exist. Yet those who actually extracted iron were at an economic advantage. Roscoe elaborated on the marketing side of the industry:

> When the smelting was finished, the iron was bought by the villagers or by other smiths who were not able to smelt, but were willing to pay a good price for the rough metal. Rough iron was worked and reworked and finally made into hoes, knives, spears, needles, fish-hooks, bells, and axes … The King had his own smiths, who made the implements required for the royal household, and each important chief had his own smiths upon his estate. These smiths worked for the poorer people, and sold their wares in the market-place, in addition to what they did for their masters … These smiths also learned to work copper and brass wire, and to make the armlets and bracelets so common among the Baganda people … All the knives, axes, and bill-hooks were made on common patterns. Copper and brass were imported, and were worked up again by the smiths into wire bracelets or the heavier kinds of bracelets …[73]

Whether or not the smiths who resided on chiefs' estates were actual smelters would clearly have depended on the location of the estate; but there was also differentiation between homestead smiths and those who were in the employ of important political figures. The latter were clearly chosen on the basis of individual ability and skill and probably, despite Roscoe's assertion that many artefacts were of uniform design, creativity. There was also undoubtedly some division of labour within the homestead forge: in addition to the *muweesi* or blacksmith himself, there was the *mukimba* or blacksmith's charge, who may have been an apprentice of sorts or simply an assistant. Many forges probably relied upon family or homestead labour, and larger and more prosperous forges would have been able to employ more charges or perhaps slaves.

Copper and, to a lesser degree, brass, because of their relative rarity, or the prestige attached to them due to the distance they had travelled, were metals and alloys normally symbolic of wealth and authority in a way that iron never was. Like many materials of great supposed value based on relative rarity, they had virtually no practical application. But the symbolic force of copper in particular was exemplified by the head of the *nsenene* clan, Mugalula, based in Gomba, who possessed large amounts of the metal. He was said to have deliberated upon a copper 'throne', and his milk container, the clan being of pastoral origin, was also made of copper. Most impressive of all were the copper spears he possessed, in many ways the most potent symbols of deep-seated power and, of course, *kitiibwa*: these suggested both military prowess, the echoes of past greatness enshrined within the memorial cavities of the clan, and the ability to accumulate and control great material wealth. Mugalula, indeed, was said never to set eyes on the *kabaka*, so powerful did he believe himself to be, a belief apparently tolerated by the *kabaka* himself.[74] Naturally, Mutesa also possessed copper

---

[73] Roscoe 1911: 382–3.

[74] Kagwa 1972: 13. As we have already seen, the relationship between the *kabaka* and Mugalula can be traced back to the reign of Chwa, to whom Mugalula gave his brother, Kalibbala, as chief herdsman. Regardless of the mythological detail, this 'gift' may be interpreted as a tacit acknowledgement on Mugalula's part of the *kabaka*'s supra-regional authority, but more generally the relationship between the *kabaka* and the head of the

spears: Speke mentions these in the context of a military review in 1862.[75] Felkin, travelling through Bulemezi in 1879, observed that all *ssaza* chiefs possessed copper-headed spears 'as a mark of honour'.[76] These again undoubtedly contributed greatly to the acquisition of *kitiibwa*. A fine example of the material symbols of authority can be seen in the badge of office of the *pokino*, governor of Buddu: Speke noted that he owned 'an iron hatchet, inlaid with copper and handled with ivory'.[77] Still, it is clear from Roscoe's account that copper and certainly brass wire were becoming common enough by the late nineteenth century, and indeed the diversity of the smith's produce is striking.

By the 1880s the blacksmith was the linchpin of Ganda material culture, and most economic activities had become dependent to some degree on the metal-worker. Hunters, fishermen, carpenters, cultivators, traders (in so far as implements forged in Buganda were exchanged both within and without the kingdom's borders) and, of course, warriors all had a common link in their local forge. A new and specialized branch of iron-working had also developed by the late nineteenth century, namely firearm repair and the manufacture of crude ammunition for guns. As early as 1862, Mutesa obtained from Speke some samples of shot and ordered 'his iron-smiths to make some like them'.[78] These workers were the forerunners of the craftsmen described by Lugard in 1892, who observed how the Ganda

> will construct you a new stock to a rifle which you will hardly detect from that made by a London gun-maker. The Fundi [= workman, from Swahili] Kisule, who learnt his art from Mackay, is an accomplished blacksmith and gunsmith, and will make a new spring or repair any damaged rifle with admirable workmanship. Their folding stools of rod iron, and their beautifully-turned-out spears, attest their ability as blacksmiths.[79]

The practical significance of guns, and therefore of the ability to repair them, is highly questionable, as we shall see in due course. Yet it was a valued skill in the 1870s and 1880s, and at the very least demonstrates the adaptability and dexterity of the late nineteenth-century representatives of this ancient profession. In the capital, where in the mid-1880s politics became an even more dangerous business and permeated virtually every aspect of urban life, skill in firearms maintenance among smiths was necessary not only to prosper but to survive. Robert Ashe reported in 1886 that although Walukaga was executed for professing Christianity – an act which itself, perhaps, signified the end of an era and which was certainly indicative of Mwanga's destructive paranoia – another principal iron-worker of Christian persuasion was spared 'solely on account of his being

---

[74] (cont.) *nsenene* clan may have been one of peers keeping each other at a diplomatic arm's length. Of course, it may not be completely irrelevant that Kagwa himself belonged to the *nsenene* clan, and that he was attempting to demonstrate that historically the *kabaka* was never so supreme that he was able to disregard all other political or regional figures.

[75] Speke 1863b: 406.

[76] CMS CA6/010/48 Felkin's Journal, 7 February 1879.

[77] Speke 1863b: 429.

[78] Ibid.: 337.

[79] Lugard 1892: 828.

able to mend guns'.[80] This would seem to be the same Matayo Kisule referred to above by Lugard. It is likely that blacksmiths based at the capital were particularly prone to conversion, as many were drawn to both Anglican and Catholic missions, intrigued by European smithing technology, the most noted practitioner of which was Mackay. It is striking that Walukaga appears not to have acquired sufficient skill in firearm maintenance to save his life, and it may be that certain traditionalist strands of the profession spurned such work. But gun repair was not the only innovation in indigenous iron-working in the last years of the nineteenth century: Ashe also noted that by the late 1880s Ganda metal-working was being influenced by implements and techniques imported by the coastal merchants. Files and instruments for boring had been introduced by Arab traders, as had the arts of brazing and tinning.[81]

Pre-colonial pottery culture

Buganda was unusual among many societies in east and central Africa in that pottery was a specialized profession, and one to which great economic and cultural importance was attached. Despite the increasing availability of coastal and European utensils from the late eighteenth century onward, the role of the indigenous potter was not seriously threatened until well after the establishment of the Protectorate. One indigenous account suggests that pottery, taking its place alongside the activities described in this and earlier chapters, was one of the oldest industries in Buganda and, as with many of the aforementioned professions, it obviously predated the kingdom itself by several centuries. Sekayala was the first potter, according to one tradition, appointed by Kintu who subsequently created the post of Sedagala in his honour.[82] Again, somewhere within this telescoped version of events, there lie the clues to the origins of a professional hierarchy and the gradual development of a guild of sorts with representatives at the metropolitan centre. The position of Sedagala – apparently a royal potter, although *mujoona* is also the term for a potter in the service of the monarch[83] – was recognized up until the reign of Kamanya in the late eighteenth or early nineteenth century. Under Kamanya, a powerful Nyoro influence was brought to bear on pottery at the capital, perhaps reflecting a similar influence on the profession in the country as a whole. A Nyoro potter, apparently a war-captive, so impressed Kamanya with his skills that he became potter to the *kabaka* and was given his own village near the royal capital. Sedagala, it seems, remained the nominal head of the profession, but his position was undermined somewhat.[84] The precise nature of this Nyoro influence is unclear and, although, ironically, a number of European commentators in the 1870s regarded Ganda pottery as superior to that of Bunyoro, this was probably less to do with pottery

80 CMS G3 A5/0 1886/308 Ashe to Wigram ? May 1886.
81 Ashe 1889: 311.
82 Kagwa 1934: 159.
83 Zimbe 1939: 428.
84 Kagwa 1934: 159.

per se than the general perception of Ganda superiority to Bunyoro in political and social terms. In 1935, Thomas and Scott wrote that '[p]articular mention may be made of the Banyoro craftsmen who manufacture a thin, black earthenware which, although brittle, is much superior to the usual manufactures in red clay'.[85] Red clay was prevalent in Buganda. In the mid-1850s, Burton reported that Ganda pottery was renowned throughout the region,[86] perhaps as a result of the injection of Nyoro ideas half a century earlier, but the Ganda also imported large amounts of earthenware, especially from Buvuma. In 1901, a colonial official observed of the Vuma that '[p]ottery is their greatest industry, and they are really very clever in this line', and indeed Vuma pots were frequently traded for foodstuffs with the Ganda.[87]

Throughout much of central and east Africa, pottery was usually associated with female labour, but there was some disagreement among nineteenth-century European observers concerning such a sexual division of labour in Buganda. Emin Pasha asserted that pottery was almost wholly a male preserve,[88] and Felkin suggested that both men and women might be potters.[89] It is difficult to resolve this question, although the social position often associated with the making of pottery might suggest that men were more prevalent in the industry; equally, however, it may have been the case that simply the most prominent potters were men. Potters in general enjoyed a privileged position in Ganda society: like iron-workers, they were exempt from arbitrary arrest. The fruits of their labour were looked upon symbolically as sources of food, and thus of civilization itself, and as such were regarded in the abstract as life-sustaining.[90] The honour bestowed on certain pots and other receptacles appears to have been common throughout the region, and even invading armies, while they might make use of the pots in a conquered village, would rarely destroy or steal them;[91] if they did, a grave violation of international conduct was regarded as having occurred. Roscoe asserted that potters were a 'distinct class of workmen, who lived with their families in communities apart from other people'. Those in the service of the *kabaka* or a chief received their own land in return for a proportion of their products.[92]

Pottery was produced in most parts of the nineteenth-century kingdom where enough *bbumba* or clay could be found. Felkin provided some detail:

> Boys and girls are at an early age initiated into the art. Two kinds of pottery, a coarse and fine variety, are manufactured. Vessels for carrying water and for cooking are made of the coarse kind ... Drinking cups and tobacco pipes are made of the finer clay. They are very thin and beautifully worked, but all the pottery is easily broken, as no flux or glaze is used. The fine clay ... is procured from the beds of streams ... The most

---

[85] Thomas & Scott 1935: 285–6.
[86] Burton 1859: 384.
[87] UNA A8/1 Tomkins to Comm., 8 November 1901.
[88] Schweinfurth *et al.* 1888: 88.
[89] Felkin 1885–6: 726.
[90] Kagwa 1934: 159.
[91] Ibid.: 160.
[92] Roscoe 1911: 399.

unusual patterns employed are circular dots, elliptical punch marks, bands, parallel incised lines, chequer concentric rings, guilloche, spiral pattern, and basketwork ... Drinking bowls and both kinds of pipes are sometimes coloured with red oxide of iron or with white colour ...[93]

Felkin's account suggests that there existed a broad range of pottery styles by the late nineteenth century, probably drawn from a number of sources across the region including Bunyoro. In general terms, however, the early pottery of the lake region has come to be known as dimple-based ware among historians and archaeologists. This is distinct, though not wholly dissimilar, from Kwale ware nearer the coast and the 'channelled' ware of Zambia and Zimbabwe.[94] The specialization of pottery in Ganda society by the nineteenth century is suggested by the existence of a pottery village near the capital, described here by A.B. Lloyd, of which there may have been many throughout the kingdom:

> Pottery also, among the Waganda, is quite a fine art. Very near to Mengo there is a whole village of pottery workers; large cooking-pots and water-pitchers, basins and cups of all shapes are made . . . The pottery is burnt after it is moulded to shape – huge fires of wood are made, a quantity of fine dried grass being mixed with it, and into the hot ash the pots are placed for an hour or two. Smoking being almost universal in Uganda, pipes are therefore made by the potter; a finer kind of clay is used, and they are coloured black, with a glazed shiny surface.[95]

This would certainly seem to support Roscoe's assertion about the tendency of potters to live in distinct communities. It is clear, then, that various qualities of clay were used in the manufacture of different implements. Emin Pasha's scientific eye observed that the 'red soil is covered by a layer of grey compact clay only in the hollows and in the declivities; the lowest stratum of this clay is free from vegetable detritus, and yields an excellent material for pottery'. He noted the existence of both red and grey clay north of the capital.[96] Felkin concurred with this analysis, remarking that '[t]he upper strata of land, for the depth of 2 or 3 feet, is a rich black alluvial soil, under which is a bed of red sandy clay averaging about 30 feet in thickness, and lower still in many places is a layer of tolerably pure porcelain earth'.[97] Although no eye-witness account or indeed archaeological evidence exists, Ganda pottery centres must have been peppered by digs or quarries several feet deep, perhaps covering considerable areas if the settlement was of long standing. If such digs did exist, it may be that they facilitated some division of labour within the profession itself, that is, that diggers and other labourers were distinct from actual potters. As with forges, the larger and more prosperous the pottery centre or community, the more people would have been employed and the more pronounced the division of labour.

Pottery was thus a significant industry, both economically and culturally,

[93] Felkin 1885–6: 726–7.
[94] Sutton 1968: 91–2; Phillipson 1985: 172–5.
[95] Lloyd 1900: 133.
[96] Schweinfurth *et al.* 1888: 125, 129–30.
[97] Felkin 1885–6: 700.

and it was certainly regarded as superior to its distant relations of basketwork and weaving. In the nineteenth century these were common homestead activities: baskets were generally made with the young leaves of the wild palm or with banana and plantain fibres.[98] Basketwork was largely a female industry, and appears often to have been associated with the poorer sections of a community, perhaps as a means of subsistence for impoverished homesteads. Roscoe asserted that the making of baskets 'was a means by which poor women were able to obtain the many little things which otherwise they would not have procured'.[99] Perhaps these were women whose plantations had suffered from lack of rainfall, or whose menfolk had been casualties of war or been pressed into the service of the state; many such scenarios are plausible, and there is no doubt that both the urban and the rural poor of pre-colonial Buganda had various means by which to meet subsistence demands. Basketwork, requiring little capital or specialization, was probably only one such option, and it may well have been critical in the evasion of bondage, which, as we shall see, was the last resort for poor individuals and homestead groups. As far as the role of women is concerned, an alternative interpretation is possible. Roscoe clearly viewed the selling of baskets by women as symptomatic of a male-dominated society, and an example of the manner in which women were essentially marginalized in economic activity. Most contemporary observers were likewise persuaded, and so modern historians are compelled to accept, through lack of clear evidence to the contrary, that this was at least superficially the case. But we need not take Roscoe's view at face value, and it is possible that he was inadvertently describing a process by which women were actually asserting their economic independence. While there are relatively few references to women in the market-place, this was apparently a situation in which women did indeed take their wares – in this case basketwork – to a local market. Indeed, although many of the economic activities and processes described in the last three chapters appear, with the exception of farming, to have been male-dominated, we need to exercise caution in our evaluation of the role of women and to be aware that there may have been many other less obvious ways in which women worked the system to their advantage. The fact that they do not loom large in the relevant sources is frustrating for historians who would want to reconstruct their past; but their lack of voice should not preclude the possibility of real economic control exercised by women in many spheres.

[98] Roscoe 1921: 221.
[99] Ibid.: 222.

Summary of Part One

The preceding three chapters represent an attempt to demonstrate, in as much detail as space and my sources permit, the complexities of Buganda's internal economic base. Certain areas of the domestic economy were subject to profound change in the seventeenth, eighteenth and nineteenth centuries; other spheres were characterized by a marked degree of continuity, and were only fundamentally altered by the onset of colonial rule. But, in general terms, Buganda's material economy was subject to the same kinds of pressures and mutations as any in other parts of the world. It changed from within, as a result of specific policies issued from the metropolitan centre, and also responded to changing circumstances outside the direct control of the territorial state: it did not exist in seclusion but was joined almost seamlessly to the surrounding region. Above all, it was complex, sophisticated and often fragile, so many spheres of industry indelibly intertwined and contributing to a coherent and perceptible whole. Clearly it was a combination of ample rainfall and prudent agricultural techniques which permitted a sophisticated urban environment and the development of homesteads not devoted solely to the growing of crops; but each sphere of the economy was dependent on every other, and as with the economy as a whole no one operated in isolation. This is not to subscribe to the thesis of the centralized political state, which points toward the domination at all levels of economic society by central metropolitan authority, by implication rendering innovation difficult if not impossible. On the contrary, the overall picture which I have tried to paint here is intended to portray not a centralized state but a loose and flexible alliance of economic and social contributions, distantly managed by a central political authority. Buganda was not a homogeneous but a composite society, tempering the demands of the state necessary to maintain the sociopolitical infrastructure by recognizing the benefits of economic freedom and the contributions made by disparate groups to the collective good.

Nineteenth-century Buganda's economic and material base was the kingdom's strength when it was successful, generating wealth and security in local communities and influencing external events through mercantilist guile; and its weakness when it failed or faltered, when natural calamities such as drought and disease sapped its productive energy, or when internal political breakdown disrupted the efficient if delicate chain of production. I have also tried, despite the difficulties posed by the nature of the sources, to portray the human dimension of Buganda's economic energy, the men and women who worked with iron, clay and barkcloth, who herded and cultivated, and who so often have been depicted either as faceless factors in a centralized political system, or as essentially unprogressive producers incapable of innovation and therefore not worthy of closer study in the way that their European counterparts might be. But the people who drove Buganda's economic machine, like those in other parts of sub-Saharan Africa, struggled and adapted and innovated within their cultural and economic framework; strove for individual security and prosperity; and invested their labour in a political system which facilitated such pursuits, thus ensuring its continued survival. Moreover, they belonged to often ancient professional genealogies, many of which were echoes of a human past much older than the kingdom itself. The hierarchies which evolved and the *kitiibwa* which was bestowed on the holders of titles were only the most obvious and public ways in which Buganda's material culture was celebrated and specialization lauded; behind it all, quiet and ageless recognition was being paid to the real builders of the nineteenth-century state, however uncoordinated and abstract the expression of the past may have been.

On a more prosaic level, it is beyond question that the organization of crop production was critical to the growth of the modern Ganda state, in terms of both land usage and labour. Intensive production in the southern *ssaza*s of the kingdom permitted the growth of quite a dense population gathered in relatively stable settlements. Yet we have also seen that intermittent crop failures led to food shortages in the nineteenth century and probably earlier: paradoxically, perhaps, these failures were felt all the more keenly precisely because a generally high level of agricultural productivity had encouraged the growth of a specialized and professional sector in society for which agriculture was much less important. The repercussions of agricultural failure were thus more profoundly felt than might have been the case in a region less densely populated and more broadly rooted in a cultivation economy. It is virtually impossible to assess the impact of such shortages earlier in Buganda's history – they may have influenced internal politics and external growth to a pronounced degree – but they were certainly of great significance in the late nineteenth century, particularly in the 1880s, when they coincided with livestock disease to seriously undermine the kingdom's productive base and, therefore, its internal security. The diversification of crop production engendered by coastal merchants at the capital from the 1860s onward failed to offset these problems, which is probably as indicative of the limited impact of such diversification as of the severity of the recurrent droughts. Food shortages and cattle disease formed part of a great concatenation of events which served to weaken Buganda in the years leading up to the establishment of the protectorate. But these events should not be viewed in isolation: as we shall see in later chapters, natural calamities intensified at a time when the Ganda army was in decline, when there were heightening political and social tensions in the capital, and when the *kabaka* himself was dying. The potency of this last factor was not diluted by the secularity of the *kabaka*'s position: his physical demise seemed to be the manifestation (and perhaps, to some extent, the cause) of the kingdom's much larger political, military and economic ailments, a comparison not lost on a number of prominent chiefs. At the same time, dwindling ivory reserves threatened commercial disaster for Buganda, as well as signifying the onset of ecological imbalance; Mutesa and Mwanga were compelled to rely increasingly upon tribute or violence or both to ensure a continued supply of ivory. Yet Buganda's ability to prosecute successful military campaigns was not what it had been 50 or even 30 years earlier, and tributary relationships were found to be less than reliable. This also had important consequences as regards the export of slaves, although time – personified by the imperial and imperious *bazungu* – was already running out for this particular commercial endeavour.

The quest for fertile agricultural land on the one hand and fine pastures on the other was one of the most important motivating factors in both the spatial and the socio-political expansion of Ganda society. In this connection, as in so many others, the annexation of Buddu was of immense significance, and the degree to which cattle was a key consideration in economic growth is reflected in Buganda's long-term interest in the lands to the west of Buddu. This interest periodically manifested itself in the dispatch of armies, not least during the eighteenth and early nineteenth centuries, but warfare was not the only means by which valued commodities were acquired: commerce at every level was probably more important still, both in the development of the Ganda economy and in the definition of Buganda's normal relations with its neighbours. The productivity of homesteads and plantations in terms of the goods and articles described in the preceding chapters is clearly only part of the story. As has already been suggested at various junctures, Buganda's economic strength and social cohesion lay in large part in the exchange system, through which passed foodstuffs, cattle and other livestock, skins and the produce of the lake and rivers. By the nineteenth century, the volume and variety of such trade goods must have increased enormously with Buganda's own expansion, which facilitated increased specialization and, through relative political security, intensive and heterogeneous settlement.

This is perhaps even more true of the industries described in Chapter 4: these were activities which not only generated wealth in the market-place, but, in the case of iron, produced the tools of violence which were necessary when commercial channels failed. The production of barkcloth was open to anyone with a plot of land; its expansion from the late eighteenth century, almost certainly linked to the acquisition of Buddu, represented a new era of Ganda economic dominance in the region. Again, as we shall see, this was especially true of the kingdom's commercial relations with its neighbours. The more specialized metal-working and pottery industries offer the best examples of how economic endeavour was rewarded with social, and often political, position: indeed, a substantial province of Ganda culture was a celebration of material culture. More tangibly, however, the textile and metal-working industries placed Buganda at the centre of a thriving regional commercial system, and it is to this system that we turn our attention in Part III. Before that, however, we examine the state's human resources, and the ways in which the utilization of human beings, unlike metals, textiles and animals, compelled Ganda society to consider such concepts as liberty and slavery.

Part Two

Labour & Liberty
The state
& its human resources

Five

Labour & Taxation

In the previous section we examined the kinds of raw materials and economic resources which the nineteenth-century kingdom had at its disposal, and how the control and utilization of these led to political, social and cultural development. We now turn our attention to the ways in which the state drew directly on its most precious resource, its human resources. I have attempted to describe how the evolution of the Ganda state owed much to the individual's relative economic freedom, in terms of both commercial activity and production. Yet the pre-colonial state tempered these individual liberties through various systems of coercion. A complex system of taxation or tribute had developed by the nineteenth century, and there can be few clearer indicators than the payment of tax – one of the two great certainties in life – of the degree to which the citizen is 'legally' bound to an exploitative infrastructure founded on the concept of mutual need. Nor was the offering of material wealth to a central system or its representatives the only manner in which the citizen of Buganda was expected to put his shoulder to the state wheel. 'Free' labour was organized by the state on a fairly regular basis to undertake public works, including the erection of buildings and, most dramatically, the construction of a network of highways linking much of the kingdom. At the extreme end of the scale, slavery ensured a subservient class, lacking the normal rights enjoyed by the broadly defined *bakopi* or free peasantry, upon which the state relied for a wide range of labour activities; slavery also served to underpin the system of professional, social and cultural deference and obligation.

Clearly, the concepts of class and obligation are of considerable importance in analysing how any given society functions, and how it enlists its members as a collective economic asset. In the broadest possible sense, class is a motivational and organizational notion critical to the effective functioning of economic and political structures. Again in a wide sense, it is fundamental to any discussion of labour organization as it implies differentiation and stratification, lending complexity to social, economic

95

and, ultimately, political relations. Yet is it possible to refer to class in nineteenth-century Buganda? The eminent anthropologist of the Lake Victoria region, Lloyd Fallers, thought not: Buganda was, rather, a classless society. The argument was that this situation came about as successive rulers sought to concentrate in their own hands the power of promotion, breeding an open and competitive society in which one could be a *mukopi* or peasant one day and the *katikiro* the next, and vice versa.[1] In this way, social strata were redundant. In theory this remained true until the late nineteenth century, although there was geographical inequality in so far as being resident nearer the capital afforded a greater opportunity to experience the vicissitudes of political life. Yet there appears to be some confusion here as to what constitutes a class: there may indeed have been fluid political mobility in theory, but this is to some extent separate from the very real social and economic structures and hierarchies, some of which have already been mentioned, which were in place by the nineteenth century. Divisions of labour had emerged, often centuries in the making, which had both social (gender, ethnicity and cultural respect) and economic (demand for produce, degree of skill and level of utility) bases. A number of people were increasingly identified by their professions. Certain professions were exclusive, and among these may be counted iron-working and pottery; some professions, or branches of those professions, for example, had been almost exclusively associated with particular clans since before 1800. Certainly, sideways movement was not so easy that such professional distinctions can be overlooked, as Fallers's argument suggested. In the early colonial period, the missionary A.B. Fisher wrote that 'crafts cannot be learned – a man must be born of the potter or blacksmith's clan';[2] ignoring his misuse of the term 'clan', this seems highly likely and meant that people of a particular lineage or in a certain community were linked to a social and economic position and rank as befitted their profession. Iron-workers who could smelt, for example, may be seen as something of a labour aristocracy compared with the comparatively humble barkcloth-maker whose wife tended their small banana plantation. Moreover, it has been demonstrated in previous chapters how professional and economic success could bring rewards both material and political, and that success in certain key professions was much more likely to attract such political and social favour than in others. This would seem to suggest that a degree of social stratification had emerged by the nineteenth century. It was of course in theory possible, as Fallers argued, for anyone to achieve high political and social rank; yet clearly such social mobility by itself did not prevent the growth of a professional, social and economic consciousness among particular groups.

There may have been considerable commercial and entrepreneurial freedom within these professions; none the less, it may be argued that socio-economic groupings based on a varying range of expectations and aspirations became perceptible by the nineteenth century. Indeed this development was probably hastened during the nineteenth century,

[1] Fallers 1959, 1964.
[2] Fisher 1912: 36.

particularly after the 1840s, which may be identified as a period of heightened economic awareness. Particular professionals were lauded above others and found themselves exempt not only from arbitrary arrest, as we have seen.[3] Other exemptions and divisions of labour further reflected Buganda's social, economic and cultural complexity. For example, it seems that state labour was not undertaken by the pastoralist community, which, as a number of observers noted, kept itself and its settlements distinct from the agriculturists. Indeed it would appear that the Hima were legally exempt from such state service, even though they were under the patronage of local chiefs. The details of the arrangement by which they held their land are unclear; however, as we have already seen, the Hima tended the cattle of the chiefly class. Exempt from war, labour and, possibly, taxation, the Hima looked after the livestock of their political masters in lieu of these other more common obligations, and were thus permitted to establish themselves on chiefs' estates. Again, the implied measure of official sanction for the pastoralists' peripheral contribution to central government suggests, perhaps, deeper historical and cultural agreements shaping the relationship between two distinct groups.

Sexual divisions of labour are also discernible, and some of these have already been examined: agriculture was largely, though by no means exclusively, a female domain. In other spheres, women often performed social and economic functions perceived as being beneath the dignity of the male. In the next chapter, we examine female slavery: here it is sufficient to state that women appear to have been more vulnerable to enslavement, however temporary, than men. Women, in theory at least, were excluded from most of the esteemed professions described in previous chapters. In nineteenth-century Ganda culture, the concept of the female as fundamentally weak or unreliable, even dangerous if not properly controlled, is underlined by the mythical story of the kingdom's creation. Of particular significance is the role played by Kintu's wife Nambi, who brought death personified, Walumbe, from heaven to earth. The parallel with the story of Adam and Eve, or that of Samson and Delilah, in which the woman is also a source of weakness and betrayal, is striking. Moreover, although the female role as giver of life appears to have been celebrated to some extent through the honour attached to the *kabaka*'s mother, the fact that disgraced soldiers were made to dress like pregnant women again implies that even (or perhaps especially) in this role women were seen as weak and decidedly inferior. One missionary claimed that labour distinctions between the sexes could be identified thus: men were engaged in

---

[3] Rusch has also argued that there was increasing differentiation within the 'broad mass' of *bakopi*: while the Ganda who relied solely on agriculture were obliged to offer their services and labour to local chiefs, professional craftsmen were often exempt from the 'indignities' of public labour and were given land in return for a proportion of their manufactures. But Rusch's Marxist perspective is both confusing and misleading. Craftsmen, he argues, despite these 'privileges', continued to be tied to the lower class because 'they too lacked the independent means of production, except for some tools or implements, and were therefore compelled to enter into a state of dependence'. The only genuine differences between various groups of *bakopi* were the ways in which each was 'exploited' by the ruling class. This interpretation of the relationship between specialized professions and chieftainship lacks both originality and evidence: Rusch 1975: English summary, 380.

house-building; women were food-providers and mothers, and collected firewood and water.[4] This is clearly a gross, and selective, oversimplification; yet it does suggest that, in a social context, men tended towards external labours and women internal. Even so, in the realm of state labour, women were not exempt: they were expected to assist in the cleaning of the public highways.[5] Sir Gerald Portal's brother observed '[g]angs of women making a great broad road, and bridging the swamps'.[6] Women were also responsible for the maintenance of the *kabaka*'s enclosure, performing such tasks as the clearing of bush and weeds;[7] they probably undertook similar roles for chiefs throughout the kingdom.

Taxation in the nineteenth century

Yet one aspect of economic and political life which bound most of the above groups together was the imposition of tax, the universality of which underlined central government's managerial role and formed a critical component of the concept of national sovereignty. One of the most critical contributions made by citizens to the state is clearly financial or material. Without this contribution, the government cannot function and the state does not exist; as the members of the state contribute the fruits of their labour to a central body, they endorse the regime. Citizens, of course, require reciprocal arrangements, and this requirement, in the case of Buganda, was no less significant for being unwritten. Taxation was the means by which the *kabaka* paid for his administration and maintained his extensive household. To some extent, it probably also permitted him and other prominent chiefs to trade externally on their own account. Equally important, it was a means of social and political control, in so far as there existed a widely held belief in the need for individual contributions to the wealth of the collective society, as personified by the *kabaka* himself. At the close of the nineteenth century, the missionary J.F. Cunningham made a fascinating, if inadvertent, comparison between state labour and tribute, asserting that '[t]he fundamental principle of the state was that all things and persons were the property of the king, and were absolutely at his disposal'.[8] This 'fundamental principle', which as a political philosophy was certainly not unique to Buganda, was the central ideology behind the organization and legitimization of state power. It should not, however, be taken at face value: while it may have been, in Buganda as elsewhere, the guiding creed of political life, it is an over-simplification of the relationship between governed and governing. It was as much a euphemism for loyalty, a pre-colonial expression of nationalism, as any clear articulation of political reality. None the less, as Cunningham implies, it was a principle which applied both to the citizen's free time, as it were, and to his or her material possessions. It is, of course, impossible to say for certain, but it may be

[4] Hattersley 1908: 108.
[5] Hattersley 1906: 57.
[6] Portal 1894: 214.
[7] Kagwa 1972: 25.
[8] Cunningham 1905: 232–4.

assumed that through such a principle the *bakopi* accepted that everything they offered was done in the name, and for the good, of the state.

Tax collection was often a complex affair by the nineteenth century, and seems to have depended on a remarkably accurate knowledge of the kingdom's resources by district. All things considered, levies of tax do not seem to have been particularly excessive, with the 'traditional' accounts, at least, markedly devoid of the kind of anti-tax uprisings with which Western history is replete. As I shall argue below, moreover, the excesses of Mwanga's reign are to some extent the exception which proves the rule. But, despite what we might call the relative fairness of the tax regime, the *kabaka*'s treasury drew considerable wealth thereby. The Ganda could be taxed in just about everything they owned or produced, which gave the nineteenth-century state considerable scope. Common articles of tax included cowry shells, pots, barkcloth, hoes and other metal implements, shields, fish and livestock. Agricultural produce was also demanded by the political establishment, underlining the extent to which by the nineteenth century the latter was the non-productive sector of Ganda society. The regularity of levies is unclear, and probably varied from one reign to another. Cunningham, again, suggested that tribute was not demanded at fixed stages, but only when the *kabaka* – or those in charge of the royal treasury, for example the *katikiro* – deemed it necessary or appropriate.[9] This was probably true in general, and sometimes political rather than economic impulses were behind the decision to tax certain districts. Certain rulers in the nineteenth century and earlier were notoriously erratic in their collection of taxes. Bloody sprees, of the kind popular with Mwanga in the mid-1880s, sometimes took the place of peaceful state intervention, but these were probably aberrations. The peaceful collection of tribute was more common, and indeed internal raids should be seen not as collections of tribute but assertions of royal potency, usually symptomatic of tensions at the centre. Moreover, the booty thus gathered rarely consisted of anything other than cattle and a few unfortunate women, which were then distributed among the faithful at the capital. It is critical, then, to recognize the distinction between plunder and the levying of tax: the Ganda themselves would certainly have known the difference. As in other spheres of Ganda life, violence had its place, but it was rarely wanton and usually confined and channelled within broadly understood parameters.

Contemporary accounts provide rich material on taxation, and foremost among these is that of Sir Gerald Portal, the first commissioner of the Uganda Protectorate in 1893; besides his own observations, he derived much of his information from conversations with other Europeans, notably missionaries, already in Buganda when he arrived. Portal, aiming to depict an impossibly top-heavy and corrupt bureaucracy which it was the British

---

[9] Ibid. Kagwa tells us that, up until the reign of Suna, the *katikiro* was in charge of the royal treasury: during that time, however, the incumbent had shown himself to be financially imprudent, and the 'treasury' was moved to the *kabaka*'s own enclosure: Kagwa 1934: 96. Although the *katikiro* seems to have retained some responsibility in this department, his position may have been gradually eroded thereafter. Harry Johnston later described the *mukwenda* as the 'treasurer' of the royal enclosure: Johnston 1902: II, 683.

duty to correct, actually provides us with a compelling account of the layers of central and local government. This 'endless and complicated network' of officials stretched from powerful provincial governors to 'the poverty-stricken headman of a miserable village'. In between were various levels of sub-chiefs whose importance in the scale was directly related to the number of people who fell under their jurisdiction. The collection of tax was one of the primary functions of this supra-regional network. Although it is unclear in what ways it changed over time, this network may be seen as the skeleton of the nineteenth-century Ganda state, representing the system by which its people could be organized as a coherent whole and made to attend to the state's needs in terms of physical labour and material wealth, not to mention, as we shall see, warfare.[10]

Portal underlines the idea that the decision to collect tax was centrally taken, the process being initiated by the royal court selecting the province to be made to pay. The centralized impetus is also described, at least in a nineteenth-century context, by Kagwa, who records that Suna appointed a chief named Lumweno, along with the *mukwenda*, to make levies of tribute,[11] perhaps as part of his tax reforms alluded to above. In the late 1860s, Mutesa sent the *kauta*, an important officer based at the royal court, to 'collect taxes from those people who had not gone to war'.[12] It seems that, certainly by the early 1890s, only one *ssaza* was taxed at any given time; this doubtless reflected the political reality of the time, with a largely figurehead *kabaka* at the head of a kingdom divided up between Protestant and Roman Catholic parties and their leaders. Portal described the process in 1893 thus:

> As soon as the king and council have agreed upon the province ... the governor is forthwith informed that he had better bestir himself, and produce what is wanted ... He, nothing loath, for he has probably even intrigued that his province may be the one selected, departs from the capital with many promises and vows of loyalty. On arrival in his district he summons before him all the most important local chiefs, and to each one assigns the amount of the contribution for which he will be held responsible. In this partition the governor is particularly careful to see that the aggregate amount, when brought in, will be more than double of what he has to pay over to the king; the rest will remain in his hands. Away go the sub-chiefs; the whole proceeding is repeated again and again in endless subdivision and gradation, and thus the hard-working peasantry, beaten and persecuted until the very last drop is wrung out of them, have to pay in the end five times, and even ten times, the amount at which their province was assessed.

In this way, Portal asserted, as little as a tenth of total tribute actually reached the royal treasury.[13] Portal's fellow officer J.R. Macdonald also claimed that the 'taxes were collected from the peasantry, and each chief, as they passed upward, deducted his own recognised percentage'.[14] This is

[10] Portal 1984: 197.
[11] Kagwa 1971: 118.
[12] Ibid.: 164.
[13] Portal 1894: 191–3.
[14] Macdonald 1897: 139.

intriguing testimony, and if accepted forces us to re-evaluate the relationship between *kabaka* and chief, between capital and district. It is, however, important to emphasize that evidence from the 1890s – the post-revolution era in Buganda – cannot be used in the context of power-politics to generalize about the nineteenth century as a whole. It may be that we can consider such evidence as relating with certainty only to the 1890s, and to speculate – nothing more – that certain elements of the 1890s situation may have their origins in an earlier era. It is clear from Portal's evidence that the *kabaka* by the 1890s was not a financially omnipotent monarch upon whom all relied for largesse and redistribution. Rather, chiefs at all levels were capable of looking after their own interests. The *kabaka's* court, according to Portal's account, was distanced and out of touch with the realities of wealth movement in Buganda after c. 1890. This is not to say that the system was corrupt as such; the system as described here may have been sanctioned from the centre, and indeed Macdonald refers to the local deduction of a 'recognised percentage', although there is no other evidence to suggest this. But it can certainly be argued that in this era the *kabaka* was a much less relevant and central figure in the control of national wealth than might be assumed. Whether this was true of an earlier era is, again, a matter of speculation, although it seems possible to consider, based on the ideas of economic freedom presented in Part I, that tax collection had always been a more complex and decentralized affair than the thesis of the omnipotent state might suggest. We can only speculate whether the monarchy in the 1890s, so reduced in terms of financial authority, really represented such a total break with the past, or whether there were already certain limitations on central authority which facilitated the situation described by Portal in 1893.

According to a report complied by Roscoe and Kagwa, moreover, the collection of tax remained an important duty of the *kitawi* or clan heads, perhaps reflecting a pre-nineteenth-century arrangement which the central kingship had gradually sought to undermine but with only limited success by the late nineteenth century. According to their findings,

> The Sekibobo (of Chagwe) when collecting taxes in his saza to this day orders his mumyuba (2nd in command) to tell the original Kitawi to collect the taxes, but of course the Sekibobo has men of his own from whom he collects direct; similarly the mumyuba would have men of his own among the Batongole & collect direct.[15]

This corroborates Portal's account in so far as it depicts the many layers of historical, geographical and hierarchical authority involved in the collection of tax; this was feeding time, it would seem, for so many elements linked to, or representing, the centralized state but basically acting on their own account.

> The King would send his messenger e.g. to Sekibobo to collect, he would put another man to go to the mumyuba, who puts his mutaba (or messenger) and the three go to the Kitawi; they had to get what they

---

[15] Roscoe & Kagwa 1906: 2.

could, they first collected one shell (or in earlier times one seed of the wild plantain) from each hut, upon this the assessment was made. Taxes were collected in kind, hoes, barkcloths, women & c. The collectors could not increase the number of barkcloths ordered, but they would add to the number of the other things composing the taxes in order to make something for themselves...[16]

Thus the decentralized ethos of tax collection in the 1890s is again suggested, although here it sounds a rather more moderate affair.

In the context of the domestic tribute system, Ganda chieftainship may be seen as having been a somewhat precarious occupation. As Portal observed, a chief had to 'exact enough from his district to satisfy not only his own requirements, but also the extortionate and constantly repeated demands of all his superiors'.[17] If he failed to produce the goods for those in authority above him, he would not last long in his position; equally, he had to be fair on his clients and retain their loyalty and support, without which his position would become just as untenable. Free *bakopi* could leave a chief's patronage without hindrance, and the steady loss of human resources would clearly be extremely damaging to a chief on several levels. Indeed, it would seem that to be a chief on any level in nineteenth-century Buganda demanded considerable ability, and that successful chiefs were consummate politicians: they needed to be. An interesting case in this context is that of the *kago*, the governor of Kyadondo *ssaza*. Kagwa asserted that the province was 'not a wealthy one, and though the county chief was the highest ranking one in the country he was often surpassed by others in wealth, because he could not raise as much in taxes'.[18] The holder of this office would have been a talented individual indeed. It is clear, moreover, that the chiefs of Buganda, both at *ssaza* and more local level, were in a very real fashion the architects of the kingdom's strength, ensuring that society and the economic infrastructure functioned as they did. On their shoulders balanced the raw military power with which Buganda faced its external enemies, the loyalty which was an essential component of this, and the economic wealth both of the districts under them and of the central government which depended on these. Little wonder that the rewards could be great, and the price of failure severe. In all of this, the *kabaka* was almost a marginal figure, at least after 1890, and the pomp and glory of the capital in many respects only the façade of a machine organized and driven by countless chiefs and sub-chiefs throughout the kingdom. Yet the power of central authority cannot be completely dismissed. As we shall see, the *kabaka*, through his perceived abuse of what was essentially a delicately balanced system of reciprocity, was still able to bring about political and social crisis; and it was a centralizing ethos which drove the system of public labour, the most dramatic consequence of which was the network of highways.

[16] Ibid.: 5.
[17] Portal 1894: 196.
[18] Kagwa: 1934: 162.

Working for the state:
the organization of public labour

The origins of state-organized labour are unclear, and may well lie in the foundation of the kingdom itself. Everything begins with Kintu, of course, and Kintu is supposed to have commanded a force of 'twelve young men' in the building of his capital.[19] One of the earliest rulers recorded making such large-scale demands is Mawanda in the early eighteenth century. According to Kagwa, Mawanda 'called upon the whole country, saying, "Come and perform duties for me. Cut down also this forest."' Possibly, this event was remembered not because the demands in themselves were unprecedented, but because several of the princes, including three future rulers, refused to obey.[20] This was tantamount to outright rebellion; the insurrection itself may have been political in origin, but it is interesting that it erupted over the issue of royal labour. Certainly, the rebels were not averse in principle to such royal prerogative: one of the princes, Namugala, who probably reigned in the 1740s or 1750s, apparently instituted the building of artificial lakes, a regular focus of royal labour. By 1800, the organization of public work teams seems to have been well established: Kamanya is remembered as having executed a number of men at the capital, believing them to be poultry-thieves. The unfortunates had protested in vain that they 'were the workers [*abakozi*]'. Kagwa suggests that such teams of state labourers, while generally not encountering such bad luck, were a common feature of urban life by the beginning of the nineteenth century.[21] The operations often took place on a large scale: Kagwa mentions that Suna 'appointed Galabuzi the *Omunaakulya* to go and cut poles from Nakalanga forest for the building of a new capital at Ngalamye'.[22] The language is almost biblical, and it was quite possibly Kagwa's intention to remind us of Solomon's temple, or the erection of a new Jerusalem. Importantly, throughout the indigenous accounts it is made clear that the organization of such labour was one of the key areas of royal authority. Undoubtedly, this was the case as far as such glorious projects as a new royal capital were concerned. However there existed, beyond the centralizing ethos, a degree of decentralization in the public labour system; this was necessarily the case, as logistically, by the nineteenth century, any kind of centralized standing labour force would have been an impossibility.

By the nineteenth century, state labour was organized largely on a local basis. In much the same way that labour armies were drafted to build enclosures for the *kabaka*, the *ssaza* chiefs and their subordinates commanded local labour on behalf of the state. The military description is important, not least because, like the majority of Ganda soldiers, state labourers were normally farmers, traders, iron-workers, and so on, required at certain junctures to put aside their private pursuits and serve

---

[19] Ibid.: 9.
[20] Kagwa 1971: 74–5.
[21] Ibid.: 108.
[22] Ibid.: 117.

the *kabaka*. Moreover, the militaristic organization of state labour is clear from Grant's description in 1862:

> One of the sights at the capital ... was to watch the crowds of men on the highroad leading to the palace; all were under officers, perhaps a hundred in one party. If wood is carried into the palace ... it must be done as neatly as a regiment performs a manoeuvre on parade, and with the same precision. After the logs are carried a certain distance, the men charge up hill ... On reaching their officer, they drop on their knees to salute, by saying repeatedly in one voice the word 'n'yans' (thanks) ... Each officer of a district would seem to have a different mode of drill. The Wazeewah [= Baziba?], with long sticks, were remarkably well disciplined, shouting and marching all in regular time...[23]

It is striking that Grant appears to be referring to the region of Kiziba, which straddled the mouth of the Kagera river on Buganda's southern flank. In the nineteenth century it was impossible to get much further from the metropolitan centre, and yet the inhabitants of this semi-autonomous province were still prone to the call to work.

Grant appears to be describing what Portal called 'corvee or forced labour': known locally as *kasanvu*, this was operated by a system by which 'men have to be supplied by the different provinces in certain proportions'.[24] The precise logistics of this state labour force are unclear, although it probably only operated in the capital. Evidence of a similar force is provided by Livinhac, who in 1879 noted that Mutesa had furnished the White Fathers' mission with 'the materials and the necessary workers for the construction of a house'.[25] It is also unclear whether it was recruited only when necessary, or whether a force of labourers, made up of men from all over the kingdom, established itself permanently in the capital. The latter scenario is distinctly possible, especially in the nineteenth century, as the urban centre expanded rapidly and became much less mobile than previously, moving within a more circumscribed geographical area. More commonly, however, the system of public labour or *kasanvu* operated on a local level. One British official noted in 1902: 'Throughout the counties I find a great objection on the part of the "Bakopi" to leave their homes and travel long distances to work off their tax. On this one point there is a very strong and general feeling that they should be put on to works which are within a reasonable distance of their villages.'[26] These feelings were almost certainly reflective of the pre-colonial system with which most Ganda in 1902, or at least their parents, were familiar.[27]

---

[23] Grant 1864: 231–2.

[24] Portal 1894: 191–3. Kagwa asserted that each *ssaza* had to contribute men to build a specified portion of the palace: Kagwa 1934: 74.

[25] White Fathers: C13/4 Livinhac to Lavigerie, 9 July 1879. Roscoe states that the construction and maintenance of buildings at the capital 'kept an army of men employed the whole year round': Roscoe 1911: 366.

[26] UNA A8/2 Wyndham to Dep. Comm., 24 October 1902.

[27] Early colonial officials to some extent saw themselves as inheriting a public labour system which could be made to serve the protectorate. There was general dissatisfaction among the Ganda, however, as Macdonald observed: 'however ready the peasantry may be to build and work for their King in accordance with historical custom, they naturally

Although the pull came from the centre, the labour itself would have been organized locally. Besides work at the capital, the primary function of this labour was the construction of roads and bridges, and occasionally public buildings;[28] the clearance of forest and bush were also common operations. The enclosures of prominent chiefs were probably built by local labour, perhaps the chief's own tenants, and this was not always directly linked to state labour as such.[29] Labour organization in the capital, however, belonged firmly in the public sphere. In the mid-1890s, one observer asserted that '[t]hree officers are employed to build houses, fences, and the like every three or four months, so that probably they find plenty of work to occupy them'. One of these officers, it would seem, was the *pokino*, governor of Buddu.[30] It is not easy to imagine that a chief as prominent as the *pokino* would have had such additional responsibilities; nevertheless, we know that *ssaza* chiefs were required to spend part of the year at the capital, and thus it is possible that these duties were circulated among the chiefs in residence there. In practical terms, however, notwithstanding Grant's evidence, it is likely that state labour at the capital was often performed by local labour, under the command of a locally based chief who perhaps specialized in construction and labour recruitment. Kagwa mentions, for example, a junior chief named Wabulakayole of the *ngeye* clan who 'took charge of thatching the houses of the late Kabakas and all the houses of his chiefs'.[31] Similarly, mention is made of the duties associated with the *ngonge* clan:

> Kisolo made his son Lutaya Sabaddu and he also put him in charge of trimming the lower part of Kintu's house. That was his basic responsibility [and] even later Kabakas observed this custom and Sabaddu Kago was in charge of building the main house of the Kabaka. It was after this model that the other big chiefs also construct their own respectable houses within their own small palaces ...[32]

Beyond the capital, patron–client relations were important. In return for land given to them by the chief on which to cultivate and establish their homesteads, local men built the chief's enclosure and repaired other

---

[27] (cont.) demurred to working in a similar way for Europeans, with their many new-fangled ideas': Macdonald 1897: 140.

[28] House-building is the prime example of private labour involving skills which were transferable into a public arena. The *bakopi* constructed their own dwellings, and they did so on a regular basis as the dwellings themselves were never built with permanence in mind. Use was made of whatever raw materials were close at hand, although better-quality materials were often sought some distance away. The basic materials included tree trunks, thinner bamboo-like poles, grass and wattle. These were collected by the men, who had the major responsibility for house-building: Kollmann 1899: 14. Tackled with skill and experience, Ganda buildings were erected swiftly: the missionary Hattersley estimated three days as being average, and also suggested that help from the local community might be expected: Hattersley 1908: 119. This private labour thus had a public dimension because of the largely moral obligations felt by the community to assist (as opposed to political or financial obligations, although clearly the economic benefits of reciprocity were influential).

[29] See for example Roscoe 1911: 375.

[30] Decle 1898: 442.

[31] Kagwa 1972: 4.

[32] Ibid.: 7.

property. Physical labour was not the only service offered to patrons by tenants: a proportion of the food produced by each homestead was regularly offered to the chief's enclosure, for example.[33] The reciprocity of the arrangement was understood, but there was no fixed duration to it; tenants could leave as freely and suddenly as a chief could evict them.[34] In the more public sphere, it is likely that responsibility for public labour levies fell ultimately on chiefs at a very local, village level: these chiefs, by the second half of the nineteenth century, were in charge of particular stretches of highway, for example. Yet the *ssaza* chief had overall authority, being the most conspicuous agent of central government. In 1893, one British official reported that, because the *kaima*, the chief of Mawokota *ssaza*, was away at the capital, no public work could be done until he returned and gave the necessary orders. The same official related how the *mukwenda* of Singo 'hears [that] orders are coming for him to do his share, but as yet they have not reached him': the work would not be done until these orders arrived.[35] The *ssaza* governor was expected to take pride, and to show an interest, in the strength and industry of his province, and thus his relationship with his constituents was critical; he also bore responsibility for the maintenance of what were essentially public highways connecting the four corners of the kingdom and linking the kingdom with the region. He was very clearly, in this sense, an agent of central government.

Understandably, however, the level of maintenance of highways, being necessarily decentralized, varied between districts, as a uniform level of energy and commitment was difficult to attain over a wide area. Thus in the late 1890s, the missionary A.R. Cook observed that 'one man might do his short bit of twenty or thirty yards excellently, while his more lazy neighbour would allow the next section to lie in disrepair or even tumble in altogether'.[36] This is a good example of how, by the end of the nineteenth century, the theory of political centralization was very clearly articulated and yet the practice was often something of a struggle. Responsibility for roads beyond the capital was clearly decentralized, but the state sought to uphold its authority through the periodical dispatch of royal inspectors whose job it was to investigate the condition of highways.[37] These inspectors were not merely sent to collect excuses; a system of fines operated to punish local chiefs and headmen who were considered remiss in the execution of their duties. Such fines may have been considerably heavier in areas where the road network was especially valued and utilized. However, one British official in 1895 was of the opinion that these fines ultimately affected the peasantry most severely, for it was they who shouldered the financial burden resulting from disputes between chiefs:

> Every chief, from the highest to the lowest, acts as 'judge', and one case I had brought before me is worthy of note: A minor chief was fined 'so many' goats for not doing certain road cleaning; he, in turn, fined the next

---

[33] Fisher 1912: 33.
[34] Decle 1898: 446.
[35] UNA A2/1 Reddie to Portal, 10 April 1893.
[36] Cook 1945: 45.
[37] Felkin 1885–6: 754.

man to him the same number of goats, for not doing his work; he again fined the next man, till it came down to the lowest chief who fined the unfortunate bakopi, and they could do nothing ...[38]

This is probably exaggerated, but some indication is given of the devolution of responsibility within the system, at least after c. 1890.

The highways of Buganda

It seems appropriate to pause for a moment and to consider the focus of much of this labour, something which the nineteenth-century state clearly believed to be of the utmost importance. In the second half of the nineteenth century, Buganda's road network drew admiration from even the most critical of observers. The communications system clearly set the kingdom apart from its neighbours. Shortly after entering southern Buddu in 1862, Speke commented: 'The roads, as indeed they were everywhere, were as broad as our coach-roads, cut through the long grasses, straight over the hills and down through the woods in the dells – a strange contrast to the wretched tracks in all the adjacent countries.'[39] The roads ran throughout the kingdom and were not confined to the environs of the capital, although apparently some of the best highways were to be found here, tending to be broader than in the outlying districts as they swept into the growing urban centre and towards, symbolically at least, the royal enclosure. These were clearly the showpiece roads of the kingdom. In 1876, Emin Pasha described the road which approached the capital from the north as 'the King's highway' and 'the Royal highway'.[40] A year earlier, Stanley had approached the capital from the south:

> As we approached the capital the highway from Usavara [near modern Entebbe] increased in width from 20 feet to 150 feet ... Arrived at the capital I found that the vast collection of huts crowning the eminence were the Royal Quarters, around which ran several palisades and circular courts, between which and the city was a circular road, ranging from 100 to 200 feet in width, from which radiated six or seven magnificent avenues, lined with gardens and huts ...[41]

But such impressive sights were not confined to the capital: L. Decle, for example, noted an 'excellent road' running through the *ssaza* of Singo.[42] Broad, straight roads, immaculately cleared of all foliage, stretched from the capital towards Kyagwe's eastern frontier: Portal suggested that they were 'from ten to twenty feet wide'.[43] Some of the outlying, less important roads were, naturally, considerably narrower: one British officer followed a 'path' to the north of the capital which was 'about 10 inches wide, bordered

[38] UNA A8/6 Report by Tomkins on tour of Kyagwe, etc. 23 March 1895.
[39] Speke 1863b: 274.
[40] Schweitzer 1898: I, 31.
[41] Bennett 1970: 222–3.
[42] Decle 1898: 432.
[43] Portal 1894: 141.

by tall elephant grass'.[44] Harry Johnston described how '[n]arrow paths may circulate between the huts of peasants or as by-ways, but as a rule the Muganda prefers to make roads as broad as those in vogue in civilised countries at the present day'; indeed, the Ganda highway was comparable to 'the old Roman road'.[45] As at the capital, the enclosures of prominent chiefs in the districts were surrounded by broad highways, which were perhaps as much an expression of grandeur as a means of communication. Approaching the enclosure of the important local chief 'Mreko' in Singo in 1876, Emin Pasha noted that 'the narrow path widened out into a well-kept broad road, bounded by trees and gardens'.[46] Two years earlier, Chaillé-Long had also met a chief named 'Morako' based near the border with Bunyoro. Chaillé-Long described an impressive crossing into Ganda territory: 'the country changed for the better, and the lowlands of Unyoro gave place … to roads well-swept, that, "Morako" tells me, have been widened and swept by orders of his great master, M'Tse … The red clay soil marked their direction for miles through a grass-covered country.'[47]

The roads of Buganda were both the lifelines of the capital, reaching outward toward the productive centres of the kingdom and the widening political and economic horizons of the nineteenth century, and the pointers towards the hub of political, economic and military power in the lacustrine region. The missionary C.T. Wilson wrote that the highways 'connect the principal villages with one another and with the capital'. As a rule, Ganda roads were remarkably straight, cutting over the crests of hills and through valleys, forests, swamps and rivers.[48] This characteristic is, perhaps, revealing of a particular Ganda attitude, especially the concept of civilization versus nature discussed in an earlier chapter. At the risk of becoming over-analytical, it might be argued that a people which determinedly pushes its roads through and across all natural obstacles is possessed, at the least, of a deep-seated stubbornness and, at worst, of an arrogance born of the belief in the superiority of its civilization. Certainly, the fact that the Ganda appeared to disregard hills, valleys, swamps and forests in their pursuit of rapid communications suggests that they were not intimidated by nature: on the contrary, this was another example of how they believed they could subdue it and impose their society on the bush. The rectilinearity of the roads may also be seen as a reflection of the Ganda predilection for social order and control. The Ganda had, of course, to wage a constant war against nature, which inevitably sought to reclaim the land over which the roads were built. Despite the regional discrepancies already mentioned, the network appears, on the whole, to have been regularly maintained and cleared of intrusive foliage, as Wilson observed, 'even in the more thinly peopled districts'. Water was overcome via bridges, which were either built on upright tree-trunks, allowing the stream or river to pass beneath unhindered, or were trunks of wild date palm laid side by side across floating vegetation, which, although sounding

[44]   Thruston 1900: 130.
[45]   Johnston 1902: II, 656–7.
[46]   Schweinfurth *et al.* 1888: 34.
[47]   Chaillé-Long 1876: 90–91.
[48]   Wilson & Felkin 1882: I, 147.

somewhat precarious, 'formed a secure and permanent road'.[49] The road on which Portal travelled from Busoga crossed several swamps, the bridges being causeways of interlaced palm logs covered with brushwood, grass and a thick layer of earth. Again, the labour which built these means of communication was organized by local chiefs in both Buganda and Busoga.[50]

Yet even the Ganda, pioneers of ascendant civilization, had to make tacit concessions to the power of nature: the maintenance of both roads and bridges was to some extent dictated by the seasons, much repair work taking place after the rains. For example, in Buddu in 1905, local chiefs reported 'that roads and bridges need repairs – damaged by the rains – towards Koki and these will have to be done now the [dry] season has set in'.[51] River-fording especially tended to be affected by the seasons. The river Katonga, in northern Buddu, was crossed by Speke in 1862, but he was told that 'it sometimes swells to the height of a man, and therefore cannot be crossed on foot'. As Speke suggested, however, this was no barrier to the river being crossed: throughout his stay in Buganda, 'there was constant communication between the palaces of Karague and Uganda, and those who went to and fro invariably forded the Katonga'.[52] Canoes, of course, were also used at times of flooding, when bridges proved impractical.

The most obvious comparison to make in a sub-Saharan context is with Asante in the nineteenth century. Wilks was able to reconstruct in enviable detail the network of 'great-roads' which spanned Asante, and any analysis of road systems elsewhere in pre-colonial Africa owes much to his impressive study.[53] The Asante great-roads were the main thoroughfares linking the political centres of the kingdom; as Wilks points out, '[t]he system of great-roads was maintained by the central government, and was to be distinguished from the many smaller and localised networks of roads the responsibility for which rested with the district authorities'.[54] This situation was not dissimilar to that of Buganda, where as we have noted stretches of road further out from the capital were the responsibility of local chiefs, ostensibly at least acting on behalf of central government. Importantly, Wilks takes a world-view of the highways of Asante. The great-roads themselves were divided into the northern and southern roads. The northern roads, Wilks explains, led to the towns on the frontiers of Greater Asante, 'where they articulated with major trans-continental caravan trails leading to the Mediterranean shores via the great entrepots of the Western and Central Sudan'. The southern roads 'linked the capital with the series of coastal ports between the Volta and Komoe Rivers, and so with the maritime highways to Europe and the Americas'.[55] Buganda's geo-political position was, perhaps, less defined than this, but a comparison is still useful. Ganda highways stretched to the south, from the

[49] Ibid.
[50] Portal 1894: 141–2, 166; Decle 1898: 435.
[51] UNA A8/6 Isemonger to Sub-Commissioner, 5 June 1905.
[52] Speke 1863a: 329.
[53] Wilks 1975: especially Chapter 1.
[54] Ibid.: 1.
[55] Ibid.

increasingly urbanized heartlands through Mawokota and Buddu, leading ultimately to the entrepôts of Unyanyembe and Zanzibar and, of course, the trade of the Indian Ocean, which also provided access to Europe and the Americas. Greater obstacles were placed in the way of the northbound roads, but, by the second half of the nineteenth century, these too led to broader horizons dominated by the Sudan, Egypt and the Mediterranean. Other roads, of course, also stretched west and east, but, though no less important in terms of regional economy and communication, they were more limited in scope; even so, the eastbound roads through Kyagwe, across the Nile and through Busoga may have been intended to eventually operate in tandem with, and perhaps even supersede, the Unyanyembe roads in connecting Buganda with the Indian Ocean. They never did so, and the route itself only took on this greater significance with the building of the East African railway from Mombasa to Kampala.

Ganda roads were clearly built with convenience and comfort in mind, and the almost exaggerated width of many, especially around the capital, suggests a less functional and more triumphalist dimension. Above all, however, they facilitated rapidity of movement, of persons, armies, news and commerce. The Ganda understood well the need for a communications network in these respects, particularly by the middle of the nineteenth century. Moreover, road construction itself was an important expression of the collective interest in Ganda society. It is significant that the local term for a public highway built by communal effort was *oluguudo lw'obulungi-bwansi*, literally meaning 'for the good of the country'.[56] As one historian has suggested, it was the existence of a relatively dense and stable population which led to the development of such communications.[57] Yet the origins of the Ganda road system are unclear. Where there are human beings there are roads, even if the latter take the form of the most barely discernible tracks maintained not by any centralized effort but by the tramp of feet. In this sense, many nineteenth-century Ganda roads must have been the descendants of older paths much more in keeping with those of the surrounding region, linking villages and districts, naturally hammered out with the expansion of human settlement. But particular circumstances facilitated the development of the nineteenth-century system: a stable and dense population, as already noted; centralized government; and a good reason for actually having roads, namely commercial expansion and the need for ever more efficient means of military movement. All of these might point, however approximately, to the middle of the eighteenth century, at least as the period in which the Ganda began to develop a road system to supplant earlier means of communication. Felkin suggested that Suna initiated the systematic building of highways; the source of this information is not disclosed, nor is the information corroborated.[58] But it is plausible: the road system may have been developed during the 1840s with the escalation of long-distance trade, when the need became apparent for a network which would facilitate the large-scale movement of, in particular, slaves and ivory. Still, it is

[56] Murphy 1972: 41.
[57] In Curtin 1978: 171.
[58] Felkin 1885–6: 754.

notable that Kagwa does not mention it, and the system may have been a much more gradual development, spanning many decades.

During the religious wars of the late 1880s and early 1890s, the road network all but collapsed, another poignant and symbolic reminder of the internal strains which had rendered Buganda's control of the environment – both human and otherwise – impossible. Moving north from Kampala in 1891, Lugard 'marched along what were once the great roads of Uganda'; they were overgrown and many had fallen into complete disrepair. It is a tribute to the earlier assiduous maintenance of the highways, however, that Lugard was still able to follow the routes due to 'the embankments which often bordered them, and the remains of culverts of palm-logs across the riverine swamps'.[59] The decline of the road network was at least in part due to population movement: depopulation in certain districts would have rendered the upkeep of parts of the network difficult, not to mention somewhat pointless.

Mwanga's reign: an abuse of the system

It is significant that among the justifications for the revolt against Mwanga in 1888 was the belief that the young *kabaka* had abused his position as guardian of the kingdom's complex, and ultimately fragile, labour and taxation systems. The potential fragility was violently exposed by Mwanga's excesses. We have already noted, for example, that from 1884 internal plundering in the name of political justice increasingly took the place of the peaceful and legitimate collection of tribute. In late 1887, Mwanga undertook two such expeditions in quick succession, seizing large numbers of livestock.[60] At the same time, he launched an ego-laden project which served as a focus of discontent among the various elements of politically ambitious chiefs at the capital. There was an enormous increase in the demand for labour at the capital, mostly, it seems, for the purpose of building the royal lake. Zimbe tells us that no one was spared: 'Everybody in the country, chief and commoner ... had to dig and carry soil on his or her head.'[61] Even allowing for this exaggeration, it is striking that Mwanga's decree was remembered in this way, indicating its excessive nature. This was an exercise in royal arrogance. Heavy fines were imposed on those who were not seen to be working hard enough; Zimbe describes how '[e]very man down from a Mutongole to a Saza chief was required to come to work before dawn. He who failed was to be fined a woman, a slave and a cow ... Indeed there were very many chiefs ... fined women, slaves, cows, goats, heaps of barkcloths, bales of clothes.' In addition, there was an excessive daily taxation: everybody was compelled to put a 'coin' (presumably a specified number of cowry shells) into baskets provided.[62] Zimbe's assertions are supported by the testimony of Ashe. The latter observed with regard to the building of the royal lake that 'if [Mwanga]

[59] Lugard 1893: II, 117.
[60] Zimbe 1939: 156.
[61] Ibid.: 148.
[62] Ibid.: 153, 156.

found the chiefs had not arrived, he inflicted enormous fines upon them, demanding something like one thousand women in all, besides valuable coloured cloths and guns'.[63]

These abuses of the taxation and state labour systems undoubtedly contributed to the overthrow, albeit temporary, of the *kabaka*. There were, of course, additional tensions and strains to those outlined above which influenced the actions of chiefs at this time; religious persuasions and an emerging political and pseudo-military culture which encouraged the ambitious to challenge the status quo were also contributory factors. But these were no more important than the perception that the *kabaka* was acting far in excess of his prerogatives and legitimate authority in taking money, goods and labour in the name of the state, thus threatening the very framework by which state and society functioned. Mwanga, of course, was under a great deal of pressure. Youth afflicted him with the heady combination of insecurity and arrogance; the volatile political situation at the capital, the legacy of his father's reign, must have heightened his awareness of the need for displays of royal potency; and from abroad came new threats of an absolutely unprecedented nature. This unique combination helps place Mwanga's seeming disrespect for the norms and institutions of the nineteenth-century kingdom in context. Still, the rebellion of 1888 was not without precedent. As we have already seen, in the early eighteenth century several princes refused to obey Mawanda's command for public labour. Indeed the parallels are noteworthy: Mawanda, like Mwanga, was also reputedly a 'notorious plunderer', as Kiwanuka has argued.[64] He was not a 'respecter of persons'; unlike Mwanga, however, Mawanda was actually assassinated by his sons.[65] Both episodes suggest the ways in which the *kabaka* might be perceived to have abused the system which sustained the state and royal enclosure; it is also clear that such abuses were tolerated by the Ganda political establishment only up to a point, while in the 1880s matters were complicated by the emergence of an almost anti-establishment coalition of religious converts and political newcomers. In this sense, the system by which the Ganda state utilized its human resources was more resilient than any individual who might temporarily control it, at least until the late nineteenth century.

[63] Ashe 1894: 93.
[64] Kiwanuka, in Kagwa 1971: 76.
[65] Kagwa 1971: 75–6.

Six

Slavery

We have seen how the state organized and utilized the bulk of its 'free' population; we now turn our attention to another significant pool of human resources in the nineteenth-century kingdom, slavery. A slave is generally defined as a person who is not free, but the problem is that freedom is relative. In nineteenth-century Buganda, there were many grades and classes of people who were not free, and in this sense they were all slaves; but their contributions and their positions in Ganda society were very different. Slavery is a complex, as well as distasteful, topic, but, at the most generalized level in the context of Ganda society, we can say that the one central tenet of the body of *bakopi* rights was the freedom of movement. Again, this is relative; but free *bakopi* could, as we have seen, enter and leave the patronage of a chief at will. They were permitted to transfer their skills and their labour according to their own needs and wishes. Slaves could not do this. In some situations they were accorded certain physical rights, but again in general terms they had no influence over their personal circumstances or geographical location. Slavery was critical to Ganda social and economic life, and we shall examine this further in the later chapter dealing with long-distance trade. In this chapter, however, we look in detail at the role of slaves and the ideology of slavery in pre-colonial Buganda, and examine the background to their commercial importance. As in many other parts of Africa, the nineteenth-century slave trade in the Great Lakes region drew on a long-established system of economic, political and social control, although, again as in other regions, the trade tended to be rather more brutal than any indigenous form of domination. Yet the significance of slavery has largely been overlooked by historians of Buganda: the existence of slaves, while accepted in the vaguest of terms, has provoked little questioning. In recent years only Twaddle has ventured to explore this important area, and he has also lamented the fact that Ganda slavery remains a subject yet to be seriously broached.[1]

[1] Twaddle 1988a, 1988b.

Slavery in Buganda can be viewed from a number of perspectives, while slaves themselves could be found in many walks of life and in many guises. E.M.K. Mulira was among the first to make clear that broad distinctions existed, describing how there were 'the *abanyage* (those stolen or pillaged in war); as well as the *abagule* (those bought). All these came into the category of *abenvumu* or true slaves, that is to say people not free in any sense.'[2] The general Ganda term for slavery or bondage is *buddu*; *muddu* referred to a male slave, and there existed by the nineteenth century a headman, whose title was the *sabaddu*, or head of the slaves of a chief who were not entitled to live within that chief's compound. It is tempting to connect the term with the *ssaza* of the same name, as Speke did in 1862:

> In the earliest times the Wahuma of Unyoro regarded all their lands bordering on the Victoria Lake as their garden, owing to its exceeding fertility, and imposed the epithet of Wiru, or slaves, upon its people, because they had to supply the imperial government with food and clothing. Coffee was conveyed to the capital by the Wiru, also mbugu (bark-cloaks), from an inexhaustible fig-tree; in short, the lands of the Wiru were famous for their rich productions.
>
> Now Wiru in the northern dialect changes to Waddu in the southern; hence Uddu, the land of the slaves, which remained in one connected line from the Nile to the Kitangule Kagera ...[3]

Speke's research was admirable, but his conclusions were inaccurate. In fact, as Wrigley has recently argued, the Nyoro form of the name Buddu was Bw-iru, which simply referred to the fact that the land was inhabited by cultivators, or *ba-iru*, who were distinct from the herdsmen predominant to the west.[4] It may have been a derogatory term, but it had little to do with slavery. Still, the problem remains of why the Ganda should eventually call the region 'Buddu'; this may indeed reflect an ancient relationship about which it is virtually impossible to know anything for certain.

In the widest possible sense slaves represented an 'underclass' in so far as they usually performed a range of lowly tasks and, with one or two notable exceptions, were liable to be bought and sold.[5] Yet many slaves enjoyed higher material standards of living, if not quality of life and notwithstanding lack of personal liberty, than the free peasantry which constituted the bulk of the population. Slavery and poverty were not necessarily connected, as is clear from the existence of well-dressed and often haughty serviles who belonged to wealthy chiefs. Clearer links, however, can be established between slavery and gender, and slavery and foreignness. Most slaves in nineteenth-century Buganda were either foreign or of foreign origin. By this time there existed a substantial slave popula-

---

[2] In Twaddle 1988b: 121.
[3] Speke 1863b: 251–2.
[4] Wrigley 1996: 218.
[5] As we shall see below, slaves were not perhaps sold as freely by their masters as might be supposed, and it may be that the internal or domestic slave market was actually fairly limited. Moreover, slaves – and in particular female serviles – who had been distributed by the *kabaka* may not have been exchanged in the market; these were, rather, expected to remain with the recipient of the gift for life.

tion which was descended from war captives, in which case the slaves were as incorporated into Ganda society as was possible for persons of their status. Buganda's reputation for being able to absorb (and often exalt) foreigners was also deserved in the realm of slavery. Clearly the fact that they were slaves meant that they never quite lost their alien dimension, but they were different from more recent imports who were still living on the edge of Ganda culture and whose alienness was as yet undiluted. Several years might pass before such recently imported slaves felt themselves an indispensable part of an extended household, if they were fortunate enough to be thus retained. It is true that a slave's life was characterized by uncertainty, but such uncertainty was exacerbated during the second half of the nineteenth century, when the large-scale export of slaves greatly widened the range of fates which might await them.

The fact that most, although by no means all, slaves were foreign to a greater or lesser degree suggests that there was indeed an ethnic dimension to Ganda slavery. As we shall see, there were circumstances in which Ganda were themselves enslaved, but non-Ganda swelled the ranks of the servile class. It is not difficult to find evidence of a sense of ethnic superiority among the Ganda; much of their military ethos was founded upon it, and important spheres of their material culture preserved notions of the innate supremacy of Ganda civilization. Such ethnic tensions are certainly present in Uganda today, with the Ganda at least implicitly, and often explicitly, presenting themselves as the vanguard of the nation, and many non-Ganda groups understandably regarding this with deep resentment. Over the past 30 years, the consequences of such tensions have often been catastrophic. These pressures may have been institutionalized and exaggerated to some extent by the creation of the protectorate in the 1890s, but they are certainly much older than this, and are reflected most clearly in pre-colonial slavery. We cannot be sure if ethnic haughtiness came prior to the systematic enslavement of foreigners, or whether it was actually prompted by increasing military success, but it seems likely that such attitudes developed in tandem with the latter and may indeed have played an important part in the binding ideology which attended the creation of the centralized political state. The term *mudokolo*, for example, an insulting and generic reference to anyone from the north, probably tells a story in itself.[6] The Hima, of course, were often described as slaves to the agricultural Ganda, which is wholly misleading, but some Ganda at least regarded the Hima as culturally inferior. Still, this contempt, where it existed, was apparently heartily reciprocated.[7] Ganda attitudes, then, may seem to have been somewhat contradictory, if we set the willingness to absorb outsiders and foreign skills in juxtaposition with this sense of ethnic superiority. On another level, however – namely that of slavery – it is clear that these attitudes were in fact perfectly complementary.

The fact that slaves in Buganda were mostly foreign in origin takes on a particular relevance when it is considered that they were employed by

---

[6] Zimbe, moreover, states that 'it was the custom of Baganda to despise other tribes, and any person of any of the other tribes they called him Munyoro': Zimbe 1939: 53.
[7] For example, Hattersley 1908: 90; Lugard 1893: I, 173.

the Ganda in times of war. It is unclear how far back this practice can be traced, but by the second half of the nineteenth century large numbers of slaves appear to have been thus utilized. In 1875, Stanley reckoned that the Ganda army was accompanied by about 50,000 slaves.[8] The improbably high figure is in this context irrelevant. Roscoe mentions that the servants of chiefs were present on military expeditions,[9] and Mackay observed the organization of an army involving the major chiefs and their slaves.[10] Slaves were used as carriers of weapons and provisions, or simply as personal attendants to various chiefly ranks in the field. The use of slaves in this way is germane to the more general question of their effective integration into Ganda society. It is difficult to imagine, for example, that the Ganda would have risked attacking Bunyoro with Nyoro slaves forming part of their military force. It seems likely that only the most loyal of slaves accompanied their masters on such expeditions: in other words, those who were descendants of war captives, and whose loyalty to their adopted culture transcended all others, or similarly were slaves captured in childhood. It is likely, however, that Ganda slaves were also employed in war.

It is impossible to assess with any exactness the extent of slave ownership in nineteenth-century Buganda, and it is difficult, indeed, to avoid reducing the discussion to one of chiefs and other powerful figures. Before arriving in Buganda in 1862, Grant was told that the average Muganda owned 100 slaves; even youths possessed 'ten or twenty ... whom they steal or kidnap in war'.[11] This was, of course, a gross exaggeration, but it conveys some idea of the impression foreigners had of Ganda slavery and its extensive nature. Perhaps the best that can be said is that while a stratum of poorer *bakopi* was probably excluded from the slave ownership system, save through participation in military campaigns, a significant proportion of wealthier peasants and non-chiefs owned at least one or two serviles. Slaves had to be fed: captured women would presumably grow their own food, but any extended household comprising non-producing slaves would need to have been at least self-sufficient in order to maintain a slave enclosure. It is probable that some chiefs faced difficulties of this nature as they accumulated slaves in the course of their careers.

Acquisition of slaves

Chiefs and peasants alike could acquire slaves by commercial means, even though, as we have already noted, the internal slave market may have been limited in comparison with other commodities. The missionary Livinhac believed that the most powerful force for slave distribution was royal patronage. Following the arrival at the capital of a batch of war captives, the *kabaka* would distribute them among successful and favoured chiefs and soldiers.[12] In other words, it was only after slaves ceased to be

[8] Stanley & Neame 1961: 99.
[9] Roscoe 1911: 350.
[10] Mackay 1890: 111.
[11] Grant 1864: 55.
[12] White Fathers: C13/5 Livinhac to Lavigerie, 24 September 1879.

the property of the *kabaka* – as in theory much war booty was – that they entered the social system and became economic commodities. This process was undoubtedly important, and was probably the norm in the capital; but it was only one of many channels through which slaves might be acquired, and should not be over-emphasized.

Slaves were brought to Buganda from throughout the lacustrine region, but they appear to have come mostly from Bunyoro and Busoga, which were clearly geographically convenient areas, although it is possible that the Ganda indiscriminately described their slaves as Nyoro or Soga; this would certainly fit in with the idea of their sweeping contempt for other nationalities. One intriguing piece of testimony dating from 1888 suggests that the Ganda had recently raided among the Nyamwezi and seized 'great numbers' of slaves.[13] This is difficult to accept, not least because, as I shall argue, at this time Buganda was scarcely in a position to organize such an ambitious operation; even so, there is little doubt that slaves were brought from considerably further afield than Bunyoro and Busoga. Nor was slave-raiding the only method by which slaves were brought into Buganda: the regional trade in slaves was a significant source by the nineteenth century. Grant depicted the Nyoro capital as the location of a thriving slave market, perhaps the most important in the region and certainly larger than anything attributed to Buganda. Grant remarked that 'Kamarasi was constantly visited by men of far countries coming to trade with him for cattle, slaves, and ivory.'[14] There is every reason to suppose that the Ganda were among these visitors. Such commerce existed at the highest level. Emin Pasha recorded that Mutesa sent commodities such as cloth, copper, brass and glass beads to Kabarega, who offered slaves in return. Notably, the slaves thus acquired were not retained domestically but were used specifically for export.[15] It is therefore possible to perceive Mutesa as the most powerful individual trader in the country, able to use his position to commercial advantage; it would also seem that he wished not to rely too heavily on the domestic slave pool for export. A balance had to be maintained between slaves retained for domestic use and those earmarked for export, although the distinction was, in practice, not always as clear as this.

The Ganda were not unique in taking foreign captives as slaves, which was practised by most of their neighbours. By the second half of the nineteenth century, the Buvuma islanders were periodically raiding the Ganda shore, mostly seizing women and children. Stanley noted an attack of this kind in 1875[16] and, during the Anglo-Ganda subjugation of Buvuma in the early 1890s, a number of Ganda were 'liberated'.[17] The Nyoro also frequently seized slaves from Singo and Bulemezi in the north, frontier districts which the centralized state was never able to completely secure: Macdonald reported that a group of Ganda who had been 'carried off into

---

[13] Middleton 1969: 396. A.J. Mounteney-Jephson passed through the area in August 1888 and was told that the attack had taken place some 18 months previously.
[14] Grant 1864: 289.
[15] Schweinfurth *et al.* 1888: 115.
[16] Stanley 1878: I, 303.
[17] Macdonald 1897: 149, 159.

slavery in Unyoro were recovered and liberated',[18] while in the early 1890s another British officer observed that, in recently fighting the Nyoro, the Ganda had succeeded in 'recovering five hundred of their countrywomen held as slaves by Kabarega'.[19] This is at least what the Ganda told the British; the opinions of the women themselves are unrecorded. A little more surprisingly, perhaps, one observer discovered around 50 Ganda slaves in Toro, women who were subsequently given their freedom by the king, Kasagama.[20] Slaving activities on the part of the Nyoro were doubtless intensified during the 1880s and 1890s, as Buganda weakened and the region became extremely volatile; but, in general, slaving was a long-established feature of warfare in the area. One British soldier remarked that the 'capture of slaves by each side ... was looked upon as the usual thing'.[21] In 1893, even though Ganda participation in the external slave trade was all but at an end, another officer noted that the Ganda welcomed 'the opportunity of ... replenishing their harems and slave establishments'.[22] It is thus clear that slavery had been a prominent feature of Ganda life long before the growth of external demand, as it continued to be for a short time after the long-distance slave trade was crushed.

Slaving activities carried out by the *kabaka* within Buganda itself were doubtless of fairly ancient standing, but they appear to have increased during the 1870s and 1880s, and particularly during the reign of Mwanga. The victims were both men and women, but especially the latter; the violent enslavement of women appears to have escalated during the later nineteenth century and was a key feature of this period. Mwanga's internal slaving operations were not, however, without precedent. Burton was told of Suna that 'when the exchequer is indecently deficient, he feigns a rebellion, attacks one of his own provinces, massacres the chief men, and sells off the peasantry'.[23] In context, it would appear that the resultant slaves were sold to the Arabs.

Apart from this kind of internal raiding, which was probably common during the reigns of Suna, Mutesa and Mwanga, the era of the inter-lacustrine slave trade, pawning or the 'human collateral' system was the main process by which Ganda were deprived of their liberty within nineteenth-century Buganda. Enslavement was often the result of economic pressures on individuals in the community, chiefly in the form of fines and debts. More affluent citizens were able to cope with these pressures by selling off the slaves they already owned, but for others the only option was to sell one's relatives or, as a last resort, oneself. Siblings and offspring often found themselves enslaved as the result of a male relative's economic difficulties; again it seems likely that women and children were the most common victims of this.[24] For example, during a food shortage in mid-1880, the missionary Pearson noted 'two or three cases

[18]   Ibid.: 320.
[19]   Colvile 1895: 134, 188.
[20]   Lloyd 1900: 163.
[21]   Ternan 1930: 188.
[22]   Thruston 1900: 129.
[23]   Burton 1860: II, 189.
[24]   White Fathers: C14/185 Lourdel to Director, 1 June 1888.

where the parents have sold their children to procure food'.[25] The phenomenon had doubtless existed since before 1800, but it may have seen an increase in the later nineteenth century, for the same reason that internal raiding also increased: as the demand for slaves for export was stepped up, ownership of people became more profitable than it had ever been before.[26] It is also highly likely that the repeated failure of crops during the 1880s, and the devastation caused by cattle disease, placed unprecedented economic pressures on the Ganda and increased the incidence of local enslavement.

In all probability, much of the selling of relatives and dependants that occurred was temporary, the victims themselves being returned once the outstanding debt had been paid or a specified service rendered. Yet this was not always the case. Lourdel observed that foreign slaves were not the only serviles to be exported; Ganda criminals who had been enslaved as a result of legal proceedings might also be sold to Arab merchants.[27] Lourdel also asserted that '[t]he chiefs sometimes also sell, by a way of a little financial adventure or simply to procure some cloth for themselves, the children and the young girls handed over to them by the people of the country'.[28] The precise meaning of this is not clear, but he appears to be suggesting that chiefs sometimes sold as slaves the children – and particularly young women – given to them by their district tenants. This may have been another form of ransom or debt repayment; it may also have been an illustration of how tenants were obliged to surrender one or more of their offspring to be the property of their local landlord. These became, in effect, the landlord's slaves, to do with as he pleased, which might involve being sold abroad. Again, this probably became more common in the second half of the nineteenth century. Before the surge in the external demand for slaves, it was probably unheard of to sell such slaves outside the kingdom. At the same time, the offering of children to the politically and socially powerful represented, to a small number of Ganda, the opportunity for what we might call privileged enslavement or indentureship.

Women & slavery

Considerable caution is required when dealing with contemporary European references to slaves in Buganda, from the point of view of general definition. The most common error – and one which was made with regard to a number of pre-colonial African societies, for example Dahomey in West Africa – was the classification of virtually all the *kabaka*'s subjects as slaves. A similar idea has already been encountered in the context of

[25] CMS G3 A6/0 1881/22 Pearson to Mackay, 29 July 1880.
[26] Perhaps the most dramatic pre-1800 example of human collateral is contained in the story of Nakibinge, the early sixteenth-century *kabaka*, and Wanema, the ruler of the Sesse islands. Nakibinge effectively exchanged his son Namuimba for Wanema's son Kibuka: when Kibuka was killed, Wanema enslaved Namuimba. See Kagwa 1972: 9–10.
[27] White Fathers: C14/185 Lourdel to Director, 1 June 1888.
[28] Ibid.

taxation and public labour, namely that everything inanimate and otherwise was the property of the *kabaka*. This was an ideological legitimization of royal power, an articulation of unwritten political philosophy, but the reality was quite different. Similarly, the *kabaka*'s subjects may sometimes have been described to Europeans as his slaves – underlining his absolute potency – and as a result, in the contemporary sources, peasants and slaves were frequently assumed to have been one and the same.[29] The term 'slave' was perhaps used most indiscriminately in the case of women. Hattersley, for example, considered that women were looked upon as slaves, because they were expected to be mothers, cultivators, provide food, water and firewood, maintain public roads and generally to be 'domestic drudges'.[30] In this sense, Ganda women had much in common with their counterparts in many parts of the world, including Europe. Yet it is clear that female labour was distinct from female slavery, even though the latter very often entailed the tasks described by Hattersley. A key feature of domestic female slavery was the harem, for which local Hima women were highly valued in particular. A *kabaka*'s, and indeed a chief's, women were drawn from a great many sources, but not all were considered slaves, as L. Schiller has recently demonstrated.[31] Many, and probably most, wives were free and could leave their husbands at will. During the eighteenth and nineteenth centuries, however, the number of women connected to the royal enclosure increased dramatically, and it is likely that a large proportion of these were indeed slaves in so far as they were seized violently and deprived of the liberties normally taken for granted by wives. This change, usually described in terms of the metropolitan centre, may be assumed to have been reflected in society more widely. The missionary J. Gorju suggested that it was in the middle of the eighteenth century that chiefs began to take as concubines foreign female slaves; he wrote that '[f]rom this era chiefs were in the habit of taking as concubines foreign women who had been seized in war'.[32] This is plausible, coinciding as it does with the era of Buganda's greatest military success. Violent accumulation of women also occurred within Buganda itself, seemingly an extreme extension of the idea that all subjects and their possessions were the property of the centralized state. Emin Pasha passed through a deserted district just inside Ganda territory where he noted that the 'housewives had been torn away from their work to increase the number of slaves in the king's household'.[33] It is interesting to note that the

---

[29] See Twaddle: 1988b: 121–2. One writer confusingly felt it necessary to describe the *mukopi* as being 'of the same race as the Baganda', which, while apparently some kind of reference to aristocracy and lower orders, is truly baffling from a historiographical point of view. The same writer barely distinguished the *mukopi* from 'the real slave, the Baddu … who was the chattel of his owner, and subject to hard usage, and whose women were degraded to the level of mere playthings', which is just about as unsatisfactory and opaque a description of Ganda (or any) slavery as one could ask for: Beachey 1976: 193.

[30] Hattersley: 1906, 57.

[31] Schiller cautions against the idea that all Ganda women were 'inferior' and subordinate to men; he argues that the more important women in Buganda were not passive actors but used their positions to manipulate the political system, most clearly by advancing the careers of their male relatives: see Schiller 1990.

[32] Gorju 1920: 123.

[33] Schweinfurth *et al.* 1888: 44.

historically insecure frontier regions were perhaps rendered even more unstable by the periodic ravages of the metropolitan centre itself.

Still, there were several ways in which women might be acquired and actually owned, as Speke described in 1862:

> If any Mkungu possessed of a pretty daughter committed an offence, he might give her to the king as a peace-offering; if any neighbouring king had a pretty daughter, and the king of Uganda wanted her, she might also be demanded as a fitting tribute. The Wakungu in Uganda are supplied with women by the king, according to their merits, from seizures in battle abroad, or seizures from refractory officers at home. The women are not regarded as property according to the Wanyamuezi practice, though many exchange their daughters; and some women, for misdemeanours, are sold into slavery; whilst others are flogged, or are degraded to do all the menial services of the house.[34]

Speke's earlier assertion that there were 'no such things as marriages in Uganda', implying that there was no such thing as a free woman, is clearly mistaken. But the above passage is nevertheless revelatory, in so far as it depicts a culture in which women certainly had fewer rights than their menfolk, even if many of them stopped short of actually being classified as slaves. Women were, so to speak, second-class citizens, and were probably more vulnerable to enslavement than Ganda men, by the very definition of their place in the social hierarchy. This was the case despite the surreptitious influences over political life, as described by Schiller, which many were able to wield.

Women, then, could be acquired through warfare, as purchases or gifts, or as part of an alliance or agreement between chiefs, or even between the *kabaka* and a particular chief.[35] Again, however, there were clear distinctions between wives and women in the service of chiefs. The brief passage below is the testimony of a Nyoro woman, apparently a runaway slave, recorded in 1903: 'When Tibashoboke [a Ganda chief] went away to German territory I went with him. I only stayed one day as I was afraid of being sold. I am not the wife of Tibashoboke but was bought by him when a small girl. I was captured during a raid [perhaps c.1890] by the Baganda in Unyoro.'[36]

Another woman, this time a Ganda, stated that 'I was not married to Tibashoboke, he bought me when I was a small girl.'[37] The Ganda chief in question had clearly expanded his harem by purchasing pre-adolescent girls, perhaps in addition to more mature women. This was doubtless viewed as economic expedience: by adding minors to his entourage, he might expect a lifetime of service. Moreover, children were theoretically less likely to attempt escape, although they might do just that when older, as in the case cited above. Children, as they grew up, might develop stronger feelings of loyalty to, and dependency on, their masters. It is

---

[34] Speke 1863b: 361.
[35] White Fathers: Rubaga Diary 1/18 January 1880.
[36] UNA A8/4 There is neither a date nor a title for this document, but it appears to have been written in late 1903.
[37] Ibid.

striking, too, that both women were unequivocal in their assertions that they were not Tibashoboke's wives; their status as slaves is clear, particularly in the case of the Nyoro woman, who feared she might be sold.

The Ganda, of course, had terms to indicate the ranking of women according to social status. The title *kaddulubaale*, meaning the principal wife of a chief or the *kabaka*, was clearly a more exalted position than that suggested by the term *muggya*, which could mean either second wife or a concubine, perhaps a telling linkage. The words *muzaana* and *nvuma* both refer specifically to female slaves, although *muzaana* tended to describe a maidservant in the royal household or that of a chief. These were usually female war captives.[38] Chiefs usually endeavoured to supply their wives with female slaves of this kind.[39] The act of handing over a woman in return for a service, or as the payment of a debt, is expressed in the verb stem *wumiriza*.

It is clearly no coincidence, then, that the noun *mwami* can mean not only chief or master, but also husband. Ganda society appears to have been male-dominated, and a large proportion of women – certain royal females being among the more notable exceptions – were regarded as being economic assets, perhaps even those who were not strictly slaves. It is unlikely that women who were involved in formal dowry marriages could be sold off by their husbands, and indeed such women were entitled to leave their husbands and return to their father's house or that of a male relative: if their grievances were upheld, the dowry would be returned, although there was in the nineteenth century a certain amount of stigma attached to this. But women who had yet to marry could apparently be sold by male relatives without recourse to any form of legal representation. The missionary Pilkington held a somewhat extreme, but telling, view, which he expressed in 1893: 'both wives and children are slaves in the eye of the law, able to be sold at the husband's will, & a woman is not set free by her husband's death, but necessarily passes with cows, goats & other property to her husband's heir ... I ought to add that the only free women in the country are the "Namasole", the "Nalinya" & the "Bambeja"; and all of these are by the law of the land not married ...'[40]

Mackay was at pains to point out that generally the lowest of female – and perhaps any – slaves were elderly women, who were often given the most degrading agricultural or domestic tasks to perform.[41] This highlights the extent to which old women, that is, women who could no longer bear children or offer sexual services, were prone to social isolation and economic hardship, despite the activities such as basketwork mentioned in an earlier chapter. This rendered them even more vulnerable to dependency. Deference to the role of motherhood, again qualified by a certain male haughtiness alluded to previously, was clearly not always sufficient to offset economic impoverishment, and one is led to question the extent to which the position of the *namasole*, the *kabaka*'s official mother, was exceptional rather than reflecting general social conditions in the nine-

---

[38] Kagwa 1934: 67.
[39] Roscoe 1911: 95.
[40] UNA A2/1 Pilkington to the Bishop, 18 April 1893.
[41] CMS Acc.72/F 10 Mackay's 'Uganda Notes in 1879'.

teenth century. The ways in which women coped with, even resisted, these economic and social pressures are a subject worthy of investigation. Again, we have already noted how women made baskets for the market-place in order to avoid destitution. Further, it is clear that women often refused to be treated as inheritance upon the death of their husband or master and simply ran away.[42] This may have been a more prevalent phenomenon in the later nineteenth century, with more fluid social conditions brought about by political upheaval, the arrival of Christian missions and the growing British colonial presence. What became of these women is uncertain, but presumably an opportunity was thus created to improve their quality of living.

Female slaves were also often dedicated by the *kabaka* to the shrines of the major Ganda deities.[43] Many of these women were designated to spend their lives in the service of particular deities, tending the grounds of the shrines and providing food for the spirit mediums and priests. In the royal enclosure itself, and presumably in the enclosures of prominent chiefs, female slaves were employed en masse in supplying the palace with food. Roscoe hints at the idea of female slaves as the real underclass in Buganda when he suggests that even male slaves within the royal enclosure had their food prepared for them by the 'King's women'.[44] This was presumably also the case on the estates of major chiefs, on which there might live 'hundreds of women and slaves'.[45] Roscoe later asserted that Mutesa 'had five hundred wives, each of whom had her maids and female slaves', and in addition there were 'hundreds' of retainers and slaves.[46] The slave population of the royal enclosure, and indeed of the capital as a whole, clearly represented a large proportion of the total by the late nineteenth century. Arab traders told Burton that Suna's harem had contained '3000 souls – concubines, slaves, and children',[47] and almost 20 years later Stanley numbered the royal women at 5,000, of whom 500 were the *kabaka*'s concubines; the rest were responsible for the maintenance of the royal enclosure.[48] None the less, the distinction between concubines and maidservants or *bazaana* is probably to some degree a false one; a woman might regularly move from one category to the other. Mutesa himself is supposed to have told Mackay 'I have no wife; my women are all slaves,'[49] which may indeed have been a characteristic of royal domesticity, although the *kabaka* may have been posturing. But both Roscoe[50] and Stanley stressed that possession of women – that is, primarily female slaves – meant economic wealth. Stanley wrote that 'large possessions' of women 'mean wealth in Uganda, for all of them have a market value, and are saleable for wares of any kind, be they cloth, cows, beads, or guns'.[51]

[42] See Roscoe & Kagwa 1906. See also Iliffe 1987: 59–60, 63.
[43] Roscoe 1911: 204, 274, 276, 297, 298, 300, 303.
[44] Ibid.: 206.
[45] Ibid.: 240.
[46] Roscoe 1921: 88.
[47] Burton: 1860: II, 188.
[48] Stanley 1878: I, 308.
[49] Mackay 1890: 129.
[50] Roscoe 1911: 246.
[51] Stanley 1878: I, 309.

Slave hierarchies

It is probably fair to say that the only feature which all slaves in Buganda had in common was a lack of personal liberty, and even this was subject to considerable variation. Otherwise, there existed something approaching a social hierarchy of slaves and many had markedly different experiences. We have already noted, for example, a prominent gender distinction: female slaves were significantly below most male slaves, many of whom were actually served by the former. In 1878, for example, Mackay asserted, somewhat simplistically but with a grain of truth, that 'work is only for the lowest class. Many slaves have slaves themselves. As a rule only the women do any work.'[52] This is a misreading of the Ganda socio-economic system, discussed in an earlier chapter, and is clearly driven by the late Victorian notion of the work-shy African. Mackay pursued the idea that 'manual labour is reckoned a disgrace' in nineteenth-century Buganda, but in this respect the Ganda 'upper class' was clearly no different from that of most other societies.[53] It is true that what particular slaves actually did would depend on the social status and professional position of their owners. There is little direct evidence to suggest that slaves were employed in more specialized professions, such as iron-working, fishing or even the manufacturing of barkcloth, although it is likely that they were. None the less, much slave labour can probably be generalized in terms of agriculture and personal services.

Freedom of movement was not, of course, the only right denied. For example, as a rule slaves were not honoured with funerals but their corpses were thrown into the forest,[54] a procedure consistent with the idea that a dead slave was an expended economic asset. Clearly in this context lack of kin was also a disadvantage. Yet slaves were often allowed to own small plots of land.[55] Lugard suggested that male slaves were often permitted to choose a wife, and, more importantly, most slaves might expect the protection – legal and otherwise – of their owners.[56] This was dependent, of course, on individual circumstances, as slaves were the property of their masters who might, for example, decide to sell them. Felkin observed that a master might kill his slave if he so desired, but that this was generally frowned upon,[57] apart from being, presumably, financially unsound. In more extended households, where there may have been a number of slaves, a hierarchy developed. According to Felkin, head slaves might be given land, permission to marry and even have slaves of their own, whom they might in theory sell. However, any offspring resulting from a slave marriage legally belonged to the head of the household.[58] The existence of

---

[52] CMS CA6/0 16/37 Mackay to Wright, 26 December 1878.
[53] Ibid. See also CMS CA6/0 16/49 (a) Mackay to Hutchinson, 11 July 1880.
[54] Felkin 1885–6: 759. According to Roscoe, even peasants were properly buried in clan burial grounds, no matter how distant the latter were from the home of the deceased: Roscoe 1911: 125.
[55] Felkin 1885–6: 743.
[56] Lugard 1893: 171–3.
[57] Felkin 1885–6: 746.
[58] Ibid.

slave hierarchies in the nineteenth century was itself indicated by the emergence of two official titles. The *sabaddu* was the title of a man in charge of the slaves of a chief who lived outside the chief's compound; above this figure in importance was the *sabakaaki*, who was the head of the slaves of a chief living within the compound. Both titles were also to be found in the *kabaka*'s enclosure.[59] It is unclear whether the holders of these titles were themselves slaves; if they were, they were clearly slaves of considerable standing. Stanley met Mutesa's 'Sabadu' in 1875, who does appear to have been more of a junior chief than a slave; he was placed in charge of a group of canoes with responsibility for locating the European at the south end of the lake.[60] This kind of responsibility is unlikely to have been given to a slave, whatever his standing. It was probably the same *sabaddu* who was part of the Ganda mission to Britain in 1879.[61] Some time after the return of this mission, in fact, there was considerable outrage that Mutesa had sent mere slaves, and not princes or important chiefs, on this journey; but this was probably figurative language. It is likely that the duties of a *sabaddu* were interpreted according to context. Zimbe noted that Ham Musaka was 'the Sabadu of the Kigalagala', suggesting authority over the royal servants or pages:[62] the status of the *mugalagala* is looked at more closely below. According to the history of the *ngonge* clan, it was a *sabaddu* from among their number who was traditionally in charge of building the *kabaka*'s main residence.[63]

Lourdel noted that the head of the *mukwenda*'s slaves also had responsibility for the protection of the *mukwenda*'s harem;[64] it is not made clear whether this 'young man' was himself a slave but again it is possible that he was drawn from the slave ranks to become an overseer. The White Fathers also recorded that Mutesa referred to a man named 'Kurugi' as his chief slave,[65] an explicit reference to slave hierarchy. In the mid-1850s, Burton was told that the *sekibobo*, the governor of Kyagwe, was in charge of 'the life-guards and slaves, the warriors and builders of the palace', which suggests that command of slave labour at the capital may have been rotated among prominent chiefs in residence near the royal enclosure.[66] At the same time, however, the *sekibobo* may also have been known as the *sabawali*, or head of the *bawali*, another name given to 'servants presented to a chief by their parents to work'. According to one testimony, the *sekibobo* was indeed the head of the *bawali* of the king.[67]

The missionary C.T. Wilson also hinted at the existence of slave differentiation:

The servants in Uganda are all slaves, the majority being born in slavery,

[59] See Murphy 1972: 512. This source specifies 'servants' rather than 'slaves'.
[60] Stanley 1878: I, 282.
[61] Kagwa 1971: 175.
[62] Zimbe 1939: 136.
[63] Kagwa 1972: 7.
[64] White Fathers: C14/24 Lourdel to Deguerry, 7 June 1880.
[65] White Fathers: Rubaga Diary 1/3 September 1880. Kulugi was Mutesa's storekeeper, and one of Kagwa's informants. I am grateful to John Rowe for this information.
[66] Burton 1860: II, 192.
[67] Roscoe & Kagwa 1906: 11. This source distinguishes three categories, namely slaves, shield bearers and servants.

and a tolerable percentage are prisoners, children mostly, taken in war. They are, as a rule, fairly well off, and are not often badly treated; but of course they are liable to be sold to the Arab and half-breed traders for guns, ammunition, cloth, etc. They often live on terms of familiar. intercourse with their masters, and are treated as part of the family ...[68]

In a domestic context, trusted slaves and those of long-standing employment were very often part and parcel of a chief's estate, as much an integral part of his property and responsibility as poor and dependent relatives. Logically enough, the loyal and devoted slave was much less likely to be sold off, even in the context of the frenzied selling of the late nineteenth century, examined in a later chapter. 'Rarely', Livinhac wrote to Lavigerie in 1879, 'do [the chiefs] give up a slave who has spent several years with them', and hardly ever did chiefs sell the children of their slaves, who were themselves born into bondage.[69] In this way slave descent groups were established in many prominent chiefs' enclosures. Roscoe is worth quoting at length:

> Slave were obtained by raids, or from wars made upon neighbouring tribes, or they were inherited from the owner's predecessors, or they were given in payment of a debt. As a rule slaves were foreigners, chiefly Banyoro and Basoga; Baganda who were slaves were treated with much consideration in their own country; they were men and women who had been sold by a relative in trouble, children who had been kidnapped, or who had been pawned to raise money in an emergency ... The status of slavery was not so dreadful in Uganda as in many other countries. In many cases the worst that could be said against it was that a slave was deprived of his freedom, that neither his wife nor her children were his own, and that his life was at his master's disposal. On the other hand if a man married his slave girl, and she had children, she became free ... They were sometimes allowed to inherit property, even though the mother was a woman of another tribe; this, however, was not a general rule ... When the King gave one of [his female slaves] away, she might become the wife of the recipient, but he could not sell her out of the land. Other slaves could be sold just as cattle, and could be put to death at the will of the owner, who looked upon them as his property. Slaves were often treated as members of the family, the only difference being ... that they could not succeed to the property, and, if women, they were handed over to the heir as part of his possessions ...[70]

It is significant that, according to this testimony, which largely corroborates that given earlier, one of the few ways the slave line could come to an end was if the master formally took one of his female slaves as a wife. In his last statement, Roscoe appears to imply that male slaves could not be inherited, perhaps becoming free upon the death of their owner, but this seems unlikely. In the context of a slave being able to inherit property, even position, it is worth quoting the story told by Speke of the slave named 'Uledi' based on the northern border of Buddu. Speke told of:

[68] Wilson & Felkin 1882: I, 186.
[69] White Fathers: C13/5 Livinhac to Lavigerie, 24 September 1879.
[70] Roscoe 1911: 14–15.

a Beluch named Eseau, who came to this country with merchandise, trading on account of Said Said, late Sultan of Zanzibar; but having lost it all on the way here, paying mahongo, or taxes, and so forth, he feared returning, and instead made great friends with the late king Sunna, who took an especial fancy to him because he had a very large beard, and raised him to the rank of Mkungu. A few years ago, however, Eseau died, and left all his family and property to a slave named Uledi, who now, in consequence, is the border officer ...[71]

Perhaps the circumstances of the case were remembered because they were so unusual; it may be that Uledi was the recipient of such good fortune because he was the slave of a favoured coastal immigrant. It is certainly striking that Uledi should not only inherit the latter's property, as well as his family, but also attain a position of local political influence. Possibly the story serves to remind us that the Ganda system was never inflexible, and that individuals, free and otherwise, might aspire to higher status whatever their starting point.

Of course, while many slaves might aspire to something greater within their servitude, others simply aspired to escape. Runaway slaves were by no means uncommon in the later nineteenth century, and presumably earlier. However, although in many circumstances it was possible to climb the slave ranks and attain a position of some importance, and although in a few situations emancipation was feasible, slaves appear on the whole to have been resigned to their status. Thus the majority of runaway slaves were merely fleeing from one master, who may have been particularly cruel or negligent, in the hope of finding the protection of another.[72] Desertions were common particularly among female slaves, notably those belonging to the *kabaka* or prominent chiefs. Livinhac asserted that 'the reason for these desertions is certainly not a love of freedom. With the Negro this is scarcely the case, and when he leaves his master, it is in order to search for another.'[73] The search for a new owner was doubtless an exercise in damage limitation, rather than being symptomatic of an antipathy towards liberty. Both male and female slaves would have been well aware that they would not stop being slaves simply by running away; lacking kin, there was therefore little alternative but to give themselves up to someone else. We are not told of the outcome of these flights. It is likely that in most cases the slave would have been returned, although they might also have been sold to the individual to whom they had fled. The experience of the White Fathers mission was that markedly little was required to prompt an escape attempt. Two of their slaves apparently fled because the bananas they were served were not cooked to their liking,[74] which is of course ludicrous and was most probably a poor excuse for opportunistic protest. Clearly, being sold to the French mission was not a normal occurrence, and it may be that the slaves were freed as a result. Lourdel suggested that some chiefs were noted for their restraint in the

[71] Speke 1863b: 276. 'Uledi' does not sound like a Ganda name, and is perhaps Swahili; it may be that 'Eseau' brought his own slave with him to Buganda.
[72] White Fathers: Rubaga Diary 1/3 September 1880.
[73] White Fathers: C13/7 Livinhac to Deguerry, 6 November 1879.
[74] Ibid.

punishment of slaves, refusing to carry out the more common forms of retribution, including the removal of ears and other facial disfigurements. The reputations of such men loomed large in the slave community at the capital, to which the French missionaries had access.[75]

Slaves at the lower end of the scale were, however, exposed to the possibility of an even worse fate than physical punishment. Human sacrifice was not uncommon in Buganda and, despite some contemporary European accounts describing innocent freemen dragged randomly from highways for this purpose, it seems likely that the practice invariably involved slaves. Students of slavery in other African societies – for example V.C. Uchendu on the Igbo and R.A. Austen on the Duala – have shown that slaves used for human sacrifice were usually fresh captives, not yet integrated into the broader society or even sold, but rather held in limbo by the state.[76] This seems to me likely to have been the case in Buganda, although other enslaved groups may also have been sacrificed. In Buganda, the Italian officer Gaetano Casati was told that Suna, when suffering from an illness, had 'ordered a hundred human victims of expiation to be killed daily to obtain his cure'.[77] It is significant that these individuals were likely to have been Ganda, as victims of expiation – in this context the surrender of personal liberty as repayment of a debt – usually were. It is unclear in this scenario whether the victims actually belonged to the *kabaka* or were offered by chiefs; however, it is possible that the legal system which sanctioned the enslavement of Ganda as ransom offered a ready pool for human sacrifice, suggesting a rather more indiscriminate system than that found in other societies, where only newly arrived aliens were used. The sacrifices mentioned by Casati lasted fifteen days, during which time, if Casati's estimations are to be believed, up to 1500 slaves may have been put to death.[78]

One imagines that valued slaves were exempt from such a tragic fate. Another sphere in which differentiation developed was that of entertainment, in which slaves played a role, particularly, if not exclusively, in the capital. Slave entertainers were frequently to be found at the royal court, for example the Soga musicians, whose talents were renowned throughout the region. Mackay suggests that wrestling contests between slaves were common;[79] slaves were regularly made to fight one another in gladiatorial contests before the *kabaka* and his court.[80] This was clearly largely for the amusement of distinguished spectators, but it may also have been linked to the appraisal of slaves in terms of their physical prowess. Slaves renowned as fighters may well have been favoured by their owners and awarded positions of privilege; such men (as men they invariably were) would certainly have fetched a good price.

---

[75] White Fathers: C14/185 Lourdel to Director, 1 June 1888.
[76] See Uchendu, 'Slaves and slavery in Igboland, Nigeria', and Austen, 'Slavery among coastal middlemen: the Duala of Cameroon', in Miers & Kopytoff 1977: 129, 316. See also Law 1985.
[77] Casati 1891: II, 51.
[78] Ibid.
[79] CMS Acc.72/F 10 Mackay's 'Uganda Notes in 1879'.
[80] White Fathers, Rubaga Diary 1/27 August 1879, 1 September 1879, 11 September 1879, 4 November 1879.

Perhaps the most visible manifestation of differentiation in servility was the growth of what might be termed privileged enslavement or indentureship in the late nineteenth century. In some respects it may be misleading to describe this phenomenon in the context of ordinary slavery, but some common features are apparent, while the development of such indentureship indicates a novel dimension to the idea of servitude in the pre-colonial kingdom. Few Ganda were involved in the system, and it should not therefore be confused with the processes by which most Ganda found themselves in bondage, as described above. None the less, its political – and, as we shall see in a later chapter, military – implications were considerable. The system basically involved the handing over of children by peasants to chiefs – or, more accurately, by relatively junior chiefs to higher-ranking chiefs – and ultimately by chiefs to the *kabaka* himself to serve as 'pages' or servants.[81] Both boys and girls might be handed over, but it is clear that the opportunities facing the former were very much greater; as we have seen, girls were usually swallowed up into the ranks of concubines or became *bazaana*. For young men, the system of socio-political indentureship produced a new breed of privileged servants, who might eventually rise to positions of considerable power; indeed, by the 1890s, they constituted a new elite in Ganda political society.

It is worth comparing the phenomenon with the *batongole*, which were created in the second half of the nineteenth century. Both privileged servants and *batongole* were pools from which the new elite, both political and military, were drawn in the 1870s and 1880s, and indeed earlier. The main and obvious difference is that, while *batongole* were freemen directly appointed by the *kabaka*, privileged servitude involved some of the features of Ganda slavery already discussed. The committal of boys to a chief's enclosure or that of the *kabaka* was both a major source of domestic labour and, more importantly for the boys themselves, a critical opportunity for social advancement. Crucially, a page was not a *muddu* but a *mugalagala*; yet the distinction was not as clear as might be supposed. Indeed, there appears to have been some confusion among the Ganda themselves concerning the legal status of the *mugalagala*. Zimbe relates the story how Kagwa, perhaps the most dramatic manifestation of social advancement, came to be in the service of Mutesa:

> It was Nzalambi the keeper of the Kabaka's mosque who persuaded Kagwa to leave his master Basude and join the Kabaka's service ... But Basude accused Nzalambi when he got a chance of seeing the Kabaka, appealing to the law forbidding mere slaves [*baddu*], for Kagwa was not his son, from serving the Kabaka. The Katikiro, Mukasa, then said to Basude: 'Do not the slaves the kabaka gives to his chiefs bring water for him?' He replied: 'They do, my lord'. Katikiro Mukasa continued: 'Do the chiefs' children bring water the Kabaka uses before prayer (Mohammedan type)?' Basude replied: 'They too can bring it but it is those who have been captured in arms that do not'...[82]

[81] The fact that certain clans are noted as having been exempted from the offering of children to the royal court suggests the general importance of the system itself. The *ngabi* and *mbwa* clans were thus exempted: Kagwa 1972: 20–21, 90.

[82] Zimbe 1939: 96–7.

There seems to have been little doubt that Kagwa was indeed considered a slave, in so far as he was in the service of Basude but was not Basude's son. Yet the term 'slave' clearly took on different meanings according to the context in which the service was being performed. The fact that Kagwa was 'persuaded' to leave his master also suggests that the former, and young men like him, enjoyed a measure of liberty not associated with the status of *buddu*. Basude did not appeal to a law which stated that Kagwa was his slave and simply could not leave his master of his own free will, but to one which stated that Kagwa and his ilk could not serve the *kabaka*; it sounds as though Basude had little legal ground to stand on.

Moreover, the careers of many of these court pages, especially those in the service of the *kabaka*, suggest that they had not been enslaved but committed to a stridently disciplinarian training school for political and social advancement. A *mugalagala* in the 1880s was sure to find a place in the *kabaka*'s personal military elite, and many were showered with favours and, in time, imbued with arrogance. Some of these were attracted to the religious factions of the 1870s and 1880s, using religious identity to win a certain leverage at the centre of power. This phenomenon, most closely associated with the later part of Mutesa's reign and that of Mwanga, will be returned to later on. In general terms, however, it may be seen at least in part as a form of privileged servitude, which ultimately backfired on those who were meant to be served. Certain young men, classed as slaves by the French missionaries, clearly possessed considerably greater freedom and enjoyed a sense of immunity as a consequence of being in the service of the *kabaka*. In late 1879, one missionary noted that '[t]wo young slaves of the king's, in my class of Bagalagala, come to ask if we can teach them to read'.[83] We cannot be sure of the extent of the liberties enjoyed by the *bagalagala* in the period of their apprenticeship, but the privilege of their position is clear. Wilson wrote in 1878: 'I am told too that many of the King's servants can read Arabic and I should like to be able to give them all Bibles ... for they are a very important class to get at for Mtesa unlike the chiefs has no slaves among his attendants, they are sons of chiefs ... these young fellows will form the future aristocracy of Uganda partly by succession, partly by creation ...'.[84] This seems an accurate assessment. These were elite servants, coming from an already privileged class to serve a period of tutelage in the corridors of power, which many would come eventually to inherit.

---

[83] White Fathers: Rubaga Diary 1/13 November 1879.
[84] CMS CA6/025/21 Wilson to Wright, 31 May 1878.

Summary of Part Two

People were pre-colonial Buganda's most valuable resource, to a degree which was remarkable even in the context of an underpopulated continent. Yet the value of human resources was directly related to the value of land in the nineteenth-century kingdom, a situation which was rather more unusual in sub-Saharan Africa. In the context of nineteenth-century East Africa, Buganda was at a decided advantage. Its relatively dense population, supported by a favourable environment and a well-developed economic system, both facilitated and, to some extent, made necessary the kind of labour system which had emerged by the eve of colonial rule. This was as complex a system of public obligation as could be found in a society without written records and permanent accounts. Nothing was written down; but there was a clear understanding of the role of the state and the public functions of those who served it and participated in it. Law and obligation were articulated by action, not by written statutes; the latter were unnecessary in a society with such a clearly defined image of itself, of how it operated most efficiently and of the roles which particular social groups were expected to perform. The kingdom was to be served, because the existence of the kingdom was in the interests of the majority; the state, the beating heart of the kingdom, ensured the growth of the principle of servitude and articulated the ideology necessary for its perpetuation.

An essential factor in understanding the pre-colonial kingdom's success, then, is the degree to which its citizens were motivated and organized to contribute to a collective whole. There was clearly a centralizing ethos in this regard, which probably developed over several centuries as the kingdom itself expanded. Yet at the same time there was a degree of decentralization, which was more pronounced than previous studies have allowed for. As in many other spheres of public life, the kingdom's labour and taxation systems were a matter for careful management rather than powerful centralized direction. This is true, for example, in the context of the road network. The impetus for the network clearly came from the metropolitan centre, which was in a position to view the long-term and long-distance opportunities presented by such a project; yet roads were maintained by district, and the level of maintenance varied as a result, despite the threats of central authority in the form of fines. The collection of tax, it seems, was also characterized by decentralization; the metropolitan centre provided the necessary impetus, and articulated the ideology underpinning the system, but certainly by the 1890s, following massive political disruption, had markedly little control over tax collection in practice. Finally, public labour more generally was also organized provincially, with public work being undertaken in the name of the centralized state rather than organized directly by it. Each of these aspects of decentralization reveals much about the efficiency with which the pre-colonial kingdom mobilized its human resources, in so far as direct and omnipresent intervention and supervision were unnecessary. In many respects the centralized state was covert rather than overt; the ethos of

131

motivation and awareness of a national cause was sufficiently developed by the nineteenth century to allow a certain decentralized approach to social and economic organization. Even so, the potential fragility of the system was exposed by Mwanga on the eve of colonial rule; but Mwanga's behaviour simply emphasizes the extent to which devolution had become necessary to the effective functioning of the system. His interference brought great damage to that system and to the kingdom more generally.

Of course, coercion or the threat of coercion was an important dynamic of the functioning society, and punishments of various kinds were meted out by the central state. The most extreme and also most visible manifestation of coercion was in the institution of slavery. Slaves formed the basis of labour in many spheres of economic life, while the immense variety within the broad category of servitude reflected great political, social and economic complexity. Moral judgements aside, it is difficult to assess how brutal Ganda slavery actually was, although it seems fair to say that in comparison with a number of other slave-owning societies, African and otherwise, the Ganda did not unduly mistreat their serviles. What is clear, however, is that, as was the case in West Africa with the growth of the transatlantic system, the life of a Ganda slave became rather more miserable with the rise of the long-distance slave trade from the mid-nineteenth century.

Part Three

Buyers & Sellers
Developments
in commerce

Seven

Domestic & Regional Trade

Trade was a major source of material strength and wealth to the pre-colonial kingdom. Its economic and social development is closely linked to the commercial ties, which grew up over centuries, and this intimate connection took on dramatic aspects during the nineteenth century with the rapid growth of long-distance commerce, namely that with the East African coast. In preceding chapters, the existence of complex trading systems has been alluded to; areas of economic activity such as food production, iron-working, pottery and barkcloth manufacturing were firmly rooted in a commercial network which was critical to Buganda's spatial and internal growth. In the late nineteenth century, and indeed through much of the twentieth, there was a profoundly mistaken view among European observers and analysts that before the arrival of the coastal merchants there was little commercial activity worthy of the name. This view seriously undervalued extant domestic and regional trade networks.[1] As I shall argue when we come to long-distance trade, the spread of goods, as well as ideas, from the coast and the inland entrepôts such as Tabora in Unyanyembe was facilitated by much older local trade networks and markets. It is therefore logical to begin by examining more regional or domestic trade networks in and around Buganda, in other words the development and operation of these systems and the ways in which the Ganda derived considerable wealth thereby. In this sense, the

---

[1] It is by no means clear that the Ganda themselves distinguished domestic trade, meaning exchange within Ganda territorial boundaries, from regional, meaning exchange between Buganda and its neighbours. The ensuing discussion focuses primarily on regional and long-distance commerce, usually trade between the Ganda and the agents of the coastal economy, who were based either at the coast or at Unyanyembe. Distinctions of this kind were suggested by Vansina: see Vansina 1962b. Nevertheless, it is necessary to take on board the criticisms of this approach made by Richard Gray and David Birmingham, who rightly suggested that such geographical distinctions frequently become blurred: they argued, for example, that there is 'remarkably little evidence to suggest that "local trade from village to village within a given population" was restricted to local products'. See Gray & Birmingham 1970.

present chapter develops some of the themes first considered by Tosh a quarter of a century ago.[2] It can be shown how long-distance goods such as particular types of metal were freely exchanged alongside local products. For Buganda as a whole, commerce was a source of strength as well as prosperity, one of the best examples of this being the lucrative regional arms trade. Private traders valued highly their ability to exchange their wares not just at local markets, but at those in neighbouring societies such as Bunyoro and Ankole. While there is no evidence of a direct tax on trade, central government acquired the fruits of such commerce through internal taxation, and indeed the *kabaka* and prominent chiefs appear to have traded on their own account.

Local commerce & commodities

Studies in other parts of Africa, as well as those in Europe, have shown that the sites of markets tend to be of ancient habitation; successful market sites stand for generations, usually centrally located or positioned at the junction of highways. Markets are conduits not only for commodities but also for ideas. The markets of East Africa were no different. By the second half of the nineteenth century, certain markets had become established as the most important in the lacustrine region. In 1876–7, Emin Pasha identified 'Werhanje' in Karagwe, 'Mpara Nyamoga' (near modern Hoima) in Bunyoro, and Rubaga, the capital of Buganda, as the major regional commercial centres. At Kabarega's capital[3] he found an exciting and cosmopolitan atmosphere in which anything and everything was brought for sale. He noted the 'restless, talkative Waganda, draped in neat tan-coloured bark cloth', who had 'brought for barter the handsome soft mats of Uganda, together with bark cloths and thick copper wire'.[4] This is a good example of the way in which regional and long-distance lines of commerce merged: the Ganda brought with them to Bunyoro both the fruits of their own industry and goods which were (probably) ultimately coastal in origin.

In an earlier chapter we saw how barkcloth was one of Buganda's oldest and most important sources of domestic wealth, and how control of the centres of the industry was one of most lucrative prizes for successive empires in the region. The value thus placed on the production of barkcloth owed much to its commercial strength. From the late eighteenth century and throughout the nineteenth, barkcloth was probably Buganda's single most important regional export.[5] It was highly valued throughout the region: Emin Pasha estimated that barkcloth 'constitutes the ordinary clothing in Uganda, and that of the better classes in Karagwa, Ruhanda, Unyoro, and Usoga'.[6] Prices varied 'considerably', depending on colour,

---

[2] Tosh 1970.

[3] For a pioneering analysis of the Nyoro economic and commercial system, see Uzoigwe 1972.

[4] Schweinfurth *et al.* 1888: 112.

[5] See Chapter 4 for a discussion of the expansion of barkcloth production under Kabaka Semakokiro in the late eighteenth century.

[6] Schweinfurth *et al.* 1888: 119.

pattern and general quality; as noted earlier, the quality of the fabric was dependent upon the age of the tree from which the original bark was taken, as this influenced both texture and durability.[7] But age was not the only determinant of market value. Dyed cloths, produced in various parts of Buganda but most likely to have come from Buddu, were the most expensive; Emin Pasha estimated their exchange value in the mid-1870s at two or three cows a piece. Cloth sold in its more 'natural' state was 'considerably cheaper' and could be 'purchased in the markets for 300 or 400 cowries'.[8] Seemingly inferior types of clothing were also traded by the Ganda: Emin Pasha mentioned the sale of several goatskins 'previously scraped down as thin as paper' and sewn together. This was apparently neither as attractive nor as durable as barkcloth, but the Ganda sold it 'at a high price' outside Buganda.[9] Some years later, the price of these garments had decreased somewhat. Lugard observed in 1891 that skins which were 'scraped very thin' were 'very cheap', being sold for 'half-a-yard of merikani [imported cloth]'.[10] Based on Lugard's pricing estimates, however, this was equal to about 250 cowries, significantly more than the 100 cowries which Grant claimed was the price of a goatskin in 1862.[11] It may have been that Grant and Lugard were quoting the domestic prices for such commodities; it seems probable, in view of Emin Pasha's testimony, that the Ganda raised their prices substantially when trading outside Buganda. At the same time, the difference in cowry value between Grant's and Lugard's estimates may be related to the devaluation of the cowry shell, which was significant by the 1890s.

By 1900, the export of barkcloth was a great source of revenue to many Ganda, particularly in Buddu. The trade between Buddu and the Banyankole was especially important in this regard. The full extent of this commerce is revealed through early colonial reports, particularly after Ganda traders were required to carry passes to enable them to travel to markets some distance away. One official at Masaka in Buddu wrote in 1901 that 'as many as fifty to sixty traders' passes have been issued at this station in one day, the bulk of the applicants proceeding to Ankole with bark cloths as their article of trade'. Mats were also traded by the Buddu merchants, but barkcloth was the prized commodity among the Banyankole, to the extent that the latter were often permitted to pay their hut tax in sheets of barkcloth.[12] The true value of this trade is further indicated by the apparently impoverishing effects of the cessation of commerce with Ankole at the beginning of 1904. The instigator of this prohibition was a German agent at Mbarara, who, according to a local British official, 'appears to have vetoed the sale of bark cloth in his district, for exchange for cattle … The natives [in Buddu] inform me that they are not allowed to sell bark cloth in exchange for cattle in Ankole. Bark cloth being the one and only

---

[7] Ibid.
[8] Ibid.: 120.
[9] Ibid.: 120–21.
[10] UNA A26/4 Lugard to Admin.-Gen., IBEAC 13 August 1891.
[11] Grant, 1864: 229.
[12] UNA A8/1 Prendergast to Jackson, 3 September 1901.

stock in trade of the people of Buddu, trade and consequently monetary prosperity have come to a standstill ...'[13]

This report surely exaggerates the extent to which trade in the area had collapsed, as many other commodities were exported from Buddu; iron, for example, remained an important trade good, being both extracted from deposits within Buddu and traded around Koki. But the Ganda traders' abrupt loss of access to the lucrative markets for barkcloth in Ankole was clearly a bitter blow.

Buddu provides perhaps the best example of how particular regions were noted for their trade in certain commodities, but there are others. The district of Bugangadzi, for example, which formed part of pre-colonial Bunyoro west of Singo, was noted in 1905 for its exports to Buganda of salt, skins, ivory, hoes, tobacco and dried fish.[14] The trade in dried fish between Buganda and Bunyoro was particularly lucrative by the nineteenth century, and was probably one of the oldest commercial interactions in the region. The Ganda carried dried fish to Buruli, north of Bulemezi, where there was a market of some renown, as one British official discovered: 'The fish market at Kisalizi, Buruli, is well patronised by the Waganda especially by those with small means as they can make a very good living out of it. I have been told by the traders themselves that out of one rupee worth of fish they make between five and six rupees profit ...'[15]

Fish were of course brought inland from lakes Kyoga and Victoria, but river fishing also played a part in this trade. Speke noted a thriving river-borne trade in 1862 between the Nyoro and the Soga, the canoes of the former being stuffed with such goods as barkcloth, dried fish, raw and cooked plantains, and beer.[16] The presence of barkcloth is certainly worthy of note: it is unclear if this was the Nyoro version of the commodity, or whether the Nyoro were re-exporting the Ganda fabric. There seems little reason to doubt that the Ganda were also involved in this commerce, particularly along the Nile, which by this time represented their eastern frontier. It also seems likely that there was a regular trade in basic food-stuffs between Buganda and Bunyoro. One report from 1894 mentions the regularity with which the Nyoro sold food to the Ganda and, although the latter at this time were attached to the British garrison at Fort Grant, it seems unlikely that the nascent colonial presence provided any significant impetus to such trade which was not already there.[17]

At the market in Kabarega's capital, Emin Pasha also noted the trade in services as well as that in actual commodities. Although Nyoro smiths were more than capable of working 'iron, copper, and brass' into spear-heads, knives and various kinds of jewellery, Ganda smiths travelled to Bunyoro 'periodically' to repair guns in the second half of the nineteenth

---

[13] UNA A8/4 Anderson to Sub. Comm., 6 January 1804. The reference to a 'German agent' at Mbarara is puzzling, although it is clear that trade restrictions between German and British territories had been imposed.
[14] UNA A8/7 Paske-Smith to Sub. Comm., 3 December 1905.
[15] UNA A8/7 Manara [?] to Sub. Comm., 3 November 1905.
[16] Speke 1863b: 476.
[17] UNA A2/3 Owen to Colvile 16 November 1894.

century. Indeed, according to Emin Pasha, these smiths charged 'exorbitant' rates, demanding, for example, 'a female slave in exchange for a gun-cock'.[18] It is clear that this would have been, even in 1877, a highly specialized profession, but its very existence on a regional scale is significant. It also hints at the existence of a commerce in ideas and expertise which almost certainly predated the arrival of firearms. Much of Buganda's development in iron-working before 1800 was facilitated by knowledge brought from Bunyoro; the repairing of firearms in the market-place by the Ganda represented something of a turnabout of commerce in skills and know-how in a late nineteenth-century setting.

It is clear that metals both in a raw state and in the form of ready-made implements were critical trade commodities throughout the nineteenth century. Brass and copper wire[19] were everyday objects of exchange, although they were in rapid decline in Buganda by the late nineteenth century. Iron, however, was the most important. Buganda derived a certain amount of its iron from tribute, but most of its imports of this material were accounted for by trade. Iron in an unworked state was carried from Kavirondo to the west, for example, and was converted into hoes once it reached the forges of Buganda.[20] Ready-made hoes were also imported. One British official remarked in 1894 how he 'bought some native [Ganda] hoes the other day but they have got rapidly ruined with digging the hard road, cutting down ant-hills etc'; however, hoes 'of a different pattern but of much harder iron' had been brought for these purposes from Busoga.[21] Hoes were regularly imported from Bunyoro, and could be found, according to Roscoe, in the numerous small markets along the frontier areas between Buganda and Bunyoro.[22] It is a striking thought that the road networks of Buganda, as well as other important public works, were carved from the soil using foreign tools. Speke describes how, when pushing north into Bunyoro, he was surrounded by a number of Nyoro who sought 'to hawk ivory ornaments, brass and copper twisted wristlets, tobacco, and salt, which they exchanged for cowries, with which they purchase cows from the Waganda'.[23] Speke may be mistaken, but the idea of the supposedly pastoral Nyoro purchasing cows from the supposedly agricultural Ganda is an appealing one, and certainly supports the idea of a thoroughly open regional market. Metals were also traded in the form of weaponry, and indeed the regional arms trade was particularly vibrant, not to mention extremely important to Buganda's military standing. Again in the border areas between Buganda and Bunyoro, territory in which the exchanged goods were so often put to good use, Nyoro traders sold spear-blades to the Ganda. In 1862, according to Grant, these could fetch 500 cowries each, while 'one cow would buy ten, or bark cloth would be taken

---

[18] Schweinfurth *et al.* 1888: 81.
[19] As discussed earlier, the origins of copper in Buganda are obscure; it may have first arrived from Katanga, but during the nineteenth century it was much more likely to have been brought from the coast.
[20] UNA A2/1 Owen to Rhodes, 29 March 1893.
[21] UNA A2/3 Ansorge to Colvile, 5 October 1894.
[22] Roscoe 1911: 456.
[23] Speke 1863b: 487.

in exchange'.[24] From the dimensions given by Grant, these blades were probably destined for use in war rather than hunting. They were 'two spans long', or around 40 cm, and 'two inches at their greatest breadth'. Spear-blades for hunting were similar in length but usually much wider at the socket.[25] Weapons were also brought up from Karagwe to be traded in the frontier areas of Buganda and Bunyoro, and again the Ganda in particular were keen buyers. Grant noted that '[e]xcellent spear-heads are hawked for sale in the southern borders [of Bunyoro], but the Waganda, a richer people, buy them up'.[26] This commercial activity took place in small local markets, away from any centralized royal control, which was in any case unnecessary. Had Buganda's internal economic base been weak, more direct royal control, might have been required to muscle in on such trade; but the strong commercial and economic position enjoyed by the nineteenth-century Ganda rendered this kind of interference redundant. Ganda traders had the wherewithal to hold their own in regional commerce.

Another of the most important articles of trade in the region was salt, trade in which was probably older than the societies involved. The Ganda produced a certain amount of their own salt, but this was too little in quantity and low in quality to free them from a heavy reliance on imported salt.[27] The major source of salt in the region was Kibiro, on the shore of Lake Albert in Bunyoro; salt had been produced there for several centuries.[28] The Ganda regularly travelled to Bunyoro to obtain it, but Nyoro traders also carried it to Buganda.[29] Emin Pasha tells us that the salt came to the market 'wrapped in banana leaves, in long packets containing four to eight pounds each'. Salt was highly valued, and this was reflected in the prices paid for it. Emin Pasha asserted that '[i]n contrast to all other goods, salt, with very rare exceptions, is sold in Uganda for cash only, that is to say, for cowries'.[30] This in itself is worthy of note; in the second half of the nineteenth century, Buganda was a relatively monetarized society, but even so most commodities had a barter as well as a cowry value. Kibiro was not Buganda's only source of salt. The Ganda also travelled by canoe to the northeast corner of Lake Victoria, apparently to the bay now known as Winam Gulf, where they obtained salt.[31] This trade was first mentioned by Speke, and was still thriving in 1898 when a British official observed that both the Ganda and the Soga regularly made voyages there. The salt

[24] Grant 1864: 271.
[25] Ibid. See also Trowell & Wachsmann 1953: 235.
[26] Grant 1864: 293.
[27] Poor-quality salt was extracted from vegetable debris, and occasionally from livestock urine.
[28] For the results of recent excavations at Kibiro, see for example Connah, Kamuhangire & Piper 1990; also Sutton 1993.
[29] Schweinfurth *et al.* 1888: 74.
[30] Ibid.: 121–2.
[31] Speke 1863b: 428–9, 434, 467; also Speke 1967: 318. Intriguingly, the Ganda apparently called this area 'Bahari Ngo', derived from the Arabic for river, which bears a striking resemblance to Baringo, about 130 miles to the east of Lake Victoria. Chaillé-Long also wrote that, from a hill near Murchison Creek, 'in the distance a small creek may be seen, like a silver stream winding through the country northward, here called "Bahr Rionga"': Chaillé-Long 1876: 109. This seems to be a reference to 'Rionga's river', Riongo being a rival of Kamurasi.

was exchanged for 'trade goods, cloth, Masai beads, white, red, and pink [beads]'.[32] This particular line of commerce has been highlighted by Kenny, who adds that 'for Ganda and Soga traders, the Lake route would surely have been more expedient, barring the political difficulties which were characteristic of the Ganda relationship to Buvuma and Busoga'.[33] Salt was also brought from the direction of Toro, or more precisely from the salt lake at Katwe. In 1901, salt caravans were reported as coming from this area to Buganda[34] and, although it is not clear that the salt caravan itself was pre-colonial in origin, the trade almost certainly was. Lugard also noted the existence of salt trade between Toro and Buganda in 1891.[35]

It is clear that there were a few major market towns in the region, one of which was the Ganda capital itself. This was especially true from the 1840s, when the capital moved within a much more limited area and expanded rapidly in size and importance as a regional centre.[36] But there is little doubt that numerous smaller markets were scattered throughout Buganda. Among the oldest markets mentioned in the indigenous sources, for example, were those on the shore of Kyagwe, which dated from at least the reign of Mawanda in the early eighteenth century and probably much earlier. A Ganda author recorded how '[t]here used to be the major markets namely, Bagegere, Bale and Nsonga. The people of Buvuma too used to sail to the shores near Kyagwe for the sale of their goods in these markets. These markets would take place for two days at a time so that men could do their selling …'[37]

Although within the capital the *kabaka* exercised a certain amount of control over commercial interaction, most obviously in the restrictions placed on certain imported goods,[38] there appear to have been few such restrictions placed on local markets outside the capital. Again, as in other spheres, metropolitan control hovered in the background but was limited. Local traders did, however, have to work within regulations, and Roscoe suggests that even markets in the outlying districts were supervised to some extent by political authority. Fees, for example, were levied on all articles brought for sale. In the capital itself, and possibly beyond, the market was under the supervision of a chief specially appointed by the *kabaka*, one of whose duties was to collect the market dues, which 'amounted to ten per cent of the value of each article sold or bought'.[39] This would have surely represented a sizeable income for the state. It is difficult to assess, of course, how much of this represented pre-colonial innovation, but it does seem likely that a special chief was indeed appointed by the *kabaka* to oversee trade in the capital, if only that with coastal merchants and if only to ensure the payment to the state of the necessary fees. In Buganda terms

---

[32] UNA A4/13 MacAllister to Berkeley, 12 September 1898.
[33] Kenny 1974.
[34] UNA A8/1 Tomkins to Comm., 3 October 1901.
[35] UNA A26/4 Lugard to Admin.-Gen., IBEAC, 13 August 1891. See also Perham 1959: II, 248.
[36] Reid 1998; Reid & Medard 2000.
[37] 'Ebye Buganda: Entabalo za Sekabaka Mawanda', *Munno* (1921) pp. 11–12.
[38] As is shown below, however, the effectiveness and range of these restrictions should not be exaggerated.
[39] Roscoe 1911: 452.

exist for an official in charge of a market – *ssentala* – and a fee imposed on sellers – *kituuza* – but it is unclear how far back these can be traced.

Similar commercial overseers may also have existed throughout the kingdom. One colonial official wrote in 1902: 'I am of opinion that five per cent is a fair due to be collected not being too severe on the natives and further one which has been charged from time immemorial in this country by the native chiefs who formerly controlled their own markets thereby giving a precedent which has become a custom.'[40]

This suggests that not only did such tolls, and presumably toll-collectors or market overseers, exist, but that markets outside the capital were responsible not to central authority but to the chief on whose land the market was located. It seems likely that this was less to do with political control per se than with the maximization of profit. Regional chiefs could draw considerable wealth from local markets, although it may be assumed that a percentage of their profits was dispatched to metropolitan government. Roscoe suggests that the location of markets was closely monitored, apparently for this reason. Markets could not be opened at random, but special permission had to be sought from a regional chief, perhaps the *ssaza* governor himself. Technically, then, such markets were under the overall supervision of the landowner. Under a system which was clearly designed to benefit chiefs financially, heavy fines were levied on those would-be traders who attempted to avoid market dues by trading outside recognized market-places; they could also expect to have their wares confiscated.[41]

These restrictions could probably only be applied to large-scale commercial centres, for example extended villages which might be centred on the enclosure of a prominent local chief, or the crossroads formed by the meeting of two major highways.[42] Private, one-to-one trading and itinerant hawking doubtless went on unchecked in more remote areas, and in the frontier regions of the kingdom, in spite of the risk of the fines mentioned above. The domestic market system in the 1890s was thus characterized by a degree of decentralization, and it seems reasonable to hypothesize that this was also true of the earlier pre-colonial period; certainly, it is likely that chiefs would have been only too happy to have a market established in their domains as it represented a useful source of income and had the potential to draw people from a considerable distance away. An example of this is provided by a British official in 1902, who noted soon after his arrival in Buddu that the market master in Masaka, which would have been the largest market in the *ssaza*, was appointed by the *pokino*, the governing chief.[43] The same official later wrote of eastern Kyagwe that 'at present market dues ... are collected by Chiefs on whose land markets have been established'.[44]

---

[40] UNA A8/1 Prendergast to Comm., 18 February 1902. 'From time immemorial' probably means 'within living memory' in this context.

[41] Roscoe 1911: 452, 456.

[42] Harry Johnston observed that '[t]he Uganda town is a series of villa residences surrounded by luxuriant gardens. Occasionally there is an open square formed by the meeting of two broad roadways, and this may be the site of a market or a place of reunion for the people': Johnston 1902: II, 656.

[43] UNA A8/1 Grant to Jackson, 1 March 1902.

[44] UNA A8/1 Grant to Jackson, 16 March 1902.

The missionary O'Flaherty described the main market in the capital as the *kabaka*'s own private market; this is certainly incorrect, but perhaps understandable as the *kabaka* apparently drew considerable revenue from it. Both Ganda and Arabs traded here, meeting at the one of the major junctions in the East African interior. O'Flaherty, who depicted a jealously guarded commerce at the capital, suggested that the collectors took 15–20 per cent of market profits, which doubtless reflected the tight control exercised over such a lucrative trade. Notably, however, he expressed doubt as to whether Mutesa was aware of this.[45] If this was indeed the case, we are confronted once again with an image of the *kabaka* as a more marginal figure than might be supposed, even in his immediate domain; he undoubtedly received a substantial percentage of dues, but, as with the taxation system, others made sure they received their cut without his knowledge. It is necessary, however, to note the important qualification that Mutesa was at this time extremely ill, and this presumably under-mined his control of trade, as of other aspects of public life. Again as with the taxation system, it is unclear whether the process by which the chiefs took advantage of Mutesa's failing powers was actually illegal, or whether it was accepted practice, with the *kabaka* having much less direct control over the generation and distribution of wealth than was assumed at the time. It does seem that in 1882 Mutesa attempted to tighten his control of the main market in the capital. As is examined below, this initiative to strengthen royal control extended to the lake ports, and in particular Entebbe, which was considered too distant for the *kabaka* to effectively control customs duty there. The missionary Girault noted in early 1882 Mutesa's declaration that no one was now permitted to buy or sell outside the main market. The *kabaka* himself would organize the collection of dues, and Girault was in no doubt that Mutesa 'has established this market because of the ivory of which he wants to have a monopoly'.[46] This seems highly likely, although the declaration that absolutely nothing was to be traded outside the main market bears the hallmarks of Mutesa's increasingly erratic behaviour, driven by incurable illness, in the last months of his life.[47] At this time Mutesa had little interest in anything other than the sale of ivory and slaves, and he was prepared to hinder all other commerce as a result. Apparently as a consequence of the *kabaka*'s orders, the cost of day-to-day provisions immediately increased, and Girault complained that such goods could no longer be bought casually around the capital, as they had been previously.[48]

It may be presumed that this situation did not outlast Mutesa's own reign, and by the early 1890s things seemed to have returned to relative normality, even allowing for the effects of civil war. Lugard observed: 'At the capital there are two regular markets, with officers to control them, collectors of the king: taxes on all produce which changes hands, viz., a small percentage on the cowrie value. Produce brought in from the

---

[45] CMS G3 A6/0 1882/56 O'Flaherty to Wigram, 15 March 1882; see also Kiwanuka in Kagwa 1971: 179.
[46] White Fathers: Rubaga Diary 2/31 January 1882, 2 February 1882, 26 February 1882.
[47] See Reid 1999a.
[48] As footnote 46.

country is sold here, and oxen slaughtered and sold retail, as in our butchers' shops ...'[49]

It is not clear what kind of distances were covered by those traders travelling to buy or sell at markets in the capital, but it may be assumed that the capital sat at the centre of a domestic network which covered most of the kingdom, even allowing for limitations on transport. The effective functioning of this network, as we have seen, was critical to the urban population, particularly in the 1880s and 1890s; the value of the trade is somehow underlined by Lugard's illustration, which depicts the selling of food even at a time of political and religious disturbance.

Pre-colonial currencies

It is clear from the various accounts of both regional and domestic commerce that barter co-existed with monetary exchange; buyers and sellers were generally flexible in this regard, although as we have seen the salt traders of Kibiro demanded cowries alone. During the second half of the nineteenth century, cowries were probably most used for the purchase of cheaper, smaller articles – foodstuffs, for example – while larger, more expensive articles were obtained by barter. This reflects the gradual but steady devaluation of cowries in the decades before colonial rule; it is also clear that certain other currencies changed in value during the nineteenth century, reflecting demand, supply and taste. The most marked decline in a standard of exchange in Buganda was that in beads. Beads had been in use, whether as a currency or as a commodity in themselves, for perhaps several centuries. The precise origins of several types of beads are unclear, but their usage and significance varied widely throughout the region. The Soga and other groups east of the Nile, for example, attached great symbolic importance to blue glass beads; as Trowell found in the early 1950s, 'a certain type of blue bead has an almost sacred value' in this area.[50] Glass beads were common throughout East Africa, and were brought in increasing bulk from Europe, in addition to those earlier brought from India, and in particular from Amsterdam and Venice, from the end of the seventeenth century onward.[51] They have been found at a great number of archaeological sites in eastern, central and southern Africa, including the east coast and Great Zimbabwe.[52] In particular, glass beads have been unearthed at Ntusi which may date back as early as the

---

[49] Lugard 1892: 831. Two maps of the capital appear in Lugard's published diaries, and only one market – that to the north of the royal enclosure – is shown in each. The White Fathers' map of the capital, however, depicts two markets, that shown on Lugard's sketches, and another in the northeast of the capital called 'marché des Basoga'. See Perham 1959: II 27, III 32; White Fathers Archive, contained in C14 'Correspondence of Lourdel'.

[50] Trowell & Wachsmann 1953: 212–13.

[51] For example, see Carey 1986.

[52] Connah, 1987: Chapters 7, 8. The archaeological evidence suggests that glass beads reached the interior via the trading towns on the east coast, where some beads were also made. Some may also have reached the interlacustrine region along the Nile via Nubia.

fourteenth century.[53] These findings seem to lend some credence to Miti's assertion that 'Kintu, as also his brother Rukedi in Bunyoro, were the first persons to import and make use of beads or other neck ornaments in this country, and by making presents of such articles to the local people Kintu won their friendship and confidence.'[54] From such evidence, oral and archaeological, it is probable that beads represented the oldest currency in the region. According to Roscoe, the blue bead 'was very rough and badly made, but ... was considered to be of great value'.[55] It was known as *lusinda* in Buganda, a term which is clearly distinct from *nsimbi*, broadly meaning money, and *ensimbi ennanda*, which specifically referred to cowries. Up until around the middle of the nineteenth century, blue beads seem to have been a common form of currency in Buganda and throughout the region.

In the early part of Mutesa's reign, they were still relatively common in local commercial interaction, but by the late 1870s their value had plummeted: Emin Pasha reported in 1877 that glass beads were no longer sought after by Ganda traders.[56] It is true that he was mostly dealing with a powerful commercial elite in the capital, but he also had experience of smaller-scale commerce. Moreover, changing values among the elite were usually shadowed by similar, if more gradual, changes among the broader populace; this is indicated in the context of cloth and indigenous fabrics. By the late nineteenth century, beads were rarely mentioned in reports relating to desirable trade goods in Buganda, although they were clearly still prevalent in Busoga and Bunyoro. Perhaps one conclusion to draw from this is that the Ganda had faster-changing needs and wants with regard to imported goods and a more volatile commercial value system. At any rate their commercial value had declined, possibly as a result of more novel, highly prized imports, such as foreign cloth, although this does not account for the relative resilience of cowry shells.

Lugard was struck by the changing economic situation in 1891:

> The first essential in Uganda is cloth, especially strong, useful calico (merikani) and finer cloths, such as bafta, joho, vitambi, & c. ... The coloured prints, red bandera, and cheap thin calicoes (ulaiti, satini, gumpti, & c.), though useful for food purchase (especially the latter), are not much sought after. Beads, and brass and iron wire, trumpery hardware, and looking-glasses, & c., are not wanted at all ... In Busoga beads and wire and trumpery goods are accepted, as also in Ankole, Unyoro, and the countries to the west.[57]

Imported cloths of all types had from the late eighteenth century been the preserve of the power elite in Buganda, as is examined below; this was only beginning to change in the 1860s, from which time cloth became in some respects a new currency, with many other commodities assessed through their value in imported cloth. As a currency, in turn, it was subject to the vicissitudes of the market-place. Elsewhere Lugard reaffirms that

---

[53] Iliffe 1995: 107.
[54] Miti 1938: I, 13–14.
[55] Roscoe 1911: 457.
[56] Schweitzer 1898: I, 39.
[57] UNA A26/4 Lugard to Admin.-Gen., IBEAC 13 August 1891.

certain 'coloured prints' were 'practically useless' in Buganda. By the early 1890s, imported cloth was measured by the *ddooti*, a coastal term, which was equivalent to about 4 yd; Lugard estimated in 1891 that one *ddooti* of 'merikani', a standard trade cloth, was valued at a little over 2,000 cowries.[58] Cloth became increasingly accessible, and the old restrictions increasingly inoperative, particularly after the upheavals of the 1880s. The complexity of the cloth-pricing system reflects in turn the sophistication of Ganda market valuation, and as such it is worthy of note, even though it developed in a colonial rather than a pre-colonial environment. Pure white cloth had a reasonably stable value in the late 1890s, while one official complained that coloured cloths 'may consist of pieces containing 5 cloths each ... In many cases in making a payment an Officer may have to deal with as many as 8 or 9 different cloths all at different prices.'[59]

The cowry shell was perhaps the most important of Buganda's pre-colonial currencies, and certainly through much of the nineteenth century would seem to have been the standard by which nearly all other commodities and products were valued. The precise origins of cowries in Buganda are unclear. Roscoe suggested that the shells were first introduced during the reign of Semakokiro in the second half of the eighteenth century,[60] but in all probability he assumed this to be the case as so many other trade goods had first appeared at that time. Tosh has suggested that, while Semakokiro acquired a number of shells, they did not become in any way current until after the middle of the nineteenth century.[61] The ubiquitous shell had almost certainly been rather more important, and for much longer, than he suggests. Certainly, large numbers of cowry shells were gathered at coastal settlements before the thirteenth century,[62] and indeed shells had reached Sanga, west of Lake Tanganyika, by the tenth century, which suggests indirect commercial contact with the coast.[63] More importantly for Buganda, seashell beads have been found at Ntusi and may date back to the thirteenth or fourteenth century: as Iliffe has suggested, these findings 'may – the point is disputed – be the earliest evidence of contact between the Great Lakes region and Indian Ocean coast'.[64]

One of the earliest references to cowries in Buganda's indigenous accounts is during the reign of an early seventeenth-century *kabaka*, Kateregga: upon his death, his jawbone was placed in a wooden bowl along with a number of shells. Kagwa commented that Kateregga 'had received these shells from the chiefs whenever they pay homage to him'.[65]

---

[58] Ibid.
[59] UNA A4/13 Smith to Comm., 7 November 1898.
[60] Roscoe 1911: 457.
[61] Tosh, 1970: 116.
[62] Connah 1987: 180.
[63] Iliffe 1995: 103.
[64] Ibid.: 107. There was also some uncertainty among Africans themselves about the origin of cowries, which may in itself suggest considerable antiquity. Speke, for example, wrote in 1861 that a 'man of Ruanda now informed us that the cowrie-shells, so plentiful in that country, come there from the other or western side, but he could not tell whence they were originally obtained': Speke 1863b: 238. At face value, this appears to suggest commerce with societies in the Congo basin, which is of course consistent with the findings at Sanga mentioned above.
[65] Kagwa 1971: 42–3.

This would seem to have been common practice. Later on, Kagwa explained the significance of the ritual with reference to a late seventeenth-century *kabaka*, Tebandeke: 'When chiefs died their successors, whether sons or brothers, had to take cowrie shells (with holes in them) and put them on the royal cushion. This was done as often as they went to pay homage to the king … If large quantities of cowrie shells and beads had been stored, the people would say, "King so-and-so was popular" …'[66]

It is not made clear if cowries were used in commercial transactions at this time, but it seems reasonably likely, even if this was not their sole purpose. They certainly possessed a recognized value. As such it is note-worthy that the *kabaka* appears not to have exercised any central controls over the shells; rather, at a time when rulers were striving to create a political system in which loyalty to them came above all else, they used cowries as a measurement of both wealth and popularity.

It may be that all this can be taken as evidence of indirect trade with the coast at least as early as c. 1600, although Iliffe's caution is surely well founded. It is likely, however, that as indirect contacts with the coast expanded over the ensuing centuries, the shell itself was gradually devalued. Eighteenth-century rulers and chiefs would have had access to consider-ably greater numbers of shells than their seventeenth-century predecessors. Importantly, too, this early long-distance contact seems to have been without restrictions on who participated. Details concerning the methods of accumulation are impossible to come by, but chiefs appear to have gathered cowries on their own account, most probably through trade. By c. 1850, virtually everything had at least a nominal cowry value; but, as cloth became more current, by the late nineteenth century cowries had gradually devalued to the point of impracticality. By the late 1890s, a single act of exchange might involve the transfer of thousands of shells and, although the *kyasa*, a string of around 100 shells, was doubtless introduced in an attempt to cope with this inflation, they became increasingly unwieldy to use. This was clearly one of the factors behind the colonial authorities' decision to introduce the rupee to the region. Even so, it was several years before the British received anything other than cowries in the payment of tax, an indication of the extent to which the cowry shell had become a staple of the local economy.[67]

Another currency which had at some point existed alongside the cowry shell, and may have predated it, was ivory. Roscoe mentions 'a small ivory disc' which he names 'sanga', *ssanga* in a more modern sense being the Luganda term for either a tusk or ivory in general. This, Roscoe claimed, was one of the earliest forms of money in Buganda; although clearly indigenous and probably much older than the cowry shell, it also had a cowry value, at least by the nineteenth century. At some point one such disc was apparently worth 100 shells,[68] although this must have changed over time. Ivory played a dual role in so far as it was on the one hand a commodity valued for its own sake, and on the other a standard medium

---

[66] Ibid.: 57.
[67] UNA A4/13 Smith to Comm., 7 November 1898.
[68] Roscoe 1911: 457.

of exchange. The former role gradually took precedence over the latter, as demand for ivory from the coast increased, so that, as the nineteenth century progressed, ivory as money all but disappeared.

There appear to have been tighter controls over ivory discs than over cowries. Roscoe wrote:

> Small ivory discs were used as currency before the introduction of cowry-shells; the ivory-worker made them for the King, though the latter had not the monopoly of making them; any skilled workman who could obtain the ivory was allowed to make discs without let or hindrance. The King, however, retained the most skilled ivory-workers in his service, and they dared not make bracelets or other ornaments without permission. The fact that most of the ivory belonged to the King also placed a restriction upon the making of discs by other people ...[69]

Thus, while the *kabaka* did not in theory have any control over the making of the currency, he did have a certain control over the materials themselves and the skills from which the discs were manufactured. Nevertheless, all a 'skilled workman' had to do was to get hold of the ivory in the first place, and one suspects that this would not have been as difficult as Roscoe suggests. In the course of hunting expeditions, ivory may have been distributed in numerous directions before any of it actually reached the *kabaka*. This was clearly the case in the 1890s, although it is again important to point out that backward extrapolations cannot be made from this era of much reduced royal authority and radically altered political structures; the most that can be suggested is that some version of this process may well have existed earlier, and that the system here described was by necessity less centrally controlled, even in normal circumstances, than has been assumed. In the 1890s, early colonial administrators, in their attempts to clamp down on the illicit ivory trade, frequently uncovered the methods and channels which chiefs at various levels used to acquire ivory for themselves. Once ivory found its way to district level, it was almost certain to be dispersed locally, either as payment for the rendering of services or as a trade good. By the 1890s, again an era in which royal authority was greatly reduced, it was in practice impossible for the *kabaka* to control every portion of ivory brought in from a hunt or military expedition, although common sense suggests that this may also have been the case earlier in the nineteenth century; still, it is worth noting that tribute became one of the most important means by which ivory was procured in the later nineteenth century, and this was easier for the *kabaka* to control. Even so, it is likely that there were far more currency-producers in pre-1800 Buganda than Roscoe suggests; and, by the time that tighter ivory control by central government was possible in the late nineteenth century, it no longer had value as a currency. Its value was now as a long-distance commercial export, and an increasingly rare one at that.

[69] Ibid.: 412–13.

Eight

The Growth
of Long-Distance Trade

The year 1844 was unquestionably a landmark in Buganda's history in many respects, not least economically. It was the year in which the first coastal merchants arrived at the court of Kabaka Suna, thus heralding a new era in the kingdom's long history of trade and foreign relations.[1] The role of these traders over the ensuing half-century will be examined in due course, but initially we shall see that the importance which one places on the events of 1844 is dependent upon two main considerations. Firstly, there is the problem of assessing the extent to which the fruits of this new direct commercial contact were shared among the Ganda, and not restricted to a political elite at the capital. In other words, attention must be paid to the role played not just by luxury items, but by goods which had a genuine material impact on the Ganda economy. Secondly, the arrival of coastal merchants in person at Suna's capital can to some extent be viewed as representing the extension of a commercial network of some centuries' standing. The year 1844, therefore, should be understood in terms of continuity rather than discontinuity. The trade routes themselves which the Arabs had used to reach Buganda had a long history and were African in origin. Moreover, Buganda had been dealing with the coast indirectly for at least a century before 1844. It can surely have come as no surprise when the agents of that culture finally arrived at the gates of Suna's *kibuga*.

Beginnings

It is, of course, difficult to say when Buganda became involved in an international trade network, but it seems likely that the cowry shell is a good indicator. As we have seen in the previous chapter, the discovery of seashell beads at Ntusi at least hints at commercial contacts dating back to the thirteenth or fourteenth century, while actual cowry shells had probably been introduced to Buganda by 1600. It has been noted how chiefs in the

[1] Gray 1947.

149

seventeenth and eighteenth centuries accumulated cowries on their own account, probably through commercial channels. What they traded in return is a matter of pure speculation. Slaves may have been a regionally based export, although ivory is likely to have been more important between 1600 and 1800. It is important to stress that this was very much an indirect trade, as the coastal market at this time was still being supplied from near interior sources. Still, there is every reason to suppose that smaller-scale transactions were carried out using local crafts, hoes and other implements, and possibly weaponry for both hunting and war. We have seen this kind of trade as it developed in the nineteenth century; these domestic and regional commercial networks were essential to the import and dispersal of such commodities as cowries, brass and copper wire, and, eventually, cloth and guns among both chiefs and the broader populace.

It was in the middle of the eighteenth century that trade with the coast entered a more intense phase. Kabaka Kyabaggu is noted as having been the 'first king to buy cups and plates', possibly during the 1750s or 1760s.[2] The notion of 'cups and plates' is probably symbolic as much as anything else, but clearly reflects the kind of luxury commodities which were finding their way to the Ganda court at this time. Wrigley has suggested that the arrival of such goods was 'incidental' and not especially important. But it seems that he underplays the significance of the commodities for the longer-term development of long-distance commercial contacts. The novelty of cups and plates is clear enough, but Wrigley seems, for once, to be taking an 'oral tradition' at face value;[3] the truth is that we do not know what other kinds of goods were reaching Buganda at this time. By the end of the eighteenth century, ivory discs had almost certainly dwindled in importance as a form of currency, but the demand for ivory in its natural form from the south had begun to increase significantly. Semakokiro, who is supposed to have been notably wealthy in ivory, had begun to send his own traders further south to meet this demand: Kagwa mentions Mangagala, who was 'the royal salesman' and whose job it was 'to sell the royal ivory'. Such traders were carrying ivory as far as Kiziba, south of the Kagera river, by the late eighteenth century.[4] The Kagera river, of course, had only recently become Buganda's southernmost frontier. Semakokiro's wealth in ivory may well have been closely connected to the fact that he 'was also the one who saved the country from being devastated by elephants, as he used to organise hunting expeditions'.[5] This is a wonderfully self-righteous interpretation of the *kabaka*'s commercial ambitions; at any rate, it is clearly no coincidence that Semakokiro was also the first *kabaka* 'to buy cotton cloth from Karagwe'.[6] Clearly, the Ganda were still relying on trade with other Africans, in the first instance the merchants of Karagwe, who for many years remained Buganda's main commercial link with the Tanzanian network. Indeed, the 'middleman period' of East Africa's commercial history never really ended, although the penetration

[2] Kagwa 1971: 99.
[3] Wrigley 1996: 232–3.
[4] Kagwa 1971: 100–1.
[5] Ibid.: 99.
[6] Ibid.

of the Arabs into the interior in the early nineteenth century was in part an attempt to avoid having to rely on African suppliers.

What is notable about the surge in long-distance commerce under Kyabaggu and Semakokiro is the apparent increase in luxury items which now came to characterize the trade. These goods were probably designed to appeal to the governing rather than the governed of the interior; but whether by design or not, the novelty goods and finery from the coast excited the avarice of African elites and marked a shift from trade between small-scale indigenous merchants to trade aimed at the heart of political establishments. In Buganda, successive rulers sought to gain control of such goods with an intensity which does not appear to have been characteristic of the earlier period of indirect contact. It would be more than 100 years before cotton cloth was anything like a common commodity in the kingdom; as we noted in an earlier chapter, it is surely no coincidence that the same Semakokiro who was so impressed by cotton garments presided over what appears to have been a large-scale escalation of barkcloth production. In the late eighteenth century, such long-distance commerce entered a rather more exclusive phase: in a general sense, wealth and, perhaps more importantly, political position were required to participate. Of course this was not always the case, and it is likely that this kind of commerce continued to affect and involve smaller-scale Ganda traders, as these remained the primary carriers of goods to and from the kingdom. But commerce was in general more elitist than previously. Cotton cloth[7] provides a good example of this process. It remained uncommon on the one hand for a very practical reason, namely the fact that it was several decades before the coastal merchants were carrying large quantities of the material to Buganda. On the other hand, it is clear that successive rulers perceived ownership of the cloth as a useful way of accentuating wealth, power and privilege, in much the same way that certain skins, notably that of the leopard, were emblems of royal blood. Cloth was a prestige good, and the *kabaka* and metropolitan establishment made strenuous efforts to control not only its import, but its subsequent distribution. However, this kind of commerce was not as exclusive as it might first appear, and smaller-scale local traders were able to take part, increasingly so as the nineteenth century drew to a close.

Coastal merchants in Buganda

The arrival of the first Arab traders in Buganda in 1844 further intensified the above process. This initial visit was probably in large part a diplomatic mission, an attempt on the part of the coastal traders to gauge the kind of society with which they were dealing in order to further commercial links. They would already have known a great deal about Buganda. The

---

[7] The term is used generically here, but there were important distinctions between types of cloth which influenced market value, and some of these have already been noted. For example, *bafuta* was a kind of thin cotton cloth, while *amerikaani* was a hard, glossy, unbleached calico; *bugibugi* and *kafiifi* were cheaper cuts; and *kaniki* was a dark blue calico or cotton cloth.

interlacustrine region had been one of the sources of ivory in the interior for the past 50 or 60 years, and indirect acquaintance would have been reasonably well established. Coastal traders had certainly reached the Nyamwezi by the 1830s, and they were doubtless drawn north by the prosperous trading activity along the Nyamwezi–Karagwe–Buganda axis. It was a logical next step in the context of their commercial exploration. The goods brought by the initial party included a number of luxury items, such as cotton cloth, mirrors and musical instruments.[8] Ganda and Arabs were doubtless mutually impressed. Suna, we are told, was struck by the beauty of the goods offered, but in particular by the guns carried by the merchants, which not long after he was able to use in a military campaign. For their part, the Arabs must have been taken aback at the size and strength of this state, which was quite unlike anything they had dealt with before. Their experience among the Nyamwezi and other groups had suggested that they might expect small-scale, often acephalous, societies which were prepared to permit them positions of political influence, or which at least were unable to prevent them acquiring such positions. In Buganda their influence would be considerable in the long term, but they would never be able to impose themselves politically.

Several more visits and almost a decade passed before the first detailed account of this early direct commercial interaction emerged. Burton did not visit Buganda himself, but at Tabora in 1858 frequently talked to Arabs who had. One such was Snay bin Amir, who travelled to Suna's court in 1852. Suna gave the greatest encouragement to the traders, bestowing generous gifts on them, often 'without expecting any but the humblest return'.[9] Of course, at this time a humble return in the eyes of a coastal merchant was probably a considerable bounty to the *kabaka*; within a few years this had changed, as the Ganda began to appreciate the value of particular commodities more on Arab terms. Snay bin Amir received a warm and elaborate welcome, being provided with specially built quarters. Readers of Tippu Tip's autobiography will recognize the manner in which Arabs, no less than Europeans, often grossly exaggerated their own importance within African societies;[10] none the less, the welcome which Snay bin Amir described undoubtedly reflects the novelty of coastal merchants at Suna's capital, and perhaps the zeal which the *kabaka* expressed concerning the development of relations with the coast. But Snay's visit was not all pomp and ceremony. At a second meeting with Suna, 'Snay presented his blackmail, which consisted of ten cotton cloths, and one hundred fundo of coral, and other porcelain beads. The return was an offering of two ivories and a pair of serviles; every day, moreover, flesh and grain, fruit and milk were supplied without charge ...'[11]

Cloth, not guns, was here the main commodity being offered by the Arab trader, in addition to beads, which were presumably still reasonably current; slaves and ivory were Buganda's most lucrative exports. It is not clear whether we can date the export of slaves from this time; there is no

---

[8] Kagwa 1971: 120.
[9] Burton 1860: II, 193.
[10] Tippu Tip 1966.
[11] Burton 1860: II, 194–5.

evidence to suggest that slaves were exported any earlier than the middle of the nineteenth century, although we cannot definitely state that they were not. Zimbe tells us that Suna 'would never allow the sale of any of his subjects to foreigners. All that could be sold was cows and goats.'[12] Indeed, as we have seen, the Ganda sold other Ganda only in exceptional circumstances, but the implication of Zimbe's remarks is that slaves in general were not on offer. This may have been the case initially, but it clearly did not take long (certainly by the early 1850s) before the Ganda realized that they could tailor their existing system of slave-gathering in war, as well as the existing institution of slavery itself, to meet the demands of the coastal traders. It seems possible that the Ganda had for perhaps several centuries been engaged in a regional slave trade, but not on such a large and organized scale as that with which they were to export them south. Slaves were, as much as anything else, commodities to be bought and sold, and there is every reason to suppose that this was carried out within both regional and domestic markets. But the idea of a slave as a marketable commodity undoubtedly took on new proportions from the middle of the nineteenth century.

Snay's visit in 1852, like those before it and many after it, was important in other ways. The merchant discussed with Suna the possibilities of a 'closer alliance' with the then sultan of Zanzibar, Seyyid Said, an alliance for which Suna expressed much enthusiasm. Indeed, the *kabaka* wanted to send back with Snay 'several loads of elephants' tusks as presents to H.H. the Sayyid', although this offer seems to have been refused on the grounds that the route would be too dangerous.[13] This seems rather strange, as presumably ivory was precisely what Snay had gone to Buganda to collect; but then again we do not know exactly what turns the conversation between trader and ruler took. In any case, there is no doubt that Suna perceived the advantages of closer links with the coast. Symptomatic of this is the fact that he refused permission, as did both Mutesa and Mwanga, for the Arabs to travel further north. The policy was met with varying success, as eventually the coastmen were able to access north-bound trade routes, which lay to the west of Buganda and reached Bunyoro. However, it was suggested to Burton that Suna considered the visits of the Arabs as 'personal honours paid to himself'.[14] Indeed, the determination to restrict the advantages of long-distance trade to Buganda was a theme running through the foreign and military policies of Suna, Mutesa and Mwanga,[15] and the most dramatic manifestation of these policies was the creation of a state fleet.

At some point during the 1850s, however, the Arab traders departed from Buganda and apparently did not return for several years. The main evidence for this is provided by Speke, who wrote, in the context of the late 1850s, that '[t]he Uganda station has been broken up by order of the king, as the Arabs were interfering too much with his subjects'.[16] Else-

[12] Zimbe 1939: 79.
[13] Burton 1860, II: 195.
[14] Ibid.
[15] See also for example Kiwanuka 1971.
[16] Speke 1864: 259.

where, Speke offers a slightly different story, or perhaps a different version of the same story, relating to the supposed expulsion of Arab traders from Ganda territory. Having crossed the Kagera into Buddu, he

> was shown by Nasib a village called Ngandu, which was the farthest trading depot of the Zanzibar ivory-merchants. It was established by Musa Mzuri, by the permission of Rumanika; for, as I shall have presently to mention, Sunna, after annexing this part of Uddu to Uganda, gave Rumanika certain bands of territory in it as a means of security against the possibility of its being wrested out his hands again by the future kings of Unyoro. Following on Musa's wake, many Arabs also came here to trade; but they were so oppressive to the Waganda that they were recalled by Rumanika, and obliged to locate themselves at Kufro ...[17]

The precise meaning of 'interfering too much' and 'so oppressive' is unclear. Some years ago Low asserted that the Arabs had been thus expelled in 1852.[18] It is remarkable that Burton, who was in much closer contact with the Arab merchants than Speke, never mentioned this supposed expulsion; this is particularly surprising in view of the fact that Burton described in detail a successful visit to Buganda by a trader in 1852. Equally striking is the fact that Speke himself, a little earlier in the same publication, had mentioned the coastal trader Musa, who 'had recently visited Kibuga [the Ganda capital], and had lived with Sultan Mtesa, the present reigning monarch in place of Sunna'.[19] Some light is shed by the following passage, also written by Speke: 'shortly after the late king of Uganda, Sunna, died, and before Mtesa had been selected by the officers of the country to be their king, an Arab caravan came across the Masai as far as Usoga, and begged for permission to enter Uganda; but as the country was disturbed by the elections, the officers of the state advised the Arabs to wait, or come again when the king was elected ...'[20]

It therefore seems likely that the Arabs were never expelled, but had been refused entry due to the temporary interregnum in the late 1850s; this has also been effectively argued by John Rowe.[21] Merchants had certainly returned by 1860 at the latest. The idea that foreigners should not be allowed in while the kingdom was politically vulnerable may also account for the fact that Suna's Zanzibari bodyguard felt obliged to leave the country upon his master's death. Speke's assertion that the Arabs had 'interfered' can probably be taken to mean that the Ganda feared the potential for outside interference if the ostensibly powerful strangers from the coast were permitted residence during such a sensitive time.

The case of Burton's 'Isa bin Hosayn' and Speke's 'Eseau', probably the same person, reveals how coastal traders or their agents could individually take advantage of Buganda's open and competitive society. Speke mentions a trader named 'Eseau', to whom we have already alluded in a different context, who had penetrated into East Africa with much

---

[17] Speke 1863b: 265. Grant also mentioned 'an old ivory depot' in the same area: Grant 1864: 193.
[18] Low 1963: I, 334.
[19] Speke 1864: 258.
[20] Speke 1863b: 187.
[21] Rowe 1966: 50.

merchandise, representing the sultan of Zanzibar, but had lost the bulk of it as a result of heavy local taxes on the way to Buganda. Fearing to return to the coast, he 'instead made great friends with the late King Sunna, who took an especial fancy to him because he had a very large beard, and raised him to the rank of Mkungu'. He sounds strikingly similar to the character described by Burton, who was also known as 'the hairy one'. Speke's 'Eseau', however, lived in Buddu, not in the capital, and Speke makes no mention of his having to flee Buganda upon Suna's death. Instead, 'Eseau died, and left all his family and property to a slave named Uledi, who now, in consequence, is the border officer.'[22] The merchant had clearly attained political position and considerable wealth. Miti's account would seem to suggest that the characters described by Burton and Speke were indeed the same person: Miti wrote that 'Isa bin Ushen' 'is said to have found much favour with the king. It is said that, as a mark of special affection, the king gave Isa bin Ushen charge of a whole village, called Kituntu, in the district of Buddu.'[23] Later examples of coastal traders settling in Buganda and reaching similar heights can be cited: Toli and Idi in the late 1870s and 1880s, for example, both led military campaigns and were given political offices.[24]

Yet the fortunes of the Arab community varied. Once the novelty had worn off and the visits of coastal merchants became more commonplace, and indeed once there was a permanent settlement in the suburbs of the capital, respect for them declined. Mutesa appears to have been markedly more contemptuous towards them than his father, although his attitude was increasingly characterized by dramatic mood-swings.[25] The merchants told Speke in 1862 that 'from fear they had always complied with the manners of the court'; in the immediate context, this involved being made to sit in the scorching sun for hours before being admitted to an audience with Mutesa.[26] By this time, their quarters had been removed to an unhealthy and disregarded area of the capital.[27] Even the supply of provisions was often problematic. In early 1878, Emin Pasha complained that the 'people are all afraid to offer us anything for sale. Mtesa sends absolutely nothing, and without his orders no one may do anything.' Moreover, 'even the Arabs, although I have repeatedly entreated them, cannot procure anything more'.[28] This is a far cry indeed from the late 1840s and early 1850s, when ample food was supplied courtesy of the *kabaka*.

By the late 1880s, Mwanga's attitude toward the coastal traders was increasingly volatile. In early 1888, he went as far as suspending all commercial operations, and prohibited the sale of food, water and other provisions to the Arabs, accusing them of having sold weapons to Kabarega of Bunyoro.[29] Mwanga, like Suna and Mutesa before him,

[22] Speke 1863b: 276.
[23] Miti 1938: I, 124.
[24] Kagwa 1971: 173–4, 177–8.
[25] Reid 1999a: 290ff.
[26] Speke 1863b: 288.
[27] Ibid.: 303.
[28] Schweitzer 1898: I, 60.
[29] CMS G3 A5/0 1888/244 Gordon to Parker, 6 March 1888.

clearly feared the wealth and, in particular, the military power which the coastal traders might pass on to his enemies. Attitudes towards the merchants were also shaped by their perceived sharp practice in the marketplace. Tellingly, the *katikiro* reportedly described Europeans as 'men of truth' because, in Mackay's words, 'our bolts of calico measured exactly as labelled; a box of gunpowder contained always the right number of tins, while no sand was to be found mixed with the powder; our guns did not explode and kill them when firing, nor did caps refuse to fire ...'[30]

Yet the underlying strength of the Arab position, in so far as they had become indispensable to the exchange economy, is clear. The diversification of local food production and trade was both a cause and an effect of this strength. As in Unyanyembe, for example, the coastal traders had introduced a number of crops to the capital, and although there is little evidence to suggest that these crops spread throughout the kingdom, many seem to have become locally important. Onions were among the new crops,[31] and the missionary Tucker observed that the Arabs had introduced to Buganda '[w]heat, rice, guavas, pomegranates, paupaws, mangoes, and other fruits'.[32] Significantly, the spread of these kinds of crops suggests commercial interaction between Arabs and small-scale Ganda traders. It is also possible that, once the new seeds were introduced, the Ganda farmers themselves gradually took over the process of cultivation.

The restrictions on imported cloth which had been in place since the late eighteenth century were strengthened once the merchants themselves actually turned up in Buganda. Burton was told that 'sumptuary laws impede the free traffic of cloth into Uganda', suggesting that the Arabs were prohibited from selling it to anyone other than Suna or his representatives.[33] But, although this particular commodity was the subject of stringent regulation, 'the imports [brought by the Arabs] are represented chiefly by beads, cowries, and brass and copper wires'.[34] The implication seems to be that these goods were purchased freely by private Ganda traders. This impression is later confirmed by Speke, who wrote that '[b]eads and brass wire, exchanged for ivory or slaves, are the only articles of foreign manufacture any Mganda can hold in his possession. Should anything else be seen in his house – for instance, cloth – his property would be confiscated and his life taken ...'[35]

Private or small-scale Ganda traders in the capital, then, did have access to the coastal merchants. In addition to ivory and, perhaps more commonly, slaves, these local traders may also have exchanged foodstuffs, a situation for which there were precedents at Tabora and Ujiji. Although the early coastal merchants were provided with sustenance by the *kabaka*, apparently free of charge, this was not the case in later years; moreover, although the Arab community did begin to produce for itself, it is likely that the bulk of their provisions came from local gardens.

[30] CMS G3 A6/0 1885/98 Mackay to Wigram ? May 1885.
[31] Schweitzer 1898: I, p.35.
[32] Tucker 1908: I, 88. See also the earlier discussion on nineteenth-century agriculture.
[33] Burton 1860: II, 196.
[34] Ibid.
[35] Speke 1863b: 345.

The capital appears to have been the only meeting point between Ganda and coastal merchants, the latter in general being restricted to the markets there. On the whole, this suited the Arabs themselves well enough, for it was at the capital that they could exchange their goods for large numbers of slaves and ivory in bulk. However, Speke mentions an Arab trader named Saim, whom he met in Buzinza and who claimed that 'he had lived ten years in Uganda, had crossed the Nile, and traded eastward as far as the Masai country'.[36] Saim had clearly been permitted to carry his merchandise past Jinja and among the Soga. It is probable that successive Ganda rulers were in fact more concerned to control the northbound trade – that is, towards Bunyoro – than that to the east. In any case, Mutesa himself was apparently keen to open a trade route to the east which bypassed the lake and represented a more direct route to the coast. In various sources, however, much is made of the supposedly traditional Ganda fear of an invasion from the east, which prompted them to close off that route to all long-distance enterprise. According to Zimbe, this prohibition dated from the reign of Suna.[37] If accepted, it is difficult to avoid the conclusion that it was related not to the threat of attack but to the control of long-distance commerce, notwithstanding the adventures of Speke's Saim; this could be more properly effected if the Arabs were compelled to use the more circuitous lake route. This was indeed the single most important factor behind the development of the Ganda navy. As we shall also see, the military capacity of Buganda at this time was not sufficient to bring a land-based eastern trade route under the kingdom's control, at least past the Nile and a few Soga chiefdoms; strategically, therefore, it made more sense to guide the Arabs towards the south end of the lake and to use naval strength to extend over a greater distance influence over commercial activity.

Before the impetus provided by the Imperial British East Africa Company in the 1890s, then, the eastern trade route was never fully developed, but in fact to a large extent for reasons beyond Mutesa's control. Central Kenya was commercially important throughout the nineteenth century, and was especially noted for its exports of ivory, but, until the 1870s or 1880s, long-distance trade routes in this region remained in the hands of African middlemen, particularly Kamba merchants. The penetration of Swahili traders was a much slower process than in Tanzania.[38] By the middle of the nineteenth century, indeed, the coastal merchants themselves had already invested too much in such entrepôts as Tabora and Ujiji to disregard them. None the less, the intricate domestic trade network in Buganda ensured that the coastal goods acquired by the Ganda in the capital would swiftly find their way into the outlying provinces. It is probable, too, that the goods brought by Arab merchants found their way into the hands of the broader populace as a result of small-scale, regional redistribution. Local chiefs may have handed out such goods to their tenants in return for the normal services, namely war, labour and

---

[36] Ibid.: 154–5.
[37] Zimbe, 1939: 126.
[38] See for example Kimambo 1970: 82–3; Jackson 1976: 217; Ambler 1988: 67–73.

provision of foodstuffs. But it is still true that such goods, even if originally derived from a redistributive process, would have retained their value as goods which could be exchanged in local markets.

An instructive comparison to draw is that with Dahomey in West Africa, as was done by Richard Waller some years ago.[39] Like Buganda, Dahomey was a relatively centralized state, and has been depicted as a society strictly organized around the role of kingship. The Dahomean king appointed officials to oversee or control commerce with European traders, although this seems often to have been ineffective as large numbers of Africans still managed to acquire wealth through involvement in the slave trade. To some extent this situation is paralleled in Buganda, as we shall see, but here the similarities appear to end. A cardinal feature of the Dahomean economy was the redistributive ceremonies regularly enacted by the monarch. These ceremonies were to a large extent a form of conspicuous consumption on the part of the ruler, but they were also the means by which a large proportion of the population came to possess articles obtained by trade with Europeans. In Buganda, the *kabaka* exercised a form of redistribution, but this seems to have been limited in scope to the upper echelons of Ganda political society. Imported cloths, for example, were distributed among chiefs who had displayed particular courage in war. The bulk of the population was excluded, at least in a direct sense, from such a system, and acquired their share of trade goods by actively participating in commercial activity, even though, as we have seen, only a small number of private and small-scale Ganda traders were actually able to engage directly with the Arab merchants.

The fact that trade in certain goods – most notably cotton cloth and, later, firearms – was restricted by the *kabaka*, and the fact that the Arabs were generally forbidden from venturing beyond the capital, should not lead us to exaggerate the control which the *kabaka* exercised over commerce among the Ganda. Similarly, the fact that local producers were often forbidden from selling provisions to Speke and Grant, as well as other travellers and foreign residents, only indicates royal control within a particular confined area; it also suggests that the *kabaka* wished to impress the Europeans with his ability to supply them with all their needs and is indicative of his jealous desire to keep them to himself.[40] Indeed, even in these objectives Mutesa was often unsuccessful: Grant was swift to point out that beads, admittedly not an especially valuable currency at this time, could be secretly used to 'purchase sufficient provisions for ourselves and men',[41] suggesting Mutesa's limited ability to suppress local trade at all levels. In any case, as with the coastal merchants, this attitude towards Europeans wore off in time, so that by the late 1870s it was commonplace for missionaries to regularly purchase their own provisions from local producers. It is clear that commercial restrictions were exceptional rather than normal. It is also true, however, that commercial life in the capital

[39] Waller offers a rather complex comparison between Buganda and Dahomey, based largely on the writings of Polanyi and Sahlins: Waller 1971: 6ff. For an excellent study of Dahomey and the operation of its commercial system, see Law 1991.
[40] See for example Speke 1863b: 268; Grant 1864: 229.
[41] Grant 1864: 229.

was not typical of that elsewhere in Buganda. Mutesa did on occasion impose bans on the sale of foodstuffs, but he would have been quite powerless to do so beyond the capital; outside the *kibuga*, economic and commercial activity went on regardless of any centralized royal control, and people could enjoy whatever fruits of long-distance trade which came their way without the occasional impediments experienced in the capital.

The Ganda position was not always characterized by mere inertia, simply waiting for the next coastal caravan to arrive. The Ganda did travel south on missions of both a diplomatic and commercial nature, and indeed the two were rarely separate in the context of nineteenth-century East Africa. We have already noted a commercial expedition south to Kiziba in the late eighteenth century, for example, and there is little reason to doubt that missions of this nature were reasonably frequent during much of the nineteenth century. During the 1850s, Speke records, 'the kings of Uganda were in the habit of sending men to Karague when they heard that Arabs wished to visit them – even as many as two hundred at a time – to carry their kit'.[42] Livingstone noted the arrival at Tabora in 1872 of a force of Ganda escorting slaves to be traded.[43] In late 1878, a band of 'Mutesa's soldiers' was reported to be returning from a mission to Zanzibar itself.[44] Perhaps more importantly, the Ganda exercised varying degrees of control over the main trading depots to the west of Lake Victoria. In particular, Speke mentions 'the Arab depot at Kufro, on the direct line to Uganda', and the trading post of Ngandu, alluded to above, which appears to have been jointly controlled by Rumanika, ruler of Karagwe, and Suna.[45] But the most dramatic example of Buganda's attempt to control the trade and deal with the coastal merchants on their own terms is the development of a navy capable of travelling the full length of Lake Victoria. In the 1870s and 1880s, the enormous canoes of Buganda featured prominently in the organization of long-distance commerce, and indeed rendered marginal the older land routes to the west of the lake.[46]

In examining long-distance or international commerce, we have focused on trade with the coast. There is little direct evidence to suggest that trade from the direction of the Egyptian Sudan, which was the other gateway to a wider world, had any real impact on Buganda. There was probably a restricted level of commercial interaction in this area, mostly indirect – that is, goods obtained by the Nyoro being traded south – but in the pre-colonial era such activity appears to have been neither regular nor substantial enough to have had a major influence. Speke heard that 'a salt lake, which was called N'yanza, though not the great Victoria N'yanza, lay on the other side of Unyoro, from which direction Rumanika, king of Karague, sometimes got beads forwarded to him by Kamurasi, king of Unyoro, of a different sort from any brought from Zanzibar'.[47] The salt

[42] Speke 1863b: 188.
[43] Waller 1874: II, 226.
[44] White Fathers: C13/282 Livinhac to Lavigerie, 20 November 1878.
[45] Speke 1863b: 201, 264.
[46] See also Reid 1998b.
[47] Speke 1863b: 89.

lake is a reference to Lake Albert or, more specifically, to the salt production centre at Kibiro. It may safely be assumed that beads of this kind also reached Buganda, but in what quantities and to what effect are unclear; we have already noted that certain beads highly valued by the Soga and their eastern neighbours may have come from the north via the Middle Nile, although they may not have caused the same level of excitement in Buganda. In the early 1880s Wilson wrote: 'There was formerly a small trade with the Soudan, coffee, tobacco, mbugu, and cattle being exchanged for fezes, calico, and red slippers. But since the evacuation of Mruli by the Egyptian troops all communication with the North is at an end.'[48] The links were always tenuous, and Sudan-based commerce remained restricted for three main reasons. Firstly, the Nyoro themselves, the most powerful middlemen along such a trade route, were consistently hostile to the Sudanese so close to their kingdom. Both Kamurasi and his successor Kabarega had numerous skirmishes with the agents of the Egyptian Sudan, naturally limiting the opportunities for peaceful commerce. Secondly, Mutesa's own attitude towards the north was characterized by suspicion and, increasingly, deep fear; when his attention was drawn in this direction, he seemed to perceive the potential for military confrontation rather than for commercial interaction. And, thirdly, when any Sudanese did travel to Buganda, for example Nur Aga and his party in 1876, they did so as soldiers, not traders, which not only severely limited the opportunity to establish trade links, but also confirmed in Mutesa's mind, and perhaps the popular Ganda imagination, the idea that they represented a military threat.

Commercial change in the late nineteenth century

One of the most important developments for Ganda commerce in the last few decades of the nineteenth century was the growth of the slave trade, which warrants separate analysis. The northern section of the East African slave trade has been rather neglected by historians in favour of studies of the trade as it affected southern Tanzania and northern Mozambique, an area for which there are, admittedly, better sources. This may also be partly connected to the fact that the systematic export of slaves from Buganda came about comparatively late. In the mid-1850s, slaves appear to have been secondary to ivory, which for several decades was Buganda's primary international export; this was at a time when slave exports from most of the rest of the eastern African interior were more important than any other commodity. None the less, even at this stage, slaves were a significant product. Burton was told that slaves were often sold for 'ten fundo of beads, and the same sum will purchase the Wasoga and Wanyoro captives from whom [Suna] derives a considerable portion of his revenues'.[49] As far as the Arab community at Unyanyembe was concerned, slaves brought from the northern kingdoms were increasingly important

[48] Wilson & Felkin 1882: I, 191.
[49] Burton 1860: II, 196.

by the 1850s. Burton suggested that the Nyamwezi themselves used slaves brought from Buganda, Bunyoro and Karagwe.[50]

In the early 1860s, it was noted that slaves transported from Buganda were regarded in Unyanyembe as being the best available, particularly the Hima women, who were also brought from Karagwe.[51] The export of slaves increased steadily through the 1860s and 1870s, reaching a peak in the 1880s, during which decade several thousand may have been exported annually. After c. 1890, Buganda's part in the slave trade was virtually at an end, and even the small-scale illicit trade which continued through the 1890s in the interlacustrine region appears to have involved very few Ganda. Two points are clear from this. Firstly and self-evidently, Buganda's participation in the East African slave trade was brief, spanning only four decades, although it was remarkably intense in its later stages. Secondly, Buganda's exports peaked at a time when the East African slave trade more generally was actually in decline, a decline due in large part to the anti-slave trade treaty signed by the sultan of Zanzibar in 1873. Buganda's anomalous position seems to have been due to the fact that, as Paul Lovejoy has pointed out, the slaves exported from the Lake Victoria region rarely reached the coast, and thus this commerce was rather unconnected to the slave-based plantation economy on the islands of Zanzibar and Pemba.[52] The precise destination of slaves bought in Buganda is unclear, but impetuses from Arab communities within the interior, rather than directly from the coast, seem to have been at work at the north end of Lake Victoria. Certainly most slaves were sent to Unyanyembe, at least initially.[53]

Slavery in Buganda, as we have seen, had existed for centuries, the Ganda having retained for economic, domestic and political purposes serviles, mostly foreign in origin, more or less since the foundation of the kingdom. Ganda themselves were occasionally enslaved by their compatriots, usually as a result of falling on hard times; however, these seem to have been traded outside the kingdom only in exceptional circumstances, although this became more common as the slave trade reached its height from the late 1870s onward. The vast majority of exported slaves were foreigners. Slaves, then, were an important by-product of war: as one British officer commented on the eve of a campaign in 1893, the Ganda welcomed 'the opportunity of ... replenishing their harems and slave establishments'.[54] The tone of this suggests that warfare was the cardinal means by which the Ganda slave population, both male and female, was sustained, and it is clear that this remained the situation in the early 1890s. In the second half of the nineteenth century, however, slaves for export were drawn from this broad group: this meant either that more Ganda had to be enslaved to sustain the indigenous slave population, or that more foreign captives had to be brought in specifically for export. What actually happened appears to have been a combination of these developments, but the latter was unquestionably the more important and dramatic.

[50] Burton 1859: 205.
[51] Grant 1864: 48.
[52] Lovejoy 1983: 151–2.
[53] For example, CMS CA6/010/13 Felkin to Wright, 1 November 1878.
[54] Thruston 1900: 129.

This did not necessarily mean that the Ganda fought more wars or carried out more slave-raiding expeditions during this period to meet demand. Twaddle, for example, has talked of a 'spiral of violence', a situation in which the Ganda made a conscious decision to 'intensify external predation in order to meet the merchants' demands for slaves as well as their own continuing need for them'.[55] There is little direct evidence for this. Wars continued to be fought, as they had been before the external demand for slaves; it seems more probable that the gathering of foreign captives became more widespread and more systematic during military expeditions than before the 1850s. On the face of it, there thus occurred something of a change in motivation behind the waging of wars; but the scale of this change should not be exaggerated. The Ganda had always waged war for economic reasons, not least, significantly in this context, because of the perceived need to maintain an enslaved underclass at home performing a broad range of tasks, for example in agriculture. For the Ganda to seize slaves abroad who were earmarked for export did not represent a major adjustment of extant principles. It must also be borne in mind that many of the wars fought by the Ganda from the 1850s onward were designed to maintain the kingdom's regional position, which was increasingly perilous. In the context of the West African slave trade, powerful states such as Benin and Asante underwent periods of expansion, in the fifteenth and seventeenth centuries respectively, which occurred for reasons of internal dynamics and not because of the magnetism of the Atlantic system. War captives which were produced as a result of expansionist conflicts were then sold to Europeans at the coast. Something similar may be said of Buganda, for whom war captives for export were often a by-product of conflicts fought for reasons of regional strategy.

The notion of a trade in slaves was already well established before the development of an external long-distance demand. The British officer Macdonald hinted at the existence of a domestic trade when he described Buganda as a country 'where a man's life was rated at the price of an ox, and a woman was an article of barter';[56] to some extent this was figurative speech, but clearly based on hard data. Women in particular were commonly traded as serviles within Buganda. In the early 1860s Grant observed how a Ganda in his party had 'kidnapped' two women, intending to sell them at 'Karee', a village in northern Singo. The price he received for these two women was ten cows, although at the capital, Grant was told, he would only have received five.[57] The commonness of a trade in female slaves is thus suggested. The Ganda may also have traded female slaves as far north as Mruli, although by the end of the 1870s, as we have already noted, this commerce appears to have dried up.[58] The existence of slave markets, as far as the term is understood in a Zanzibari context, is not so clear. Roscoe, for example, suggested that slaves were commonly sold 'by private arrangement'.[59] As we shall see, however, within or in the suburbs

[55] Twaddle 1988a; 119, 122.
[56] Macdonald 1897: 143.
[57] Grant 1864: 258.
[58] Wilson & Felkin 1882: II, 32.
[59] Roscoe 1911: 456.

of the capital there were compounds for recently captured slaves, which the coastal merchants visited before making their purchases. Hima women were in demand both domestically and externally as slaves. They were often bought or seized as concubines for chiefs or to be sold to the coastal traders, and were regarded as being exceptionally beautiful.[60] The high price paid for Hima women reflected the value placed on them: the missionary Girault observed that a Hima woman might fetch anything between five and 50 cows in the domestic market, while a Ganda woman in the same position was worth only one.[61] All of these quoted prices must, of course, be regarded with some scepticism, and for our purposes are purely impressionistic. Women from a pastoral background were clearly more valuable than their agricultural counterparts. Grant does not specify whether the purchased women in question were Hima, but, if we assume that they were not (as such an identification was usually made when appropriate), then Girault's estimates suggest that inflation had taken its toll: in 1862, a woman was worth at least two cows in the metropolitan market, and in 1880 only one. Whether women had become less valuable generally, or cattle more so, is a matter of speculation. Accepting that the domestic slave market for both sexes must have been reasonably buoyant in 1880, taking into account external demand, then we might assume that cattle had become more valuable, perhaps as a result of the livestock disease which was spreading at that time.

By the early 1880s, anything from 1,000 slaves were probably being exported annually. Precise figures for the East African slave trade generally are impossible to come by, particularly for the entrepôts of the interior. But, to place the Buganda figure in some kind of comparative context, some 20,000 slaves may have been sold annually in Zanzibar during the 1860s.[62] Lovejoy has suggested that the coast retained some 188,000 slaves during the 1870s. Yet he also points out that by the late 1860s 95 per cent of Zanzibar's slaves came through Kilwa to the south, which clearly had nothing to do with the northern interlacustrine trade.[63] So it is extremely difficult to contextualize figures for Buganda, however tentative. Having said this, in the light of Lovejoy's calculations it seems likely that Buganda's exports in the early 1880s were actually substantial in the context of the northern lake region.

Mackay stated unequivocally that '[t]he demand for slaves in Uganda itself is very great, it being only the surplus which is carried off by the Arabs. Every year some 2,000 slaves, as nearly as I can estimate, are purchased by Arabs, and conveyed by water from Uganda to Usukuma.'[64] One cannot be sure of Mackay's methods of calculation, but he was certainly in a position to regularly observe slave transactions both north

[60] For example, Peters 1891: 402;. Junker 1892: 550.
[61] White Fathers: Rubaga Diary 1/18 January 1880.
[62] Sheriff 1987: 60, 224–30.
[63] Lovejoy 1983: 151–2.
[64] Mackay 1890: 435. It is interesting to note that according to Mackay only the surplus was sold to the Arabs. This goes some way to contradicting Mackay's official line as a bitter opponent of the slave trade that slave-raiding was carried on virtually at the behest of the Arabs themselves; indeed, it was supposedly the Arabs who supplied the Ganda with firepower to do so: 1890: 438.

and south of the lake. It is also significant that his figure was based solely on the lake route, although in late 1879 it was reported that the land route was virtually closed, and that all caravans bound for Buganda went directly to Kagehyi on the south shore of the lake.[65] Another missionary estimated that by 1880 around 1,000 slaves left Buganda by the lake route alone, regardless of any being transported through Karagwe.[66] Breaking down this sample figure, which was rather more conservative than that offered by Mackay, an average of 80 slaves per month were being exported across the lake, and the slave canoes observed by the same missionary crossing the lake with 200 slaves would have taken around ten weeks to fill. Comparative figures for the land route are unavailable. If we assume the figure of 1,000–2,000 slaves a year to be an approximate average, this represents over a period of several years a significant regional population drain, even allowing for the fact that the region was relatively densely populated. The figure clearly does not include those who were killed in the process of slave-gathering. The slave trade must therefore be regarded as the first in a series of catastrophes, including the ravages of rinderpest and the outbreak of sleeping sickness, which served to depopulate many parts of the northern interlacustrine region in the late nineteenth and early twentieth centuries.

The reality of slave accumulation at the lake shore probably involved coastal merchants often having to wait months for fresh slaves to arrive from the interior. In 1883, Mackay noted that '[t]here have been three Arabs waiting for months at Buganga [on the lake shore] with some two hundred tusks and as yet they have only ten canoes'.[67] On another occasion, in early 1880, the Arabs were refused permission to gather up canoes because the god of the lake, Mukasa, was about to visit the capital. An interesting ideological struggle ensued between Mutesa and several leading chiefs, the former demanding that commerce should be allowed to continue, the latter pleading respect for Mukasa. It seems that the chiefs' arguments held sway.[68]

By the early 1880s, groups of slaves consisted of boys, young men and comparatively smaller numbers of young girls. Generally, mature females were originally retained in Buganda and served to bolster harems of varying sizes across the kingdom. Notwithstanding our earlier speculations concerning the price of women, Felkin suggested that the price of slaves had risen fourfold between 1870 and 1880.[69] Emin Pasha corroborates this to some extent, stating that 'in the year 1876 a girl of ten to twelve years was exchanged for thirty to forty ells [= almost two feet] of madapolam [= foreign cloth] of the ordinary kind, two years later the price had risen to nearly as much again; but since then it seems to have remained almost stationary'. It would appear that female slaves in particular had become more expensive, largely because of the increased preference for them

---

[65] CMS CA6/016/42 Mackay to Wright, 2 November 1879.

[66] Wilson & Felkin 1882: I, 189–91.

[67] CMS G3 A6/0 1883/120 Mackay's Journal, 29 June 1883.

[68] CMS CA6/016/43 Mackay to Wright, 7 January 1880. For a more detailed examination of the Mukasa debate of 1879–80, see also Reid 1999a: 285–6.

[69] Felkin 1885–6: 746.

among coastal traders.[70] This might seem to be in contradiction to the earlier tentative assessment that the price of women had fallen overall between the early 1860s and c. 1880; but this contradiction may be explained by making a distinction between the domestic market, to which Grant appears to have been referring, and the export market. It is also important to remind ourselves that the exchange good by which we evaluated the price of women in the domestic market was cattle; we probably have a situation, therefore, in which cattle had become more valuable rather than women having become less valuable. The value of cattle rose at a time of livestock disease; but the fact that this value held despite strong market competition from women, an export commodity in increasing demand, perhaps suggests which of these commodities – livestock or domestic slaves – was regarded as fundamentally more important by 1880.[71]

In general, slave prices in Buganda are extremely difficult to assess. Contemporary Europeans provided a bewildering array of prices in their accounts, and it seems likely that slaves were exchanged for a wide range of commodities. Cloth has already been mentioned, although even in the early 1880s this was still confined to a relatively small elite. Increasingly, guns and ammunition were required by smaller-scale traders. On the whole, however, it is clear that by the early 1880s female slaves were fetching the best prices. Girls and slightly older women, the latter being increasingly exported rather than retained for the domestic market, were in general more expensive than their male counterparts.[72] It is important to note the coastal merchants' demand for females. Females of any age appear to have been more valuable because they were not only of use in the sphere of manual labour, but could also perform sexual services. Concubinage, indeed, was a major motivating factor, and had a much greater significance for the external East African slave trade than for that of West Africa. Crucially, circumstances in Buganda lent themselves to the meeting of this demand. The generally subordinate role of women in society, as we have seen, meant that the Arabs were tapping a ready-made system of inequality and domination, while the already fluid domestic trade in female slaves made the task of both buying and selling much easier.

Two missionaries were of the belief that by the 1880s more slaves were being exported than were being retained for domestic use in Buganda. The Ganda apparently bemoaned the fact that ivory was becoming increasingly scarce, and so their desire for foreign goods – most notably cloth and guns – was leading them to sell their slaves, more so than they would normally have done. As a result, the slave population was actually in decline.[73] This is certainly possible. Felkin observed that '[t]he slave population is diminishing, and the Waganda are beginning to feel that the exportation of slaves must cease, for if not, they will be compelled to do manual labour work themselves, which work they strongly object to'.[74]

---

[70] Schweinfurth *et al.* 1888: 117.
[71] This was of course before the outbreak of the pleuro-pneumonia or rinderpest panzootics.
[72] Felkin 1885–6: 753–4.
[73] Ibid.: 746; Wilson & Felkin 1882: 190.
[74] Felkin 1885–6: 746.

This somewhat amusing image undoubtedly reflects a genuine concern among many Ganda. Livinhac also observed in 1879 that demand was exceeding supply and that slaves were in fact something of a scarce commodity.[75] Several years later, in 1886, Lourdel noted that slaves were much easier to procure;[76] nevertheless, it is possible that increasingly the Ganda were struggling to meet demand and in the process selling more domestic slaves than would otherwise have been the case. What the evidence does suggest, moreover, is that ever greater numbers of Ganda were participating in the slave trade, albeit often on a small scale, perhaps selling one or two slaves at a time to coastal merchants eager to fill their caravans or canoes quickly. There is little doubt that the majority of slaves carried away by the Arabs were bought in bulk, but smaller, individual transactions undoubtedly took place. The French missionaries, who made it their policy to buy slaves with a view to liberating and converting them, quickly discovered that local slave-owners were only too willing to exchange their serviles for guns and sundry other goods.[77]

Social perceptions of slave-selling and wealth accumulation in the capital are to some extent revealed in an incident related by Lourdel. It involved the condemning to death of two youths at the *kabaka*'s court, the punishment for selling a young slave belonging to the *katikiro* to the Arabs. The youths had decided to seize and sell the slave in return for 'the luxury of several lengths of white cloth'. Significantly, Lourdel suggested that this kind of behaviour was not uncommon.[78] Indeed, the expansion of the slave trade in the 1870s and early 1880s seems to have prompted a wave of lawlessness around the capital. Slave-stealing and kidnapping increased, Lourdel noting that 'some people seize the unfortunate slaves by force and immediately afterwards go to sell them at the Wangouanas' [= coastal merchants] place or guard them until their master has replaced them'.[79] The Arabs themselves appear not to have been overly fussy about the origins of the slaves thus acquired.

The excitement generated by the arrival of a new batch of slaves in the capital is clear from contemporary missionary accounts, with both Ganda and Arab traders examining and discussing the best specimens, haggling over prices and selling and reselling their captives. One missionary described how, with a campaign in Busoga having recently ended, the slaves were assembled and selected:

> Three large courtyards were full of old women, and women with children, some of them in the most shocking condition ... Three or four coast men were there bargaining ... On going in the shamba I met a troop of boys, about thirty, not more than four years of age, lean, lank, & hungry looking, some mere skeletons. They were being led out by one of the king's own men whom I have often seen at the palace. When I had finished my business here, I went on to the palace and saw this same troop of boys coming out from being inspected by M'tesa. These were part of the

[75] White Fathers: C13/5 Livinhac to Lavigerie, 24 September 1879.
[76] White Fathers: C14/139 Lourdel to his brother, 15 October 1886.
[77] White Fathers: C13/1 Livinhac to Lavigerie, 2 July 1879.
[78] White Fathers: C14/185 Lourdel to Directeur, 1 June 1888.
[79] White Fathers: Rubaga Diary 2/12 August 1881.

captives made in Usoga, and what about the men and younger women [sic]. It was said that wives were very cheap in Uganda now![80]

A year later, the same missionary witnessed the arrival of another batch of Soga slaves:

> I saw the remains of the King's share of women going to the palace, over three hundred wretched creatures ... There ought to have been five hundred but death by hunger and fatigue had so reduced them. It is stated that one thousand captives died on their way here ... All the best of the women were taken by the chiefs. The number taken must have been great. The Arabs are in full feather [?] and great slave buying is going on ...[81]

The figure of the *kabaka* now appears to have been relegated almost to a background role, simply taking his pick of the new slaves and distributing or selling them to the Arabs as he saw fit, and leaving the merchants to carry on.[82] The apparent rise in lawlessness was symptomatic of the freedom accorded to the commercial arena, even in the comparatively tightly controlled environment of the capital. As we have seen in the context of the market-place, Mutesa did attempt to impose restrictions on exchange in the capital, but it seems likely that this was a desperate measure by an ailing *kabaka* to use political force to secure personal economic interests. Moreover, he did so in a sphere of Ganda life which was traditionally free from political constraint, excepting the restrictions placed on such imported goods as cotton cloth dating from the late eighteenth century, which might explain why he was only marginally successful. In any case, the policy of monopolizing the ivory trade, which we have already noted, was the only area in which Mutesa could hope to have some success. All in all, the *kabaka* by the early 1880s was little more than the most powerful and important of a great many Ganda traders eager to do business with the coastal merchants.

Although cloth was becoming increasingly widespread through the 1880s, firearms were perhaps the most important goods demanded by African sellers of slaves. In 1880, Mackay observed that a 'host of traders who arrived in Buganda shortly before I left, brought almost no barter goods, but an immense supply of guns and powder'; at Kagehyi on the southern shore of the lake he wrote that '[e]ight canoes arrived last week, and the chief refused to take any of our goods to Buganda, but took the traders with as much of their guns & c as the canoes could carry'.[83]

The mortality rate must have been a significant factor in the transport of slaves, and it was presumably a factor which was allowed for, among both the Ganda who escorted slaves from the war-zones to the trading areas and the Arabs who supervised their transport south. The lake route in particular was hazardous, and conditions on board the great slave canoes themselves were markedly unhygienic: Lourdel noted that slaves were piled virtually one on top of the other to maximize space.[84] On the

---

[80] CMS CA6/019/13 Pearson to Wright, 29 September 1879.
[81] CMS G3 A6/0 1881/22 Pearson to Mackay, 29 July 1880.
[82] White Fathers: Rubaga Diary 1/16–17 July 1880.
[83] CMS G3 A6/0 1881/9 Mackay to Wright, 24 September 1880.
[84] White Fathers: C14/185 Lourdel to Director, 1 June 1888.

overland route, rather more care was taken to ensure against escape than against death, captives being joined by the neck with long wooden forks. Many were also made to carry baggage.[85] The coastal traders took great risks on the lake itself, as is shown by the fact that in 1887 numerous slaves and considerable quantities of ivory were lost in a storm which wrecked the traders' hired canoes.[86] In the light of this information, it seems that the conservative figure of 1,000 slaves being exported a year during the 1880s might represent no more than half of the slaves actually involved in Ganda slave-gathering and marketing. This estimate clearly excludes those killed during the military operations themselves, deaths en route to Buganda and fatalities on the lake, not to mention those slaves retained in Buganda for domestic use.

It is likely that the wars of the late 1880s further multiplied the ways in which slaves were acquired, while the fighting itself generated new sources of slaves. Kabaka Kiwewa, who reigned briefly following Mwanga's deposition, promised an end to the duty imposed on coastal merchants,[87] although it is unclear whether this promise was kept. The coastal merchants themselves may well have taken advantage of the political turmoil by helping themselves to local slave supplies, perhaps even carrying out their own raids. In 1889, Lourdel noted the arrival at the south end of the lake of a group of Ganda who he claimed had been enslaved by the Arabs.[88] The idea of the Arabs actually enslaving anyone was certainly novel, since in Buganda they had occupied the position of buyers only, although this was the period of Muslim ascendancy during the civil conflict in Buganda. But even more striking is the fact that these slaves were described as Ganda, rather than Soga or Nyoro as was usual. Less conclusive, but also suggestive of the upheaval in the region at the end of the 1880s, is Lourdel's remark that not all slaves were being sent south: rather, 'an ever greater number have been driven north, into Bunyoro, where they are exchanged for ivory'.[89] This may have been because the southern routes were largely controlled by Christian enemies in the civil war;[90] yet coastal merchants may again have been taking advantage of political upheaval by plying their trade more directly with the Nyoro, who were by this time the biggest suppliers of ivory in the region, and who represented a market to which the Arabs had previously been allowed only limited access. This probably also reflects the declining importance of the slave trade itself. The coups of 1888–9 clearly had important economic dimensions. On the African side, the coastal traders represented the promise of the firepower which had become so highly valued.[91] The Arabs themselves welcomed the opportunity of at last influencing political conditions as they had elsewhere in eastern Africa, with a view to establishing more favourable terms of trade.

---

[85] Ibid.
[86] CMS G3 A5/0 1887/141 Gordon to Mackay, 14 November 1887.
[87] CMS G3 A5/0 1889/62 Mackay to Ashe, 11 November 1888.
[88] White Fathers: C14/190 Lourdel to Superior-General, 8 June 1889.
[89] Ibid.
[90] See also Twaddle 1993: *passim*.
[91] This is more closely examined in a later chapter.

Much of this activity, however, represented something of a last throw for organized slave-trading. By March 1890, Mwanga, recently reinstated, had announced the abolition of the slave trade, if not of the institution of slavery itself.[92] The declaration had little immediate impact, and six months later there were reports of slaves for export being brought down from the border areas of Bunyoro, generated by the ongoing war in that area.[93] It was, however, the beginning of the end, and the increasing British presence in Buganda precluded the majority of Ganda from participating even in the smuggling of slaves in the long run.

In more normal circumstances, it is difficult to see how any *kabaka* could have ended Buganda's participation in the slave trade, so critical was it to Ganda political and economic structures, as well as to the *kabaka* himself, of course. Both domestically and internationally, the slave trade was a dominant feature of economic life from the 1850s onward. Mutesa allegedly once declared: 'If the Queen of England would help me as she helps Sayyid Barghash of Zanzibar, certainly I would abolish slavery. But the power of my chiefs and my people depends on this traffic and I have no right to hinder it.' He also, again reportedly, put it another way: 'I could easily prevent the Arabs from coming here or expel them when they arrive; but who then will supply us with foreign goods, who will satisfy the aspirations which have risen in the hearts of my chiefs and my people?'[94] The *kabaka* is also supposed to have said to O'Flaherty in 1883, with regard to the slave trade, 'What can I do? ... Those cursed slave dealers really rule my people. This I myself formerly encouraged, but it has assumed such dimensions that it cannot I fear be stopped.'[95] There are of course several examples of such sentiments being expressed by pressurized nineteenth-century African rulers concerning the inimical export trade, a fact which lends Mutesa's reported remarks further credibility. In 1886, the Lozi king Lewanika was allegedly deeply disturbed by the heavy reliance of his people on the ivory trade, for example.[96] Even more pertinent is the example of Gezo, king of Dahomey, who told a British envoy in 1848 that he could not possibly give up the slave trade: the army had to be kept active and, if Gezo himself tried to alter 'the sentiments of a whole people', Dahomey would be thrown into anarchy and revolution, which 'would deprive him of his throne'.[97] Mutesa's own remarks may be evidence of a certain amount of political manoeuvring, but one suspects that Mutesa was not merely posturing here. It was an unashamed admission as to the importance of the coastal merchants to the kingdom's economy; Buganda had become involved in international commerce and could not now withdraw from it. The ability of the people to sell their

---

[92] White Fathers: Rubaga Diary 4/12–16 March 1890.
[93] White Fathers: Rubaga Diary 4/4–9 August 1890.
[94] Reported in *Les Missions Catholiques* 14 (1882): 89–90. Around the same time, the Anglican missionaries reported similar remarks: CMS G3 A6/0 1881/75 O'Flaherty to Hutchinson, 12 July 1881.
[95] CMS G3 A6/0 1883/71 O'Flaherty to Wigram, 28 February 1883.
[96] Roberts 1976: 172.
[97] B. Cruikshank, 'Report of his Mission to the King of Dahomey', in 'Missions to the Kings of Ashanti & Dahomey: Dispatches from the Lieutenant-Governor of the Gold Coast', *British Parliamentary Papers – Colonies (Africa)* Vol. 50: 17.

slaves had become critical to the functioning of the local economy. This was increasingly the case as ivory became more scarce and as most Ganda no longer had ready access to it. Nor were the Ganda purely the victims of the international market. Long before the arrival of the coastal traders, the ability to own and sell slaves meant social and economic power and reinforced critical ideas of domination, particularly, though not exclusively, along lines of gender and ethnicity. The injection of long-distance commercial impulses served to strengthen these ideas, and indeed made the selling of slaves even more lucrative, particularly in the two decades before the colonial period.

By the final third of the nineteenth century, the elephant was fast disappearing from Buganda. Therefore, as we have noted, ivory was becoming harder to procure, which was unfortunate for Buganda as on an international level it would supersede slaves as the most valuable regional export. By the end of the 1870s, most of Buganda's supplies were coming from Bunyoro and Busoga, some of it in the form of tribute, or as a result of regional commerce, or as war booty. As far as most Ganda were concerned, ivory was thus increasingly scarce as a trade good. One missionary noted in 1879 that Mutesa sold his ivory to the Arabs at inflated prices,[98] probably because it was in such short supply, while Mutesa himself had a virtual monopoly of its supply, although it was a monopoly largely by default. Later on, as we have noted, he attempted to establish even closer control over its acquisition, but by this time supply was so irregular that slaves had become the primary export anyway. Years earlier, when ivory was more abundant, such a monopolistic policy would have been rather more difficult, if not, as we have seen, impossible, to implement. It would also, presumably, have been less desirable, considering the rising value of ivory by the late nineteenth century. In the last years of Mutesa's reign, as Felkin observed, ivory supplies were 'coming fast to an end', with greater effort made and greater distances travelled for their collection.[99] Even so, one Arab merchant boasted privately to O'Flaherty that he sold his guns to Mutesa 'at more than 20 times their value' and received in return 'ivory less than 20 times its value'.[100] Yet this is clearly in comparison with conditions prevailing in Zanzibar. In general the prices paid for ivory in Buganda appear to have been as little as a tenth of that which might be paid at the coast.[101]

According to Mackay, supply problems meant that 'Mutesa always keeps the Arabs waiting a year or two before he pays them their ivory',[102] although this may also have been a deliberate policy aimed at detaining the merchants in Buganda for as long as possible. Still, Mwanga was faced with similar problems in 1885: 'there were many Arabs crying out for their ivory, due them before Mutesa's death, and Mwanga had promised to pay them when Wakoli, king of half of Busoga, arrived with his yearly tribute

---

[98] CMS CA6/010/48 Felkin's Journal, 17 March 1879.
[99] Ibid.
[100] CMS G3 A6/0 1881/70 O'Flaherty to Hutchinson, 18 April 1881.
[101] CMS G3 A5/0 1887/367 Mackay's Journal, 25 June 1887.
[102] CMS G3 A6/0 1884/55 Mackay's Log, 5 January 1884.

of tusks. Wakoli however did not come, either with or without ivory, to render his homage to the new king.'[103]

Mwanga was also unable to pay ivory owed to the missionaries, a debt which partly went back to Mutesa's reign; it was eventually paid in part in cowries.[104] Regular tribute as a source of ivory was increasingly important by the early 1880s, and thus Mutesa was ever more dependent on Busoga. In early 1880, for example, a supposedly tributary Soga chief was condemned to death for refusing to pay ivory to the *kabaka*, who 'appointed' the chief's son in his place. A missionary remarked that the new chief immediately 'set about furnishing his Majesty with hundreds of elephant tusks'.[105] Still, at the end of that year, Livinhac observed that 'the Arabs do not stop asking for their ivory. His Majesty promises and never gives.'[106] Inability to compete in the international ivory trade meant that by the beginning of the colonial period Buganda was increasingly sidelined. One British official wrote in 1893 that 'there has been quite a rush of traders from Tabora for Unyoro via Karagwe'. One such trader had recently returned from Bunyoro 'with forty frasala of ivory, as the proceeds of thirty loads taken from Tabora'.[107] Indeed, by the early 1890s the Ganda themselves were trading guns for ivory in Busoga.[108]

Buganda on the eve of colonial rule, therefore, had become to a very real extent commercially weakened. The political establishment had been able, by and large, to control the traders; it had been unable to control the export trade itself, or to guide it to the kingdom's advantage. It is usually, and correctly, argued that unlike the successful Akwapim cocoa farmers of the Gold Coast the Ganda experienced no economic continuity between the pre-colonial and colonial eras, although of course the banana plantation straddled both. But it seems clear that, stripped of its key nineteenth-century commercial assets, Buganda was ready for the introduction of a new commodity through which they could recapture some of their former commercial glory. The British eventually encouraged cotton, and the alacrity with which the Ganda took up cotton production is unquestionably linked to the trauma of economic isolation, notwithstanding continued involvement in the ivory trade, experienced by the beginning of the 1890s.

---

[103] CMS G3 A6/0 1885/98 Mackay to Wigram, ? May 1885.
[104] CMS G3 A5/0 1886/99 Mackay to Lang, 10 December 1885.
[105] White Fathers: Rubaga Diary 1/2 April 1880. This, indeed, emphasizes Buganda's heavy reliance on external sources, as well as the unreliability – or at best unpredictability – of such sources.
[106] White Fathers: Rubaga Diary 1/29 October 1880.
[107] UNA A2/1 Munworthy to Williams, 1 February 1893.
[108] UNA A2/1 Memo by Williams, 1 March 1893.

Summary of Part Three

The complexity and vitality of commerce, both regional and domestic, are clear. The importance of trade to the pre-colonial Ganda economy is also beyond question. It is equally clear that the growth of long-distance trade from the late eighteenth century onward transformed commercial relations both within Buganda and between the Ganda and their neighbours. The kind of commodities demanded – chiefly slaves and ivory – brought great wealth to a number of Ganda. Yet Buganda also found itself in a potentially precarious position. The struggle to secure ivory was increasingly difficult as elephants were driven beyond the kingdom's frontiers. Moreover, ever greater numbers of slaves were required for export at a time when Buganda's military strength was being sapped by tensions and misjudgements at the centre. Indeed military weakness and ultimately civil war also affected the kingdom's ability to acquire ivory through tribute. At the same time, Buganda had to strike the delicate balance between the export of slaves and retention of war captives for use within the kingdom. The slave trade, therefore, in which the Ganda were for the most part enthusiastic participants, threatened long-term economic doom, as it had for a number of African societies in the nineteenth century, a fact implicitly recognized by Mutesa himself. The threat was only effectively removed with the establishment of the protectorate, although it is important to qualify the notion of imperialism to the rescue by pointing out that the British would come to award commercial middleman status on a racial basis, thus handicapping Africans.

Examination of the development of commerce also shows that the *kabaka*'s control over the economic lives of his subjects should not be exaggerated. Indeed, relatively free and unhindered trade was essential to a large number of ordinary Ganda producers, and in this sense Buganda had developed, by the nineteenth century, a remarkably exchange-oriented economy. This situation probably precluded the need for what might be termed professional traders. We have already seen how politics and economics might be closely intertwined; but, in the context of trade, economics and domestic politics were almost entirely separate, except of course where political disputes prevented commercial movement. The *kabaka* was to some extent only the most powerful and privileged Ganda trader in the capital between c. 1850 and c. 1890, after which, of course, he was not even this. It is true that in the early 1880s Mutesa did attempt to exercise some control over local markets; by this time, too, a royal monopoly in ivory had been effected. Yet such controls achieved only very limited success, while the ivory monopoly had come about largely by default. The capital was indeed the most important centre in the kingdom, not because it was the seat of an omnipotent ruler, but because it was the commercial gateway to exciting and apparently lucrative new horizons.

It is clear, however, that war and commerce were inextricably interwoven. The failure of commercial relations often prompted military action, but military expansion could open up commercial opportunities. The attempt to control trade, and to impose favourable trading conditions, itself often led to conflict. Most obviously, the slave trade could scarcely have flourished as it did in Buganda without the military operations to fund it. In Part IV, we examine military developments in Buganda: it will be seen how economic or commercial considerations almost always played a significant part in Ganda expansion, whether the annexation of Buddu, or the development of a powerful canoe fleet, or military operations south of the Kagera river. Yet this is not to ignore the importance of war, which, by itself, was a critical activity in the growth of the Ganda state.

Part Four

War & Peace

Nine

The Rise & Decline
of Ganda Military Power

War and militarism have been studied, in a broader context if not for their own sake, in a number of pre-colonial African societies. In the southern part of the continent, the Zulu have been seen as epitomizing a society organized around militaristic principles, using warfare to effect change both internally and externally. In eastern Africa, Mirambo and Nyungu-ya-Mawe have received similar treatment. Comparison between these societies and Buganda helps shed light on the latter and highlights important questions about the nature of military structures and strategies. Among the Zulu, or more correctly among the Mthethwa under Dingiswayo, the creation of age regiments ensured that war was a way of life rather than an occasional occupation. A standing army put the Zulu on a permanent war-footing. This was not the case among the Ganda, who despite having developed an efficient military structure never went as far as establishing permanent regiments or professional soldiery. At the same time, the Ganda and Zulu shared a certain parasitic character. The latter incorporated conquered peoples into their army and fleeced their districts of cattle, while the former used cattle, slaves, women and ivory as the rewards for military success and, in a more long-term context, actively sought to exploit the natural economic resources of conquered or tributary regions. As with the Ganda, indeed, the Zulu army cannot be studied in isolation; social, economic and ecological factors are critical to understanding the wars in southern Africa in the nineteenth century, and this has been persuasively argued by historians such as Jeff Guy, J. Cobbing and P. Maylam.[1]

It is, however, a historian of West Africa, Robert Smith, who has written most comprehensively on pre-colonial African warfare in its many dimensions.[2] Many of the questions he poses serve to guide other historians, including the present writer, in their examinations of different regions of Africa. Smith highlighted the difficulties of analysing pre-colonial tactics,

---

[1] Guy 1979; Cobbing 1988; Maylam 1986.
[2] Smith 1989; Smith & Ade Ajayi 1971. There are also some excellent essays in Falola & Law 1992.

particularly with regard to the role of firearms. Guns had a longer and somewhat more varied history among the Yoruba than among the Ganda, but clearly applicable to the latter is Smith's assertion that '[t]he use of firearms influenced not only decisions on the battlefield but also, and perhaps to a greater extent, the political course of events'.[3] Smith also sought to clarify the terminology of war: 'Skirmishes, battles, and even campaigns, are not wars but incidents comprised within a war. A war may, though rarely, be decided by a single battle, but that battle is something less than the total state of hostility within which it takes place.'[4] He also had difficulty with the fact that 'European observers have often used such limited terms as "raid", "expedition" or "campaign" to describe the wars of West Africa.'[5] These are, of course, terms of convenience, but Smith is correct to suggest that they can often blur our understanding of warfare. Such terms are all used in the present study, usually because within the context they seem to mostly aptly describe the nature of the offensive or attack being mounted; but this should not then be taken as meaning that the Ganda did not practise 'war'. There is undoubtedly some validity in Smith's assertion that 'a state of general hostility between adversaries might indeed last, though with only intermittent action, for several years'.[6] It may be suggested that this be applied to relations between Buganda and Bunyoro at various stages in their histories. The question of terminology does, however, lead to one of interpretation of motivation, which is why the present study has striven to avoid the term 'raid' as much as possible. 'Raid' implies a more short-term approach to Ganda warfare than was normally the case. The Ganda fought wars for a number of reasons, with both short- and long-term gain in mind. The mistake must not be made of assuming that the immediate and most tangible yields of a battle – for example, cattle, women and slaves – represent the final desired result, although such booty was clearly important. This was particularly true in the later nineteenth century, with the increased demand for slaves among the coastal merchants, although the argument that the Ganda fought more wars at this time to fulfil this demand is unconvincing and unsubstantiated. In a wider perspective, however, it is clear that warfare was of greater significance to the kingdom of Buganda than the booty which resulted from it.

Warfare is clearly fundamental to the process of state-building, to the material basis of state power and to internal cohesion; this is as true in Africa as in Europe. Yet European observers, then as now, tended towards a dismissive and ignorant attitude regarding the nature and ethos of African warfare. As Bethwell Ogot pointed out, the study of European history is in large part a procession through a gallery of war-leaders and momentous battles;[7] such personalities and events were accepted as having been instrumental in the flow of social, economic and political history in the West. War was rational, often noble, usually inseparable from the growth of nationhood, and the most dramatic – indeed the most effective

---

[3] Smith & Ade Ajayi 1971: 20.
[4] Smith 1989: 41.
[5] Ibid.: 41–2.
[6] Ibid.: 42.
[7] Ogot 1972: 3.

– expression of political and economic will. This may be something of an exaggeration, but the point is clear enough. As Ogot argued, poignantly in 1972 and hardly less so a generation later, Africa is frequently depicted as 'a continent of warring natives'.[8] The most common characteristics of such warfare were bloodthirstiness, economic and social irrationality and a paucity of grand strategies or even, often, limited objectives. It was, in effect, predation, not war. Slave- and cattle-raids could scarcely be described as powerful determinants of social, political or economic change; they did, however, lend weight to Hugh Trevor-Roper's famous description of African history as the 'unrewarding gyrations of barbarous tribes'.[9] No continent, surely, is without its history of unrewarding gyrations – western Europe between 1914 and 1918 leaps immediately to mind – but only the African past has been so arbitrarily and completely dismissed.

The current work, as well as that of the authors mentioned above, demonstrates that warfare was a major factor in political and economic change in pre-colonial Africa. Although European observers in the nineteenth century refused to credit African warfare with anything approaching the supposed nobility and higher purpose, never mind larger strategic aims, of European war, the evidence they left behind in fact contradicts itself. Even while Europeans were contemptuously dismissive of African warfare and armies, their reports on both suggested that their contempt was utterly misguided. The detail contained within many of these primary sources undermines the overall viewpoint of the authors, and demonstrates that war was both rational and imbued with a sense of higher purpose. It is not our purpose here to laud conflict, but to emphasize its enormous significance as an agency of change and national self-expression in the context of Buganda.

Ethos & motivation

The Ganda had incorporated a strong strand of militarism into their culture by the nineteenth century. The use of arms played a critical part in the foundation myths of the kingdom, and participation in military campaigns was, by the nineteenth century, a fundamental part of male life. War in a more general sense also had a significant impact on women, as it was usually they who were left to maintain the domestic economy in the absence of the men, of whose labour they might even be deprived in the case of death or severe injury in action. Female responsibility for agricultural production, for example, was clearly even greater than in 'peacetime'. But the extent to which combat itself was a masculine activity is suggested by the fact that cowards or deserters were made to dress in the manner of pregnant women, or were forced to undertake work usually performed by women in the service of braver, more honoured warriors.[10] War was instrumental in Buganda's historical development, in both an external and internal sense. With a carefully structured army, Buganda

[8] Ibid.: 3.
[9] Quoted in Hopkins 1973: 32.
[10] Kagwa 1934: 93.

was able to expand steadily, taking advantage of Bunyoro's difficulties, especially in the seventeenth and eighteenth centuries. By the middle of the nineteenth century, Buganda was the most powerful kingdom in the lacustrine region, and the Ganda had recorded their military history in various forms of martial celebration.[11]

The symbols and regalia of war played a critical role in Ganda culture. The decision to wage war was itself taken amid elaborate ceremony, which indicates not only the historical importance attached to warfare but also, perhaps, the extent to which the decision to fight was not taken lightly. One of the most important pieces of ceremonial equipment, for example, and one which also served a very practical function, was the drum *mujaguzo*. This enormous drum was beaten primarily to announce an imminent war, and thus probably served to attract a number of warriors from the vicinity of the capital at least. Significantly, it was a general public declaration, reflecting the degree to which the Ganda regarded war as a communal activity, binding the community in collective action. This in itself probably stemmed from a time in Buganda's early history when war affected ordinary people far more profoundly than it did in the eighteenth and nineteenth centuries. Notably, however, one indigenous source suggests that *mujaguzo* is not, relatively speaking, particularly old, dating back to the reign of Kabaka Mutebi in the middle of the seventeenth century.[12] It seems highly likely that drums of a similar kind existed before this time, and that Mutebi simply 'institutionalized' the practice. *Mujaguzo* was also used to announce events of national importance, such as the coronation of the new *kabaka*, or the death of an old one. It seems likely that the name *mujaguzo* was actually applied not to one drum but to a large set; a recent lexicographer defined *mujaguzo* as consisting of 93 drums, all under royal control.[13] The *kabaka* alone was supposed to own the means of such public address, but *ssaza* chiefs had access to similar drums to convey information on a national scale. It is unclear how practically important such drums were by the nineteenth century, when the kingdom, at its greatest territorial extent, would have needed a much more elaborate and reliable system of conveying news and metropolitan decisions. But it is clear that, during war itself, drums in the nineteenth century remained practically important, as well as being sources of inspiration around which soldiers rallied. On the battlefield, according to Burton, the drumbeat often set the tempo of the fighting; he was told that the army engaged the enemy for as long as the drums were sounded and, once the drums stopped, the soldiers knew to withdraw from the action.[14] It should be noted, however, that none of my other sources – the first-hand accounts of the 1880s being the most important – mention the use of drums in actual

[11] The militaristic overtones of the *kabaka*'s coronation provide one of the best examples of this. Newly appointed rulers swore, for example, to fight and die for the kingdom in the event of invasion. By the middle of the nineteenth century this was largely irrelevant, but the historical symbolism remained important.

[12] Zimbe 1939: 19.

[13] Murphy 1972: 357. The word itself comes from the verb stem *jaguza*, to rejoice or celebrate.

[14] Burton 1860: II, 189.

combat. Whether Burton was misinformed, or whether the practice some-how disappeared between the 1850s and the 1880s, is a matter of speculation.

By the nineteenth century political leadership was also imbued with the symbolism of war; the *kabaka* came to be seen as being by necessity a worthy military leader, even if by the nineteenth century this was largely ceremonial rather than functional. The historical and cultural importance of this is reflected in the fact that long after military leadership had ceased to be a practical function of kingship, rulers were none the less surrounded by a militaristic aura. Zimbe, for example, describes how Mutesa, towards the end of his reign, took the young Mwanga under his protection and began to promote him as his successor. Mutesa asked his chiefs, "Can't he lead an army successfully?' The chiefs answered, 'Yes, Your Lord, he certainly can do so.' The chiefs, of course, had as little idea as Mutesa himself about Mwanga's military skills, but this was irrelevant. A statement concerning Mwanga's military prowess needed to be made to indicate the young prince's suitability to succeed his father. It was a metaphor for what it meant to rule the kingdom of Buganda.[15] Mwanga also had to participate in a mock battle, the *katikiro* urging him to '"Fight your enemies and conquer Buganda", for a Kingdom is always conquered not succeeded to.'[16] This may tell us something about post-colonial politics, and it may be that this essential principle of governance was scarcely dissipated by the relatively brief interjection of colonial rule. Later on in the ceremonies, the young *kabaka* was told to 'always be brave in fighting for your country'.[17] None the less, Mwanga was probably the first ruler not to lead an army of foreign invasion in any sense at all; even Mutesa had been known to set up camp at military headquarters and direct the campaign locally, albeit at a safe distance.[18] Although this may be a reflection of Buganda's military decline in this period, it is more likely to have been a symptom of the decidedly sedentary kingship which had developed by the late nineteenth century. Yet the symbolism of war continued into the twentieth century. The coronation in 1993 of Kabaka Mutebi II was accordingly replete with militaristic regalia and the echoes of battles past, as the commemorative booklet shows.[19]

There was an important spiritual dimension which bound myth and symbol together and which provided the kingdom's military adventures with a more profound, indeed extra-terrestrial, justification. In Buganda there were two principal gods associated with war. The more famous, and the one to which appeals for advice and assistance were more regularly made, was Kibuka. This deity apparently oversaw campaigns to the west of Buganda and against Bunyoro, although he could also be called upon in other directions. Nende, believed to be the son of the lake god Mukasa, was approached on the eve of wars to the east – chiefly Busoga[20] – and

[15] Zimbe 1939: 83.
[16] Ibid.: 107.
[17] Ibid.: 109.
[18] Stanley 1878: I, Chapter XII.
[19] See the *Coronation Special Souvenir* (Kampala, 1993).
[20] It should be pointed out that to talk of Busoga in this context is something of a misnomer.

accordingly his temple was in Kyagwe. It is striking that the Ganda thus made a distinction between, in effect, wars against Bunyoro and those against Busoga. Although the belief system was the same, two separate deities were required with the needs of the different war-zones.[21] The advice rendered by the gods was very often taken seriously and even heeded. However, there seems little doubt that often the spirit mediums, perhaps being in touch with the kingdom's military needs and strengths, or at least with feelings among the *kabaka* and chiefs at the royal court, would tailor their celestial messages accordingly. The gods often told the chiefs what they wanted to hear, followed the prevailing wisdom, or simply pronounced common sense.

However, such counsel, although usually sought, was not always followed, and this was probably increasingly so in the late nineteenth century, a period of new religions as well as heightened scepticism. In 1884, for example, while leading a disastrous campaign to the east against Budama, the commander of the army was 'told' by Nende to retreat to Buganda. The commander, not apparently noted for his strength of character, was all too keen to heed his advice, but several other chiefs in positions of command refused to countenance such an idea. As Zimbe wrote, 'Nobody would agree to the recommendation of returning without battle. It is impossible to do such a thing. How can the men of victorious Mutesa return at night? What shall we say if we are asked about the war? We had better be buried rather than run away.'[22] The god Nende had allegedly advised a course of action which ran contrary to the Ganda military ethos. The commander may well have elicited from the spirit medium his desired response. Nevertheless, rather than expounding and upholding Buganda's military ethos, the god was seen by implication to have done a disservice to the brave warriors proud to be fighting under the colours of Mutesa. An example is thus provided of how spirit mediums were capable of giving advice so partial and tailored to suit particular commanders that no self-respecting Ganda soldier could possibly follow it. What is also striking about this illustration is the fact that Nende's message caused such deliberation among the commanders; the gods clearly still had a certain amount of influence in the mid-1880s, and their counsel could not easily be dismissed. On this occasion, the problem was perhaps made more complex by the fact that the overall commander favoured Nende's proclamations. Eventually, the commander did in fact flee, leaving behind a number of Ganda soldiers and chiefs. When next the enemy force attacked, the divided and severely depleted Ganda force was badly beaten with heavy casualties inflicted. The moral dilemma had apparently been the army's downfall. For the soldiers who remained, their loyalty to the *kabaka* and to their perceived military tradition ultimately overrode all else, including deities with dubious counsel. Mutesa later judged these men to

---

[20] (cont.) Strictly speaking, Busoga was to a large extent a colonial invention. In a pre-colonial context, the territory east of the Nile was divided between a number of political entities, many only loosely affiliated to one another. To some degree, therefore, Soga was something of a generic term.

[21] Zimbe 1939: 84.

[22] Ibid.: 85.

have taken the righteous path. As Zimbe explained, the commander caused 'because of his timidity, the death of so many people', and accordingly 'was fined 40 women for the Kabaka by the Katikiro Mukasa while others who had fled with him were fined a total of 200 women'.[23] The fact that the commander could claim to have merely been following higher orders was clearly seen as irrelevant. Counsel obtained through spirit mediums was important only in so far as it upheld Buganda's military pride and dignity: this had retained its original potency, even if the Ganda army itself had not.

Gods were consulted throughout the campaign and not only at its outset. Spiritual matters were probably most important on the eve of a war, but spirit mediums were an indispensable part of the commander's entourage, and were consulted regularly on the feelings and advice of whichever god was represented as the war progressed. In addition to Kibuka and Nende, Mirim, supposedly another son of Mukasa, was of some importance. Kagwa wrote: 'Mirim went to the front himself in time of war. He would go into the camp of the enemy at night and steal a warrior's spear and bring it back saying, "Here is an enemy's weapon. I give it to you as a sign that you will win the battle tomorrow." If he failed to steal anything, the warriors were all very much depressed and were therefore easily defeated …'[24]

The question of morale was clearly significant and was often connected to religion. The passage quoted here indicates how an army's performance in the field was seen, at least in theory, to be influenced by apparently small but vital acts of considerable portent. Of course it is almost impossible to judge to what extent this was, in practice, true; one suspects that, although these acts may have been frequently performed, the relevance attached to them must have varied among individual soldiers. This was probably particularly the case in the late nineteenth century, by which time traditional or indigenous belief systems had been thrown into flux somewhat by the arrival of new religions, although doubtless Christianity and Islam were themselves adapted by individual Ganda to meet the needs of warfare.

It is probably true, indeed, that the bonds between warfare and religion had been gradually weakened over several centuries. As Buganda became more powerful, a more pragmatic cynicism may have dictated military conduct; in all probability, the idea developed that sound strategy and superior weaponry, not the propitiation of particular gods, made for successful war-making. Religion and spiritual observances continued to play a role, as we have already seen, but by the nineteenth century this role had declined in importance. Early in Buganda's history, there had been a clear connection between religion and war in that certain hills, scattered throughout the kingdom, had been both places of worship – where the shrines to certain deities were located – and places of sanctuary in time of foreign attack. A great many of these hills were located in Singo and Bulemezi, for several centuries the front-line provinces in the intermittent struggle between Buganda and Bunyoro; but they were also found in the

---

[23] Ibid.: 85–6.
[24] Kagwa 1934: 121.

more central areas of Busiro, Kyadondo and Kyagwe.[25] It is unlikely that it was mere coincidence that these important local shrines were also last points of defence. However, as Buganda grew stronger and less prone to serious attack from without, the significance of these religious and military sanctuaries declined, although their spiritual relevance may have been relatively unaffected. Certainly the dual importance of such hills lessened over time.

In other spheres, the motivation behind war and indeed its very nature changed over time. Motivation is often difficult to analyse; actions are not always true indicators of motive, although they are often all that is available for close examination. Confusion concerning the motivations behind warfare is evident from some late nineteenth-century writings. Roscoe felt qualified to declare that '[t]he hope of spoil made every man anxious to be sent on a punitive expedition'.[26] Yet he was also keen, doubtless from his position as a missionary as well as in the context of the anthropological research he was undertaking on behalf of Sir James Frazer, to promote the idea that all military campaigns were initiated by the kingdom's deities:

> A messenger sent from the War-god to the King advocating a punitive expedition was often the first step in preparation for war. Chiefs were then sent by the King with presents to the gods, to ask their advice as to the conduct of the war and the choice of a leader. The gods would name the person who was to be chosen as general, and would send their blessing, and also some fetish by the hands of representatives who were to accompany the army; these representatives had charge of the special emblems from the temples, by which to divine, when necessary.[27]

This may indeed have been the official, though obsolete, system by which decisions were reached, but it is most unlikely that it had much practical significance. Roscoe was not unique in his attempt to depict African warfare as driven by superstition without any basis in rational motives or objectives. To put it mildly, it is difficult to conceive of a situation in which a military organization as structurally advanced as that of Buganda in the nineteenth century would have relied on such a whimsical methodology by which vital decisions were reached. Again, this is not to dismiss out of hand the role of religion but merely to place it in its proper context. Roscoe's assertion, mentioned earlier, concerning the economic motive of the average soldier certainly has a solid basis in fact. Economic gain in general was an enormously influential factor in waging war, as it always has been, and soldiers could certainly expect to reap some form of material reward for their part in a campaign, as we shall see. Of course material gain was only part of the story. From the example of the disastrous war of 1884 – probably the last of Mutesa's reign – there were often deeper, less tangible motivations for soldiers in the field. This was true among chiefs, for whom the available sources speak loudest, and there seems little reason to doubt that the same applied to lowly peasant-soldiers. While wars are rarely fought without some economic motive, it is equally

---

[25] Ibid.: 123–4.
[26] Roscoe 1911: 346.
[27] Ibid.: 348.

rare to discover a war devoid of passion, pride and some spiritual element perhaps comprehensible only to the participants. Some distinction should also be made between individual and collective motivation; Ganda must usually have identified with both their own personal positions and with that of the broader community and even of the state itself.

Recorded tradition suggests that from the earliest times Buganda faced a territorial struggle. The dominance of Bunyoro through the fifteenth and sixteenth centuries meant that, if Buganda was to expand, even survive, military confrontation was inevitable. Herein lay the origins of the modern Ganda army and military organization, with an essentially defensive ethos: an army was required if the society was to flourish. This is, of course, somewhat simplistic, as armies also have social and political roles to play. For example, soldiers may offer their loyalty to the political status quo or to the ruler himself, which has profound implications for the development of the society as well as the state. The ruler or ruling group may develop an army precisely for this reason. Primarily, however, in the case of Buganda an army was born out of what might be called aggressive defensiveness. At some point in Buganda's history, this defensiveness became aggression; in other words, the need to wage war was at least equalled by the desirability of doing so. During the nineteenth century, by which time Buganda had reached its greatest territorial extent and the height of its material potency, war was still necessary to maintain regional hegemony, although there is clear evidence that the kingdom was in military decline by this time. In this later period, military activity was motivated more by internal political, social and economic factors; none the less, the need to express the military ethos, which was as old as the kingdom itself, remained.

Military growth before the nineteenth century

For data on Buganda's pre-1800 military history, we must rely on recorded oral sources, largely those of Kagwa; and, regardless of the reliability of such sources, they are extremely dense with tales of battles and outstanding heroes, to the extent that discerning the significant and even seminal military encounters is often problematic. There is hardly space here to analyse all of the early data, nor would it be particularly profitable to do so; however, careful reading of these sources does suggest that the period of what seems to be the sixteenth century may reasonably be regarded as marking the beginning of the kingdom's modern military history. One of the most important wars in Buganda's early history was that with Bunyoro under Nakibinge, probably in the sixteenth century;[28] it was important not because the Ganda won but exactly the reverse. In the course of the crushing defeat inflicted by the Nyoro, the cult of Kibuka was born; moreover, as we have already seen, Ganda weapon production entered a significant new phase. Nakibinge is remembered as reigning through dramatic events and one of the most important periods in the kingdom's history. Economic and military processes were set in motion at this time

---

[28] For a full discussion of both the king and the conflict, see Reid 1997.

which would lead ultimately to Buganda usurping Bunyoro's position as the most powerful state in the northern lake region. The profound importance of Nakibinge's conflict with Bunyoro is underlined by the accession ceremonies undertaken by Mwanga in 1884. According to Zimbe, the *mugema*, the governing chief of Busiro *ssaza*, handed to the new *kabaka* a bow and arrow, a weapon known to, but not used by, the Ganda.[29] Mwanga was then required to stab a young Nyoro male, presumably a slave or recent war-captive, in the chest. Zimbe explained:

> This taboo has two significant points. By this the Kabaka is paying back the Banyoro who fought and killed Sekabaka Nakibinge; the new Kabaka won't fail to fight and defeat the Banyoro. The bow and arrow used were those Sekabaka Nakibinge fought with. The second aim was to encourage the Kabaka by showing he was now a grown up man who could even kill a man.[30]

The great struggle to which Nakibinge gave his life had lodged itself in Buganda's collective memory, and the Nyoro had been identified as the old enemy, as it were, although it is also possible that Nyoro was used as a generic term, encompassing all enemies of Buganda. The Nyoro were, in any case, the *sine qua non* of Ganda militarism. It is striking too that Nakibinge is supposed to have made use of a bow and arrow, although this is not mentioned in any of my other sources. Some confusion may have developed over the ensuing centuries as to what the bow and arrow actually represented. Perhaps the Nyoro themselves used the weapon; it also seems likely that Kibuka and his fellow Sesse warriors may have brought bows and arrows with them in aiding Buganda.[31]

It is probably from around 1700 that we can safely date Buganda's modern military ascendancy. The reasons for this ascendancy are not always easy to define, but certain key themes can be identified. Buganda's position in 1700 was markedly different from that in 1500. We have already noted how the kingdom had gradually built up a position of some economic as well as military strength, facilitated by an efficient and centralized socio-political structure. During the eighteenth century, as Kiwanuka has argued, the *kabaka* increased his authority by expanding the *ssaza* system and by creating the *batongole* or royally appointed chiefs.[32] It is clear that these chiefs also had a growing military role, and that military organization was increasingly efficient. It is indeed important to note the great significance of the *batongole* in this respect, as in the second half of the nineteenth century the changing political and military nature of this 'class' of chiefs had a detrimental effect on Buganda's overall military performance. From the point of view of the material basis of warfare, the lessons of Nakibinge's reign had clearly been learnt. One of these lessons was the need for an efficient, well-organized army which could be quickly

---

[29] The apparent absence of the bow and arrow, and Ganda weaponry in general, is examined below.
[30] Zimbe 1939: 111–12.
[31] Kibuka was supposedly sent by the ruler of Sesse, Wanema, to help Buganda against Bunyoro: see for example Kagwa 1971, 1972: 9–10; Stanley 1878: I, 349–50.
[32] Kiwanuka 1971: 112ff.

assembled. The Ganda had also recognized the need for adequate raw materials in successfully prosecuting large-scale campaigns. Iron was clearly among the most important of these raw materials, and certain types of wood were also seen to be of great significance in the construction of spear-shafts, shields and, later, war-canoes. By the early eighteenth century, Buganda had succeeded in extending its reach towards these resources, taking advantage of Bunyoro's relative decline. It produced, indeed, a snowball effect: the increased accessibility of these resources fuelled military success, which in turn led, in the second half of the eighteenth century, to the capture and annexation of Buddu. Buddu clearly contributed enormously to Buganda's war resources and indeed its domestic economy generally.

Under Mawanda in the early eighteenth century, Buganda expanded to the east, securing much of Kyagwe; Ganda influence was also strengthened to the south and southwest, particularly in Buddu. It was Kabaka Junju, however, who capitalized on gains made in Buddu in the earlier part of the century; the leading character in the Buddu drama was Luzige of the *diga* or sheep clan.[33] He was sent to wage war 'against all the people of Buddu county', and was apparently successful, as he 'defeated them wholly'.[34] Junju consolidated his control over Buddu by distributing various villages, mostly famed for their manufacture of fine barkcloth, to several of his relatives.[35] Indeed the incorporation of Buddu into what might be called greater Buganda probably involved both military conquest and local political alliances, the latter facilitating the positioning of Ganda royalty alongside local elites. Junju had planned, moreover, to link his seizure of Buddu with an annexation of Mawogola to the west, hence incorporating a huge area formerly under the sway of Bunyoro. In this, however, he was no more successful than his predecessors. Although the extension of Ganda power throughout Buddu probably placed Mawogola in some form of tributary position, formal rule – which seems to have been Junju's objective – could not be achieved. Buganda's expansion was thus checked in the west, and remained so until the second half of the nineteenth century when Mutesa achieved some military success against the peoples bordering Buddu,[36] although even this does not seem to have involved formal political control. Nevertheless, the mass attack organized by Junju to capture the whole of Buddu – surely one of the largest in Buganda's history – was also felt much further afield. Doubtless as part of his plan to impose Ganda authority throughout the region, Junju sent regiments across the Kagera river into Kiziba, and out past Mawogola against Busongora.[37] The project proved too ambitious, and indeed over-ambition was by this time becoming a defining characteristic of Ganda military organization. Such long-range regiments might cause considerable damage in the target areas, as well as to and from their objectives; but logistically they were difficult to maintain, and their presence in a particular area alone was not sufficient to

---

[33] 'Luzige' was the title of a chief of this clan, with estates in both Butambala and Kyagwe.
[34] Kagwa 1972: 71.
[35] Ibid.: 108.
[36] Zimbe 1939: 16.
[37] Kagwa 1971: 91.

bring about political hegemony, contrary to Ganda expectations. Peoples living a sufficient distance from the Ganda heartlands learnt to take the blows of the Ganda army and wait until it had withdrawn, developing political and economic systems which enabled them to withstand periodic Ganda assaults. In this way the Ganda expansionist edge was blunted after the mid-eighteenth century. We see a similar phenomenon with the Zulu in the early nineteenth century: by the end of Shaka's reign, Zulu armies were having to cover ever greater distances in their pursuit of enemies, producing logistical problems which made the Zulu less devastating than before. Moreover, surrounding peoples had adapted their political and military structures to withstand Zulu attacks.

Following these military operations, which probably lasted several months, Junju turned to concentrate on developing the administration of Buddu and, alongside this, pursuing the economic exploitation of the new *ssaza*. It can be seen that the political as well as economic incorporation of Buddu into Buganda, while largely attributed to Junju, was a gradual process spanning several decades; none the less, it provides us with the most dramatic example of the expansion of Ganda power in the eighteenth century. It was fundamental to the creation of modern Buganda, most significantly in its economic dimensions, and in the sense that it gave the kingdom extended reach southwards and a valuable stretch of shoreline. Buganda would not acquire so much territory so relatively quickly until the capture of the Nyoro 'lost counties' under the British at the end of the nineteenth century.

As seems to have been the pattern through much of Buganda's history, the reign of a particularly aggressive *kabaka* was followed by that of a consolidator: thus Junju was succeeded by his brother Semakokiro. Semakokiro, however, had to contend with a series of counter-attacks by Bunyoro, probably in response to the recent losses of ground which that kingdom had suffered at the hands of Junju. This sequence of conflicts would have been particularly galling for Semakokiro as they were largely instigated by his rebellious and disaffected son Kakungulu. Following insurrectionary activity in Buganda, the latter fled to Bunyoro, as many bitter and disappointed Ganda had over the centuries, and was given charge of a large army by the *mukama* of Bunyoro with which to invade Buganda. Again, this was common enough practice in the region, and clearly the Nyoro were attempting to install a favourable ruler in the kingdom that was expanding at their expense. In the first of these attacks, the Nyoro penetrated much of Singo before the *mukwenda*, as governor of that *ssaza*, could muster an army. In the initial clash, the Ganda were heavily beaten, apparently through simple lack of preparedness; it seems that Kakungulu's army came uncomfortably close to Buganda's core area before it was finally repulsed.[38] The subsequent history of the region would have been quite different if Kakungulu had been able to seize power with Nyoro help; he was, however, largely staved off for the remainder of Semakokiro's reign, although, as we shall see below, he was still active during the reign of Kamanya.

---

[38] Ibid.: 97–8.

Semakokiro's attention was also drawn south of the Kagera river, to where a military expedition was dispatched in order to protect commercial interests along the increasingly active and lucrative trade routes west of Lake Victoria. There is little doubt that such commercial activity was already expanding under Junju, and that this was one of the motivations behind his thrust towards the Kagera; moreover, Junju was also engaged in military activity in Kiziba, again probably with control of trade as one of the key factors. But both commercial and military operations in the area intensified under Semakokiro. When Mangagala, a trader whom Kagwa describes as the *kabaka*'s 'salesman', was killed by local traders in Kiziba who had suspected him of cheating in their commercial dealings, Semakokiro sent an army to the area, presumably to persuade the locals of Buganda's omnipotence and commercial hegemony. The plundering of slaves and cattle, as so often, was a by-product of the attack, but it was certainly not the primary motive. Semakokiro had recognized the importance of defending Buganda's economic interests even in areas in which he had no direct control.[39] Commerce and local economic interests in general may also have been behind Semakokiro's attack on the Nile entrepôt of Bulondoganyi,[40] which seems to have been in effect an invasion of Bugerere. This was a district divided roughly between Bunyoro, Busoga and Bukedi, which was eventually marked as a *ssaza* by the British. There was less success in this direction, however, and for reasons unspecified the invasion was swiftly abandoned.[41]

Although it is clearly chronologically convenient to draw a line under the reign of Semakokiro, the bulk of his successor Kamanya's reign lying in the nineteenth rather than the eighteenth century, it is also true that with the close of the eighteenth century, a discernible middle period in Buganda's history came to an end. During the preceding three centuries, Buganda achieved considerable territorial expansion. While Kamanya was a warrior-*kabaka* of some repute, much of Buganda's military history in the nineteenth century is characterized by consolidation and the perpetual attempt to maintain the status quo. Lack of territorial conquest may not itself signify military decline; more importantly, maintenance of the external status quo became increasingly problematic. Between the reigns of Nakibinge and Semakokiro, the Ganda had developed a dynamic military policy aimed specifically at the expansion of their borders, in search of both security in their foreign relations and economic wealth, and at replacing Bunyoro as the dominant power in the northern lake region. By 1800, this had largely been achieved, although Bunyoro and a host of smaller but no less difficult enemies were still very much present. Even by 1800, certain trends had appeared which did not bode well for the future. One obvious characteristic was the arrogance of the Ganda military ethos, and the over-ambition which it bred. Grandiose territorial aspirations would later lead to the development of a canoe fleet; but even this did not offset problems on land, which reflected both errors on the battlefield and

---

[39] Ibid.: 100.
[40] The importance of this area, especially in the nineteenth century, is examined in Chapter 11.
[41] Kagwa 1972: 52.

tensions at the political and military centre. During the nineteenth century, Buganda's military position gradually became less secure; the determination with which the Ganda defended their earlier gains was increasingly undermined by an almost supine belief in their own superiority and by changes in the balance of political and military power.

'Restless warfare': conquest & consolidation under Kamanya

Because there is much data on Mutesa, and thus on the glorification of militarism which was closely observed during his reign, it might easily be assumed that Mutesa was one of the most militarily successful rulers in Buganda's history.[42] A number of authors have made this assumption, and that Buganda under Mutesa was at the height of its power. Military leadership was not among his talents. Mutesa was, rather, a custodian of earlier gains, and while he appears to have fulfilled this role reasonably well in general – Buganda did not, for example, suffer a territorial collapse – there is clear evidence to suggest that the kingdom by the early 1880s was in military decline. The decline was gradual and was due to a wide range of factors; but the nineteenth century was ushered in by one of the kingdom's more successful military leaders, Kabaka Kamanya (c. 1790s–1820s). He was certainly the last of the kingdom's great warrior-kings, his reign being noted for the feats of the army; we may consider this period to have witnessed the peak of Buganda's regional power. Kamanya's evident appetite for military adventures probably stemmed from his own struggle for power following the death of his father Semakokiro. His eventual success in what seems to have been a grim and protracted civil war was due in large part to the high pedigree of military chiefs who had supported his colours. The *mukwenda*, a veteran of numerous campaigns, among which was the defence of Singo against Kakungulu, was one such supporter, and Kagwa also mentions Kasujju Wakayamba of the *mamba* clan as being among the 'bravest chiefs'. Kamanya's forces 'also contained men who were renowned fighters'. Once the civil war was won, Kamanya, recognizing both his debt to these soldiers and the need for a loyal army, groomed and developed Buganda's military organization.[43] In other words, a powerful and influential military element was incorporated into Kamanya's government.

This influence was reflected in Kamanya's foreign policy. During his reign, there were a number of campaigns against the Soga, and he was clearly seeking to make secure, or even to advance, Buganda's eastern frontier. During this series of wars, Kamanya also moved to crush both disloyalty and cowardice in the army, perhaps indicating a desire to control those elements which may have become excessively powerful. A strong army command was to Kamanya's benefit, but it was also a potential difficulty for him. When a junior chief, Sewankambo, brought

---

[42] See Reid 1999a.
[43] Kagwa 1971: 103.

allegations of cowardice and corruption against his commander, the *sekibobo*, the latter was dismissed and then executed by an enraged Kamanya.[44] Presumably there was evidence to support the allegations, although Kamanya was possibly only too prepared to rid himself of a potentially over-powerful military and political chief. Sewankambo was the beneficiary of the affair, as indeed he may have anticipated, and Kamanya doubtless felt more confident of his loyalty. He was promptly promoted to lead an army against Busongora,[45] part of Buganda's ongoing programme to extend its influence in the west. This campaign, however, was ill-timed: not long after the army's departure to the west, Kakungulu, Kamanya's brother and the scourge of Semakokiro's reign, appeared on the horizon once more at the head of a Nyoro army. Indeed, this may not have been coincidental, while a large Ganda force was heading in the other direction along the Katonga river valley. Before the Ganda could mobilize, Kakungulu had pillaged a district of the kingdom and withdrawn safely.[46] Kakungulu certainly seems to have developed these tactics fruitfully: he later repeated the success, attacking and pillaging an area around Bulondoganyi, killing a number of Ganda in the process. Again, the Ganda army arrived on the scene too late.[47] Such guerrilla tactics suggest that Kakungulu had modified his earlier ambition of winning the Ganda throne, and was now dedicating his career to undermining Ganda security. None the less, Kakungulu's success on this score exposed a weakness in Ganda military organization, a weakness which would become ever more significant as the nineteenth century wore on. The problem which Kakungulu revealed was that the Ganda army was becoming too cumbersome, hierarchical and slow to react; this problem was not addressed, and seems in fact to have become even greater by the time of Mutesa's reign. Weaker enemies who were exposed to the full weight of Buganda's military might would suffer the consequences; but, as will be demonstrated in other circumstances, smaller and apparently less powerful societies in the surrounding region were learning how to avoid being thus exposed, adopting guerrilla tactics and small-scale lightning attacks, or using their knowledge of home geography to conduct solid defence.

Kamanya's response to Kakungulu's attacks was to strengthen the river port of Bulondoganyi by establishing *batongole* there. The precise role of this administrative garrison is unclear, but in the context it seems to have been of a primarily military nature, turning Bulondoganyi into a kind of frontier post representative of the Ganda desire to control an important point of commercial and cultural interchange. Reading the available sources, this seems to be one of the earliest references to a *kabaka* setting up a permanent military post, and suggests that reform was being initiated. We shall return to this process later on, but for now it is sufficient to note that during the nineteenth century, a succession of rulers created more specifically military appointments within the class of *batongole*. This is not to suggest that the *batongole* had previously been purely political or adminis-

44 Ibid.: 104.
45 Ibid.: 105.
46 Ibid.
47 Ibid.

trative, but rather that there was a new military emphasis on a number of appointments during the reigns of Kamanya, Suna and Mutesa.

Notably, Kamanya did not launch a retaliatory attack on Bunyoro; instead, he dispatched Sewankambo, who had by this time established himself as Buganda's premier military commander, to attack the Soga. This conflict was clearly regarded as being of great urgency, as there was 'a concerted campaign throughout the country to recruit as many people for the war as possible'. This was most likely to have been during the early or mid-1820s; notably, we are told that a young prince named Suna, the future *kabaka*, participated in some way.[48] It may seem inexplicable that Kamanya should choose to attack in the direction of Busoga and not Bunyoro; it is conceivable, however, that a number of Soga principalities were in league with Kakungulu and the Nyoro at this stage. As we shall see below, we know that they were allied to Kakungulu later on. Kamanya may therefore have attacked in the east in the belief that the Soga were softer targets than the Nyoro.[49] If so, he was mistaken: following a prolonged and bitter conflict, the Ganda were defeated, suffering the ultimate humiliation of having their war regalia captured by the enemy. This again did not bode well for the future, for despite the 'concerted campaign throughout the country' Buganda was unable to overcome a coalition of regional opponents. A sense of desperation perhaps set in soon after: Kamanya was quickly on the offensive again, and once more Sewankambo led an apparently enormous army, being described by Kagwa as consisting of the 'whole of Buganda', or *Obuganda bwonna*. The scale of the conscription was clearly unusual, and strongly suggests the importance attached by the Ganda to the threat posed by the Nyoro–Soga alliance. On this occasion, however, the Ganda were successful, and the Soga capitulated to Sewankambo's forces. Once more we are told in Kagwa's *Kings* that this marked the end of Soga resistance, reflecting the tendency of the Ganda to declare what amounted to total victory over areas which they were unable to politically or administratively subjugate. In the 1820s, this was clearly not the case, as subsequent events were to prove; rather, Soga chiefs periodically agreed to acknowledge Buganda's hegemony and pay tribute, but this may be seen as a short-term measure to provide relief from Ganda incursions. The Ganda, moreover, seemed content to accept these limited overtures.[50] Both sides implicitly recognized the Nile as a permanent barrier to the formal extension of Ganda territorial control. Buganda's inability to impose a long-term settlement on the Soga was clear by the early nineteenth century; under Kamanya Ganda power may be said to have reached its zenith, but from the zenith it is also possible to identify limits, and these were being forced on the Ganda by this period.

Indeed, shortly after the events described above, the Soga were once again pressing on the eastern frontier, and again allied to the roving Kakungulu. But, although Kamanya sent scouts to ascertain the positions of the enemy forces, he declined to launch an attack: whether he was fearful of engaging his opponents, or whether he did not take the so-called

[48] Ibid.
[49] See also Cohen 1977: 75–7.
[50] Kagwa 1971: 106.

rebellion seriously, is difficult to establish. It seems, however, that for whatever reason Kamanya was reluctant to pursue his wayward brother, and for this period the Ganda appear to have maintained defensive positions.[51] Their stance undermined somewhat the description the Ganda had of Soga activity as a rebellion, suggesting that the region of Busoga was under Ganda control, which it was not; it is true, however, that the Ganda may have viewed the refusal of tribute as a form of rebellion. None the less, in terms of their oral history, the Ganda certainly knew how to construct the language of empire, even while they were unable to extend their domains on the ground. However, a number of campaigns were later carried out against the Soga, and also against Buruli, bordering Lake Kyoga. These were clearly aimed at the maintenance of the external status quo rather than the extension of territorial control, and were also perhaps carried out to appease the influential military element in Kamanya's government. This element appears thus to have been becalmed, as there then ensued what Kagwa describes as 'many peaceful years', during which Kamanya presumably sought to consolidate his position. His last major military outing was probably against Buruli once more, and at the same time Bukedi or Lango. During this conflict, canoes were carried in pieces northward to Lake Kyoga: here it is sufficient to state that Kamanya's use of canoes signified their growing importance to Buganda's military machine, and on this occasion the Ganda were successful.[52] There was an interesting aftermath to this war in that Sewankambo, the veteran army commander, faced popular outrage because he had ordered the canoes to be dragged overland, an act which was seen as breaking the back of the *lubaale* Mukasa. Kamanya withdrew favour from Sewankambo, who was plundered of his war spoils, thus blighting an illustrious career which had spanned much of Kamanya's reign.[53] Notably, Sewankambo had come to hold one of the major political titles in government, that of the *sekibobo*. This suggests that not only were the holders of such titles often expected to have military abilities, but it was also possible for specialized military chiefs to attain political and social positions. As with the political chiefs, however, favour could be withdrawn from such figures remarkably suddenly.

Kagwa offers the following summary of Kamanya's reign:

> [Kamanya] was a brave man and desired to expand his kingdom. He therefore organised several expeditions which followed one another in rapid succession so that the men were always in the field. He himself did not take part in the fighting. His wars came to be known as 'restless warfare', because the men were not permitted to rest and even children of fourteen were required to carry each his two spears and shield to war. By

---

[51] Ibid.: 106–7.

[52] Ibid.: 109–10.

[53] Ibid.: 110–11. It is not clear if this actually ended Sewankambo's career. Kagwa mentions Sewankambo during the early part of the reign of Kabaka Suna, suggesting that he may have survived Kamanya's wrath. Someone of that name, for example, is mentioned as being second-in-command of an army sent by Suna against Sesse, although this might represent something of a demotion. However, it is unclear if Kagwa is referring to the same person: Ibid.: 119, 125.

this means he widened the bounds of his kingdom, which was pressed in the Banyoro ...[54]

Under Kamanya, the process begun in the eighteenth century may be seen to have been completed, whereby the Ganda shifted from having to fight wars to survive to fighting them aggressively and on their own terms. Even so, no state can ever remove the possibility of war through necessity in favour of war through choice. 'Restless warfare' did not involve the establishment of a standing army, but clearly an army was permanently active for a substantial part of Kamanya's reign. The stress laid upon 'restless warfare' by Kagwa suggests perhaps its novelty in the early nineteenth century; the youth of many of the combatants likewise seems to have been without precedent. Many of these conflicts were indeed wars of aggression; yet the sources themselves may lead us to over-simplification. Buganda in this period was faced with a coalition of enemies, an alliance which it was not always able to overcome; the kingdom was in many respects forced on to the defensive by Kakungulu, and Kamanya may have had recourse to such huge levies of men (and children) through sheer desperation to maintain the kingdom's regional position. In general, however, it may be argued that Kamanya was able to hold fast Buganda's position as the dominant military power in the region, even if problems were looming on the horizon. He built on the territorial achievements of the previous century, although it is unclear what territory Kamanya himself added to the kingdom: a later translated edition of Kagwa's *Kings* which was used in the present study suggested that Kamanya took formal control of Buwekula, formerly a Nyoro province to the west of Singo and Gomba.[55] Kamanya, then, carried the kingdom to its peak; but limits and weaknesses also now appeared, in the form of powerful and determined regional opponents and organizational inadequacies.

Stability & decline in the nineteenth century
1: the reign of Suna

Kamanya's son and successor Suna appears to have been less of a warrior. One indigenous account describes him as being 'a peaceful and able ruler', and although courageous, an almost obligatory attribute, 'he was excessively interested in women'.[56] 'Peaceful' is, of course, a relative term, and wars were regularly fought under Suna, most frequently against the Soga beyond the unsettled eastern frontier.[57] Another account lists a series of campaigns against Gambalagala (the Luganda term for the area around the foothills of the Ruwenzoris, and therefore representative of long-distance warfare), Bukedi and Busongora.[58] Like Kamanya, Suna faced the real or perceived problem of cowardice in the army in the early part of his reign; for

---

[54] Kagwa 1934: 43.
[55] Kagwa 1971: 114.
[56] Kagwa 1934: 50–51.
[57] Ibid.: 51.
[58] Kagwa 1971: 115–16.

cowardice in this context, as in the case of Kamanya, we can perhaps read disloyalty and the fear that a military force must not develop as a potential source of opposition or alternative source of authority. This has been a problem with which many of the post-colonial leaders of Uganda are all too familiar. Of course the practice of exposing cowardice in the army was also useful in so far as it reinforced the Ganda military ethos and the idea of the strength of arms, so critical in the pre-colonial nationalism of the Ganda. During the war against Busongora, for example, cowardice was deemed to be rife among the chiefs; the accused were forced to drink doctored beer, though the details of the test are unclear. Those who failed it, however, were condemned as cowards.[59] Thus were Suna's authority and the purity of the military spirit simultaneously strengthened.

Suna's reign was of revolutionary significance in military terms in that it witnessed the introduction of two new types of weaponry.[60] The first was indigenous or at least African in origin: this was a small, light spear, which appears to have been standard equipment from around the 1830s or 1840s onward, although precise dating is clearly out of the question. It first appeared during preparations for a campaign against Busagala, and was reportedly a great success.[61] Its influence on Ganda warfare is unclear, but by its very nature it probably facilitated closer if not hand-to-hand combat, and may have been used in following up an initial, more long-range assault. Its provenance is unclear. Much later in the nineteenth century, Ashe recorded that 'after a Baganda army had been annihilated by the naked Bakede, who only use the assegai or light throwing spear, of which they carry several, the Baganda set to work to make spears like those of the Bakede'.[62] This is intriguing, though uncorroborated, evidence. The weapon sounds strikingly similar to the Zulu stabbing spear which had so forceful an impact on southeastern Africa, although there is clearly a difference between short 'stabbing' and short 'throwing' weapons; the question is, could it have been introduced by northwards-migrating Ngoni groups? On the face of it, this seems unlikely. If we use a very approximate chronological structure based on the indigenous account, it might reasonably be assumed that the weapon was present in Buganda by around 1840. The bulk of the Ngoni, under the leadership of Zwangendaba, crossed the Zambezi river in 1835; they had reached the region of southwestern Tanzania by the late 1840s, and on Zwangendaba's death in 1848 the main Ngoni body broke up, with one faction raiding into the north of Tanzania. This seems somewhat late for the Ngoni to have influenced Ganda weaponry north of Lake Victoria. Nevertheless, as stated above, a precise date for the Ganda development is out of the question. Although nothing can be proven, and while Buganda may indeed have been the scene of a separate and unrelated innovation, the simultaneous appearance of a short stabbing spear in Tanzania and Uganda may not be coincidence. What is certain above all is that, whatever the provenance of the weapon, it had a major impact on Ganda warfare.

[59] Ibid.: 116.
[60] This is also examined in Chapter 10 below.
[61] Kagwa 1971: 117.
[62] Ashe 1889: 297–8.

Yet the second weapon, the firearm, was to have a much more profound long-term impact. It was probably introduced by coastal merchants
in 1844, when the first traders arrived in the kingdom; it is possible that
guns were carried northwards by African merchants before this time, but
no mention is made of what would have been a momentous event in the
indigenous accounts. Within a short time, at least three of these early
visiting merchants participated in a campaign against Bunyoro, having
four guns between them. It is unclear whether they volunteered their
services, or whether Suna requested their assistance, but the potential
power of the gun was clearly demonstrated. The Nyoro must have been
terrified, and it was perhaps the psychological impact which impressed the
Ganda most of all. The campaign was successful: the Nyoro were heavily
defeated and much booty was seized, and Kagwa states that this was
accomplished 'with the aid of their four guns'.[63] As we shall see, the
acquaintance of the Ganda with the firearm was to transform, slowly but
irrevocably, their military organization, and not for the better.

Another military innovation under Suna, which coincided approximately with, but was initially unconnected to, the introduction of the
firearm, was the creation of new *batongole*. The two developments were
later to become closely linked. Suna is credited with the establishment of a
number of new *batongole*, or chieftaincies directly answerable to the *kabaka*.
The nature of these posts is not made entirely clear in the indigenous
sources, but, in addition to their civil and political functions, there appears
to have been a greater emphasis on military duties.[64] Although it is unlikely
that this represented the establishment of a standing army, it clearly
increased the manpower which the *kabaka* had at his disposal. Suna may
well have created these chieftaincies to enlarge the pool of potential soldiers
which he would be in a position to recruit, but the most immediate, and
indeed the most permanent, outcome was the growth of a class of chiefs
who regarded themselves as potentially powerful military and ultimately
political figures. During one war against the Soga, the men of the *ekitongole
ekisigula* raided a small island without the *kabaka*'s prior knowledge. Suna
was enraged by this unsanctioned act of plunder and executed many of
those involved, thereafter launching his own attack on the same island.[65]
This episode indicates the military nature of these new offices. It also
suggests that Suna had created chiefs who were either more powerful than
he had intended, or at least believed themselves to be to some extent
independent of royal authority. There would later be a conjunction of this
process with that of the creation of the *bagalagala*, or privileged servitude.
Both groups would come to enjoy both political and military power; both
groups developed an arrogance and sense of immunity which were detrimental to the collective ethos; and both groups would come to be identified
with the cult of the firearm, which, in their role as military chiefs, served to
undermine the success of Ganda arms in the later nineteenth century.

There appears to have been a period of relative peace, possibly in the
late 1840s, after which, and in the later years of his reign, Suna became

[63] Kagwa 1971: 123.
[64] Ibid.: 124. For an analysis of this development, see for example Southwold 1961.
[65] Kagwa 1971: 128.

somewhat more aggressive and fought some of his more notable wars. Among the relatively minor campaigns were attacks on Sesse and several of the islands just off the shores of Buganda and Busoga. It was no coincidence that these were carried out by a *kabaka* noted for his interest in developing the Ganda navy and, simultaneously, long-distance lake trade routes:[66] here it is sufficient to state that, with the arrival of the first coastal merchants in Buganda and their increasing presence south of the lake, the 1840s saw the beginning of a period in which waterborne communications took on a particular importance. Suna recognized this, and his campaigns along and off Buganda's lakeshore reflected a concerted effort to secure Ganda control of the north end of the lake and, thereby, of lake traffic. These campaigns, taken as a whole, are a good example of how war was expected to bring both short- and long-term gain: as slaves and other booty were acquired, the Ganda were attempting to improve their overall economic and strategic position. During the latter stages of his reign, Suna was increasingly preoccupied with taking full advantage of the southbound trade routes, and, like Semakokiro against the Ziba half a century earlier, was prepared to use military force to secure Buganda's interests. One such expedition was against Koki, on the Kagera river, where commercial interests were of the utmost importance. Suna apparently, and unusually, led the army in person. The campaign yielded much livestock,[67] but undoubtedly its primary function was to remind the peoples of the western shore of the lake that Buganda aimed to be paramount in the region, and that the *kabaka* was capable of punishing anyone who appeared to forget this.

In a similar vein, another war of significance took place in the mid-1850s, and was ostensibly motivated by sheer avarice. A report reached the capital 'that a Muzong'ola called Kataba had a palace with all the porches made of copper'. Suna dispatched an army – actually to Kiziba, on the southern bank of the Kagera river, and not, as one might assume, to Busongora – apparently against the advice of his chiefs, who feared the effects of famine and disease, which were then prevalent in Buganda. Indeed, the attack failed, according to Kagwa, largely, it seems, because of the soldiers' hunger.[68] The incidence of 'famine' is noteworthy in itself, and clearly illustrates the obvious point that the success of the army was as dependent on an ample harvest in the soldiers' homesteads as on the quality of their weaponry or fighting spirit. Stanley's version is somewhat different, and he relates that 'Kytawa, the mighty king of Uzongora', was eventually defeated by Suna.[69] Kagwa's telling of the tale is clearly allegorical. Copper may be seen as a symbol of coastal trade, the effects of which had clearly begun to be felt among the states west of Lake Victoria, such as Kiziba. We have already observed, in an earlier chapter, how much prestige was attached to copper, which was associated with political authority. Suna's attack may have been an attempt either to warn the Ziba not to partake in the commercial system which he himself sought to

---

[66] See also Reid 1998b.
[67] Kagwa 1971: 131–2.
[68] Ibid.: 134–5.
[69] Stanley 1878: I, 375–6. It is unclear why Kiziba and Busongora are confused in these accounts: see for example Kiwanuka's notes in Kagwa 1971: 100.

control, or at least to demonstrate to the agents of coastal commerce that it would be better for all concerned if they dealt only with him. Successive Ganda rulers could not rid themselves of the fear that this new imported wealth, and the improvements in material culture, not to mention prestige, which it brought, might be shared between weak and strong in the region. This fear was even more characteristic of Mutesa's reign.

Stability & decline in the nineteenth century
2: the reign of Mutesa

Suna died during or shortly after the 'copper war', and it fell to Mutesa to ensure that Buganda's interests were protected in the context of the new world advancing from the south and, to a lesser extent, from the north. Again, many more military encounters are recorded for Mutesa's reign than for any reign previously. It is possible that this accounts for the higher proportion of wars between the 1860s and 1880s which seem to have ended in failure; but this phenomenon is none the less impossible to ignore, and rather seems to suggest military decline. Mutesa conducted enough successful campaigns to maintain Buganda's position in the region; in the early years of his reign, these included wars with Bunyoro, Buruli and Busoga. Yet the number of failed expeditions suggests that Buganda was over-reaching itself in the second half of the nineteenth century. Early in Mutesa's reign, for example, he dispatched an army to aid the ruler of Karagwe, Rumanika, in fighting a rebellion. The details are obscure, and Rumanika was clearly ultimately successful, as he ruled Karagwe until 1878, but not before the Ganda force was defeated and ignominiously ejected from the country.[70] In the mid-1860s, the Ganda also suffered a series of defeats at the hands of the Soga, although in the last of these campaigns Mutesa achieved some success, thus at least maintaining the kingdom's eastern frontier.[71]

Over the next few years, Mutesa did have more success, notably in an attack on Busagala, which reportedly, and again unusually, he led himself,[72] and his intervention in the Nyoro civil war, in which he backed the winning side led by Kabarega.[73] Yet two wars in the 1870s tell a different story. The first can be seen in the context of Mutesa's recurrent attacks on Koki and his attempt to secure influence in Karagwe; these represented the ongoing effort to strengthen Buganda's control of trade routes both on the lake and to the west of it. An expedition was planned against Buzinza, at the south end of the lake. The army, however, 'stopped on the way because it was too large and therefore it could not get enough food to eat'.[74] There were clearly immense logistical problems in the movement of large numbers of soldiers over long distances; these problems

---

[70] Kagwa 1971: 153.
[71] Ibid.: 156.
[72] Ibid.: 158.
[73] Ibid.: 159. Even so, the success in Bunyoro turned out to be bitter-sweet, as Kabarega was not as favourable to Ganda interests as Mutesa presumably anticipated.
[74] Ibid.: 163.

must have been particularly galling to Mutesa, who was repeatedly frustrated in his attempts to extend Buganda's control over an ever larger and more lucrative area.[75] The development of the navy, as we shall see below, represented an attempt to compensate for military failure on land.

The second war was the one so dramatically described by Stanley against the island of Buvuma in 1875. The explorer's account was, as ever, written with literary effect in mind, but, even accepted as a rough impression, it makes sorry reading from Buganda's standpoint. Here was a war personally overseen by Mutesa, involving at the most conservative estimate several thousand Ganda soldiers, which ended in ignominy for the most powerful state in the region. While it is true that Buvuma did eventually offer to pay tribute, the manner in which this was done suggests that they were by no means a beaten people. The Vuma, over a period of several weeks, successfully repelled wave after wave of well-armed Ganda, the latter led by some of the most prominent military chiefs in the kingdom.[76] Mutesa's reaction to continued failure, again even allowing for Stanley's sometimes histrionic reportage, reveals an angry and almost resigned frustration, in a speech redolent with poignant rhetoric:

> 'Wherein have I been unkind to you, that you will not fight for me, for my slaves who were sent to Usoga have returned saying there was not a man but either had joined me or had already joined the Wavuma? Who gave you those clothes that you wear? Who gave you those guns you have? Was it not I? Did Suna my father give his chiefs such fine things as I give? No; yet they fought for him ... Am I not Kabaka? Is this not Uganda, as well as my capital? Have I not my army here? And you, Katekiro, were you not a peasant before I dressed you and set you up as chief of Uddu? And you, Chambarango, who made you a chief? And you, Mkwenda, and you, Kimbugwe, Kitunzi, Kaeema, Kangau, Kagu, speak, was it not Mtesa who made you chiefs? Were you princes, that you came to be made chiefs, or peasants whom it was my pleasure to make chiefs?'[77]

This is a telling oration. It may be that Buganda's inability to over-whelm Buvuma was not, in the grand scheme of things, very important, but the island continued to be not only a thorn in Buganda's side but also a serious impediment to its control of the northern shore through the 1870s and 1880s. It is clear that there were limitations to Buganda's military potency. As we have already noted, these limitations had been realized several decades earlier, when the Soga blocked further advance to the east, but in the second half of the nineteenth century they were particularly relevant and, indeed, more obvious. The tactics of blending defensiveness with sporadic guerrilla activity which characterized Buvuma's soldiery in 1875 and on other occasions in which the Vuma clashed with the Ganda lead one to ask questions about Buganda's own tactics and military organization. The Ganda army seems to have become excessively organized, burdened by hierarchy and obsessed with structural detail; this may have been a reflection of the socio-political system in the same period.

---

[75] For a fuller analysis of some military and diplomatic aspects of this period, see also Reid, 1998a.
[76] Stanley 1878: I, 304ff.
[77] Ibid.: 330.

It is striking that a mightily regimented army could not defeat a comparatively tiny force consisting, essentially, of fishermen. A less cumbersome and more flexible Ganda force might have succeeded. Similarly, the army sent to attack Buzinza was the product of an ambitious plan, but the plan failed to some extent because of its sheer size and unwieldiness. It is worth noting that, in Mirambo and his force of Nyamwezi, we have an example of a smaller army, well structured but operating in smaller units, covering an arguably far wider area than Buganda ever managed to do. The same might be said of Mirambo's contemporary and neighbour, Nyungu-ya-Mawe.[78]

It is true that the Ganda continued to achieve success with smaller armies and, possibly, in more prolonged campaigns, although on occasion they also had success with smaller strikes. The war against Busoga and Buvuma in 1879 appears to have involved at the most some 10,000 soldiers – considerably lower than Stanley's estimate for the 1875 war of 100,000–200,000 – and lasted at least six months, during which slaves were sent back from the battle area.[79] Indeed, the events of 1879 prompted the French missionary Livinhac to declare that hardly a week went by without an army returning with the spoils of war.[80] The successes of the late 1870s – the campaigns against Busoga, as well as a strike force against the island of Ukerewe in the south of the lake – spurred Mutesa once more on to greater things. The army returned from Busoga in September 1879. Within four months, another force had been dispatched, this time apparently to Rwanda,[81] an expedition which in terms of distance alone was a major undertaking. It involved 'large quantities of warriors', and its purpose, according to Pearson, was 'to bring back cattle', although it seems there had been a diplomatic dispute between the two kingdoms.[82] Details are non-existent, but the timing of the war suggests that it may have been connected to the movement of the first coastal merchants towards the borders of Rwanda in the late 1870s. Two months later, Pearson reported news 'of the utter rout of the Waganda and that the remnant of the army was on its way back despoiled rather than bringing back cattle & slaves'.[83] It is unclear whether the Ganda actually reached Rwanda; indeed, few wars between the two states are recorded.[84] Yet this was clearly an ambitious long-distance campaign which had failed miserably. As news of the calamity filtered in, Pearson was moved to write that 'the prestige of Waganda warfare has begun to fade'.[85] It would have been clear to Mutesa that Buganda had once again over-reached itself.

These setbacks did not, however, slow down the frequency of military

[78] See Roberts, 'The Nyamwezi' and Shorter, 'The Kimbu', in Roberts 1968: 96–116, 117–50; also Reid 1998a, *passim*.
[79] CMS CA6/010/48 Felkin's Journal, 14 February 1879, 22 April 1879; CA6/019/14 Pearson to Wright, 10 March 1879; CA6/019/15 Pearson to Wright, 29 September 1879.
[80] White Fathers: C13/1 Livinhac to Lavigerie, 2 July 1879.
[81] CMS CA6/019/18 Pearson to Wright, 7 January 1880.
[82] Ibid.
[83] CMS CA6/019/19 Pearson to Wright, 5 March 1880.
[84] Neither the attack by the Ganda in 1880 nor the dispute which preceded it is mentioned in the major works on Rwanda: see Kagame 1963; Vansina 1962a.
[85] CMS CA6/019/19 Pearson to Wright, 5 March 1880.

expeditions during the early 1880s. Indeed, the ailing *kabaka*, in the twilight of his reign, actually increased the number of campaigns in search of popularity and, no doubt, security at home.[86] Zimbe attests to this:

> [Mutesa] understood people were tired of him and therefore that it was possible to assassinate him. He saw that there were many people, that the princes could form an army, that the men in the homes of his chiefs could do so too. To decrease these numbers he decided to wage several wars and in this way put off the hatred they bore him by providing them with an occupation. Thus, 5 wars were carried out against Ankole, Bunyoro, Busoga, Bukedi, Toro and Kalagwe ...[87]

The range of these conflicts is staggering, covering as they do almost every stretch of Buganda's frontier. This is indicative of the sense of desperation behind them; yet Zimbe, whose own bias is revealed, suggests that the military policy proved unsuccessful as 'his men were always victorious and returned without loss of numbers'. The veracity of this last assertion is open to serious doubt: missionary accounts suggest that in the early 1880s, the Ganda met with extreme difficulties in their intervention in the politics of Karagwe, and a heavy defeat was inflicted by the Nyoro.[88] But Zimbe's earlier comments are telling. Mutesa was faced with increasing failure abroad; the resultant restlessness at the capital was also doubtless connected to his prolonged illness[89] and his perceived inability to take control of the new influences penetrating his kingdom. He was not only trying to divert attention and energies away from home; he was making an increasingly desperate search for some great success abroad which would rekindle respect for and loyalty to the *kabaka*.

Mutesa feared what were perceived to be growing pockets of alternative authority, in the form of ambitious young men, often identifying with one or other of the religious factions at the royal court,[90] armed with guns, the weapon which had come to symbolize power, freedom, adventure and escape from inhibiting tradition. Guns may not have been effectively used on a practical level before around 1890, but on another level they may be seen to have had only a detrimental effect on Buganda's military performance. Ironically, perhaps, soldiers armed with spears and shields had rarely been anything other than loyal to the *kabaka*; by the early 1880s, many younger chiefs, if not ordinary peasant-soldiers, were acquiring firearms. Access to guns, originally the consequence of royal favour but increasingly the result of commercial access, bred arrogance and a lack of regard for traditional authority. Moreover, the traits of personal courage and reputation as a warrior were being increasingly ignored in the 1880s. The men who formed the military elite now had guns rather than spears;

---

[86] For a fuller analysis, see Reid 1999a: *passim*.

[87] Zimbe 1939: 82.

[88] CMS G3 A6/0 1883/104 O'Flaherty to Wigram, 19 June 1883.

[89] Mutesa may at this time have been suffering from psychological disorders as a result of syphilis, and encroaching madness would have weakened his authority even more than any physical ailment: see Reid 1999a: 292–4.

[90] See Twaddle 1993: *passim*, for a thorough account of these developments. Chapter 1 of the present study also offers a rather more brief survey of the religious factionalism and the literature dealing with this aspect of late nineteenth-century Ganda politics.

yet this elite had acquired their weaponry through court intrigue and patronage, as well as through commerce, not through proving their valour and worth in the tradition of Kibuka, previously the essence of the Ganda military ethos. This trend undoubtedly weakened the calibre of the Ganda army, quite apart from the fact that few knew how to use the gun effectively, and that the guns themselves were often sub-standard. This is returned to in the next chapter.

The proposed attack on Mirambo clearly shows that Buganda's projects were now considerably greater than its ability to carry them out.[91] The plan was stimulated by the perceived need for ever greater control of East Africa's trade network. Mackay, who also spent time among the Nyamwezi, believed that such an attack would probably come to grief; Mutesa's soldiers were acquainted with neither the territory south of the lake, nor the strength of Mirambo's forces.[92] In July 1880, Pearson learnt that an expedition against Mirambo was 'in active preparation', and that the *katikiro* had been appointed to lead it, joined by 'all the great chiefs'. The East African Arab community was also to play a significant role. A mammoth operation was envisaged, with the Ganda in league with the Arabs of Unyanyembe, the latter intending to attack Mirambo from the south and east.[93] Antipathy towards Mirambo among both the Ganda and the Arabs stemmed from his stranglehold on key trade routes between Karagwe and the coast. Ill-feeling dated back to 1871, when the Nyamwezi warlord had made his presence felt west of Unyanyembe. There is no evidence to suggest that an attack on the scale of that proposed in 1880 was envisaged nearly ten years earlier, although in 1872 David Livingstone, who was then at Tabora, recorded that soldiers had arrived from Buganda to aid the Arabs against Mirambo.[94] Reports of similar activity reached the coast, prompting one consular official to write that 'the King of Uganda is dispatching a force of 17,000 men to assist in carrying on the war against Mirambo'.[95] But the grand assault planned in 1880–81 proved to be little more than bellicose rhetoric. Mutesa could take comfort from the fact that Mirambo had made strenuous efforts to placate him. Several years earlier, Stanley had witnessed Mirambo's ambassadors 'kneel and tender their allegiance' to the king of Buganda,[96] which was classic East African diplomacy; and towards the end of 1881 it was reported that the Nyamwezi leader 'was willing to accept Mutesa's Brotherhood'.[97] This did not disguise the fact that the proposed attack on Mirambo ended up looking like a gigantic bluff. Buganda was no more

---

[91] Again, see also Reid 1998a: 82–5.

[92] Ibid. Mackay's assertions are not entirely correct. There is evidence that the Ganda had some knowledge of the area south of the lake, which they had visited in both a military and a commercial capacity; moreover, they may well have met with Mirambo's forces in the 1870s, and would at least have been possessed of detailed intelligence regarding the latter's military organization.

[93] CMS G3 A6/0 1881/22 Pearson to Mackay, 29 July 1880.

[94] Waller 1874: II, 226–9.

[95] *British Parliamentary Papers Relating to the Slave Trade*, Vol. 54, First Section, Prideaux to Derby, 21 May 1874.

[96] Stanley & Neame 1961: 71.

[97] CMS G3 A6/0 1882/14 O'Flaherty to Wigram, 25 December 1881.

capable of subduing Mirambo's power than that of Rwanda.

It may seem apt, therefore, that Mutesa's last major campaign ended in a rout. The *kabaka*, close to death, sent out an army against the 'Kedi',[98] beyond Lake Kyoga, although the army itself was bitterly divided over the predictions of the spirit mediums that the campaign would end in disaster; indeed, we have already noted this war in examining the role of such spiritual advisers. Although a number of soldiers remained loyal to the *kabaka*, the commander and several other chiefs abandoned the attack, severely depleting the force. The Kedi attacked and killed a large number of Ganda, including several of the remaining chiefs, and the expedition collapsed in failure.[99] In the middle of 1884, Ashe, presumably describing the same conflict, reported that a Ganda war party had been 'cut to pieces'.[100] This is confirmed by O'Flaherty's description in July 1884 of a campaign in which a 'large army' was sent in support of the Soga chief Wakoli 'to pillage the Basoga & the Bakedi not subject to him', an occurrence apparently not uncommon. Initially successful, the Ganda were attacked on the way back, laden 'with much spoil & slaves', by a Kedi force. The result was that '[s]ix chiefs & 46 subchiefs & many, many of the King's pages & innumerable Bakopi or peasants were killed'. O'Flaherty was happy to announce that he had dissuaded Mutesa from launching a revenge attack on Christian grounds;[101] the *kabaka* was probably even happier to use the *muzungu*'s arguments as an excuse. Mutesa lived long enough to punish the commander for his 'timidity'; but, as Zimbe tells us, '[t]his was the last war of Mutesa the conqueror for his illness became worse and soon he died'.[102] The description used by Zimbe is certainly a misnomer. Mutesa had presided over a clear decline, and Buganda's position was significantly weaker in 1884 than it had been in 1857, the year Mutesa had succeeded Suna. Miti was closer to the mark than Zimbe when he wrote that '[t]here were also a number of military expeditions in [Mutesa's] last years, not all of which were victories, though in the main they sustained Buganda's authority among surrounding territories'.[103] There is something glum in this statement which suggests a harsher reality.

An interesting aspect of Mutesa's reign was the infrequency of military engagements between Buganda and Bunyoro; this was a period in which relations between the two countries were characterized by a kind of cold war. Since the later years of Suna's reign, Buganda's military preoccupations had moved southward, despite the presence of the Egyptians to the north. Out of 25 references to wars by missionaries between 1878 and 1883, for example, only three relate to Bunyoro. This is in stark contrast to Kagwa's writings, which are replete with references to wars with Bunyoro during the eighteenth and early nineteenth centuries. This comparison is

---

[98] The term 'Kedi' probably refers to the people of either Lango or Teso. As Kiwanuka points out, the Ganda often used descriptions such as 'Bakedi', 'Basoga' and 'Banyoro' indiscriminately: see Kiwanuka's notes in Kagwa 1971: 98.
[99] Zimbe 1939: 85–6.
[100] CMS G3 A6/0 1884/111 Ashe to Lang, ? June 1884.
[101] CMS G3 A6/0 1884/115 O'Flaherty to Wigram, ? July 1884.
[102] Zimbe 1939: 86.
[103] Miti 1938: I, 224.

purely impressionistic, of course, but it does further suggest that Buganda was attempting to assert itself to the south as long-distance commerce expanded. An additional factor, perhaps, was Nyoro resurgence during this period, and the Ganda may have begun to shy away from confrontation with its increasingly powerful northern neighbour. Relations between the two kingdoms were, however, in perpetual flux during the 1870s and 1880s, in large part because of the shared fear of the foreign power approaching from the north. At the end of 1879, Mutesa had declared himself ready to stand alongside Kabarega in order to expel the Sudanese from Mruli,[104] although in the end Kabarega appears to have achieved this by himself. Within the space of a few months in 1880, Kabarega had wanted to launch a massive attack on Buganda, and then had requested Buganda's assistance and even shelter against the Sudanese, which Mutesa had promised to provide. Mutesa had long feared the armed presence of the Egyptians and Sudanese to the north, even though, in true Machiavellian style, he had employed a number of them as drill-instructors. In 1882, reports abounded that the route north to Lado was closed due to the 'constant wars' between the Nyoro and the Sudanese;[105] Mutesa must have listened to these reports with growing apprehension.

From the end of Mutesa's reign onward, however, there appears to have been a resurgence of conflict with Bunyoro; Kabarega may have detected that Buganda was weaker than it had been for several decades, while taking advantage of the fact that a young and inexperienced *kabaka* had just taken power. During the 1886–8 period, a number of particularly bloody encounters with Bunyoro were reported; for the Ganda, these were at best inconclusive, and at worst further evidence of Ganda decline. In 1886, Lourdel, who received his information from the Christian 'readers' who frequently participated in these conflicts, noted that Bunyoro was becoming more powerful and would soon be able to hold its own against Buganda.[106] This betrays, perhaps, the fears of the soldiers themselves. In mid-1887, there were rumours that Mwanga was proposing an alliance with Kabarega, with the intention of attacking Stanley, who was then leading the expedition to 'rescue' Emin Pasha.[107] It is difficult to know whether there was any truth behind these rumours and counter-rumours. Joint action never materialized, however, and Kabarega himself vacillated for some time during the Ganda 'religious wars' before finally deciding to send armed support to Kalema, the *kabaka* installed by the 'Muslim' party of Buganda, in 1890. This was a reversion to the pre-colonial device of supporting one side against another in a neighbouring kingdom's internal strife, as Mutesa had done when Kabarega himself was fighting for power 20 years earlier.[108] But events overtook Kabarega, and he quickly found himself confronted by an enemy with the support of the British, who may be seen as arriving in timely fashion to rescue Buganda from possible military and territorial collapse. The Ganda, adaptable as ever, seized the

[104] White Fathers: Rubaga Diary 1/19 December 1879.
[105] White Fathers: C14/130 Lourdel to his brother, 4 May 1882.
[106] White Fathers: C14/64 Lourdel to Levesque, 28 June 1886.
[107] White Fathers: C14/178 Lourdel to Superior-General, 1 July 1887.
[108] White Fathers: C14/192 Lourdel to Superior-General, 25 January 1890.

great opportunity thus presented, despite misgivings in certain quarters, and were able to once again impose their military and political influence over much of the region, notably in the seizure of Nyoro territories, the 'lost counties', which they claimed as their own. If the British had arrived ten years later, events might have been very different, and there might be a 'Republic of Unyoro' in the region at the time of writing rather than the 'Uganda' which serves as a monument to Ganda military good fortune.

Ten

Developments in Organization, Tactics & Weaponry

In the previous chapter, an outline of basic chronology in terms of key wars and general trends was presented; in this chapter, we examine the structure of the army, its tactics and weaponry, the ways in which it was recruited, and of course changes in all of these as far as they can be identified by the late nineteenth century. In this chapter, we shall also return to several themes alluded to above, notably the development of a class of chiefs and pages equipped with firearms who came to be seen as the new elite, and who can also be studied in the context of the growth of what was at least nominally a royal bodyguard. Such themes, as well as the impact of the firearm, are critical to our understanding of Ganda military development in the nineteenth century, which is itself central to a study of the material basis of the state. Other aspects of military organization lend themselves less easily to the charting of change over time, due to the silence of my available sources, most of which tend to depict the army's structure as static over several centuries. This it almost certainly was not, and it may be assumed that changes in political organization, as well as in foreign relations and the external environment generally, would have been reflected in the structure of the army and in the nature of its recruitment.

Structure & hierarchy

The basic mechanism of recruitment, levies made by regional chiefs, probably dates back to the kingdom's foundation. It seems logical, then, that as the *kabaka* assumed ever greater political control, the concept of a supra-regional army, marching under the colours of regional chiefs but with the *kabaka* at its head, developed accordingly. Even by the nineteenth century, however, armies were still to a considerable extent regionally based, with particular districts being selected to contribute soldiers for particular wars, in much the same way as taxes and labour were organized. Regions within the *ssaza* system remained the basic units of military organization, but the increasing authority and importance – both functional and symbolic – of the *kabaka* ensured coherence and unity of purpose. Exceptional instances of wayward commanders and local initiatives notwithstanding, this system had reached a peak of efficiency by the early nineteenth century. It is possible that, at the outset of this process, the *kabaka* commanded his own private army, recruited in a manner similar to those of the regional chiefs; in this sense, a royal bodyguard had probably existed since before 1800. During the nineteenth century, this bodyguard, which may be regarded as something of an elite force, was developed by both Mutesa and Mwanga and seems to have been merged with the growing number of armed pages prevalent in the capital. It is important to see these men as distinct from the regular military chiefs, most of whom, in times of peace, held major political positions, often as *ssaza* governors. These belonged to the longer-standing military establishment. The increasing preoccupation with firearms, the lavish favour poured upon young and usually militarily inexperienced pages, and the consequent rivalry between them and the more professional war chiefs were factors in Buganda's declining military competence immediately before the colonial period. The *kabaka*'s ability to appoint chiefs who would be loyal to him seems to have served Buganda well in the seventeenth, eighteenth and early nineteenth centuries; ironically, this system would ultimately serve to undermine the kingdom's fighting capacity, as loyalty to the *kabaka* was increasingly lauded above military professionalism, while in time such loyalty could not necessarily be relied upon.

With the exception of a possible royal bodyguard, there was no standing army in pre-colonial Buganda, and therefore the size of armies varied considerably according to need. Depending on the scale of the war or the particular expedition, they usually numbered several thousand, although contemporary (but not necessarily eye-witness) reports often offer more extravagant estimates. In the mid-1850s, for example, Burton was told by his Arab informants that the Ganda army numbered 'at least 300,000 men'.[1] Buganda's population could in theory have yielded such a figure, but it is extremely unlikely that an army of this size was ever operational. Stanley was told that Mutesa once sent 100,000 men against Busongora to the west.[2] This again sounds exaggerated, although the idea that the Ganda army was large in an interlacustrine context is effectively conveyed. The largest first-hand estimate was made, again, by Stanley, who on the eve of the war against Buvuma in August 1875 reckoned that Mutesa had mustered a force of 150,000 men.[3] The desire for dramatic effect undoubtedly prompted Stanley to suggest such an improbable figure, although he estimated that Mutesa's army of 125,000 had been bolstered by 'quotas furnished by Karagwe, Uzongora, Ukedi, Usoga, Sesse, and the islands of the lake', these totalling around 25,000 men.[4] The extent to which Ganda armies were strengthened by foreign regiments is unclear; it may have been a common enough practice, although the

---

[1] Burton 1860: II, 189.
[2] Bennett 1970: 266, 271.
[3] Stanley 1878: I, 304.
[4] Ibid.: 306.

collaboration of some of the states mentioned by Stanley seems unlikely. The size of armies also leads us to the question of casualty figures; unfortunately there is almost no evidence for this. We may state, very obviously, that, just as the size of armies varied considerably, so did the number of casualties in particular engagements. Taking into account small populations, and the frequency with which wars were fought in the nineteenth century, it may be assumed that casualty figures were usually small, at least with regard to deaths, as in terms of demographics alone the region could not have sustained a high death toll. The sources, especially those of indigenous provenance, occasionally offer phrases such as 'many were killed' or 'there were a great many deaths', but these are clearly unhelpful, as they are both relative and of course imprecise. People clearly died, but rarely, it seems, in sufficient numbers to dissuade the authorities from fighting, or from pursuing war rather than peace if the former suited their interests better. For an army to suffer large casualties was sometimes taken as an indication of defeat, as loss of people seems to have been regarded as much more significant than the failure to capture substantial amounts of booty.

The lack of a standing army meant that there was no title denoting overall military command. Instead, chiefs, often the governors of *ssaza*s, were appointed on merit to lead campaigns; it is clear that particular chiefs built up reputations as soldiers and leaders of men, qualities which often led to political promotion itself. In the mid-1850s, the *sekibobo*, as already noted, seems to have had such a reputation. In the early 1860s, a chief whom Grant names 'Kamaraviona' was noted as an outstanding military commander.[5] This is a corruption of the title *kamalabyonna*, a variation of *katikiro* or 'chief minister'.[6] Stanley's description of the war against Buvuma in 1875 provides some valuable data on the organization of the army in action. In the mass parade which preceded hostilities, Stanley noted the contingent commanded by the *mukwenda*, who guarded 'the frontier between the Katonga valley and Willimiesi against the Wanyoro'.[7] 'Willimiesi' is a corruption of Bulemezi, the neighbouring province to that of the *mukwenda*, Singo. The *mukwenda* is described as being 'accomplished with the spear' and as having 'much experience in wars', and was clearly a respected military figure. Stanley also mentioned the 'old general Kangau', whose normal military brief was the defence of Bulemezi.[8] In 1862 Speke also wrote of 'Congow, a young general, who once led an army into Unyoro',[9] and in 1874 Chaillé-Long described 'Kongowee' as the 'General-in-Chief of the army'.[10] While the *kangawo* mentioned by Stanley and Chaillé-Long was probably the same person, it would seem that several men held the title during the 1860s and 1870s.[11] Any civil chief or *ssaza* governor, then, could also be an army commander, and again it is likely that many attained political importance as a result of their exploits on the battlefield.

[5] Grant 1864: 220, 231.
[6] *Kamalabyonna*: lit., 'finishes-all-things'. See Murphy 1972: 150.
[7] Stanley 1878: I, 306.
[8] Ibid.
[9] Speke 1863b: 359.
[10] Chaillé-Long 1876: 102, 128.
[11] Kagwa states that Mutesa had five *bakangawo* during his reign: Kagwa 1971: 185.

The selection of command was mostly based on merit and personal courage, at least up until the late nineteenth century; this may have been true of the lower ranks as well.

It is significant that the governors of Singo and Bulemezi should be described to Stanley not as the pillars of government which they undoubtedly were, but as military commanders in charge of certain stretches of frontier. This is likely to have been a form of war-speak: in wartime, the *kangawo* was not only the chief of Bulemezi but also the defender of the kingdom along the border covered by his province. His position, as it were, underwent militarization. It is also worth noting that his military responsibilities were described in purely defensive terms: this is probably less to do with a desire to conceal the kingdom's conquering ethos than the need to emphasize sovereignty and the territorial unity of the state. It is also worth considering that, while the description of regional chiefs as 'defenders of frontiers' may have reflected their skills in war, it may equally have reflected only their theoretical responsibility for the military operations and recruitment within a particular district. Although it was generally the case that such positions were militarized, however, it is clear that in 1875 both the *mukwenda* and the *kangawo* were particularly honoured military leaders. What is also clear is that the position of commander itself was highly coveted, largely because it carried the potential for great financial reward and the opportunity for political promotion based on the prestige of a successful campaign; direct royal command was, for much of the nineteenth century at least, relatively rare.

In his description of the war against Buvuma, Stanley noted that just about every major provincial chief held a position of command. Besides the *kangawo* and the *mukwenda*, mention is made of the *pokino* (who at this time also held the post of *katikiro*), the *kaima*, the *kitunzi*, the *kasujju*, the *kago*, the *kimbugwe* and the *katambala*. Even Mutesa's mother and uncle were represented by officers, having placed forces in the field.[12] Roscoe claimed that the *katikiro* and the *kimbugwe* had additional responsibilities in that they were consulted by the *kabaka* from the outset as to the number of soldiers required, and also on the choice of commander,[13] although it is likely that the *kabaka* himself had the final say in this matter. What Stanley appears to describe, then, is a truly national army, but this may not have always been the case. Armies often consisted of soldiers from only a few districts; it may even be that Mutesa laid on this great military display purely for the benefit of his European guest, although this seems unlikely.

It was the stress on merit which made Buganda such an effective military power at its zenith; conversely, it was the gradual disregard for merit which contributed to the downturn in the kingdom's military fortunes. As with the hierarchy of command, so it was with the rank-and-file soldiers: Stanley, for example, noted 'about 2000 chosen warriors'.[14] The presence of soldiers ranked higher than others on the basis of their specific abilities on the battlefield suggests a level of professionalism even

---

[12] Stanley 1878: I, 305.
[13] Roscoe 1911: 348.
[14] Stanley 1878: I, 306.

though no professional army existed. Indigenous histories are replete with tales of individual derring-do by men who raised themselves to prominence through military endeavour.[15] Rank-and-file soldiers took up the colours of their local chief and offered their services for the forthcoming war. This apparently simple procedure was multifaceted. Soldiering was one of the most important services offered by a tenant to a patron. There was a risk of death, of course, but, for the farmer as much as the chief, war was an economic adventure, and even a semi-successful campaign would yield some form of booty, as we have already noted. The fact that a tax was often levied on those who stayed at home was an additional, though negative, economic incentive to participation;[16] indeed the existence of such a tax suggests something of a voluntary dimension in recruitment, although this doubtless varied according to circumstances. The possibility of social advancement was another incentive, again already noted. These motives to fight, however, seem to some extent to apply only to a society in full control of external circumstances. In very general terms, up to the reign of Kamanya armies were frequently raised to defend the kingdom from outside attack, a very different form of motivation. For at least 200 years, war was a means of survival for the Ganda, and for much of that time they were militarily inferior to Bunyoro. During the seventeenth and eighteenth centuries, however, military organization had become a means not only of the extension of national power, but of the accumulation of wealth and the maintenance of a favourable external status quo. For much of the nineteenth century, war was a reaction to impulses within the state rather than threats from without. The kingdom's military decline modified this somewhat, as external threats once again became real, especially in the second half of the nineteenth century. But, in whatever ways the nature of both individual and collective motivation changed over time, the philosophy of masculinity was a binding force; ultimately, men and war were as naturally bound as women and the bearing of children.

Structure & tactics

Roscoe drew a firm distinction between actual soldiers, who are depicted as being at least semi-professional, single-minded and, above all, out-

---

[15] Often these men are described as having phenomenal physical strength, able single-handedly to fight off thousands of enemy soldiers; interestingly, they are also often associated with periods of military hardship and national crisis. Kibuka is the most celebrated example of this. Another notable instance is provided by Stanley, who was told of the achievements of Kasindula during the reign of Suna. Although Kasindula was a sub-chief in Kyagwe, he 'had neither pride of birth nor riches to boast of'; determined to demonstrate his loyalty to Suna, he gathered a small army and defeated the Soga in a series of battles. Returning to Suna's capital with his booty, he is credited with a stirring speech: 'My dear Lord, Namujurilwa [the *pokino*] and Setuba [either *luwekula* or *mukwenda*?] are great chiefs, and stand in your presence daily, but I am only a Mtongoleh under Sekebobo. I have neither farm nor house, wife nor child, and my only wealth consists of my spear and my shield, and my only cloth is this rotten mbugu. Namujurilwa and Setuba brought slaves and cattle by hundreds, but the kopi Kasindula brings his thousands to Suna. Behold where they stand! Kasindula gives them all to Suna ...' See Stanley 1878: I, 372–5. This also seems to be an example of the local initiative alluded to earlier.

[16] Kagwa 1934: 94.

standing specimens of manhood, and the general rabble who accompanied the former to war but who had a somewhat lower status. He explains that '[t]hough warriors were armed with spears and shields, peasants who joined them as bearers or as followers had only clubs or heavy sticks; these men were the looters, who robbed the dead and the wounded of their clothing, and plundered the houses in conquered districts'.[17] These men are clearly depicted as the dirty underside of the military machine, although they were also critical to the overall success of a campaign. The distinction between warrior and follower is not explained, however; men who were probably social equals became differentiated in the bearing of arms. Clearly, from among the enormous social group termed *bakopi*, there were men who were known to their local chiefs as being particularly skilled or courageous in war. These were the men who owned fine spears and shields, weapons which 'were always kept in good condition',[18] and who were presumably called upon by the local chief when he himself was required to provide a contingent for the national army. This was a measure of specialization which probably remained unchanged over several centuries; by the 1880s, however, the peasant-soldier had been to a large degree supplanted by the ambitious musketeer at the capital.

We have already noted some of the logistical problems experienced by Ganda armies during the nineteenth century. Paucity of evidence for before 1800 prevents a comparison between the size of armies in that period and those in the nineteenth century, but it is clear that large armies after 1800 were often cumbersome and difficult to feed. Food provision for an army on the move while still in friendly territory was in the hands of the locals, and was undoubtedly a burden on regional resources. We have noted Roscoe's assertion that a section of the force was responsible for the gathering of food. In enemy territory, this involved plunder. According to Roscoe, who relied on a variety of Ganda informants, the commander of the army would arrange for different chiefs to use separate roads in advancing towards the point of rendezvous, so as not to drain completely the food resources of one area. This in itself may have been one of the motives behind the extension of the road network in the nineteenth century. Once in enemy territory, the ordinary soldiers were supplied through plunder, and chiefs usually had their own supply carried with them, often by their wives and concubines.[19] Typically, a period of several days was allowed for the army to gather in or near enemy territory, during which time reconnaissance missions were dispatched to collect information about the enemy's state of preparedness, military concentrations, and so on. As the attack was initiated, the commander was positioned at a vantage point from which he could survey the main action and send reinforcements where they were needed. The first line of the force would attack, then withdraw to the main body while a second line attacked, and so on. Each regimental or sectional chief had men who carried reserve weaponry. When long-distance missiles – spears – were exhausted, hand-to-hand fighting ensued; in a successful engagement, the soldiers would

[17] Roscoe 1911: 352–3.
[18] Ibid.: 353.
[19] Ibid.: 351.

pursue the fleeing enemy while club-wielding auxiliaries rounded up women, cattle and various other forms of booty. To some extent, the collection of such spoil was the standard by which immediate success was measured, for it was only when the commander 'thought that he had as much spoil as was possible to obtain, he beat his drums, recalled his forces, waited for the various parties that had been sent out to loot, and began his march back'. Roscoe, like other writers of the period, does not acknowledge long-term strategic objectives. Throughout the engagement, the *kabaka* would have been kept informed, by means of runners of athletic renown,[20] of developments concerning the course of the fighting and the spoil being accumulated,[21] and also, though of course Roscoe does not mention this, whether the true strategic objectives of the war had been achieved.

Further information on Ganda tactics is provided by first-hand European accounts dating from the 1890s, when the Ganda military machine was revitalized in the process of acting as the agency of British imperialism. Although during this period the nature of Ganda warfare was clearly in flux, certain aspects of organization were plainly rooted in the pre-colonial era. Lugard, for example, suggested that the Ganda only waged war at particular times of the year. In April 1891, the army encountered almost impassable rivers and swamps flooded by recent rains, and food for the expedition was difficult to come by as the crops 'were only just springing up'.[22] In what was probably southwest Singo, Lugard wrote:

> The Waganda called a council of war ... but only came to the resolution that they would halt the next day and discuss it, being completely at a loss what to do. My suggestions of endeavouring to effect a crossing at several points simultaneously was opposed, on the grounds that they dare not divide their force, even into two parties; that it is the custom of the Waganda to fight en masse only; and that if one party were driven in they would never rally, but would be utterly dispersed, and never stop running until they reached their homes ...

Lugard's plan to advance to Kabarega's capital also met opposition, and even he had to bow to the superior knowledge and experience of the region among the Ganda:

> They informed me that there were three very large swamps, one they said absolutely impassable at this season; and they had news that the enemy had prearranged to make a stand there if defeated in the first battle. They also said that there was no food whatsoever ...[23]

---

[20] These runners or messengers were identified in 1880 as *bakayungirizi* by the missionary Livinhac. They were trained from an early age in prolonged, rapid marches, moving night and day with only short breaks; Mutesa had a number in his service. See White Fathers: Rubaga Diary 1/27 June 1880.

[21] Roscoe 1911: 355–9. It is clear that Roscoe is describing a single battle, which was sometimes what a war might amount to, but more often wars probably comprised several such engagements. Moreover, the importance attached to booty would have depended on the circumstances in which the war was fought; to reiterate the point, graver issues were usually at stake.

[22] UNA A26/4 Lugard to Admin.-Gen., IBEAC 13 August 1891.

[23] Ibid. These accounts appear to relate to Lugard's advance through Singo in April–May 1891, a time of year when rainfall is both regular and heavy: see also Perham 1959: II, 144ff. Kabarega's capital was close to modern Hoima.

By this time, of course, guns were becoming dominant, and had a significant impact on tactics. Here it is sufficient to note that firearms had little direct or practical influence on combat and tactics before the 1870s. But it is clear that by the 1890s guns had altered tactical arrangements. The following account by Macdonald relates to 1893–4:

> They were drawn up in a number of parallel columns, each headed by its chief, and the front rank of which contained the best armed men, while behind them followed the spearmen. The attack was most impetuous, but, as they did not understand the use of supports or reserves, anything more than a temporary check was likely to involve the retreat of the whole force, until they had time to reform ...[24]

Other evidence, already noted, suggests that the Ganda understood very well the use of reserves; moreover, a force which allowed itself time to fall back and re-form could hardly be described as impetuous. It is striking, however, how tactics and formation had altered. The idea of spearmen waiting for those with guns to win the battle was unquestionably a new development. At one time, the spearmen had been at the forefront of the attack and were served by lowlier peasants with clubs; now the riflemen were perceived as the main assault soldiers and were served by the spearmen. But it is insufficient to suggest simply that one technology had been replaced by another. There were many more spearmen in the 1850s than there were riflemen in the 1880s and 1890s, and any one of the former was likely to have been a more accomplished warrior than his counterpart a generation later. The technology had become more sophisticated, but the potency of the Ganda army had been undermined and, to a large extent, the military ethos cheapened. Technological complexity was not sufficient in itself to maintain the march of progress, although many Ganda were understandably impressed by it. But, as we shall see below from the comments made by one Ganda soldier in 1887, guns were not universally perceived as a good thing. Nevertheless, although spears remained the numerically predominant form of weaponry even after 1890, both the ideological and tactical emphasis had begun to rest on the firearm from the 1870s onward. Kiwanuka, however, rightly cautions historians not to exaggerate the practical importance of the firearm, suggesting that 'the spear and other traditional weapons remained the masters of the battlefield until the 1890s'.[25] It has often been argued that European imperialism and all that accompanied it interrupted, in many spheres of life, Africa's 'natural' development; one wonders whether the Ganda adopted firearms with excessive and unjustified enthusiasm, regarding them too much as a panacea for all their military and external ills. Whatever the case, however, it is clear that the leaders of Buganda in this period really had little choice.

[24] Macdonald 1897: 142–3.
[25] Kiwanuka 1967: 72. Yet Kiwanuka contradicts himself by implicitly conceding that it was precisely because the Ganda used guns that they were often unsuccessful in the second half of the nineteenth century. He asserts, for example, that 'Muteesa's failure to subdue the Bavuma remains one of the classic examples of how the mere possession of firearms without training in using them had little advantage over the traditional weapons and methods of warfare': Kiwanuka 1971: 145. By extension of the argument, possession and use of guns were surely a decided disadvantage.

The new elite: from bodyguard to vanguard

The soldiers based at the capital, whose primary role at least in theory was the defence of the *kabaka*, were distinct from the fighting army. A bodyguard surrounding the political elite had probably existed since the Kintu era, reflecting a period in the kingdom's history when the capital was under threat of direct attack, and the importance and size of the bodyguard undoubtedly grew as the *kabaka*'s authority increased. During the nineteenth century, a police force of sorts also developed from the bodyguard. Burton mentions the reported presence of '2000 guards armed only with staves' surrounding the hall in which the coastal merchant Snay bin Amir met Suna in 1852.[26] These probably took no part in military campaigns. Burton also claims to have been told by the Arabs that 'guards in hundreds attend [Suna's enclosure] at all hours. They are commanded by four chiefs, who are relieved every second day'.[27] Mention was also made of the 'Sakibobo or commander-in-chief, who has power over the Sawaganzi, the life-guards and slaves, the warriors and builders of the palace'.[28] This description seems somewhat muddled, which is hardly surprising considering its provenance and the fact that it may be second- or even third-hand. The *sekibobo*, the governor of Kyagwe, may at that time have been a noted military leader, and possibly such men were periodically required to command the bodyguard, perhaps as part of their period of residence in the capital. The reference to the Sawaganzi is puzzling: the *sabaganzi* was the title of the eldest brother of the *kabaka*'s mother, apparently established by Suna himself, and a figure of some authority.[29] It may be that Suna created the title with the bodyguard in mind, and perhaps the members of this corps were generally referred to by the same title, reflecting the extent to which they were a favoured elite. It is clear, in any case, that the royal bodyguard was well regimented, with a command structure of its own, and was permanently on duty. Almost 20 years later, the number of personal guards surrounding the *kabaka* had increased, Stanley noting some 3,000 in the presence of Mutesa, although it is clear that not all of these were military personnel.[30] This armed corps, notably, was also open to foreigners. An inner circle of the bodyguard, apparently some 200 strong, included 'renegades from Baker's expedition', Zanzibari deserters and disillusioned (or desperate) coastmen, and 'the elect of Uganda'.[31] By the mid-1870s, possession of a firearm and indeed some skill in using it were a sufficient qualification for entry. The precedent had been set by Suna, who favoured a coastal merchant and placed him in a position of some authority.[32]

Clearly, one of the most important developments in military organization during the nineteenth century was the growth of a new elite of gun-

[26] Burton 1860: I, 194.
[27] Ibid.: 188.
[28] Ibid.: 192.
[29] See for example Murphy 1972: 512. *Muganzi* means a favourite person.
[30] Bennett 1970: 219; Stanley 1878: I, 193.
[31] Bennett 1970: 221; Stanley 1878: I, 198.
[32] Burton 1860: II, 193.

wielding young men in the service of the *kabaka*. The royal regiment, if it can be described as such, had several overlapping functions: it was a branch of the army, a police force and, at least in theory, a bodyguard. As we have already noted, it seems to have originated under Suna, whose *batongole* appear to have taken on increasingly military dimensions and grown into something of an elitist corps with an ethos characterized above all by a sense of self-importance. That this development occurred at all, however, has not been universally accepted. Low wrote of 'Suna's and Mutesa's reforms of the military system, with the creation of the Mujasi and his professional subordinates' as evidence of Buganda's 'commitment to war'.[33] Kiwanuka, however, later complained that '[o]ne finds ... writer after writer repeating that Kings Suna II and Mutesa I organized the army and created a special force under the Mujasi. Yet nowhere in Kaggwa's *Basekabaka be Buganda*, our best source, is it said that there was a reorganization of the army.'[34] Elsewhere, Kiwanuka asserted that the foundation of the *ekitongole ekijaasi* had been misunderstood, that it had 'nothing to do with the reform of the military service as there was none during the reign of Muteesa' and that, in any case, the *mujasi* rarely commanded military expeditions.[35] The *ekitongole ekijaasi* refers to the special force mentioned by Low under the command of the *mujasi*, and we shall return to the post of *mujasi* below. A third writer, C.P. Kottak, drawing heavily on the work of Southwold, considered Mutesa's reign 'to be a culmination of the Ganda state', asserting that Mutesa 'reinforced the traditional military authority by the creation of a standing army and the allocation of estates to warriors as a regular reward in lieu of pay in money or kind'.[36]

I agree with each of these arguments up to a point. Kottak, however, overstates the extent to which the army in its entirety was reorganized, although there were important implications for the national army, and he virtually ignores the non-military functions of the new force in the capital. The evidence suggests that a multifaceted new elite had emerged by the 1870s, but, as Kiwanuka rightly points out, the description of this force as a standing army is exaggerated. Michael Wright is among those who suggest that a standing army was created; even so, his argument that a new military element grew out, at least partly, of what was originally a royal bodyguard is surely sound.[37] Kiwanuka himself ignores the evidence for, and thus the relevance of, this development and its longer-term implications for the army as a whole, which in structural terms remained essentially unchanged.[38] Kagwa's failure to make it explicit that such changes were taking place in his *Basekabaka be Buganda* is scarcely reason to dismiss the entire argument. Kagwa fails to mention many events and developments which we know from other evidence took place.

After 1884, Kabaka Mwanga established enclosures throughout the king-

---

[33] Low 1963: I, 335.
[34] See Kiwanuka's 'Preface' in Kagwa 1971: i–ii.
[35] Kiwanuka 1967: 73.
[36] Kottak 1972: 376.
[37] Wright 1971: 25.
[38] Kiwanuka 1971, especially the later chapters which move beyond 1884, the stopping point for his works cited in footnotes 34 and 35.

dom which were occupied solely by what might be termed royal soldiers and which were virtually independent of the *ssaza*s in which they were located.[39] The head of this increasingly nationwide force carried the title of *mujasi*, who was often mistaken by contemporary observers as the commander of the regular army. He was, rather, the head of a royal army with an apparently omnipotent brief and a close relationship with the *kabaka* himself.[40] The position was established by Mutesa in the early stages of his reign. According to Kagwa, there was up until the 1850s a post which has been translated as that of Lieutenant-General, or the *kalabalaba*. Literally translated, this meant 'the one who sees sharply', and this high-ranking scout marched to the right of the commander himself. The title 'was conferred upon a favourite by the king himself'. The *kalabalaba* was also a bodyguard of sorts. The post was, however, abolished by Mutesa, who instead created – or at least upgraded – the title of *mujasi*, previously the 'chief of police' (to use the translation of Kagwa's phrase), to permanently occupy the role.[41] The title clearly carried explicitly military responsibilities but, although the *mujasi* often took part in military campaigns, it was not in this context an especially high-ranking position. The *mujasi*'s importance lay in his role on the general staff, as it were, but it would probably be more appropriate to describe him as a kind of political commissar. Mackay described the *mujasi* as 'the captain of the bodyguard';[42] Lourdel used the phrase 'one of the chiefs of the king's soldiers'.[43] The importance of the title seems to have increased over time: Lourdel clearly refers to him as only one such chief, while Zimbe, writing of the early and mid-1880s, similarly implies that there were several other chiefs of equal standing.[44] Yet even at this stage Zimbe refers to the title as denoting a commander-in-chief,[45] and the stature of the holder of the title had grown significantly by the early 1890s.

There is little first-hand evidence relating to these royal soldiers outside the capital, but in and around the royal enclosure they were well observed. They were a permanent feature at the capital by the time British and French missionaries had arrived in the late 1870s. They were distinct from the bulk of the Ganda army in that they were armed with guns; they were also dressed in a uniform of sorts which appears to have been influenced by both coastal and Western military culture, betraying the admiration Mutesa had for the latter in particular. Foreign influence was also apparent in the formation of these soldiers: they were usually drawn up in lines in Western fashion, not in the indigenous manner of parade and salute which involved waves of warriors approaching the *kabaka* and waving their spears in his direction as a sign of undying loyalty. The soldiers were, perhaps, most distinguishable from the bulk of the army in

---

[39] This was, of course, in theory true of all *batongole*.

[40] UNA A1/1 IBEAC Report 1891–2.

[41] Kagwa 1934: 90. Murphy lists 'bodyguard', alongside 'best man at a wedding', among possible interpretations of *kalabalaba*: Murphy 1972: 143. Twaddle suggests that the *kalabalaba* was the second-in-command during a campaign, and 'took control when the commander became indisposed': Twaddle 1993: 51.

[42] CMS G3 A6/0 1885/98 Mackay to Wigram, ? May 1885.

[43] White Fathers: Rubaga Diary 2/14 May 1881.

[44] For example, Zimbe 1939: 49.

[45] Ibid.: 49, 153.

terms of attitude. The missionary Gordon, for example, noted the 'saucy young recruits who form the body guard', observing that they were 'only too ready for the opportunity of mischief & the sport of firing off their guns'.[46] The immediate context of this observation was the confiscation of a wayward chief's property, suggesting that these young men were as much an increasingly self-governing police force as a military elite. There can be little doubt, however, that – their ferocity and apparent conviction during the civil war notwithstanding – they were much better at internal pillage and 'firing off their guns' in sport than at fighting external enemies.

Mackay describes how he and his fellow missionary Ashe were set upon by a small force commanded by the *mujasi* at a time when Mwanga's anti-Christian policy was gaining momentum. The *mujasi*'s role as commander of a civil police is clear. Mackay also mentions that in 1885 the *mujasi* was sent 'far off to the borders of Bunyoro to plunder a chief who had been arrested for appropriating some of the king's cattle'.[47] This was plainly less of a military operation than a political matter, a punitive expedition within the kingdom's boundaries. None the less, it seems to me that increasingly the *mujasi* and his men formed the spearhead of military operations. Lourdel described one prominent member of this force as having distinguished himself in a war with Bunyoro.[48] The *mujasi* himself was a divisional commander and, on one occasion when he was called to the royal enclosure to relate his personal feats in a military engagement, it was noted in the Rubaga Diary that his name alone as chief of police inspired great fear.[49]

The rivalry between the favoured young men and the older chiefs representative of the military establishment grew as the former were accorded greater responsibility in actual warfare. Zimbe states that '[w]hen after a war the old chiefs came back defeated, the bitongole of the young men jeered them very much. The Kabaka always appointed young men to distribute what booty the old chiefs had brought back and he always gave them power to jeer them.'[50] It is clear that these changes at the centre had a detrimental influence on Ganda military performance during the last few decades of the pre-colonial era. The attraction of guns and European uniform had proved stronger than the desire to maintain an effective rank-and-file army. It may be that after c. 1850 Buganda's rulers became increasingly complacent over the kingdom's invincibility; this is particularly apparent during the reign of Mwanga. Both Mutesa and to an even greater extent Mwanga bastardized the kingdom's military tradition; we have already noted how the idea of war was in many respects as important as war itself, and political leaders in the 1870s and 1880s to some degree undermined even this ethos. First Mutesa and then Mwanga were increasingly preoccupied with power struggles and loyalty at the court, and with displays of armed strength rather than the exercise of it.

[46] CMS G3 A5/0 1888/241 Gordon to Mackay, 31 December 1887.
[47] CMS G3 A6/0 1885/98 Mackay to Wigram, ? May 1885.
[48] White Fathers: C14/182 Lourdel to Superior-General, 12 September 1887.
[49] White Fathers: Rubaga Diary 3/7 April 1886, 28 April 1886, 30 April 1886.
[50] Zimbe 1939: 174.

The tools of war: weaponry & the role of firearms

The most basic early development which can be identified in the context of weaponry is the transition from wood to iron. It was apparently, as might be expected, during the Kintu period that a chief of the *kkobe* clan, Magere, began to make wooden spears for the *kabaka*. This in itself appears to have been an innovation, presumably involving a new type of spear or perhaps a more effective type of wood. During the reign of Kintu's supposed successor, Chwa, iron spear-blades were first manufactured.[51] At some point, the position of weapon-maker to the *kabaka* (at a time when he still needed one) was transferred from Magere to Walukaga of the *kasimba* clan,[52] and Walukaga, of course, is elsewhere noted as having been the head of all blacksmiths in Buganda. Ganda spears, along with drums, came to be among the great standards of material culture; the admiring descriptions of European observers suggest that spears were not always constructed with combat in mind but were also works of art. The reign of Nakibinge in the sixteenth century represented a watershed in Buganda's military history, and it seems that this was also true with regard to the concept of weaponry and the raw materials required. The disastrous war against Bunyoro at this time drove home, perhaps for the first time, the need for an ample supply of iron for the manufacture of weapons. It is recounted how, following the death of Nakibinge in battle, the *kabaka*'s chief wife Nanono supervised the sharpening of reeds to be used as spears.[53] This last-ditch innovation appears to have saved Buganda from total annihilation, but it is clear that the technological revolution begun during the Chwa period was not yet complete. From the reign of Mulondo onwards, Buganda actively sought to secure sources of iron as part of its military policy.

By the 1850s, when the first contemporary report emerged, the average weaponry for a Ganda soldier consisted of at least one long spear, two lighter spears, a dagger and a shield.[54] Spare weapons were carried on longer campaigns. The lighter, smaller spears mentioned by Burton had only very recently been introduced under Suna; again, as we have seen, the inspiration behind their introduction remains unclear. As though to test the new weapons, immediately after their appearance Suna plundered an estate in Bulemezi; apparently satisfied, he appointed the *pokino* to lead an army against Busagara. The war was successful, and the small spear became standard equipment.[55] By the nineteenth century, most spears were constructed of wooden shafts and iron blades, but some were still made wholly from wood, with the sharpened end hardened in the fire; the local name for this was *maguma*, according to Mackay.[56] The bow and arrow, though relatively widespread in pre-colonial Africa, were not used by the Ganda in either warfare or hunting. The absence is not easily

---

[51] Kagwa 1972: 78–9.
[52] Ibid.: 63.
[53] Ibid.; also Reid 1997.
[54] Burton 1860: II, 189.
[55] Kagwa 1971: 117.
[56] Mackay 1890: 222. This is probably derived from the Luganda verb stem *guma*, to be solid or firm.

explained, and the sources are regrettably silent about Ganda views on the subject. It is clear, however, that, although arrows may be cheaper missiles than spears, they are not necessarily more efficient. In some cases, bows and arrows require more rigid attack formations and, depending on size, they can only efficiently be used from a motionless position.[57] Spears can offer greater flexibility of movement, and allow the carrying of a heavy shield, which was also a standard piece of Ganda military equipment. Moreover, as Smith has shown in a West African context, spears are often cultural symbols, or standards of office and honour.[58] This was undoubtedly true of Buganda, where the spear and shield were, as Speke put it, 'the Uganda cognisance'.[59] Only during Nakibinge's war with Bunyoro do the bow and arrow seem to have figured with any importance. The Sesse warrior Kibuka used bows and arrows during this conflict, and the weapon consequently took on a symbolic significance. During Mwanga's accession, the new *kabaka* was required to go through the motions of killing a Nyoro youth with a bow and arrow; the weapon was held to be that used by Nakibinge himself.[60] Although the weapon was not standard Ganda army equipment, in 1862 Speke described Mutesa and several attendants holding archery practice, each taking turns to shoot arrows at a shield. Speke, a professional soldier, exclaimed that 'they were such bad shots that they hardly ever hit it'.[61] Archery may have been regarded as sport; in any case, proficiency in the use of the bow and arrow was perhaps not such as to warrant their widespread adoption in warfare.

According to Speke, Mutesa then 'ordered sixteen shields to be placed before him, one in front of the other, and with one shot from Whitworth [rifle] pierced the whole of them, the bullet passing through the bosses of nearly every one'. This feat prompted the *kabaka* to gesture triumphantly towards the rifle and declare to his chiefs, 'What is the use of spears and bows? I shall never fight with anything but guns in future.'[62] Whether Mutesa actually uttered these words is doubtful, but the sentiments were probably expressed, and an obsession had clearly been born. Yet Mutesa's obsession with the firearm was one thing; the widespread adoption of guns and the complete retraining of the army was another. Again, assessing the impact of firearms is sometimes problematic.[63] Guns were never imported in sufficient numbers to be widely used by the Ganda army, but by the 1870s they were numerous enough to influence the nature of warfare. Their symbolic importance was immense; indeed, the overall influence of the gun was grossly out of proportion to its successful utilization. As Twaddle has suggested, guns, even by the 1880s, 'were still used as much

---

[57] See for example Keegan 1993: 162–3.
[58] Smith suggests that the spear 'was a symbol of honour and office as well as a weapon of war, being carried into battle as a standard, while spears handed down from ancestors, or symbolic representations of these, more decorative than useful, form part of the regalia of kings and chiefs': Smith 1989: 68.
[59] Speke 1863b: 255, 291.
[60] Zimbe 1939: 111.
[61] Speke 1863b: 397.
[62] Ibid.
[63] Indeed, it is a problem which has been addressed with regard to much of nineteenth-century Africa. See for example Smith 1989: 80–6; Roberts 1971.

for psychological effect as for actual destruction'.[64] In practical terms, there were clear limitations to the effectiveness of firearms in battle, as we shall see. The gradual 'firearm revolution' can be said to have begun in the mid-1840s with the arrival in Buganda of the first coastal merchants. It seems likely that small groups of Arab traders participated in military campaigns alongside the Ganda during the reigns of both Suna and Mutesa, although the nature and frequency of their involvement are less clear. Arab participation was certainly prevalent during the 1880s, and Kabarega himself is supposed to have complained that coastal merchants were allying themselves with Ganda expeditionary armies. Presumably both Mutesa and Mwanga would have welcomed armed support from traders who were more skilled in handling firearms than the Ganda. During the war against Bunyoro in the early months of 1886, three Arabs were apparently killed; these probably belonged to a larger detachment of merchant adventurers linked to the Ganda army.[65] The motives behind such involvement, with its attendant risk of death, are not entirely clear, but economic incentives must have been predominant; traders might expect to receive a share of the spoil, and campaigns to the north in particular would have provided an opportunity to explore an otherwise prohibited region and perhaps assess its commercial possibilities. Military involvement would also have been an effective way of currying favour with the *kabaka* himself. However, before the religious wars, the military role of the Arabs was markedly less dramatic than it was among the Nyamwezi, for example, where the loosely defined state allowed the powerful strangers to take advantage of fissures in the polity.

By the time Speke arrived in Buganda in 1862, guns, though still novel, were clearly becoming more common. Even so, just south of Karagwe in late 1861, Speke was met by Mutesa's emissary, Irungu, to whom he offered a rifle to take to the *kabaka* as a gift. Irungu refused, 'lest his master, who had never seen such a wonderful weapon before, should think he had brought him a malign charm'.[66] Rumanika, the ruler of Karagwe, also later told Speke that Mutesa might be frightened by the gun, 'considering it a charm of evil quality, reject us as bad magicians, and close his gates on us'.[67] This is somewhat mystifying, but it was probably less to do with the fact that Speke wanted to send Mutesa a gun than that he himself was a stranger and, moreover, a *muzungu*. Moreover, it might have been Irungu and, to a lesser extent, Rumanika who were frightened by the gun. Paradoxically, Speke later wrote: 'At Rumanika's request I then gave Mtesa's pages some ammunition to hurry on with to the great king of Uganda, as his majesty had ordered them to bring him as quickly as possible, some strengthening powder, and also some powder for his gun.'[68] Firearms were already established at the Ganda capital, if not exactly commonplace.

The demand for guns in Buganda was insatiable in the second half of the nineteenth century. The value placed on them by the Ganda matched

[64] Twaddle 1993: 9.
[65] White Fathers: C14/61 Lourdel to Bridoux, 6 April 1886.
[66] Speke 1863b: 187.
[67] Ibid.: 215.
[68] Ibid.: 245.

that in other parts of the continent; still, in terms of the volume of guns arriving in Buganda, exact figures are impossible to come by. In 1880, Mackay was of the opinion that 10,000 guns per annum were being brought from the coast to Unyanyembe.[69] From Unyanyembe these guns travelled in several directions but, from Mackay's estimate, it seems unlikely that less than 2,000–3,000 guns thus found their way to Buganda, or at least the lake region.[70] Certainly Buganda must have been the single most important market for the Arabs' trade guns, particularly after they had frozen sales to Mirambo, although the latter retained control over sections of the critical trade routes south of the lake.[71] In early 1887 Mackay reported that coastal traders tended to carry with them more guns than cloth for exchange: 'Within the last month ... a great number of *loads* of breech loading rifles have come into Buganda alone!' A smaller number of repeating rifles, more advanced and more reliable, were also being brought by coastal merchants.[72] The Arab traders themselves recognized the importance which Mutesa placed on these relations. In 1881, a merchant arrived in Buganda with some 400 guns, 300 of which he claimed were a gift from Sultan Barghash to persuade Mutesa to join him in fighting Mirambo. Lourdel was able to reveal, however, that the Arab bore neither gift nor message, but was in fact a private trader.[73]

During the 1870s, guns became an established feature of life at the capital, and had begun to influence the development of a new military elitism. In 1872 Samuel Baker was told by traders that Mutesa 'had a regiment armed with a thousand guns, in addition to the numerous forces at his disposal'.[74] The distinction between the newly armed regiment and the bulk of the Ganda army is critical. By the end of the 1870s, this royal corps probably numbered around 2,000 fusiliers, mostly located in the capital. The extent to which firearms found their way into the districts as part of the new military *batongole* expansion is unclear, although important chiefs may have had their own stocks in regional estates. The gun had certainly become a great object of desire, and small-scale commercial transactions with both Europeans and Arabs were probably common: Lourdel, for example, recorded that he was able to acquire three child slaves for a rusty and antiquated gun.[75] By the time of Mwanga's accession in 1884, according to Zimbe, 'there were about 4,000 people in the palace all of whom had guns'.[76] Even so, guns were too few in number to have an impact on the rank and file of the army.

The relative rarity, in the context of the army as a whole, of guns notwithstanding, the formation of Ganda armies was increasingly based around the select few who possessed guns. This was to the detriment of the army as a whole. The firearms which arrived in Buganda were usually

---

[69] CMS CA6/016(a)/46 Mackay to Hutchinson, 11 June 1880.

[70] It is true, however, that Mackay had every reason to exaggerate his figure: the gun was for him the root of all evil in Africa.

[71] CMS CA6/018/6 O'Neill to Wright, ? October 1877.

[72] CMS G3 A5/0 1888/194 Mackay to Ashe, 17 April 1887.

[73] White Fathers: Rubaga Diary 2/1 January 1881, 3 January 1881, 14 January 1881.

[74] Baker 1874: II, 98.

[75] White Fathers: Rubaga Diary [Annex Lourdel 12 June 1879].

[76] Zimbe 1939: 100.

archaic and often downright dangerous; some probably did not work at all. This was the case in many African societies during the nineteenth century and earlier. It was of course safer, and more profitable, for traders to hand over to unsuspecting indigenous buyers outdated and unreliable models. But this trickery was not wholly by design: clearly, as new types of guns were constantly being produced in Europe, many older models became surplus to requirement, and in Africa there was a ready market for these weapons. At the beginning of the 1890s, most firearms in Buganda were still muzzle-loaders, less reliable and often more dangerous than breech-loaders, which were increasingly common after 1890.[77] It was the muzzle-loader which Lugard labelled the 'curse of Africa'; it was readily available via the trade routes of Ankole and Buddu and, later, the lake route. These older firearms often failed to work at all, or might explode in the user's hands. Moreover, one missionary in 1877 noted the pre-dominance of flintlocks among the palace guard.[78] By this time the flintlock was also an outmoded weapon: a spark struck from a flint in the stock of the gun lit the gunpowder, and thus the gun was fired. At best it was unreliable, at worst it could maim the gunman. Moreover, during the wet season, gunpowder was often rendered useless, and would similarly have affected the operation of the spark or the creation of an open flame from matches. Throughout the 1880s, incidents were recorded in which stocks of powder or ammunition at the capital exploded as a result of lightning striking storage huts and starting fires; many guns and crates of powder were lost in this way.[79]

The frequent shortages of both bullets and powder also contributed to the ineffectiveness of firearms in the hands of the Ganda. Mutesa's eager-ness to acquire powder from Speke has already been noted. Much later, Lugard was compelled to supply the *katikiro* with 'thirty kegs of powder' with which to load his guns,[80] despite the fact that powder for muzzle-loaders was apparently stored in 'enormous quantities' by the chiefs of Buganda.[81] Wright has suggested that ammunition was sometimes made locally 'by cutting iron rods into lengths in imitation of rifle bullets'.[82] To some extent, at least initially, ammunition and powder were centrally con-trolled, but by the 1880s efforts by the *kabaka* to this end were clearly less successful; the *kabaka* did, however, possess a substantial personal supply.[83] Guns could be acquired by chiefs and appear not to have been royally controlled, although the *kabaka* did distribute guns as largesse and as an individual trader he had a clear advantage in bargaining power. In 1880, Girault recorded that a number of chiefs were eager to acquire firearms

---

[77] UNA A26/4 Lugard to Admin.-Gen., IBEAC 13 August 1891. Breech-loading rifles, which fired more rapidly than any gun previously, were developed in Europe in the mid-nineteenth century, and were associated in particular with the Prussian army in their defeats of Austria (1866) and France (1870).

[78] CMS CA6/025/8 Wilson to Wright, 6 July 1877.

[79] For example, White Fathers: Rubaga Diary 3/23 February 1886.

[80] UNA A26/4 Lugard to Admin.-Gen., IBEAC 13 August 1891.

[81] Ibid. Interestingly, Lugard indicates that many chiefs actually traded their surplus powder for ivory, apparently to the north.

[82] Wright 1971: 67.

[83] CMS G3 A6/0 1885/98 Mackay to Wigram, ? May 1885.

and ammunition from Europeans and coastal traders in the capital, as they were preparing for a military campaign.[84] How successful they were in their quest is unclear; in any case, for this particular engagement Mutesa handed out guns and ammunition from the royal stocks,[85] suggesting that, although in theory anyone could trade for guns on their own account, the *kabaka* endeavoured to ensure that his was the lion's share.

It is clear that the Ganda scarcely knew how to use guns properly, compounding the problems outlined above. It is true that a new branch of the iron-working industry developed around firearms, and as we have seen a number of blacksmiths, at least at the capital, became gunsmiths.[86] The fact that a number of Ganda could now repair firearms went some way to ensuring that a proportion of the weapons continued to function. However, the effective utilization of any firearm requires training, and in Buganda, as elsewhere in Africa at this time, this did not exist in any real form.[87] In the last years of Mutesa's reign, it was common to hear guns being fired into the air as a rallying call, or as a noisy accompaniment to a celebration. Yet it was relatively easy to parade guns around the royal enclosure; as Zimbe tellingly, if unwittingly, wrote, the royal bodyguard 'all appeared very nice to look at'.[88] It was a different matter to load, aim and fire repeatedly and in order in the heat of battle. By the late 1870s, a detachment of Sudanese or 'Nubians' were serving, according to Zimbe, as 'the instructors of the Kabaka's soldiers', as they were 'experts in the gun exercises'.[89] Indeed, they appear to have attached themselves to the *kabaka*'s entourage at the invitation of Mutesa himself, who clearly valued, and probably feared, their technical knowledge and military background. The military impact of this foreign assistance was minimal, although Zimbe tells us that one of the officers of the royal bodyguard, Kapagala, was 'very skilled in gun exercises'. What these exercises actually entailed is unclear, but they appear to have consisted of nothing more useful than marching up and down, blowing trumpets and shouldering arms. Still, the Ganda took them very seriously. Soldiers of lower ranks wore cartridge belts, and those of more responsible station were equipped with swords as well.[90] Kiwanuka has argued that the real aim in developing these regiments 'was to have trained men who could march, play drums and blow trumpets and present arms'; the new *ekitongole* was 'in fact a collection of bandsmen designed to impress foreign guests rather than a special armed force'.[91] Yet it seems that Mutesa intended much more than this. The pomp and ceremony at court conceal the fact that these soldiers were being used to fight, and that their role was fundamentally altering the nature – and the outcome – of Ganda warfare.

---

[84] White Fathers: Rubaga Diary 1/3 March 1880.
[85] White Fathers: Rubaga Diary 1/16 March 1880.
[86] See for example Lugard 1892: 828.
[87] See however Legassick 1966: 95–115.
[88] Zimbe 1939: 45.
[89] Ibid.
[90] Ibid.: 45–7. Swords were purely decorative; though highly prized as a trade good, they were never used in battle.
[91] Kiwanuka 1967: 73.

It is clear that Mutesa regarded guns as critical to Buganda's military development. A deputation sent to him by Kabarega in 1879 was deliberately equipped with firearms in what amounted to a show of strength,[92] although by this time guns were also reaching the Nyoro in increasing numbers.[93] By the 1870s, then, a few men were carrying guns into battle as part of a larger army; increasingly, the prominence given to firearms in the army's formation actually served to impede the fluency of the attack. The interests of the larger force were not served by even a partial reliance on weapons which were ill-used and untrustworthy. Mutesa was not alone in his enthusiasm for guns: clearly many Ganda were only too keen to discard indigenous weaponry and take up less effective but superficially more impressive technology, and the army's overall performance suffered as a result. None the less, even the gun enthusiasts must have had their doubts about the efficiency of their weapons in certain situations. The deputation sent to Bunyoro mentioned above, which apparently amounted to a small army, fought with the Kedi on its return, using not its guns but 'sticks'. Zimbe, who claims to have been present, explains that 'we fought the Bakedi using our sticks, because amongst us there were two very brave people in fighting with sticks namely Somera and Mbazira'.[94] People who were 'very brave' in fighting with guns had presumably yet to emerge. Ironically, when the deputation arrived safely back at the capital, Mutesa distributed rewards of guns and bullets.[95] The distribution of firearms to favoured young chiefs and pages at the royal court was increased by Mwanga, who did so with the intention of empowering his army and winning the loyalty of these ambitious and increasingly powerful men; clearly, despite the commercial availability of guns, many will still have been attracted by the prospect of receiving firearms free in return for at least outward displays of loyalty. Regardless of the practical functions of the gun itself, it became a symbol of autonomy and authority. The new technology came to represent to those who owned guns their widening opportunities in the fluid society in the capital which characterized the 1870s and 1880s. The original motives of Mutesa and Mwanga can be understood, but the plan was to backfire on the latter. The firepower of the new elite may have been more symbolic than real, but events were to prove this irrelevant. The combination of the gun culture and the creation of a new class of chiefs with the introduction of new religious loyalties in the form of Catholicism, Protestantism and Islam would prove explosive.[96]

Some had misgivings about the ways in which firearms were altering warfare. By the mid-1880s, as the Nyoro brought their guns to bear on the armies of Buganda, bullet wounds had become common among returning soldiers. Yet the Nyoro seem to have relied less on guns than the Ganda, perhaps because they possessed considerably fewer; at any rate, their

[92] Zimbe 1939: 49.
[93] Dunbar 1965: 42; Dunbar 1960: 73. On Nyoro military organization more generally, see for example Beattie 1971: 128, 253.
[94] Zimbe 1939: 51.
[95] Ibid.: 52.
[96] Ibid.: 165, 174. For an unsurpassed account of the political and religious backgrounds to the subsequent coups at the capital, see Twaddle 1988c: 81–92.

military organization appears not to have experienced anything like the crisis of adaptation of the Ganda. In 1887, a French missionary recorded the unease expressed by a chief known as the *kyambalango*, one of Buganda's most prominent war heroes of the time.[97] The year before, he had been involved in a particularly bloody campaign against Bunyoro in which he had sustained two bullet wounds. In an account of the war made before the royal court, the *kyambalango* claimed to have told the *katikiro* on the eve of his departure for battle that the Ganda were no longer in the era of man-to-man combat, where the warrior could rely upon his own strength, his bravery in battle and his skill in handling his weapons. They had entered 'a new *genre* of battle', in which the hand of a coward hidden in the bushes could put an end to the most courageous soldier. Thus, he declared, they were going to fight with the gun, 'since the gun is the fashion'.[98] A military revolution was under way, a revolution that not only was undesirable but was undermining the great Ganda warrior tradition. Guns were in fact incompatible with indigenous methods of fighting, but they had come to be perceived as necessary; their adoption, indeed, was inevitable.[99] The *kyambalango*, who was, it would seem, a relatively young man and not a veteran in whom opposition to change might have been more natural, went on to describe his own injuries from Nyoro gunfire. The Nyoro may have had fewer guns than the Ganda, but the implication is that they possessed better models which they were able to put to more effective use. None the less, according to the *kyambalango*, the Ganda felled many Nyoro with their own steady fire.[100]

By the 1890s, the number of guns in Buganda was increasing rapidly, despite the efforts of a fledgling British administration to control the flow. In 1893, for example, it was reported that individual Ganda were exchanging firearms, probably for ivory, with the Soga, suggesting the extent to which guns had begun to be common currency.[101] A British-led force in 1894 consisted of around 1,000 soldiers with guns out of a total of a little over 5,000.[102] Zimbe asserted that by 1890 there were around 10,000 firearms in the kingdom;[103] Lugard was somewhat more conservative, estimating in 1891 that there was a total of 5,700.[104] Perhaps Zimbe had

---

[97] It seems to have been a title of some importance, although details are difficult to come by. On first arriving in Buganda in 1875, Stanley counted 'Chambarango' among the eminent chiefs of the kingdom. The 'tall and handsome Chambarango' played a major part in the war against Buvuma that year; he was, indeed, a 'general', while Stanley also described him as 'Chief of Usiro', meaning that he probably commanded soldiers from that *ssaza*, although he may also have been the *mugema* or governing chief of Busiro: Stanley 1878: I, 189, 302, 305. After 1894, the *kyambalango* was made chief of Buyaga *ssaza*, one of the districts wrested from Bunyoro and incorporated into Buganda by the British.

[98] White Fathers: Rubaga Diary 3/21 March 1887.

[99] An almost identical situation had provoked the 'warrior crisis' of sixteenth-century Europe. The biographer of the sixteenth-century warrior Louis de la Tremouille wrote: 'What is the use, any more, of the skill-at-arms of the knight, their strength, their hardihood, their discipline and their desire for honour when such [gunpowder] weapons may be used in war?': quoted in Keegan 1993: 333.

[100] White Fathers: Rubaga Diary 3/21 March 1887.

[101] UNA A2/1 Memo by Williams, 1 March 1893.

[102] UNA A2/2 Diary of expedition to Mruli, 29 April 1894.

[103] Zimbe 1939: 287.

[104] UNA A26/4 Lugard to Admin.-Gen., IBEAC 13 August 1891.

better information than the *muzungu* newcomer. At any rate, there were more guns in Buganda than in any other state in the region, and Lugard remarked that 'the large number of guns [the Ganda] possessed ... rendered them invincible to their enemies'.[105] If anything, the opposite was true.

Nevertheless, the balance of guns took on a new significance during the political and religious upheavals of the late 1880s and early 1890s, as Twaddle has demonstrated.[106] In 1889, the forces gathered around Kalema reportedly possessed around 2,000 guns, while Mwanga's dispersed and depleted forces could barely muster 300 and suffered from a severe shortage of powder. Mwanga was at a disadvantage in that the agents of the firearm trade, the coastal merchants, were ranged against him.[107] By the end of the year, however, Mwanga's forces had recouped somewhat and boasted around 2,000 guns. Spears and shields were still, of course, the predominant form of weaponry, but Mwanga had been able to take control of firearm supply routes.[108] Yet the Muslim party remained a force to be reckoned with. The missionary Livinhac reported that Kalema commanded 5,000 guns, with a substantial reserve of ammunition, as a direct result of his alliance with 'the merchants of Zanzibar'.[109] It is ironic that the coastal merchants found themselves in a position to challenge indigenous authority, considering that Mutesa had perceived his kingdom's military development to be directly linked to the firearm, and that the acquisition of guns was to a very real extent dependent on the Arab community in Unyanyembe and, ultimately, Zanzibar. Yet Mutesa did not foresee the role to be played by the British. Mwanga was finally reinstated by 1890 and over the next few years the British gradually established a presence in the kingdom; a new source of military hardware, organizational skill and both moral and practical support, the British offered an opportunity for regional resurgence which Mwanga, at least initially, was eager to grasp. His rebellion in 1897 signified the final passing of Buganda into the colonial era, an era in which regional dominance was guaranteed but in which the price for success was loss of sovereignty, engendered by the very power from which the Ganda themselves had benefited.

[105] UNA A26/4 Lugard to Admin.-Gen., IBEAC 24 December 1890.
[106] Twaddle 1993: 35–6.
[107] White Fathers: C14/191 Lourdel to Superior-General, 18 September 1889.
[108] Ibid.
[109] White Fathers: C13/117 Livinhac to Lavigerie, 12 December 1889.

Eleven

Lake Victoria,
the Final Frontier

Attention has been drawn in previous chapters to the development of a waterborne commerce and to the use of canoes in war. In this chapter,[1] which brings together many of the themes followed through the book, we shall expand on the enormous significance of Buganda's lakeside location, examining both the broader economic importance of canoes, and more particularly the development and organization of the Ganda fleet. It is clear that the history of the Ganda canoe in the nineteenth century is inextricably linked to key developments discussed earlier, the most important of which were the growth of long-distance trade from the 1840s and Buganda's military stagnation. Canoes, and the creation of a canoe fleet in the service of the state, became critical in the attempts both to control the former and to overcome the latter.

Few pre-colonial societies south of the Sahara possessed a more developed naval organization, or were more intimately attached to a lacustrine or coastal position, than Buganda. Navies, indeed, are not readily associated with African civilization, for a number of reasons, not least of which is the fact that Africa's strikingly regular coastline allowed for few natural protected ports. Yet several historians have demonstrated that water transport was important in a number of regions, usually inland. In West Africa, canoes were vital for commerce on Lake Chad, sections of the Volta river, and along the more sheltered estuaries and lagoons of the Atlantic coast; moreover, the middle section of the Niger was, according to Hopkins, 'one of the great centres of pre-colonial trade in Africa', thanks to the canoe.[2] Fishing in canoes along the Zaire river and its major tributaries was an important economic activity in the area, and water-

---

[1] This chapter is closely derived from my article 'The Ganda on Lake Victoria: a nineteenth-century East African imperialism' (Reid 1998b). I would like to thank Cambridge University Press for their kind permission to reprint some of the material.

[2] Hopkins 1973: 72–3.

borne trade also flourished.[3] Again in West Africa, naval warfare was also practised, along the protected lagoons, in the Niger delta as well as further upriver, and on Lake Chad. As Smith has demonstrated, canoes were used both for transporting and supplying armies on distant campaigns, and as weapons of war in themselves.[4] In Buganda, as we shall see, fishing, transport and war were activities in which canoes were vital. The lake itself was a critical part of Ganda life and culture, offering a livelihood in the form of fishing to shoreline communities, which also supplied the hinterland; the lake was also the home of the kingdom's most potent deity, Mukasa. In military terms, the Ganda were able to extend their hegemony by using the lake; at the height of its naval power, Buganda was suffering a series of setbacks on land and this served to underline the importance of the navy, for the lake represented, to Mutesa in particular, the only remaining route by which the kingdom could extend its control or influence beyond extant territory.

Canoe construction

By the second half of the nineteenth century a wide variety of canoes were being built along the Ganda lake shore and on the islands. Many of the canoe types had been in use for several centuries, and others were of more recent origin. The Ganda employed a correspondingly broad range of wood types in construction; particular regions were noted for their abundance of materials, and Buganda was in general extremely well wooded. Even so, wood was undoubtedly one resource which influenced the direction of Ganda expansion. The Sesse islands, for example, represented an important source, being described by one missionary as 'splendidly timbered'.[5] Specifically, *mpewere* was widely used, and was found around the Katonga valley, in northern Buddu and Mawokota.[6] Roscoe noted the prevalence in canoe-building of *muvule*, which was comparable with mahogany in that it hardened in water; this wood is resistant to termite attack and is a useful substitute for teak.[7] *Muvule* was indigenous throughout the lake region: according to colonial forestry surveys, it was common in Bunyoro, Ankole and Busoga.[8] It was found in most wooded districts in Buganda.[9]

Kagwa suggests that for canoes made from planks, or the vessels which comprised the bulk of the Ganda *mpingu* or navy, the wood types *emiyoru* and *nkoba* were preferred for the sides of the vessel, being hard and thus resistant to violent weather and leakage.[10] The Minziro forest system in

[3] Vansina, 1990: 91, 94; Harms 1981: *passim*.
[4] Smith 1989: 51–2.
[5] CMS CA6/025/17 Wilson to Wright, 19 April 1878. The Sesse group comprises one large island and numerous smaller ones. The large island is generally known as 'Sesse', and thus gives its name to the group; the people of the whole group of islands are known as the (Ba-) Sesse.
[6] Thomas & Scott 1935: 160.
[7] Roscoe 1911: 385.
[8] Thomas & Scott 1935: 163ff.
[9] Eggeling 1940: 234–7.
[10] Kagwa 1934: 151.

central and southern Buddu contained *nkoba*, which was also located in abundance in the Mabira forest of southern Kyagwe, quite close to the lake. The term *emiyoru* used by Kagwa is more commonly interpreted as *miovu*, which was also found in the forests of Kyagwe.[11] Use was made too of *musizi*, a wood common in Buddu but again also found in Kyagwe.[12] Drawing tentative conclusions, it seems likely that up until the second half of the eighteenth century the Ganda relied heavily on Kyagwe for wood for canoes. The acquisition of Buddu, as in so many other spheres of economic activity, was a significant boost, opening up considerably the range of suitable wood types for canoe construction.

There is little evidence for the impact of canoe construction on local environments. Ecological damage may have resulted in a number of areas, especially in the last decades of the nineteenth century as canoes were built ever larger and at a faster rate. A colonial report from 1901 suggested that 'during the last few years', meaning since the early 1890s, some 10,000 canoes had been built by the Ganda. Many of these vessels each required three trees, 'as only two planks are got from one tree'. As a result, the author of the report surmised, anything up to 30,000 trees had been felled during this period alone.[13] Although this is probably exaggerated, it does suggest that some forest areas may have been seriously depleted; and, although the Ganda probably made use of the leftover wood from canoe construction, there is no evidence to suggest that they attempted to replenish forests by rotating their source areas.

There were obvious variations in construction styles. The *mmanvu*, or dugout canoe, was distinct from the larger vessels constructed from planks: an entire tree might be dug up, roots and all, apparently to minimize the risk of splitting the wood. The required length and diameter were measured and the tree was fashioned accordingly. Kagwa suggests that the inside of this canoe was on average 10–15 ft in length. The trunk was hollowed, the ends tapered and the bottom flattened, whereupon the canoe was rolled on logs to the shore: clearly the closer the materials were to the water, the better.[14] Roscoe states that they could be anything up to 20 ft in length and 4 ft wide, and many contained flattened floors to facilitate the transport of cattle across rivers or shallow bays off the lake.[15] In general, dugout canoes were used for short trips, as ferries across the inland arms of the lake, and for shallow-water fishing both along the lake shore and on rivers further inland, as well as on Lake Wamala in southern Singo. This type of vessel was not unique to Buganda, and was probably of a common design; the Vuma also built canoes capable of carrying livestock between the island and mainland.[16] Chaillé-Long, travelling in such canoes along the Nile from Bulondoganyi, opined that river canoes were inferior to those on the lake;[17] yet, given the contrast in the elements each had to face,

[11] Thomas & Scott 1935: 161–1, 534.
[12] UNA A8/1 Prendergast to ?, 2 July 1900.
[13] UNA A8/1 Tomkins to Commissioner, 13 November 1901.
[14] Kagwa 1934: 151.
[15] Roscoe 1911: 385–6.
[16] UNA A4/8 Report on the Caravan Route from Mombasa to Kampala, by Hobart 15 July 1897.
[17] Chaillé-Long 1876: 155.

this is hardly surprising. In addition to these dugout vessels, the Ganda also made use of the *kadyeri*, a small raft; this was made by lashing together palm-leaf stems, and was used for fishing short distances off shore or for laying traps in shallow water.[18] Both the *mmanvu* and the *kadyeri* were probably older and more common than the larger vessel built from planks, which was known to contemporary Europeans as the Uganda canoe. The latter was clearly deliberately developed in the nineteenth century with both warfare and long-distance trading expeditions in mind. Kenny, however, has suggested that what he calls the 'sewn-canoe' was also found among the Kerebe and the Soga;[19] clearly, then, although the vessel was not unique to the Ganda, they none the less developed the technology to a higher level and utilized it on a much grander scale than any of the other lacustrine peoples.

The building of these vessels was the true glory of the industry in the nineteenth century. Emphasizing the time-honoured skills involved in canoe-building, Kagwa wrote that '[t]he King's boats and some of the others were constructed by experts who were trained in the trade from childhood. Different parts required different experts ... Special tools belonged to each of these.'[20] These divisions and the specialization of labour serve to underline the complexity involved in canoe construction, and stress the exclusivity of the profession and of shoreline communities in general. It is likely that there was a class of skilled men whose reputations went before them; many of these would have been engaged by the *kabaka* to construct the best vessels. The construction of larger canoes in the second half of the nineteenth century was clearly the most recent branch of the industry; the industry itself was the preserve of families long settled along the shore or on the islands.

A high degree of competence in carpentry is evident from Kagwa's descriptions of the exact measurement and weighing of the various boards and planks required for the larger canoes. Planks were held together by pegs or skin thread, pulled through holes made by hot spikes,[21] and a kind of creeper was also sometimes used for stitching, which was in turn covered with a finer creeper for protection. The stitching itself was caulked with tree fibre.[22] The canoe itself was often covered with a dye derived from red clay, found in the surface soil around iron formations; this, mixed with oil or beer, hardened and served to protect joints and seams.[23] Among the final touches, particularly to the larger vessels, was the fixing of animal horns to the prow, which was supposed to symbolize strength,[24] and which may have been connected to the Ganda ideology of civilization's conquest of nature. In 1862 Speke described a flotilla of canoes thus: 'They were all painted with red clay, and averaged ten to thirty paddles, with long prows standing out like the neck of a syphon or swan, decorated on the head with the horns of the Nsunnu (lencotis) antelope, between which was stuck

---

[18] Roscoe 1911: 391.
[19] Kenny 1979: 99.
[20] Kagwa 1934: 151.
[21] Ibid.: 152.
[22] Roscoe 1911: 388–9.
[23] Ibid.: 390. It is unclear whether oil was a pre-colonial ingredient, although castor-oil plants did grow in Buganda.
[24] Kagwa 1934: 152.

upright a tuft of feathers exactly like a grenadier's plume.'[25] Many of the larger vessels were fitted with what was effectively a battering ram, protruding up to 5 ft in front.[26] The launch of a canoe was an occasion of great excitement attended by the builders and their wives.[27] When not in use, canoes would been pulled on to dry land; strenuous efforts were made to conceal them and, if not on land, they might be sunk with large stones,[28] presumably as a precaution against robbery or sabotage.

By the second half of the nineteenth century, the size of canoes varied enormously. Roscoe recorded that larger canoes could carry 'twelve to fourteen loads each', and smaller vessels managed on average four loads: a 'load' was generally 60–70 lb in weight.[29] The largest vessel recorded seems to have been that described by Mackay in 1883, which was apparently 80 ft long and 5 ft wide.[30] Stanley noted a canoe which was 72 ft in length, over 7 ft wide and 4 ft deep.[31] At the south end of the lake, Stanley also observed 14 large Ganda canoes, 'with ample storage room, and all the goods, ammunition, and asses, and all the timid men, women, and children, and Wanyamwezi, were placed in these'.[32] These magnificent vessels were clearly built with long-distance transport in mind, but would also have served as war canoes; other canoes described by Stanley during the war with Buvuma in 1875 were 50–70 ft in length, other varieties again 30–50 ft. The smallest war canoe on this occasion was 18 ft long.[33]

Naval developments c.1700–c.1840

Smaller-scale activity involving the littler vessels described above had existed before the nineteenth century. In commercial terms, the salt trade centred on the northeast corner of the lake, as discussed in an earlier chapter, is just one example of a canoe-based exchange system which doubtless existed before naval expansion in the second half of the nineteenth century.[34] The Ganda also used canoes in warfare before the reign of Mutesa, in both a lacustrine and a riverine context. Kabaka Mawanda, probably in the 1720s or 1730s, used a 'fleet of canoes' to fight the people of Bugerere, north of Kyagwe. A prince named Namatiwa led the fleet

---

[25] Speke 1863b: 390–1. The *nsunu*, or more commonly *mpala*, is the Uganda kob, a large antelope, after which modern *Ka-mpala* ('place of the antelope') is named.

[26] Roscoe 1911: 386.

[27] Kagwa 1934: 152.

[28] Roscoe 1911: 391. Kagwa claims that anchors were attached: Kagwa 1934: 152.

[29] Roscoe 1921: 64.

[30] CMS G3 A6/0 1883/120 Mackay's Journal, 6 July 1883.

[31] Stanley 1878: I, 314.

[32] Ibid.: 293.

[33] Ibid.: 314.

[34] Salt was almost certainly only one among many commodities traded by canoe, although lack of concrete evidence renders this speculative. Stanley, for example, noted that at Musira Island, off the western lake shore south of the Kagera river, 'we found four or five canoes from Kamiru's country loaded with coffee and butter'. The Ganda may also have been involved in such commerce: Stanley 1878: I, 218.

into enemy waters, probably via the Nile, and on this occasion Bugerere was subdued.[35] It may indeed be possible to date the origins of Ganda naval power in the nineteenth century from the reign of Mawanda, who is credited with the complete subjugation not only of Kyagwe '[from] the shores up to the limit of Bugerere', but also of the critical river port of Bulondoganyi and the surrounding district, at or near the modern site of Nabuganyi.[36] Bulondoganyi was of great commercial and military importance through the eighteenth and nineteenth centuries. Commercially, it was located at the junction of several societies, including those of the Ganda, the Nyoro and the Soga, and as such attracted traders from a wide area. Its economic significance in turn lent it military importance, for control of the district meant control of a considerable portion of Nile trade as well as of a strategic frontier post in a region bordered by several, often warring, peoples. Its capture by Mawanda would have been a major boost to Ganda naval and commercial strength in the region.[37] Moreover, we have already noted the importance of Kyagwe in supplying wood for the building of canoes; the extension of Ganda power into this region would have transformed canoe construction.

Around 1800, a military campaign involving canoes was undertaken by Kamanya against the Kedi or Langi. This war was noted for its ferocity and, according to the version told to Stanley, Kamanya became so exasperated at his inability to overcome the enemy that a grand council was held to discuss tactics. Significantly, the geography of the enemy territory was daunting to the Ganda, the land being intersected by 'broad rivers' and the eastern arms of Lake Kyoga. The use of canoes as instruments of war was clearly seen as unconventional:

> Stimulated by large rewards, the chiefs proposed various tactics for retaliating upon the enemy; but it was the plan of the grandfather of Sabadu the historian [who told Stanley this and many other stories] that was deemed the best. This person advised Kamanya to command 100 canoes to proceed by water to Jinja, where they might be taken to pieces and conveyed overland through Usoga to the Nagombwa river, whence, after reconstruction, they could proceed to attack the Wakedi in the rear, while the king himself could proceed with his army to Urondogani, along the western bank of the Victoria Nile, and menace Ukedi from that side. This wise counsel was loudly applauded and at once adopted, the charge of the canoes being given to Sabadu's grandfather himself.[38]

The battle which ensued was eventually, if not easily, won. Kagwa's version does not differ substantially, although one or two details are worth noting. Although the *gabunga* was ordered to 'build canoes' rather than simply collect them, it was Sewankambo the *sekibobo* who was given command of them. In terms of organization, this is worthy of note, as we

[35] 'Emmamba ye Namukuma: Kabaka Mawanda awangula e Kyagwe', *Munno* (1913) p. 111.
[36] 'Ebye Buganda: Entabalo za Sekabaka Mawanda', *Munno* (1921) pp.10–11.
[37] Village ports along this stretch of the Nile had probably been in existence for several centuries. One of the earliest references to Bulondoganyi in this regard is in a mid-seventeenth context: Kagwa 1971: 50.
[38] Stanley 1878: I, 361.

shall see below. Moreover, the canoes were used for ferrying the soldiers and were not directly involved in the fighting.[39]

The next large-scale naval campaign appears to have taken place during Suna's reign, and was directed against the Soga, who had fled to Kitente island in the Buvuma channel and established themselves there in defiance of Ganda authority. It is clear from accounts of this conflict that the Ganda frequently relied on friendly islands to supply them with both crews and vessels; Buvuma, at peace with Buganda on this occasion, offered up to 100 canoes, manned by crews from nearby islets, and several other islands, those of the Sesse group included, supplied 200. Out of a force said to consist of some 500 canoes, probably an exaggerated figure, the remainder came from the Ganda mainland. The Soga, aided by other island allies, apparently managed to muster an equal number. According to Stanley's version, the Ganda felt diffident about fighting on water; it was not universally accepted that canoes and warfare were naturally compatible. The fact that Ganda soldiers were willing to fight on water at all, of course, suggests a certain versatility, which doubtless lent a particular potency to the kingdom's military effort, although this was scarcely a substitute for competence. For one month the Ganda were unable either to overwhelm the Soga canoes, or to land on the island itself. Suna then decided to besiege the island, preventing the Soga from obtaining supplies from the mainland; the conflict lasted a further two months until, on the verge of starvation, the Soga capitulated.[40] The idea of a naval blockade may not have been entirely novel, but on this occasion it was carried out to great effect, demonstrating the utility of the canoe as an instrument of war.

It was no coincidence that such expeditions were carried out by a ruler noted for his interest in developing a state fleet and long-distance trade routes simultaneously. Although the Ganda had had indirect dealings with coastal traders since the late eighteenth century, the arrival of the first such merchants at Suna's court in 1844 provided commerce with a new impetus.[41] With their arrival and increasing presence south of the lake, the 1840s saw the beginning of a period in which waterborne communications took on an unprecedented significance. Suna recognized this, and his campaigns along and off Buganda's lake shore represented a concerted effort to secure Ganda control of the north end of the lake and, thereby, lake traffic. As we shall see, it is a matter of debate whether this was wholly achieved. Nevertheless, these campaigns are a good example of how war was expected to bring both short- and long-term gain; while slaves and other booty were acquired, the Ganda were attempting to improve their overall economic and strategic position. During the last years of his reign, Suna was increasingly preoccupied with the southbound trade routes and was prepared to use military force to secure Buganda's interests. Suna's son and successor, Mutesa, carried this policy even further.

---

[39] Kagwa 1971: 109–10.
[40] Stanley 1878: I, 365–7.
[41] The standard account is by Gray 1947.

The growth of naval power from c. 1840

Canoes, then, were used but infrequently in war before c. 1840, and it was only in the second half of the nineteenth century that attempts were made to use them to extend Ganda military power over long distances. The building and manning of canoes in the nineteenth century remained specialized professions, as they had been before 1800. However, I propose that from the 1840s onward there was a dramatic increase in both the number of canoes constructed and the scale of the vessels themselves. The canoe became a more overt instrument in the extension of state power, both in a physical, territorial sense, and in the marshalling of labour and raw materials for state service. There were two main reasons for this surge: the expansion of long-distance commerce following the arrival of coastal merchants in Buganda in 1844; and the gradually declining success rate of the Ganda army on land, for which naval expansion was in the first instance supposed to compensate. It may also be suggested that the control exerted by Mirambo over the Unyanyambe–Karagwe route forced Mutesa to rely increasingly on waterborne transport during the 1870s.[42]

The precise origins of longer-distance canoe journeys remain unclear, as the relevant sources are not specific. But it seems reasonable to suppose that the first such voyage had been made by at least the early 1850s. Suna is credited with the establishment of a naval force capable of launching attacks against the Soga and even further east. Burton described how the 'merchants have heard that Suna, the late despot of Uganda, built *matumbi*, or undecked vessels, capable of containing forty or fifty men, in order to attack his enemies, the Wasoga, upon the creeks which indent the [eastern] shores of the Nyanza'.[43] Suna also sent canoes as far south as Umara and perhaps Ukerewe.[44] Certainly, we can ignore Stanley's claim to have prompted Mutesa to open trade links with the south end of the lake.[45] The second half of the nineteenth century saw a remarkable increase in the use of the lake as a trade route, so much so that in 1871 Mutesa sent a mission to Zanzibar requesting, among other things, that the sultan send ship-building experts to Buganda to help him navigate the lake, although the Ganda were already capable of this.[46] By the 1880s, coastal merchants were commonly choosing waterborne transport, normally in the form of Ganda canoes, although occasionally their own dhows, rather than the land route through Karagwe.[47]

Slaves and ivory were the primary commodities exported from Buganda by canoe. The journey from the Ganda ports to Mwanza took on average three or four weeks, the canoes hugging the western shore; remaining close

---

[42] Hartwig 1970: 552. Hartwig later enlarged on some of the themes discussed in this article: see Hartwig 1976. See also Reid 1998a.
[43] Burton 1860: II, 212.
[44] Hartwig 1970: 542. James Grant was told that Suna sent canoes 'to the country of Umara, east of Uganda and near to the Masai': Grant 1872: 267.
[45] Hartwig 1970: 536.
[46] Grant 1872: 265–6.
[47] The first Arab dhow appeared on the lake in 1881 and belonged to the trader Said ibn Seif: Hartwig 1970: 546.

to land was essential in order to acquire supplies and to avoid the storms that might loom on the horizon. The advantages of the lake route included lower porterage costs and a minimal risk of slaves escaping; in addition there was the motive of avoiding the centre of Mirambo's empire, as noted earlier.[48] Arab traders also had to pay considerably less in local *hongo* or customs duty. As we have noted in an earlier discussion, the importance of the land route had dwindled by the end of the 1870s, and some 2,000 slaves a year may have been transported by canoe during the 1880s. However, as we have also seen, the lake route had perils of its own, as storms could appear with terrifying abruptness in certain seasons. On the Buddu shore, for example, winds are calm to moderate during February–March and September–October; at other times of the year, north-northeast winds die down in the early morning to be replaced by south-southeast trade winds that can reach gale force during the day.[49] These difficulties, combined with the fact that travel of this magnitude required considerable stamina and certain navigational skills, probably meant that the voyage was the preserve of a small group of people even during the 1870s. A number of Europeans claimed in the 1870s to have experienced considerable difficulty in either getting access to the lake or rounding up sufficient boats and crews. They may have been exaggerating, but it seems to have been the case that Ganda themselves often expressed reluctance to have anything to do with the lake.[50] A voyage from one end of the lake to the other was never one to be taken lightly, as we have already seen in the context of commerce. In 1877, for example, the missionary Wilson was transported in a canoe from Mwanza to Buganda and described how the pilots on two occasions lost their way, mistaking islands for the Ganda shore.[51] Trepidation doubtless accompanied all such trips, which makes it all the more remarkable that Ganda were prepared to push these voyages into commercial and military spheres.

Prompted by repeated military failure on land and by ever greater commercial rewards, the Ganda navy was at its most powerful in the 1870s and 1880s. To some extent, Mutesa was able to offset the limitations imposed by land warfare by adopting a policy of informal empire. Perhaps the best instance of this was the influence exerted over Lukonge, the ruler of Ukerewe. The attack made by a Ganda fleet in that direction in 1878, supposedly in response to the killing of two European missionaries there, was actually made in reply to Lukonge's request for assistance against his rebellious brother. The insurrection was put down and the Ganda withdrew, the status quo maintained and Buganda's reputation intact.[52] At the same time, naval strength led the Ganda to respond positively, even violently, to commercial developments. In 1878, a missionary noted that a Ganda canoe had been 'prowling' off the southern shore of the lake, near

---

[48] Mirambo's polity was concentrated west and northwest of Unyanyembe; the land journey from the southern shore of the lake still meant moving along the fringes of his domains, but this was clearly preferable.

[49] Chorley 1941: 77.

[50] For example, Chaillé-Long 1876: 141; Stanley 1878: I, 214.

[51] Wilson & Felkin 1882: I, 101–2.

[52] Kagwa 1971: 174.

the creek known as 'Jordan's Nullah', capturing people along the shore and selling them as slaves to the Arab trader Songoro.[53]

In 1883, Mackay noted that a great many of the smaller islands down the western side of the lake had been 'devastated' by the Ganda and were now deserted.[54] To be sure, these were soft targets, but they were none the less stark reminders of Buganda's naval power. That year, there were also reports of large-scale naval expeditions led by the *gabunga*, the chief who was, in theory at least, in charge of all canoes. According to Ashe, one of these was against 'Kutahala';[55] the precise direction of the attack is unclear. It was often the mercenary dimension of their activities which lent the Ganda their naval potency. Requests for Ganda assistance in local conflicts went some way to ensuring Ganda hegemony. In 1883, a chief named Rwoma on the southwest shore of the lake, hearing of an impending attack by a Ganda fleet, hastily dispatched a placatory gift of ivory. He also requested Ganda assistance in reducing a rebellious island under his suzerainty. The Ganda obliged, were successful and returned home.[56] By this means, as in the earlier case of Ukerewe, Mutesa was able to extend his influence over areas that would otherwise have remained outside Buganda's reach.

Yet it seems likely that Mutesa was frustrated by his inability to strengthen his control over the southern part of the lake, particularly the mainland. Contemporary Europeans, relying on Ganda informants, tended to exaggerate the extent to which various peoples around the lake owed allegiance to Buganda. Livinhac noted in 1882 that Mutesa regarded the ruler of Karagwe as tributary to him.[57] The White Fathers were also given the impression that the rulers of Mwanza and Sukuma were tributary to Buganda.[58] Although the region may have intermittently fallen under Ganda sway, the term 'tributary' is a gross overstatement of the relationship.

It was much closer to home that the tensions between ambition and reality were most evident. The campaign against Buvuma in 1875 is perhaps the most famous – and certainly the best documented – example of how the fleet was used in war and of the fleet's limitations as an instrument of war. Mutesa was continuing the struggle begun by Suna to pacify the northern shore of the lake; it was a struggle that, on the evidence of the 1875 campaign, Buganda was ultimately unable to win. In this war, which came about because of Vuma raids along the Ganda shoreline, canoes of varying sizes were deployed against the Vuma. The most important vessels, however, were those that, according to Stanley, could carry 60–100 soldiers exclusive of crews. These were formed into what amounted to squadrons of 50–100 vessels, each under the command of a prominent military chief. The squadrons then advanced en masse across the channel

[53] CMS CA6/01 [Letters from the Foreign Office] 3A Kirk to Derby, 1 April 1878.
[54] CMS G3 A6/0 1883/120 Mackay's Journal, 15 July 1883.
[55] CMS G3 A6/0 1884/38 Ashe to Lang, ? November 1883. Ashe also mentions an attack against 'Kunyagga', which is a Luganda word meaning to raid or plunder; he presumably misunderstood.
[56] CMS G3 A6/0 1883/120 Mackay's Journal, 4 September 1883.
[57] White Fathers: C13/37 Livinhac to Lavigerie, 30 April 1882.
[58] White Fathers: C14/38 Lourdel to Superior-General, 24 March 1882.

separating Buvuma from the Kyagwe shore, the oarsmen squatting at the sides of the canoes and the soldiers standing upright, wielding spears and shields. In military terms, the campaign against Buvuma was at best inconclusive; although the Vuma agreed at length to pay tribute to Mutesa, this result was achieved at great cost. The smaller and quicker vessels of Buvuma repeatedly dodged the more cumbersome Ganda canoes, enabling them to launch lightning attacks and then swiftly withdraw.[59]

The Vuma, it is true, were no novices at waterborne activity; even in the 1890s, Europeans noted the size of their canoes and the skill with which they handled them.[60] Yet something of a paradox remains. The Ganda had increasingly used canoes in warfare since the early eighteenth century; yet, even in the 1870s, comparatively few Ganda appear to have been adept at water-based military operations. Tactically, they appear to have remained undecided about the precise role of the large canoe. The problem of whether it should be employed simply as a troop transport or as a weapon in itself perhaps undermined the development of a truly effective naval strategy. Certainly, by the second half of the nineteenth century, the Ganda were capable of building vessels that could travel the length of Lake Victoria at the behest of the state; but they were unable to use such technology to overcome small local islands. This had wider implications, for such unresolved conflicts on occasion paralysed the entire commercial system, leaving merchants stuck on one shore of the lake or the other waiting for their transport to be freed from local military operations.[61] This said, the failures of Ganda lacustrine imperialism should not overshadow the complexity and the force of the system of exploitation that lay behind it. The fact that the state was able to marshal the resources for such a project and organize the fleet and army in tandem is alone worthy of examination.

'The helots of Uganda': the Sesse & Ganda naval expansion

Buganda's canoe technology developed unevenly. After c. 1700, the Ganda gradually attempted to link together two separate spheres of activity, namely military expansion and fishing, for which they had long made use of smaller canoes. Efforts to use the skills of fishing communities for military expansion met with variable success. Even in the late nineteenth century,

---

[59] Stanley 1878: 301–41. The 325 canoes counted by Stanley on the Ganda side represented a markedly smaller force than that used against Busoga by Suna perhaps 30 years earlier. This may seem strange considering that by the 1870s large-scale naval expansion had taken place, but it is very likely that by the 1870s many more vessels were involved in operations beyond Buganda's home waters than had been the case in the 1840s and 1850s, when the vast bulk of naval resources were concentrated around the Ganda shoreline. Moreover, we do not know what kind of vessels were employed during Suna's expedition; presumably there were considerably fewer large canoes than in the 1870s.

[60] For example, UNA A4/8 Report on the Caravan Route from Mombasa to Kampala, by Hobart, 15 July 1897.

[61] For example, CMS CA6/09/6 Copplestone to Wright, 24 June 1879.

it was often an uncomfortable pairing, using experts among the Sesse islanders, who had little experience of transporting large numbers of men in battle conditions, and soldiers, who like the majority of Ganda had little direct experience of the lake and even less of fighting on water.

Nevertheless, the development of Ganda naval power was closely linked to the Sesse islands, strategically located and rich in expertise and raw materials. The historical relationship between the islands and the mainland is not, however, very clear; it is not obvious when Buganda formally extended its rule over Sesse, although Kiwanuka argues that this 'probably' occurred in the sixteenth century.[62] Although details are difficult to come by, it is likely that the Ganda appointed chiefs from among their own governing class to manage Sesse affairs. Indeed, a number of prominent nineteenth-century mainland chiefs had enclosures on the island shores and these probably made use of local collaborative elites. Yet, even during Mutesa's reign, the Ganda were known to launch armed expeditions in the direction of Sesse, suggesting that this combination of collaboration and coercion did not always function smoothly.[63] It seems likely that, before the British intervened, Sesse retained a degree of political, and certainly cultural, autonomy from the mainland. Perhaps it was their historical experience as an island people that as much as anything else engendered the entrenched feelings of separateness among the inhabitants of the Sesse group. Roscoe tells us that up until the late nineteenth century many Sesse had never visited the mainland, and a journey to the capital of Buganda amounted to the trip of a lifetime.[64]

The islands had probably been brought into some form of tributary relationship with Buganda by the middle of the eighteenth century. The original impulse behind the development of canoe transport in Buganda did not come from Sesse, but the economic and professional benefits of closer cooperation between mainland and islands undoubtedly stimulated the rapid growth of the state fleet in the nineteenth century. The origins of mainland expertise are unclear, although Roscoe noted a tradition that the principal canoe-builders of Buganda arrived during the reign of Kintu 'from the north of the lake'. As a geographical expression this is hardly revealing, but these early canoe-builders and oarsmen were apparently the forefathers of the *mamba* clan, traditionally associated with lacustrine affairs and from the Kintu period onward the most prominent representatives of the profession on the mainland. Moreover, it was from their ranks that the *gabunga*, the 'chief of canoes', came.[65] According to one Ganda source, Kintu crossed Lake Kyoga by way of a port named Podyo, implying that canoe technology and a transport network had already emerged in the region.[66] None the less, developing links with the Sesse islands represented an ongoing investment for Ganda leaders. Roscoe gathered that the Sesse people led their field as 'experts in canoe-building, while as sailors they also possess an accurate knowledge of the geography and physical features of

[62] Kiwanuka's notes in Kagwa 1971: 9; Kiwanuka 1971: 66.
[63] For example, Kagwa 1971: 160–1.
[64] Roscoe 1921: 61–2.
[65] Roscoe 1911: 383.
[66] Zimbe 1939: 9.

the lake'.[67] Had not Sesse skills and natural resources been harnessed by the Ganda, it is unlikely that the latter would have been able to develop the naval power they did in the nineteenth century. The skill of the Sesse in canoe construction was to some extent rivalled by that of the Vuma and the Soga, who had more timber than the other shores of the lake, but only the Sesse and Ganda, forming an unequal partnership, managed to build vessels capable of moving considerable distances from their territorial waters.[68]

By the 1870s, the Sesse islands were a crucial pool of canoe-builders and oarsmen; yet their importance to Ganda naval development contrasted with the economic and cultural gulf that existed between the islands and the mainland.[69] Stanley wrote that the islanders, 'because of their coal-black colour, timidity, superstition, and general uncleanly life, are regarded as the helots of Uganda'.[70] Undoubtedly exaggerated, this still suggests something of the relationship between the Ganda and the Sesse. Kenny reminds us that mainlanders regarded islanders with deep suspicion, and that the Sesse were considered cannibals.[71] The sense of separateness was probably reinforced by the roles fulfilled during naval campaigns; Sesse were oarsmen and Ganda were warriors and, of course, mostly landlubbers. It is likely that the arrogance inherent in the Ganda military ethos led many soldiers to look down upon the Sesse, who were more often than not merely their means of transport. Sesse did not normally participate in the fighting. Perhaps because of this, Sesse also had a reputation for abject cowardice. Livinhac wrote in 1889: 'The oarsmen, inhabitants of the Sese islands, whose cowardice is proverbial, were terrified by the gun-shots and threw themselves into beating a retreat. In order to retain them, Gabriel [the Ganda commander] was forced to have recourse to the most terrible threats.'[72] Whether deserving or not, this characterization is revealing of Ganda attitudes.

At the end of the nineteenth century, tensions between the islands and the mainland persisted, and indeed the nascent colonial presence offered the Sesse an opportunity to voice their dissatisfaction with their position in this relationship. In 1898, some Sesse chiefs presented a list of grievances to the British agent Wilson, among which was the fact that 'the Island race is regarded in Uganda as being inferior and subordinate to that country'. Moreover, canoe-building had temporarily ground to a halt because of the 'severe strain upon the Island labour resources'. This discontent was considered 'so serious as to endanger the existence of the canoe service, now so essential with the increasing demands on the Victoria Nyanza lake transport'. The fact that local taxation often took the form of canoe labour reflected pre-colonial arrangements between Sesse and their mainland

[67] Roscoe 1921: 61.
[68] Ibid.: 62.
[69] Stanley 1878: I, 212–14.
[70] Ibid.: 214.
[71] Kenny 1977: 721.
[72] White Fathers: C13/115 Livinhac to Lavigerie, 3 November 1889. This reputation for timidity is all the more perplexing considering that the principal Ganda god of war, Kibuka, is supposed to have come from the Sesse islands. It is, however, also worth noting that a number of Sesse islanders were renowned for their ritual power; this might help explain their low status, which was often associated with such roles.

overseers.[73] By 1900, according to a contemporary report, a number of Sesse had 'emigrated' to the mainland, 'where they find ... more freedom from the power of the Chiefs than they have on the islands, where they are constantly called, by the Ba Ganda chiefs, to man canoes for transport of Government and other loads ... [Such work] takes them from their homes, I believe, as long as seven to eight months in the year ...'[74]

Even allowing for recent changes wrought by the protectorate government, these grievances had clearly been festering for some time. The precise relationship between chiefs and canoeists is unclear, but many contemporary accounts suggest that Sesse oarsmen were miserable and subservient, with virtually no rights over their own labour and little recourse to the freedoms enjoyed by the Bakopi on the mainland. Mackay wrote in 1881: 'The canoes are all built by the Basese, who are the very slaves of slaves. At the point of a spear, on Mutesa's orders, they are obliged to leave their homes and paddle all the way to Usukuma & back, receiving *no pay* and *no food* for any journey.'[75] Mackay exaggerated when he claimed that all canoes were built by the Sesse, as there were also mainland centres of construction; but the significance here lies in the exploitation of their labour. Similarly, another missionary suggested that they were expected to provide their own food on long voyages, could anticipate little payment and above all had no choice in undertaking the journey itself. In sum, 'the Msese must feel greatly honoured and must give thanks for performing the work of the king for free!'[76]

Even by the late nineteenth century, long-established fishing communities remained largely separate from the blossoming profession of long-distance lake travel. Still, it is likely that in the case of the Sesse islands, the constant drafting of professional oarsmen had an adverse effect on the local fishing economy. The drain on Sesse labour would clearly have interfered with the local economic infrastructure. Worse, the men were often absent for at least two or three months, while the labour itself received little or no remuneration. It might be suggested that the islands in the second half of the nineteenth century represent a classic case of underdevelopment; the islanders themselves were closely involved in the expanding cycle of long-distance commerce that was seen to bring economic advancement to Buganda, but they received none of the benefits.

The expansion of ports

Canoes, particularly the larger vessels, needed ports for landing, collection and, indeed, construction. Before the second half of the nineteenth century, there were few ports between the Nile and the Kagera river, the latter approximately representing Buganda's southern extremity. There existed, instead, numerous smaller landing stages, which were used according to season. Many of the shoreline fish markets – notably those in Kyagwe –

---

[73] UNA A4/12 Wilson to Berkeley, 4 September 1898.
[74] UNA A8/1 Pordage to Acting Dep. Comm., 14 August 1900.
[75] CMS G3 A6/0 1881/66 Mackay to Hutchinson, 20 April 1881.
[76] White Fathers: C14/167 Giraud to Bridoux, 24 July 1885.

were probably located in villages which stretched to the water's edge and contained landing areas for fishing canoes. Many of these were also probably centres of construction, at least for smaller vessels. In some areas, seasonal flooding may have prevented the establishment of permanent ports. Emin Pasha believed that regular rises in the level of the lake could produce flooding for up to 2–3 miles inland, creating marshy ground amid the low hills, which in some areas stretched almost to the water's edge.[77] This made the landing of canoes extremely difficult. In other areas, steeper shores prevented flooding and made possible the establishment of landing areas.

In the late 1870s, Emin Pasha observed a point along the shore which he called Usavara where the incline to the water was steep and where there was a shelf 'which for about forty feet is absolutely bare of vegetation'. This allowed 'the boats to come right up to the landing-stage, and hence Usavara is the usual starting-place for voyages on the lake'.[78] Usavara probably lay close to Entebbe, then beginning to emerge as a long-distance port. While the shelf itself was natural, it was probably cleared of vegetation by hand. In 1875, Stanley asserted that Usavara (or Busabala, now Kaazi), which he described as 'the Kabaka's hunting village', was located on the east side of Murchison Bay. It was here that Stanley first landed in Buganda and it was clearly quite a large settlement. The drawing accompanying Stanley's text plainly illustrates the cleared landing area described by Emin Pasha. The broad, neat approach to the water, the huts depicted to the left of the landing area and the fact that the forest is shown to be some distance away suggest that Usavara was an important collection point for canoes.[79] Further south, there may have been an important port at Buganga, at the mouth of the Katonga, although this lay close to marshy ground liable to flooding during the wet season.[80] Canoes were ordinarily collected here to transport men and livestock across the Katonga itself.[81] As well as a port, it may also have been an important centre of canoe construction. Lugard wrote of the Buganga promontory in 1891, 'there is here a land-locked harbour, and the opposite shore of Bunjako is the main timber supply of this part, from whence came most of the large forest trees used for making canoes and planks'.[82] Passing through the 'Katonga valley' in 1862, Speke also wrote of the 'magnificent trees' which 'towered up just as so many great pillars, and then spread out their high branches like a canopy over us'.[83] This

---

[77] Schweinfurth *et al.* 1888: 126. Of the shoreline of southern Buddu, Speke wrote: 'Indeed, it appeared to me as if the N'yanza must have once washed the foot of these hills, but had since shrunk away from its original margin': Speke 1863b: 265–6.

[78] Schweinfurth *et al.* 1888: 126.

[79] Stanley 1878: I, 186–8.

[80] UNA A4/8 Hobart to Comm., 15 July 1897.

[81] UNA A6/9 Cunningham to Comm., 24 September 1894.

[82] UNA A26/4 Lugard to Admin.-Gen., IBEAC 13 August 1891. Lugard drew attention to the abundance of construction wood in Buddu generally, and implied that the only other *ssaza* which was as rich in this respect was Kyagwe.

[83] Notably, Speke and his party waded across the Katonga instead of using canoes. He wrote that 'instead of finding a magnificent broad sheet of water, as I had been led to expect by the Arabs' account of it, I found I had to wade through a succession of rush-drains divided one from the other by islands'. He did, however, use canoes to cross the Kagera: Speke 1863b: 263, 277–8.

area, indeed, may be an example of the manner in which particular ports were under the command of local naval commanders. Stanley, for example, described a journey to Jumba's Cove. The *jumba*, discussed more fully below, was a vice-admiral in the European sources, and was in charge of the district of 'Unjaku', which was 'a headland abutting on the left or north bank of the Katonga river'.[84]

By the late nineteenth century, the port of Munyonyo had also become established on the eastward-facing shore of the peninsula between present Entebbe and Kampala. The origins of this port are unclear, but it first came to prominence in the late 1860s, when Mutesa established one of his capitals there. For several years the *kabaka* regularly travelled to this spot to observe Ramadan.[85] Speke may have been describing Munyonyo when in 1862 he accompanied Mutesa to 'the royal yachting establishment, the Cowes of Uganda', apparently located 'down the west flank of Murchison Creek'.[86] In 1875, Stanley mentioned Monyono Bay as being the location of the *kabaka*'s 'favourite canoes'.[87] Twenty years later, British officials were also impressed with the site as a port. Ternan noted a 'good approachable foreshore for boats and steamers', the fact that the ground was 'well raised above the level of the lake – a very gentle slope' and the ready availability of timber nearby.[88] In the later nineteenth century, Munyonyo became noted primarily as the base for the *kabaka*'s 'pleasure trips' on the lake. Roscoe noted that the *kabaka* kept a large number of canoes at the 'King's port', almost certainly Munyonyo, enabling him 'to go at pleasure to the lake and spend some time in the water'.[89] The tradition of royal pleasure-boating at Munyonyo remains strong. The recent souvenir book cele-brating Mutebi II's coronation alleges that a canoe regatta was founded by Mwanga in the late 1880s. There is no evidence for this; it is more likely to have originated under Mutesa. Throughout the twentieth century such events have been closely associated with the *kabaka*; in 1993 a regatta took place amid much publicity.[90] Munyonyo, however, had an additional, less frivolous, function: royal canoes were maintained here which in the event of an emergency – namely rebellion or foreign invasion – could facilitate the *kabaka*'s hasty departure.[91] The port itself may have existed for this purpose since before 1800.

Finally, the origins of Entebbe are, again, unclear, although there can be little doubt that a fishing settlement had existed near modern Entebbe for several centuries. Kagwa offers one of the earliest references to Entebbe when he suggests that Kabaka Kiggala, perhaps in the mid-fifteenth century, sought sanctuary there upon hearing of his brother's rebellion.[92] Little mention is made of Entebbe in any source as a major port until the

[84] Stanley 1878: I, 212.
[85] Kagwa 1971: 158, 161.
[86] Speke 1863b: 389, 391.
[87] Stanley 1878: I, 186.
[88] UNA A4/5 Ternan to Berkeley, 19 August 1896.
[89] Roscoe 1921, 62–3.
[90] *Coronation Special Souvenir* (Kampala, 1993) p. 25. A copy of this entertaining and often informative booklet is held by the author.
[91] Roscoe 1921: 89.
[92] Kagwa 1971: 20.

late nineteenth century, and its development was probably directly linked to the growth of long-distance canoe travel. Even then it seems to have been, for several years, less important than Munyonyo or Usavara (Busabala). In 1879 a French missionary described it thus: 'The port of Mteve is large and very well-sheltered; on the shore there are no more than three or four poor houses for travellers; the village of Mteve is some distance from there.'[93] Mutesa seemed reluctant to lend his support to the development of Entebbe as the main arrival point of coastal merchants. Girault suggested in 1882 that the *kabaka* was anxious to control customs duty on the incoming traders, and that Entebbe was regarded as being too distant from the capital for this to be done effectively.[94] None the less, Entebbe also had the major advantage of being well served by local timber,[95] and this was doubtless a significant factor in the settlement's emergence; still, Entebbe's later pre-eminence was largely based on its selection as the capital of the British colonial administration.

The organization of the fleet

In theory at least, the *gabunga*, the state official responsible for canoe traffic, was at the pinnacle of Buganda's naval hierarchy. In practice, his authority was often limited, and probably did not usually extend beyond control over the *kabaka*'s favourite vessels. His responsibilities depended on current circumstances. It seems likely, for example, that his position was gradually undermined during the age of long-distance travel after the 1840s. This was largely because the uses to which naval technology was put at this time demanded either commercial or military expertise; there is little evidence that the *gabunga* was expected to have either. In the 1870s and 1880s, it may have been his job to look after Europeans on the lake, overseeing the arrival of missionaries and their goods. Increasingly, however, although he did on occasion lead military expeditions, it was a largely honorary position, and the importance of the holder should not be exaggerated. One of the problems in analysing his role is the extent to which he was able to organize large concentrations of canoes. His main enclosure was in the *ssaza* of Busiro, where, according to Roscoe, he was virtually as important as the county chief, the *mugema*. In theory, he 'controlled all the traffic on the lake', and a great many chiefs were under his authority, as were hundreds of canoes. Thus, he was 'often called upon to furnish the means of transport for troops on their way to attack [the south end of the lake]'. His authority in peacetime is suggested by the fact that he 'also provided canoes for people who wished to visit the more remote parts of the mainland, which could be reached more easily by water than by making a long over-land journey'.[96] Roscoe may well have been describing the duties of

---

[93] White Fathers: Rubaga Diary 0/17 June 1879.
[94] White Fathers: Rubaga Diary 2/17 February 1882. Mutesa appears to have favoured, for a while at least, a point closer to Lweza, about which little is known. In 1875 Mutesa apparently went to Lweza 'to consult the god Wannema': Kagwa 1971: 166.
[95] UNA A4/19 Whyte to Ternan, 26 July 1899.
[96] Roscoe 1911: 254.

the *gabunga* in a past era, rather than those of the later nineteenth century.

The fishing and canoe industries were traditionally linked to the *mamba* clan, whose foundation, again, was supposedly contemporaneous with the arrival of Kintu. The *gabunga* is generally regarded as the head of the clan, although his claim is disputed by the chief Nankere. According to one version, Kintu asked the *gabunga* where in Buganda he wanted to settle, to which the latter replied 'near the lake'. Thus, as Kagwa wrote, '[t]he main function of the Mamba clan was to construct Kabaka's canoes and Gabunga took sole charge of all the canoes that were on the lake'.[97] Theoretically this may have been true, but there was little evidence of it by the nineteenth century. As we have noted, the position of the *gabunga* was probably undermined by the linking of maritime culture to warfare and commerce. Yet, as early as the mid-seventeenth century, the *gabunga* was experiencing political vicissitudes. At this time, according to one indigenous account, Kabaka Kayemba favoured Lugumba, a sub-chief of the *nvubu* clan, and gave him 'the leadership of the canoes'.[98] It is not clear how long this appointment lasted, or indeed what exactly it entailed; the *gabunga* had presumably re-established his position by the end of the eighteenth century, when he took a limited part in Kamanya's war against Bukedi, discussed above.

Moreover, although the *mamba* clan may have had an older claim to naval responsibility, they did not have a monopoly of it, or of water-based activities generally. One of the most important clans in this context is that of the *nkima*, and we return to this below. The *nvuma* or *katinvuma* clan also stress the importance of canoes in their heritage. The sub-chief Munyagwa appears to have been in charge of canoes at Bulondoganyi on the Nile, a responsibility which would have increased in importance as Bulondoganyi itself grew in significance and as Ganda control in the area was consolidated. In addition, Munyagwa 'was also in charge of transporting the Basoga from that side to Buganda and likewise he transported Baganda who left to fight in Busoga. His canoe is claimed to have been very large.'[99] It is impossible to place these duties in a historical context, but their relevance is clear. Members of the same clan had also come to the attention of Nakibinge in the early sixteenth century because 'they protected him to and from Ssese'.[100] Their canoe heritage embraced both riverine and lacustrine transport. A chief of the *kasimba* clan, Kabazzi or Kabuzi, claimed to be in charge of the *kabaka*'s canoe *Nakawungu* – many vessels had names – of which he was the chief rower.[101] The 'fox' clan were also closely associated with maritime culture, having supposedly come from an island off the mainland and settling originally along the Kyagwe shore.[102] Finally the *nkejje* clan established their naval prowess in the early eighteenth century under Kabaka Mawanda. The case of the *nkejje* is striking because it explicitly makes the link between fishing and naval war-

[97] Kagwa 1972: 34–8.
[98] Ibid.: 85.
[99] Ibid.: 58.
[100] Ibid.
[101] Ibid.: 63.
[102] Ibid.: 87.

fare. Mayemba, the clan head, 'was an expert at sailing and he constructed two canoes Nalubugo and Nalugo both of which he used for fishing'. But he was able to apply these skills to fighting when Mawanda decided to make war on Busoga. Mayemba distinguished himself – indeed conquered the Soga army single-handed, according to the clan history – and Mawanda rewarded him with a copper paddle. We have already noted the significance of copper, and the reward was clearly of considerable value. After the Soga campaign, Mayemba built a number of canoes at Namukuma in Kyagwe and was apparently greatly favoured by the king.[103] It is significant that these events occurred during the reign of Mawanda, who, as we have noted, was probably the first *kabaka* to encourage the development of naval power as an extension of military strength. What is clear is that all of these clans, or sections of them, were mobilized by the state in the nineteenth century to contribute to naval expansion.

The *gabunga* might be described as the senior naval chief, but other chiefs were in charge of local fleets. Chiefs whose estates bordered the lake had such responsibility, and indeed it was probably these men in whom real naval authority was vested. Early colonial officials, for example, clearly felt little need to use the *gabunga* to collect canoes for them. In 1896, one officer, wanting 20 canoes to travel down river to Mruli, 'called the principal chiefs together, and explained to them the nature of the undertaking required of them. They at once issued orders for 20 canoes to be at Fouira in 24 days.'[104] One of these chiefs may have been the *jumba*, noted in the previous section: in 1862, the *jumba* was placed in charge of organizing canoes to take Speke east to the Nile. Speke described him as 'the fleet admiral', and a junior chief named Kasoro, who was 'a lieutenant of Jumba's', was ordered to provide the European with canoes at Bulondoganyi.[105] Stanley also later mentioned the *jumba*, which he described as 'the hereditary title of one of the junior admirals in command of a section of the imperial canoe fleet', based in the district of 'Unjaku' on the north bank of the Katonga river.[106] The *jumba* appears to have been an important figure. It was the hereditary title of a chief of the *nkima* clan; the main enclosure associated with the title was in Bunjako in the *ssaza* of Mawokota. According to Kagwa's history of the *nkima* clan, the *jumba* was historically a very powerful character who 'would not see the Kabaka' and who was extremely wealthy. He was more or less the social equal of the *kaima*, the governor of Mawokota.[107] Notably, the clan history gives no indication of the *jumba*'s naval responsibilities, which may only have been conferred in the nineteenth century. The office retained authority through the 1880s and 1890s, however, and in 1897 was still a prominent naval position.[108] Stanley also mentioned 'Magura', who was 'the admiral in charge of the naval yards

[103] Ibid.: 106.
[104] UNA A4/6 Wilson to Comm., 17 September 1896.
[105] Speke 1863b: 446, 449, 453.
[106] Stanley 1878: I, 212–14.
[107] Kagwa 1972: 19.
[108] UNA A4/9 Pordage to Wilson, 4 September 1897. In 1897 the *jumba* was a Christian named Noah Naluswa.

at Sesse'.[109] This man does not appear in any other source under this name, but his responsibility would have been considerable.

Kagwa suggests that there were around 100 specially made canoes for state service, each with its own name and captain, belonging to a particular clan and stationed at its own mooring site. These were the pride and joy of the Ganda fleet, which when launched in full, and inclusive of 'all the additional vessels of the chiefs and the fishermen', probably numbered thousands of canoes.[110] To talk of an operational fleet numbering thousands of vessels is, however, surely mistaken. It is highly unlikely that such a number of vessels ever acted in concert. Nor is it clear that fishing vessels were regularly requisitioned for military service, although this seems to have been the case during the war with Buvuma in 1875, when Stanley noted among the assembled fleet small vessels each carrying between three and six men.[111] None the less, canoe-builders, oarsmen and actual canoes were doubtless pooled for naval campaigns in much the same way that large-scale armies were. The state fleet had numerous vessels at its disposal between the mainland and the islands, and a flotilla of 'a hundred strong could easily be collected in two or three days'.[112] Chiefs based on the islands were obliged to have ready at all times a number of canoes for use in the service of the kingdom – military campaigns or long-distance commercial missions – and punishment could be expected if such canoes were not in good condition.[113]

Moreover, such chiefs were expected to cooperate with the military establishment as need arose. Once again, Stanley's account of the war against Buvuma in 1875 is illuminating as it shows the organization of the fleet at war, as well as the ways in which the army worked in tandem with the navy. The fleet was basically at the army's disposal; it formed part of the resources utilized by the army, and was not capable of independent action, nor was it expected to be. In 1875, the *Sekibobo* was in command of both the army and the assembled canoes. Including some 150 canoes, the fleet totalled over 300 large and small vessels, of which Stanley reckoned 230 to be 'really effective for war'. About half were manned by the Sesse, the rest having crews from other islands tributary to Buganda and the mainland shores. These had apparently been hand-picked by the *kikwata*, another 'vice-admiral'.[114] The *kikwata* was later described by a British official as 'the man in charge of the canoes at Munyonyo'.[115] The *jumba* and *gabunga* had also collected crews from the islands and mainland. The *gabunga* was indeed the grand admiral of the fleet, but in a joint action with the army he could not hold a position of supreme command. In wartime, the fleet appears to have been relegated to a subordinate position within the great hierarchy of responsibility, and it was the *gabunga*'s duty 'to convey the orders of the fighting general to his captains and lieutenants'.

[109] Stanley 1878: I, 212–14.
[110] Kagwa 1934: 153–6. Kagwa's figure of 'ten thousand' is presumably notional.
[111] Stanley 1878: I, 314.
[112] Roscoe 1911: 384.
[113] Ibid.: 384–5.
[114] Stanley 1878: I, 312–13.
[115] UNA A9/1 Comm.'s Office to Collector, 30 July 1801.

Stanley suggests that the principal reason for this was that the oarsmen rarely fought, except in dire emergency, and thus were denied the glory of fighting rank. There were parallel lines of command, however, and the internal structure of the fleet was respected in joint actions. The soldiers transported in each canoe only took orders from their supreme commander – in 1875 this was the *sekibobo* – and the oarsmen only obeyed the *gabunga*, who himself, of course, received instructions from the *sekibobo*.[116] Whether this lent itself to efficiency in operations is another question; it is probable that a joint expedition was a cumbersome affair indeed, undermining the overall effectiveness of the operation itself. Cooperation of this kind was made possible by what might be described as the Ganda deference to the ideals of hierarchy. Care may have been taken not to offend prominent naval personages; yet one might contrast this with the haughty disdain directed toward the Sesse oarsmen. Campaigns of a different nature may have afforded the *gabunga* greater authority, although where a substantial military presence was involved, this was probably rare. Even so, we have already noted the campaigns led by the *gabunga* in late 1883 and early 1884. O'Flaherty observed him on the eve of one of these expeditions, 'surrounded by several thousands of his choicest warriors' and being blessed by various priests. The campaigns were apparently successful, although the *gabunga* himself died on the journey back to Buganda.[117]

In 1875, more junior land-based commanders were given charge of various sections of the naval advance. The *kyambalango* was in charge of the right flank, consisting of 50 canoes. The centre was under the command of the *kauta*, who had responsibility for 100 vessels. The *mukwenda*, commanding 80 canoes, led the left flank.[118] Estimating that the three categories of larger canoes had on average crews of 20, 40 and 50 respectively and estimating the total number in each of these categories, Stanley produced the figure of 8,600 as the aggregate number of naval personnel involved in the war against Buvuma.[119] Stanley implies that the war was indeed one of great importance, but this may reflect his desire to be seen at the centre of great events rather than the reality of the war itself. Bearing this in mind, we should read with caution Stanley's calculation that the Ganda were capable of putting on the water a force of 'from between 16,000 to 20,000 ... for purposes of war', including the soldiers in the canoes.[120] None the less, a large force requiring close collaboration between two separate agencies of power in Buganda – the army and the canoe fleet – was clearly gathered in 1875 and, as we have noted, the long-term failure of operations along the northern shore was symptomatic of a much greater malaise, regardless of the significance of the 1875 campaign in particular.

There can be little doubt, then, that during the nineteenth century the Ganda developed water transport into an invaluable resource for economic and military expansion, and attempted to convert fishing skills into long-distance navigational and military skills. There was no ready

---

[116] Stanley 1878: I, 313.
[117] CMS G3 A6/0 1884/79 O'Flaherty to Wigram, 1 April 1884.
[118] Stanley 1878: I, 331.
[119] Ibid.: 314.
[120] Ibid.

bridge between the two, and so the story of Buganda's naval expansion is to some extent the story of the struggle to link the old with the new, to pull what was perceived to be ready-made labour from among the shoreline communities and place it in a radically different context. On one level, the success of the endeavour is hardly in question; Buganda became the dominant naval power on Lake Victoria, extended its influence beyond the confines of land-based military operations and was almost unrivalled in the volume of trade that it carried from one end of the lake to the other. Yet the lake continued to be treated with great respect, and the uncertainty of naval tactics, combined with the diffidence of many Ganda on the water, prevented the complete military domination for which the fleet seems to have been designed. One should not read too much into European tales of the incompetence of oarsmen and the dread expressed by many about long-distance voyages, but it is clear that, although the Ganda had the most powerful claim, no one could describe the lake, as the Romans did the Mediterranean, as *mare nostrum*.

The heavy reliance on Sesse labour demonstrated the vigour and ruthlessness with which the Ganda exploited the human resources and raw materials at their disposal. Yet this exploitative system was also a source of potential weakness. Despite their highly specialized skills and the great value that the Ganda attached to them, the Sesse appear to have been treated little better than slaves. The ruthless and grinding process by which Sesse labour was utilized was not perhaps the most efficient way of developing a motivated maritime class; the undermining of the indigenous Sesse economy and the exclusion of the islands from the benefits of commerce can scarcely have inspired the Sesse to commit themselves whole-heartedly to Buganda's programme of military and commercial expansion.[121] Finally, the Ganda fleet moved with impunity in those areas of the lake bordered by societies with no naval technology of which to speak (for example, the islands off the western shore noted by Mackay in 1883), enabling the Ganda to extend their influence through mercenary activity. Elsewhere, effective challenges were mounted. Buganda's inability to completely pacify the northern shore meant that valuable naval resources were often tied up in struggles with the Soga and the Vuma. Missionaries and coastal traders alike were often stranded at both ends of the lake precisely because of this insecurity. The failure to overwhelm Buvuma in 1875 typifies this. Ironically, perhaps, the Ganda fleet had more success in the southern, more distant waters of the lake, but here also the Ganda were unable to impose the authority that Mutesa desired and of which their technology suggested they were capable.

[121] In spite of this, it is interesting to note that, during the civil war, the Sesse rallied to support the deposed Kabaka Mwanga.

Summary of Part Four

Buganda's military achievements were indeed remarkable; its expansion over some 200 years was achieved by force of arms, and the position in which the kingdom found itself in 1800, as the dominant military state in the region, was in large part a credit to the organization and motivation of the military establishment. Its success, clearly, must be studied as a fundamental component of the process of Ganda state formation, and it needs to be acknowledged that war was critical to the state. But an important argument running through the preceding section has been to demolish the myth of Ganda military prowess. In the decades after the onset of colonial rule, the idea of Ganda military supremacy became more or less set in stone, largely because of their mutually advantageous alliance with the British. By the time the first Europeans arrived to provide eye-witness accounts, the kingdom was already experiencing serious problems; but, in what was perhaps a credit to Ganda military organization even in decline, they tended to report what the Ganda army was and not what it had been.

Although in general the methods of organization and recruitment, with their origins before 1800, appear to have remained fairly constant during the nineteenth century, we have seen how political and military changes were taking place from the 1850s onward. This is mirrored by the fact that, although indigenous weapons remained predominant, guns – in all their variety – were seen to represent a new genre of battle. Both changes were detrimental to Buganda's fighting capacity. I have also argued that military decline coincided with the expansion of long-distance trade and of the lucrative commercial connections to the East African coast. From this point on, therefore, Ganda foreign policy was driven by two main objectives: firstly, to reap the greatest possible benefits from the coastal traders, preferably by controlling the routes as well as the traders themselves; and, secondly, to overcome the stagnation, and later what we can call active decline, experienced by Ganda armies abroad.

The answer, it seemed, lay in the development of the Ganda fleet. If the Ganda could harness their advantageous lakeside position with their renowned military prowess, the lake might be controlled and Ganda influence extended far beyond the confines imposed by land warfare. Moreover, the same canoes which carried soldiers to the battle zone might be used to carry traders and their goods huge distances, giving the Ganda maximum control of lucrative long-distance commerce. These aims were perfectly complementary. In securing the lake by force, the Ganda would make it safe for commerce, and more importantly on their terms. This was the East African variety of the imperialism of free trade made famous in connection with Britain's global position in much the same period; Lake Victoria, therefore, was the final frontier for Ganda imperialism, and it was on the waters of the lake that the kingdom made its last bid for pre-colonial hegemony. The development of a canoe fleet was indeed an innovation, but the policy behind it was consistent with earlier phases of expansion. Continuity, rather than discontinuity, is the key theme. Naval expansion, however, met obstacles of its own. Ultimately, the success of this remarkable endeavour was overshadowed by a series of failings in naval strategy and by the uncertainty attendant in the largely unprecedented transfer of skills from one sphere of activity to another. But the entire exercise is a critical one on which to finish any study of the Ganda state, as it brings together the themes of commercial enterprise, organization of labour, state utilization of natural resources, the exploitative nature of the Ganda state and the centrality of military activity to the kingdom's existence. Symbolically, as well as in practical terms, the story of Buganda's material and military progress culminates in what might be termed the kingdom's naval period. The Ganda attempt to expand via the waters of Lake Victoria was the last great innovation of the pre-colonial era; it was an operation which, over the final decades before colonial rule, symbolized many of the strengths as well as the weaknesses of the pre-colonial kingdom.

Twelve

Conclusions

I have argued that Buganda's growth was inextricably linked to economic and military developments, and how the material basis of political power, both internal and external, was on many levels the *sine qua non* of the state. An understanding of this material basis is clearly critical to unravelling the complexities of the state and of the expansion of the state, both physical and abstract. Much of the success of the political state was founded on its ability to marshal human and material resources for what was perceived to be the common purpose, even allowing for the fact that there was a marked degree of decentralization in terms of organization and considerable scope for individual initiative in many spheres of economic activity. The ethos of state organization manifested itself in a number of ways, the recruitment of armies perhaps being the most dramatic. In other spheres of public life, the collection of tax in a wide range of local produce was a critical component of the relationship between governed and governing; the construction of a fleet of canoes represented a deliberate attempt to join raw materials with ancient skills for the purpose of extending state influence and making the most of the commercial and military opportunities presented by long-distance trade. Yet such centralization was, again, balanced by a marked degree of commercial freedom. The ability of the Ganda to trade freely in an enormous range of products – from foodstuffs to textiles to human beings – was to a great extent the true basis of Ganda wealth. In this context, the breadth of Buganda's productive base was striking. Even so, the need to defend commercial strength and the restless search for secure supplies of raw materials strongly influenced the nature of Buganda's relations, both peaceful and bellicose, with its neighbours for much of the nineteenth century.

In the opening chapter, we noted that the unifying theme of the book is the way in which the Ganda state utilized its human and material resources in order to attain three main and interrelated goals: profit and economic growth; internal cohesion; and external security. Individually, the Ganda traded and produced freely in most spheres of economic activity, with a few exceptions; at the same time, however, this freedom was more often than not to the benefit of the state. Buganda's strong commercial position, based on the activities of a multitude of private traders and producers, contributed as much as military organization to the kingdom's regional domination for much of the nineteenth century; the state intervened in the progress of commerce when the kingdom's regional position was threatened, as was the case with the development of long-distance trade from the 1840s. The Ganda empire of the nineteenth century was less formal than informal, while Ganda military imperialism was inextricably linked to the desire for commercial and economic hegemony. We have seen, moreover, that through the commercial and productive freedom of the individual, the state derived considerable wealth through taxation.

Yet the state intervened in private life in other ways and, although internal cohesion was an aim in itself, it was in another sense – what we might call pre-modern nationalism – the means to an end, namely external security. The highways of Buganda represented the combination of these aims. Roads were built to facilitate human traffic and the transport of goods and people; clearly, then, they aided the pursuit of profit and enabled the Ganda to seize the opportunities presented by commerce. Roads were also critical to the rapid recruitment and deployment of armies. At the same time, the state's ability to marshal the kind of public labour required in road-making was critical in the search for both internal cohesion and external security. Political authority was underpinned by such labour, as it was by the organization of peasant armies. Slavery was also a critical part of this system, forming a central component of economic, social and political life; the fact that slaves were mostly foreigners further reflected Buganda's desire for external control on an internal level. Slavery as an institution was as elaborate as it was ancient in Buganda and, while the situation became even more complex with the growth of a long-distance slave trade, such complexity reflected the Ganda desire to utilize the kingdom's human resources, free or unfree, to the maximum advantage. From such an efficient organizational base, the kingdom strove to secure the external environment to its own advantage. Internal cohesion was essential if the kingdom was to control, or exercise an influence over, the external status quo. As we have seen, internal cohesion had begun to dissipate by the time British imperialism appeared on the horizon; the ability of the Ganda to maintain some form of control over these new circumstances, by acting as the 'sub-colonists' of the British, is a credit to the resilience of the pre-colonial political system.

It is clear that Buganda's regional power was based not simply on the resources it was able to derive from other societies, although imports and tribute were clearly essential, and the celebration of material culture was of profound importance within the pre-colonial state. In the case of barkcloth production, the Ganda themselves possessed the means of commercial hegemony. Ganda producers of this valued textile traded throughout the region during the nineteenth century, and derived much wealth from it. This was as clear an indication of the material basis of Ganda power as were the military expeditions which often travelled in the same direction. Yet these two expressions of Ganda expansionism were rarely far apart. Semakokiro's revolution in indigenous fabric production at the end of the eighteenth century was almost certainly linked to the military seizure of Buddu by his brother a few years earlier. Buddu produced some of the finest barkcloth in the region. There were many advantages to territorial expansion in this direction; but there was no greater prize than barkcloth, one of the less dramatic but certainly no less significant determinants of Ganda regional strength by the early nineteenth century. It was the British, not the coastal Arabs, who eventually destroyed this industry, by which time – the early twentieth century – it had in any case lost its *raison d'être*.

We have also noted the importance of iron in Buganda's growth by the nineteenth century. Iron was both the cause and the effect of expansionism. Iron was found in the Ganda core area, but it was particularly abundant in the lands to the west; it was the quest for this critical raw material, as well as for barkcloth and cattle, that drew Buganda's attention in that direction. The cultural and social importance of blacksmiths themselves suggests the reverence with which the Ganda treated the profession and the metal. This was particularly the case in the late nineteenth century, with the development of a branch of the profession which dealt in the repair of firearms. In a general sense, metal-working and pottery were probably the two most celebrated professions in Buganda, and this celebration of material culture speaks volumes about the ways in which the Ganda themselves perceived the kingdom's growth and development. Great warriors, while rewarded with political position and material wealth, were rarely as lauded as the humble smith. The former were certainly not exempt from the arbitrary power of the *kabaka* in the way blacksmiths and potters were. The individual endeavour of the local forge was seen as the means by which economic and material greatness could be attained; and the Ganda appear to have acknowledged this manifestation of greatness above all others.

Fabrics and metals, meanwhile, were among the commodities which placed Buganda at the centre of a complex and flourishing trading system. Buganda's central and often dominant position in this network was the key to the kingdom's material strength vis-a-vis its immediate neighbours. Moreover, the promotion and protection of commerce were the driving forces behind Ganda diplomatic, military and technological policy in the second half of the nineteenth century. This was consistent with the kingdom's objectives since around the middle of the sixteenth century, although clearly the scale of the objectives, like the kingdom itself, had expanded. Yet recognition of this basic continuity must not detract from our appreciation of the degree to which the Ganda innovated to meet the challenges of long-distance trade. Theirs was a positive response: the presence of Ganda on the southern shore of Lake Victoria, in Tabora and even on Zanzibar itself is indicative of the alacrity with which Suna and Mutesa seized their opportunities.

Yet the tensions inherent in Buganda's position after c.1850 are clear. Militarily, the kingdom was not the power it had been in 1800. The army frequently over-reached itself, and changes in military organization at the centre, initiated perhaps in the 1840s, served in the long term to impair the effectiveness with which the army operated on the battlefield. The militarization of junior chiefs and pages – both *ebitongole* and, later, *bagalagala* – introduced conflict into command structures and signified the *kabaka*'s attempt to strengthen his own position politically. European military uniforms at the capital were no mere triviality: in a sense they represented much deeper changes in the military ethos at the capital, where social and political positioning combined with a detrimental gun culture to weaken the army more generally. There is also little doubt that, as pointed out in the opening chapter, these metropolitan tensions were closely intertwined with the introduction of foreign religions; yet religious factionalism was not the cause but rather the symptom of such tension. These difficulties could scarcely have come at a worse time for Buganda, when slaves were increasingly important as export commodities and as the kingdom's own reserves of ivory were dwindling rapidly. Indeed, the expansion of the slave trade itself may have undermined the effective functioning of the internal labour base; it certainly weakened internal cohesion, generating a level of lawlessness as people scrambled to acquire the goods offered in exchange for human beings.

We have seen how war and commerce had long been closely inter-woven in the kingdom's development; both Suna and Mutesa frequently resorted to conflict to establish favourable trading conditions. The development of a fleet of canoes, some of enormous dimensions, was the most dramatic expression of this policy. The long-term objectives of this pro-gramme from the 1840s onward were the control of vital lake trade routes and the restoration of Ganda military power in the region. It was clearly believed that the fleet could overcome the obstacles imposed by land war-fare. There is little doubt that the fleet did indeed serve to extend Ganda influence. It also almost certainly prolonged Ganda power and significance in the region; without canoes, Buganda's geopolitical position on the eve of colonial rule would have been considerably weaker. But the renewed confidence which the fleet gave to successive rulers often proved unfounded and revealed, as on other occasions in the later nineteenth century, the Ganda tendency to over-confidence and even complacency about their ability to control the external environment. There is a clear, and on one level pathetic, paradox in the fact that as the Vuma were repelling Ganda attacks and even raiding the Ganda shoreline for slaves, the *kabaka* was drawing up grandiose plans to invade Buzinza and subdue Mirambo. As we have seen, the evidence suggests that this was not mere talk, at least initially, although subsequent events reduced the plan to exactly this. Through the fleet the Ganda were able to take control of vital trade routes, but even here they were, in a sense, exposing their own weaknesses.

The reliance on the slave trade, brief but intense, was inimical to the kingdom's long-term economic development; at the same time, the exaltation of the firearm, perhaps the most valued trade good, led to enervating political factionalism and the blunting of the army's effectiveness on the battlefield. None the less, the development of the fleet provides an excellent example of the ways in which the Ganda state sought to channel its material and human resources into the extension of power and influence and the generation of wealth. We have seen, in this context, the significance of public labour in the construction of highways which stretched throughout the kingdom. In this way Buganda connected itself to the outside world, a new horizon of increasing significance from the middle of the nineteenth century, as well as facilitating communications within the kingdom; at the same time, roads were unifying themes, providing the foci for social and political cohesion. The fleet can also be seen in these terms, though in practice rather more complex and, perhaps, less successful. The attempt to transfer the skills and labour of fishing communities, on both the mainland and the Sesse islands, on to a wider economic and military stage met with limited success. But, even within these limits, it was a remarkable achievement and an even more remarkable endeavour.

Buganda on the eve of colonial rule was experiencing a series of crises, serving to undermine both internal cohesion and prosperity and the kingdom's ability to control the external environment. The first such crisis was recurrent food shortage from at least the early 1880s onward. It seems that food shortages or even full-blown famines were not unknown to Buganda before Mutesa's reign; what is clear is that the agricultural base remained potentially fragile, as the widespread hunger of the 1880s indicates. This fragility was further exposed by the religious wars of the late 1880s and early 1890s, during which time crops and plantations throughout the kingdom were destroyed or abandoned. There can be little doubt that this situation eased the entry of the IBEAC, and influenced Ganda policy towards the British. At the same time, a wave of cattle disease had struck, possibly as early as the late 1870s; this was followed by the continental outbreak of rinderpest in 1889–90, but in Buganda, at least, much of the damage had already been done. Buganda was not, of course, as reliant on livestock as many other East African societies, many of which were reduced to mere shadows of their former selves as a result of rinderpest; but again the impact of the disease on Buganda has been underestimated, and the timing misunderstood. The death of livestock on a massive scale was a crippling blow to the economy and combined with food shortage to produce a catastrophe of epic proportions; again, the Ganda entered the colonial period struggling not only to come to terms with this catastrophe, but to assert themselves in a new and potentially hostile political environment.

By the 1880s, the fact that sources of ivory had become severely restricted also had implications for Buganda's economic and political base. The value of ivory had changed markedly throughout the period under examination; formerly a variety of currency, it had been overtaken in this regard by the cowry shell, but from the mid-nineteenth century, if not earlier, the new demand from the coast re-established ivory as one of Buganda's most valuable material assets. Elephant-hunters represented an increasingly important and indeed elite profession. But the elephants themselves were rapidly disappearing from Ganda territory by the 1870s, with damaging repercussions for the kingdom's political, commercial and ecological base. As we have seen, the scarcity of elephants in all probability increased the incidence of the tsetse fly, which, deprived of its preferred and relatively impervious host, searched for what were less resistant carriers, namely cattle. Certainly the incidence of cattle disease – probably trypanosomiasis – escalated during this same period, although this wave of disease doubtless paled in significance alongside the rinderpest pandemic which arrived a few years later. Commercially, too, Buganda was weakened: deprived of regular supplies of this most valued trade commodity, the Ganda were restricted to the export of slaves. During this period, coastal merchants were increasingly looking towards the more lucrative ivory markets, such as those in Bunyoro, to meet their demands. The Ganda could no longer hold the attention of these traders through their own resources; even the *kabaka*, who alone by the early 1880s could offer ivory in any kind of volume to the Arabs, was hard pushed to round up sufficient amounts. Mwanga, for example, was almost wholly dependent on supplies from Busoga. But the irregularity of such tribute merely served as a reminder that Ganda influence east of the Nile was not only waning, but had never been as powerful as the Ganda themselves had led others to believe. When the early colonial authority tried to gauge Buganda's influence in the young protectorate, the Ganda chiefs were extremely, and understandably, keen to press the traditional tributary obligations of the Soga, and indeed a number of other peoples. Again, however, this represented to some extent a sense of desperation among a Ganda elite determined to seize the opportunity presented by the British arrival.

The consequences of these ecological, agricultural and pastoral crises were many. Obviously the most dramatic and tangible of these was widespread mortality. Pastoral communities were devastated, and in this sense the cattle catastrophe of the late nineteenth century represented another blow to the Hima in Buganda, whose numbers may well have been decreasing throughout the nineteenth century. At a deeper level, the outbreak of cattle disease and the failure of successive crops in the 1880s not only undermined Buganda's economic base, but doubtless weakened the kingdom's social and political structures. The inability of Mutesa and Mwanga to feed their vast entourages adequately and to ensure the supply of food from the countryside to the capital almost certainly weakened the position of kingship at a time when tensions of a political and religious nature were already in evidence. We have noted, for example, how the conspicuous consumption and distribution of food at the *kabaka*'s enclosure had served to underline his authority; inability to do so can only have damaged perceptions of the kingship. Similar consequences would have resulted from cattle disease. Cattle were clearly critical as sources of food for a select few, and as trade commodities more generally; they were, moreover, symbols of wealth in themselves, and ownership of large herds was an essential part of Ganda chieftainship. Political power and its material basis were therefore thrown into flux. This is no less true of the *kabaka* himself, whose control of vast herds and regular distribution of cattle formed an important part of royal potency.

Military decline compounded Buganda's crisis in this period; moreover, Mwanga's mismanagement at home, particularly in his abuse of the long-standing public labour and taxation systems, fomented a crisis of political unity whose origins, nevertheless, lay in the reign of Mwanga's grandfather Suna. All of this combined to place Buganda in a precarious position on the eve of colonial rule. For at least 200 years, the kingdom had striven for hegemony through a combination of commerce and conflict; perhaps its greatest weakness was its periodic inability to achieve the required deft balance between the two, and this was especially true after c. 1850. Yet much of Buganda's history is characterized by a striking ability to expand at the expense of neighbouring societies, to marshal raw materials and natural resources in the pursuit of productive growth and commercial gain, and to control or at least influence the external environment. The expansion of the fleet represented the kingdom's last flourish in the last decades before colonial rule, a final attempt to harness and manipulate developments and circumstances far beyond its borders. Indeed, the attempt to control Lake Victoria may also be seen in the context of the concept of nature versus civilization so important in Ganda culture and historical development. Yet, by the end of the 1880s, the external environment was changing too quickly for even the Ganda to control, and ever more powerful influences were being brought to bear on the region. There were new challenges to be met, and still further innovation was essential; but, as the study of the pre-colonial past demonstrates, this, at least, was to Buganda's advantage.

Sources & Bibliography

Unpublished & archival material

Church Missionary Society (CMS) Archives, University of Birmingham, UK
G3 A5/0 1880–1934 Original Papers, Incoming
CA6/0/1–25 1876–1880 Original Papers, Incoming
G3 A6/0 1880–1885 Original Papers, Incoming
Acc.72 1876–1890 A. Mackay: papers including correspondence with missionaries and officials in East Africa
Acc.84 1894–1953 Rev. B. Fisher: correspondence, diaries, papers: 2 boxes

Makerere University Library, Kampala, Uganda
A. Kagwa [tr. J. Wamala], 'A Book of Clans of Buganda', manuscript, 1972
B.M. Zimbe [tr. F. Kamoga], 'Buganda ne Kabaka', manuscript, 1939
Munno (Luganda language periodical), for the years 1913, 1914, 1916, 1921

National Library of Scotland, Edinburgh, UK
Mss 4872–79 Manuscript and proofs of Speke's 'Journal'
Ms 17909 Grant Papers
Ms 17915 Manuscript of Grant's 'African Journal'

Public Record Office, London, UK
Series FO881 Africa

Rhodes House Library, Oxford, UK
John Roscoe and Apolo Kagwa, Mss.Afr.s.17 Enquiry into Native Land Tenure in the Uganda Protectorate (1906)

School of Oriental and African Studies Library, London, UK
J. Miti, manuscript, 'A History of Buganda', n.p., 1938 (3 vols)

Uganda National Archives (UNA), Entebbe, Uganda
A1 General Correspondence
A2–3 Staff and Miscellaneous, Inward
A4 Staff Correspondence, Inward
A6 Miscellaneous Correspondence, Inward
A8 Buganda Correspondence, Inward
A9 Buganda Correspondence, Outward
A26/4 Papers relating to the Mombasa Railway Survey and Uganda

White Fathers Archives, Rome, Italy
C13 Correspondence of Mgr Livinhac 1875–92
C14 Correspondence of Mgr Lourdel 1872–90
Rubaga Diary 1879–98
Les Missions Catholiques, vols 11–24

Published primary sources

Ashe, R.P. *Two Kings of Uganda*, London, 1889
—— *Chronicles of Uganda*, London, 1894
Austin, H.H. *With Macdonald in Uganda*, London, 1903
Baker, S. *Albert Nyanza, Great Basin of the Nile*, 2 vols, London, 1866
—— *Ismailia*, 2 vols, London, 1874
Bennett, N.R. (ed.) *Stanley's Despatches to the* New York Herald, *1871–72, 1874–77*, Boston, 1970
British Parliamentary Papers: Relating to the Slave Trade and *Colonies (Africa)*, reprinted in Dublin by the Irish Universities Press
Burton, R.F. 'The Lake Regions of Equatorial Africa', *Journal of the Royal Geographical Society*, 29 (1859) pp. 1–454
—— *The Lake Regions of Central Africa* [2 vols, London, 1860]; repr. one vol., 1995
Casati, G. *Ten Years in Equatoria*, 2 vols., London & New York, 1891
Chaille-Long, C. *Central Africa: Naked Truths of Naked People*, London, 1876
Colvile, H. *The Land of the Nile Springs*, London & New York, 1895
Cook, A.R. *Uganda Memories 1897–1940*, Kampala, 1945
Cunningham, J.F. *Uganda and its Peoples*, London, 1905; repr. 1969
Decle, L. *Three Years in Savage Africa*, London, 1898
Felkin, R.W. 'Notes on the Waganda tribe of Central Africa', *Proceedings of the Royal Society of Edinburgh*, 13 (1885–6) pp. 699–770
Fisher, A.B. *Twilight Tales of the Black Baganda*, London, 1912
Gorju, J. *Entre le Victoria, l'Albert et l'Edouard*, Rennes, 1920
Grant, J.A. *A Walk Across Africa*, Edinburgh & London, 1864
—— 'Summary of observations on the geography, climate, and natural history of the lake region of Equatorial Africa', *Journal of the Royal Geographical Society*, 42 (1872) pp. 243–342
Gray, J.M. (ed.) 'The Diaries of Emin Pasha', *Uganda Journal*, 25 (1961) pp. 1–10, 149–70; 26 (1962) pp. 72–95
Harford-Battersby, C.F. *Pilkington of Uganda*, London, 1898
Hattersley, C.W. *Uganda by Pen and Camera*, London, 1906
—— *The Baganda at Home*, London, 1908; repr. 1968
Jackson, F. *Early Days in East Africa*, London, 1930
Johnston, H.H. *The Uganda Protectorate*, 2 vols, London, 1902
Junker, W. [tr. A.H. Keane] *Travels in Africa during the years 1882–1886*, London, 1892
Kagwa, A. [tr. E.B. Kalibala, ed. M.M. Edel] *The Customs of the Baganda*, New York, 1934
—— [tr. & ed. M.S.M. Kiwanuka] *The Kings of Buganda*, Nairobi, 1971
Kitching, A.L. *On the Backwaters of the Nile*, London & Leipzig, 1912
Kollmann, P. *The Victoria Nyanza*, London, 1899
Lloyd, A.B. *In Dwarf Land and Cannibal Country*, London, 1900
—— *Uganda to Khartoum*, London, 1906
Lugard, F.D. 'Travels from the East Coast to Uganda', *Proceedings of the Royal Geographical Society*, 14 (1892) pp. 817–841
—— *The Rise of Our East African Empire*, 2 vols, Edinburgh & London, 1893
Macdonald, J.R. *Soldiering and Surveying in British East Africa*, London, 1897
Mackay, A.M. [ed. by his sister] *Pioneer Missionary in Uganda*, London, 1890
Middleton, D. (ed.) *The Diary of A.J. Mounteney-Jephson: Emin Pasha Relief Expedition 1887–1889*, Cambridge, 1969
Mounteney-Jephson, A.J. *Emin Pasha and the Rebellion at the Equator*, London, 1890
Nicq, A. *Le Père Simeon Lourdel*, Algiers, 1906
Parke, T.H. *My Personal Experiences in Equatorial Africa*, London, 1891
Perham, M. (ed.) *The Diaries of Lord Lugard (East Africa 1889–1892)*, vols 1–3, London, 1959
Peters, C. [tr. H.W. Dulcken] *New Light on Dark Africa*, London, 1891
Portal, G. *The British Mission to Uganda in 1893*, London, 1894
Roscoe, J. *The Baganda: an Account of their Native Customs and Beliefs*, London, 1911
—— *Twenty-five Years in East Africa*, Cambridge, 1921
Schweinfurth, G. *et al* (eds) *Emin Pasha in Central Africa*, London, 1888

Schweitzer, G. (ed.) *Emin Pasha: his life and work*, 2 vols., London, 1898

Schynse, A. *A Travers l'Afrique avec Stanley et Emin-Pacha*, Paris, 1890

Scott Elliot, G.F. *A Naturalist in Mid-Africa*, London, 1896

Speke, J.H. 'The upper basin of the Nile from inspection and information', *Journal of the Royal Geographical Society*, 33 (1863a) pp. 322–34

—— *Journal of the Discovery of the Source of the Nile*, Edinburgh & London, 1863b

—— *What Led to the Discovery of the Source of the Nile* [London, 1864]; repr. London, 1967

Stanley, H.M. *Through the Dark Continent*, 2 vols, London, 1878; repr. 1899

—— *In Darkest Africa*, 2 vols, London, 1890

Stanley, R. & Neame, A. (eds) *The Exploration Diaries of H.M. Stanley*, New York, 1961

Ternan, T. *Some Experiences of an Old Bromsgovian*, Birmingham, 1930

Thruston, A.B. *African Incidents*, London, 1900

Tippu Tip [tr. W.H. Whiteley]. *Maisha ya Hamed bin Muhammad el Murjebi yaani Tippu Tip*, Nairobi, 1966

Tucker, A.R. *Eighteen Years in Uganda and East Africa*, 2 vols, London, 1908

Vandeleur, S. *Campaigning on the Upper Nile and Niger*, London, 1898

Waller, H. (ed.) *The Last Journals of David Livingstone in Central Africa*, 2 vols, London, 1874

Wilson, C.T. & Felkin, R.W. *Uganda and the Egyptian Soudan*, 2 vols, London, 1882

Unpublished secondary sources

Kiwanuka, M.S.M. 'The traditional history of the Buganda kingdom: with special reference to the historical writings of Sir Apolo Kagwa', PhD thesis, University of London, 1965

Low, D.A. 'The British and Buganda 1862–1900', DPhil thesis, University of London, 1957

Reid, R.J. 'Economic and Military Change in Nineteenth-Century Buganda', PhD thesis, University of London, 1996

Rowe, J. 'Revolution in Buganda 1856–1900: Part One, the reign of Kabaka Mukabya Mutesa 1856–1884', PhD thesis, University of Wisconsin, 1966

Twaddle, M. 'Slaves and peasants in Buganda', paper given at the African History Seminar, School of Oriental and African Studies, London, 23 June 1982

Waller, R.D. 'The Traditional Economy of Buganda', MA thesis, University of London, 1971

Willis, J. 'Clan and history in Western Uganda: a new perspective on the origins of pastoral dominance', Annual Lecture of the British Institute in Eastern Africa, London, 2 February 1996

Published secondary sources

Alpers, E.A. 'The nineteenth century: prelude to colonialism', in B.A. Ogot & J.A. Kieran (eds), *Zamani: a survey of East African history*, Nairobi, 1968, pp. 238–54

—— *Ivory and Slaves in East Central Africa*, London, 1975

Ambler, C.H. *Kenyan Communities in the Age of Imperialism*, New Haven & London, 1988

Ambrose, C.H. 'Archaeology and linguistic reconstructions of history in East Africa', in C. Ehret & M. Posnansky (eds), *The Archaeological and Linguistic Reconstruction of African History*, Los Angeles & London, 1982, pp. 104–57

Anon, *Coronation Special Souvenir*, Kampala, 1993

Apter, D.E. *The Political Kingdom in Uganda*, Princeton, 1961

Arnold, D. *Famine: Social Crisis and Historical Change*, London, 1988

Atkinson, R.R. 'The traditions of the early kings of Buganda: myth, history and structural analysis', *History in Africa*, 2 (1975) pp. 17–57

Austen, R. 'Patterns of development in nineteenth-century East Africa', *African Historical Studies*, 4:3 (1971) pp. 645–57

Beachey, R.W. 'The arms trade in East Africa in the late nineteenth century', *Journal of African History*, 3 (1962) pp. 451–67

—— 'The East African ivory trade in the nineteenth century', *Journal of African History*, 8

(1967) pp. 269–90

—— *The Slave Trade of Eastern Africa*, London, 1976

Beattie, J. *The Nyoro State*, London, 1971

Beinart, W. 'Production and the material basis of chieftainship: Pondoland c. 1830–1880', in S. Marks & A. Atmore (eds), *Economy and Society in Pre-Industrial South Africa*, London, 1980, pp. 120–47

Bennett, N.R. 'The Arab Impact', in B.A. Ogot & J.A. Kieran (eds), *Zamani: a Survey of East African History*, Nairobi, 1968, pp.216–37

—— *Arab versus European: Diplomacy and War in Nineteenth-century East Central Africa*, New York & London, 1986

Bourgeois, R. *Banyarwanda et Barundi*. Vol. 1: *Ethnographie*, Brussels, 1957

Buchanan, C. 'Perceptions of interaction in the East African interior: the Kitara complex', *International Journal of African Historical Studies*, 11 (1978) pp. 410–28

Carey, M. *Beads and Beadwork of East and South Africa*, Aylesbury, 1986

Chorley, C.W. 'Winds and storms of Lake Victoria', *Uganda Journal*, 8:2 (1941) pp. 76–80

Cobbing, J. 'The *mfecane* as alibi: thoughts on Dithakong and Mbolompo', *Journal of African History*, 29:3 (1988) pp. 487–519

Cohen, D.W. *The Historical Tradition of Busoga*, Oxford, 1972

—— *Womunafu's Bunafu: a Study of Authority in a Nineteenth-century African Community*, Princeton, 1977

Connah, G. *African Civilizations: Precolonial Cities and States in Tropical Africa. An Archaeological Perspective*, Cambridge, 1987

Connah, G., Kamuhangire, E. & Piper, A. 'Salt production at Kibiro', *Azania*, 25 (1990) pp. 27–39

Cox, A.H. 'The growth and expansion of Buganda', *Uganda Journal*, 14:2 (1950) pp. 153–9

Curtin, P., Feierman, S., Thompson, L., and Vansina, J. *African History: From Earliest Times to Independence*, London & New York, 1978; 2nd edn, 1995

Dunbar, A.R. 'Emin Pasha and Bunyoro-Kitara, 1877–1889', *Uganda Journal*, 24:1 (1960) pp. 71–83

—— *A History of Bunyoro-Kitara*, Nairobi, 1965

Dupuy, R.N. & Dupuy, T.N. *The Collins Encyclopaedia of Military History, from 3500 BC to the Present*, London, 1993

Eggeling, W.J. *The Indigenous Trees of the Uganda Protectorate*, Entebbe, 1940

Ehrlich, C. 'The economy of Buganda, 1893–1903', *Uganda Journal*, 20:1 (1956) pp. 17–26

Eldredge, E. *A South African Kingdom: the Pursuit of Security in Nineteenth-century Lesotho*, Cambridge, 1993

Fallers, L.A. 'Despotism, status and social mobility in an African kingdom', *Comparative Studies in Society and History*, 2:1 (1959) pp. 4–32

—— 'Social stratification in traditional Buganda', in L.A. Fallers (ed.), *The King's Men*, London, 1964, pp. 64–117

Falola, T. & Law, R.C.C. (eds) *Warfare and Diplomacy in Precolonial Nigeria*, Madison WI, 1992

Feierman, S. *The Shambaa Kingdom: a History*, Madison WI, 1974

Ford, J. *The Role of the Trypanosomiases in African Ecology*, Oxford, 1971

Gee, T.W. 'A century of Muhammedan influence in Buganda, 1852–1951', *Uganda Journal*, 22:2 (1958) pp.139–50

Goody, J. *Technology, Tradition and the State in Africa*, London, 1971

Gray, J.M. 'Mutesa of Buganda', *Uganda Journal*, 1:1 (1934) pp. 22–49

—— 'Early history of Buganda', *Uganda Journal*, 2:4 (1935) pp. 259–71

—— 'Ahmed bin Ibrahim – the first Arab to reach Buganda', *Uganda Journal*, 11:2 (1947) pp. 80–97

—— 'Trading expeditions from the coast to Lakes Tanganyika and Victoria before 1857', *Tanganyika Notes and Records*, 49 (1957) pp. 226–46

—— 'Arabs on Lake Victoria: some revisions', *Uganda Journal*, 22:1 (1958) pp. 76–81

Gray, R. & Birmingham, D. 'Some economic and political consequences of trade in Central and Eastern Africa in the pre-colonial period', in R. Gray & D. Birmingham (eds), *Pre-Colonial African Trade*, London, 1970, pp. 1–23

Gutkind, P.C.W. 'Notes on the *kibuga* of Buganda', *Uganda Journal*, 24:1 (1960) pp. 29–43

Sources & Bibliography

—— *The Royal Capital of Buganda: a Study of Internal Conflict and External Ambiguity*, The Hague, 1963

Guy, J. *The Destruction of the Zulu Kingdom: the Civil War in Zululand, 1879–1884*, London, 1979

—— 'Ecological factors in the rise of Shaka and the Zulu kingdom', in S. Marks & A. Atmore (eds), *Economy and Society in Pre-Industrial South Africa*, London & New York, 1980, pp. 102–19

Hailey (Lord), *An African Survey*, London, 1957

Hansen, H.B. *Mission, Church and State in a Colonial Setting: Uganda 1890–1925*, London, 1984

Harms, R. *River of Wealth, River of Sorrow: the Central Zaire Basin in the Era of the Save and Ivory Trade, 1500–1891*, New Haven & London, 1981

Hartwig, G.W. 'The Victoria Nyanza as a trade route in the nineteenth century', *Journal of African History*, 11:4 (1970) pp. 535–52

—— *The Art of Survival in East Africa: the Kerebe and Long-distance Trade, 1800–1895*, New York & London, 1976

Henige, D. 'Reflections on early interlacustrine chronology: an essay in source criticism', *Journal of African History*, 15:1 (1974) pp. 27–46

—— '"The disease of writing": Ganda and Nyoro kinglists in a newly literate world', in J.C. Miller (ed.), *The African Past Speaks*, Folkestone/Hamden, 1980, pp. 240–61

Holmes, C.F. 'Zanzibari influence at the southern end of Lake Victoria: the lake route', *African Historical Studies*, 4:3 (1971) pp. 477–503

Hopkins, A.G. *An Economic History of West Africa*, London, 1973

Iliffe, J. *The African Poor: a History*, Cambridge, 1987

—— *Africans: the History of a Continent*, Cambridge, 1995

Jackson, K. 'The dimensions of Kamba pre-colonial history', in B.A. Ogot (ed.), *Kenya Before 1900*, Nairobi, 1976, pp.174–261

Kagame, A. *Les Milices du Rwanda Precolonial*, Brussels, 1963

Karugire, S.R. *A History of the Kingdom of Nkore in Western Uganda to 1896*, Oxford, 1971

Kasozi, A.B.K. 'Why did the Baganda adopt foreign religions in the nineteenth century?', *Mawazo*, 4 (1975) pp. 129–52

Katoke, I.K. *The Karagwe Kingdom*, Nairobi, 1975

Keegan, J. *A History of Warfare*, London, 1993

Kenny, M. 'Salt trading in eastern Lake Victoria', *Azania*, 9 (1974) pp. 225–8

—— 'The powers of Lake Victoria', *Anthropos*, 72 (1977) pp. 717–33

—— 'Pre-colonial trade in eastern Lake Victoria', *Azania*, 14 (1979) pp. 97–107

—— 'Mutesa's crime: hubris and the control of African kings', *Comparative Studies in Society and History*, 30 (1988) pp. 595–612

Kimambo, I.N. 'The economic history of the Kamba, 1850–1950', in B.A.Ogot (ed.), *Hadith 2*, Nairobi, 1970, pp. 79–103

Kiwanuka, M.S.M. 'Sir Apolo Kagwa and the pre-colonial history of Buganda', *Uganda Journal*, 30:2 (1966) pp. 137–52

—— *Muteesa of Uganda*, Nairobi, 1967

—— *A History of Buganda: from the Foundation of the Kingdom to 1900*, London, 1971

Kjekshus, H. *Ecology Control and Economic Development in East African History*, London, 1977; 2nd edn, 1996

Knappert, J. *African Mythology: an Encyclopaedia of Myth and Legend*, London, 1995

Kottak, C.P. 'Ecological variables in the origin and evolution of African states: the Buganda example', *Comparative Studies in Society and History*, 14:3 (1972) pp. 351–80

Langlands, B.W. 'Early travellers in Uganda', *Uganda Journal*, 26:1 (1962) pp. 55–71

—— 'The banana in Uganda 1860–1920', *Uganda Journal*, 30:1 (1966a) pp. 39–63

—— 'Cassava in Uganda 1860–1920', *Uganda Journal*, 30:2 (1966b) pp. 211–18

Lanning, E.C. 'Bark cloth hammers', *Uganda Journal*, 23:1 (1959) pp. 79–83

Law, R.C.C. *The Oyo Empire c.1600–c.1836*, Oxford, 1977

—— 'Human sacrifice in pre-colonial West Africa', *African Affairs*, 84 (1985) pp. 53–87

—— *The Slave Coast of West Africa 1550–1750*, Oxford, 1991

Legassick, M. 'Firearms, horses and Samorian army organisation 1870–1898', *Journal of African History*, 7 (1966) pp. 95–115

Lovejoy, P. *Transformations in Slavery*, Cambridge, 1983

Low, D.A. 'The northern interior, 1840–1884', in R. Oliver & G. Mathew (eds), *History of*

East Africa, vol.1, Oxford, 1963, pp. 297–351

—— *Buganda in Modern History*, London, 1971

Low, D.A. & Pratt, R.C. *Buganda and British Overrule 1900–1955*, London, 1960

MacKenzie, J.M. *The Empire of Nature: Hunting, Conservation and British Imperialism*, Manchester & New York, 1988

McMaster, D.N. 'Speculations on the coming of the banana to Uganda', *Uganda Journal*, 27:2 (1963) pp. 163–75

Mair, L. *An African People in the Twentieth Century*, London, 1934

Mayanja, A.M.K. 'Chronology of Buganda 1800–1907, from Kagwa's *Ebika*', *Uganda Journal*, 16:2 (1952) pp. 148–58

Maylam, P. *A History of the African Peoples of South Africa*, London, 1986

Medard, H. 'Epidémies, développement du commerce et pratiques médicales au Buganda précolonial', in F. Raison Jourde (ed.), *Hygiéne et Epidémies dans l'Océan Indien*, Paris, 1996, pp.1–19

Miers, S. & Kopytoff, I. (eds) *Slavery in Africa*, Madison WI, 1977

Mukasa, H. 'Some notes on the reign of Mutesa', *Uganda Journal*, 1:2 (1934) pp. 116–33; 2:1 (1935) pp. 65–70

Murphy, J.D. *Luganda-English Dictionary*, Washington, 1972

Musere, J. *African Sleeping Sickness: Political Ecology, Colonialism and Control in Uganda*, Lewiston, 1990

Ogot, B.A. (ed.) *War and Society in Africa*, London, 1972

Oliver, R. 'The royal tombs of Buganda', *Uganda Journal*, 23:2 (1959) pp. 124–33

—— 'Discernible developments in the interior c.1500–1840', in R. Oliver & G. Mathew (eds), *History of East Africa*, vol. 1, Oxford, 1963, pp. 169–211

Peel, J.D.Y. 'Conversion and tradition in two African societies: Ijebu and Buganda', *Past and Present*, 77 (1977) pp. 108–41

Phillipson, D.W. *African Archaeology*, Cambridge, 1985

Ray, B. 'Royal shrines and ceremonies of Buganda', *Uganda Journal*, 36 (1972) pp. 35–48

—— *Myth, Ritual and Kingship in Buganda*, New York & Oxford, 1991

Reid, R.J. 'The reign of *Kabaka* Nakibinge: myth or watershed?', *History in Africa*, 24 (1997) pp. 287–97

—— 'Mutesa and Mirambo: thoughts on East African warfare and diplomacy in the nineteenth century', *International Journal of African Historical Studies*, 31:1 (1998a) pp. 73–89

—— 'The Ganda on Lake Victoria: a nineteenth–century East African imperialism', *Journal of African History*, 39 (1998b) pp. 349–63

—— 'Traders, chiefs and soldiers: the pre-colonial capitals of Buganda', *Les Cahiers de l'Institut Français de Recherche en Afrique*, 9 (January–February 1998c) pp. 4–22

—— 'Images of an African ruler: *Kabaka* Mutesa of Buganda, c.1857–1884', *History in Africa*, 26 (1999a) pp. 269–98

—— 'War and militarism in pre-colonial Buganda', *Azania*, 34 (1999b)

Reid, R.J. & Medard, H. 'Merchants, missions and the remaking of the urban environment in Buganda c. 1840–c. 1890', in D.M. Anderson & R. Rathbone (eds), *Africa's Urban Past*, London, 2000, pp. 98–108

Richards, A.I. 'Authority patterns in traditional Buganda', in L.A. Fallers (ed.), *The King's Men*, London, 1964, pp. 256–93

—— *The Changing Structure of a Ganda Village*, Kampala, 1966

Richards, A.I., Sturrock, F. & Fortt, J. *Subsistence to Commercial Farming in Present-Day Buganda*, Cambridge, 1973

Roberts, A.D. 'The sub-imperialism of the Baganda', *Journal of African History*, 3 (1962) pp. 435–50

—— 'Firearms in north-eastern Zambia before 1900', *Transafrican Journal of History*, 1:2 (1971) pp. 3–21

—— *A History of the Bemba*, London, 1973

—— *A History of Zambia*, London, 1976

Roberts, A.D. (ed.), *Tanzania Before 1900*, Nairobi, 1968

Rowe, J.A. 'Roscoe's and Kagwa's Buganda', *Journal of African History*, 8 (1962) pp. 163–6

—— 'Mika Sematimba', *Uganda Journal*, 28:2 (1964a) pp. 179–99

—— 'The purge of Christians at Mwanga's court', *Journal of African History*, 5 (1964b) pp. 55–72

—— 'Myth, memoir and moral admonition: Luganda historical writing 1893–1969', *Uganda Journal*, 33:1 (1969) pp. 17–40

Rusch, W. *Klassen und Staat in Buganda vor der Kolonialzeit*, Berlin, 1975 (with English summary)

Schiller, L. 'The royal women of Buganda', *International Journal of African Historical Studies*, 23:3 (1990) pp. 455–73

Schmidt, P. *Historical Archaeology*, Westport, CT, 1978

Seligman, C.G. *Races of Africa*, London, 1966

Sen, Amartya. *Poverty and Famines*, Oxford, 1982

Sheriff, A. *Slaves, Spices and Ivory in Zanzibar*, London, 1987

Smith, R. *Warfare and Diplomacy in Pre-Colonial West Africa*, London, 1989

Smith, R. & Ade Ajayi, J.F. *Yoruba Warfare in the Nineteenth Century*, Cambridge, 1971

Southwold, M. *Bureaucracy and Chiefship in Buganda*, East African Studies, 14, Kampala, 1961

—— 'Leadership, authority and the village community', in L.A. Fallers (ed.), *The King's Men*, London, 1964

—— 'Succession to the throne of Buganda', in J. Goody (ed.), *Succession to High Office*, Cambridge, 1966, pp. 82–126

—— 'The history of a history: royal succession in Buganda', in I.M. Lewis (ed.), *History and Social Anthropology*, London, 1968, pp. 127–51

Steinhart, E.I. *Conflict and Collaboration: the Kingdoms of Western Uganda 1890–1907*, Princeton, 1977

—— 'From "empire" to state: the emergence of the kingdom of Bunyoro-Kitara, c.1350–1890', in H.J.M. Claessen & P. Skalnik (eds), *The Study of the State*, The Hague, 1981, pp. 353–70

Sutton, J. 'The settlement of East Africa', in B.A. Ogot & J.A. Kieran (eds), *Zamani: a Survey of East African History*, Nairobi, 1968, pp. 69–99

—— 'The antecedents of the interlacustrine kingdoms', *Journal of African History*, 34:1 (1993) pp. 33–64

Sutton, J. & Roberts, A.D. 'Uvinza and its salt industry', *Azania*, 3 (1968) pp. 45–86

Thomas, H.B. & Scott, R. *Uganda*, London, 1935

Thomson, A.D. 'Barkcloth making in Buganda', *Uganda Journal*, 1:1 (1934) pp. 17–21

Tosh, J. 'The northern interlacustrine region', in R. Gray & D. Birmingham (eds), *Pre-Colonial African Trade*, London, 1970, pp. 103–18

Toussaint-Samat, M. [tr. A.Bell] *A History of Food*, Oxford, 1994

Trowell, M. 'Some royal craftsmen of Buganda', *Uganda Journal*, 8:2 (1941) pp. 47–64

—— 'Clues to African tribal history', *Uganda Journal*, 10:2 (1946) pp. 54–63

Trowell, M. & Wachsmann, K. *Tribal Crafts of Uganda*, London, 1953

Twaddle, M. 'The *Bakungu* chiefs of Buganda under British colonial rule, 1900–1939', *Journal of African History*, 10:2 (1969) pp. 309–22

—— 'The Muslim revolution in Buganda', *African Affairs*, 71 (1972) pp. 54–72

—— 'On Ganda historiography', *History in Africa*, 1 (1974a) pp. 85–99

—— 'The Ganda receptivity to change', *Journal of African History*, 15:2 (1974b) pp. 303–15

—— 'The ending of slavery in Buganda', in R. Roberts & S. Miers (eds), *The End of Slavery in Africa*, Madison, 1988a, pp. 119–49

—— 'Slaves and peasants in Buganda', in L.J. Archer (ed.), *Slavery and Other Forms of Unfree Labour*, London, 1988b, pp. 118–29

—— 'The emergence of politico–religious groupings in late nineteenth-century Buganda', *Journal of African History*, 29:1 (1988c) pp. 81–92

—— *Kakungulu and the Creation of Uganda*, London, 1993

Uzoigwe, G.N. 'Pre-colonial markets in Bunyoro-Kitara', *Comparative Studies in Society and History*, 14:4 (1972) pp. 422–55

—— *The Anatomy of an African Kingdom: a History of Bunyoro-Kitara*, New York, 1973

Vansina, J. *L'Evolution du Royaume Rwanda des Origines à 1900*, Brussels, 1962a

—— 'Long-distance trade routes in Central Africa', *Journal of African History*, 3:3 (1962b) pp. 375–90

—— *Paths in the Rainforests: Toward a History of Political Tradition in Equatorial Africa*, London, 1990 van Zwanenberg, R., with King, A. *An Economic History of Kenya and Uganda 1800–1970*, London, 1975

Wainwright, G.A. 'The coming of the banana to Uganda', *Uganda Journal*, 16:2 (1952) pp. 145–7

—— 'The diffusion of *-uma* as a name for iron', *Uganda Journal*, 18:2 (1954) pp. 113–36

Webster, J.B. (ed.) *Chronology, Migration and Drought in Interlacustrine Africa*, London, 1979

Were, G.S. 'The western Bantu peoples from AD 1300 to 1800', in B.A. Ogot & J.A. Kieran (eds), *Zamani: a Survey of East African History*, Nairobi, 1968, pp. 177–97

West, H.W. *Land Policy in Buganda*, Cambridge, 1972

Whitehead, N.L. & Ferguson, R.B. (eds) *War in the Tribal Zone*, Santa Fe, 1992

Wilks, I. *Asante in the Nineteenth Century*, Cambridge, 1975

Wright, Marcia. 'Ecclesiastical records and their part in an Eastern African data bank', *Histoire Sociale de l'Afrique de l'Est*, Paris, 1991, pp. 437–52

Wright, Michael. *Buganda in the Heroic Age*, Nairobi, 1971

Wrigley, C.C. 'Buganda: an outline economic history', *Economic History Review*, 10 (1957) pp. 60–80

—— 'The Christian revolution in Buganda', *Comparative Studies in Society and History*, 2:1 (1959a) pp. 33–48

—— 'Kimera', *Uganda Journal*, 23:1 (1959b) pp. 38–43

—— 'The changing economic structure of Buganda', in L.A. Fallers (ed.), *The King's Men*, London, 1964, pp. 16–63

—— 'The kinglists of Buganda', *History in Africa*, 1 (1974) pp. 129–39

—— 'Bananas in Buganda', *Azania*, 24 (1989) pp. 64–70

—— *Kingship and State: the Buganda Dynasty*, Cambridge, 1996

Yoder, J. 'The quest for Kintu and the search for peace: mythology and morality in nineteenth-century Buganda', *History in Africa*, 15 (1988) pp. 363–76

Index

agriculture 2, 20-32, 124, 155, 156: collapse of 36-9, 119, 179; *see also* bananas; barkcloth; coffee; cotton; famines; food; pastoralism; sweet potatoes; tobacco

Albert, Lake 160

animals: 55-60; *see also* cattle; elephants; hunting; livestock; skins

Ankole 21, 30, 40, 44, 45, 52, 60, 137, 138, 145, 201, 228

Arabs 27-8, 50, 86, 118, 119, 123, 143, 151-8, 159-61, 163-4, 166, 167, 168, 170, 202, 220, 221

armies 179-80, 185, 186-8, 189, 190, 191, 192, 193-4, 197-202, 206-17, 221, 224, 246-7; *see also* soldiers; war; weapons

Asante 109, 162

Ashe, Robert 8, 48, 60, 66, 75, 85, 86, 111-12, 195, 203, 217, 236

Baker, Sir Samuel 6, 221

bakopi (peasants) 4, 59, 72, 75, 78, 95, 100, 102, 104, 106-7, 113, 114, 116, 211, 213

bakungu 4 *see also* chiefs

bananas 21, 22-5, 26, 27, 28, 29, 31, 33, 35, 36, 37, 38, 47, 77, 138

barkcloth 22, 52, 70-6, 136-8, 151, 187

Baskerville 38

basketwork 89, 122, 123

bataka (clan heads) 3, 80; *see also* chiefs

batongole 3, 129, 186, 192-3, 196, 215, 216, 221; *see also* chiefs

Beachie R.W. 120

beads 144-5, 152, 156, 158, 159, 160

beans 27, 29

Beattie, J. 40

beer 29, 138

blacksmiths 79, 80, 81, 82, 83, 84, 85, 86, 138-9, 218

brass 84, 139, 150, 156

British 6, 7, 38, 39, 99-102, 118, 123, 125, 147, 169, 189, 204-5, 226

Budama 182

Buddu: acquisition of 3, 5, 74, 76, 78, 82,

187; agriculture 20-1, 22, 24, 29, 30, 38, 39; barkcloth 70, 71, 72, 73, 74, 75, 76, 137-8; chief of 4, copper 85; highways 109; iron-working 82, 138; mining 77, 78; pastoralism 43, 44, 45, 47, 53; trade 137-8; wood 228-9, 241

Bugerere 231-2

Bujaju 73, 75

Bukedi 194, 201, 244

Bulemezi 4, 21-2, 29, 37, 44, 45, 53, 63, 71, 75, 85, 117, 183, 209

Bulondoganyi 43, 67, 189, 191, 232, 244, 245

Bunyoro: agriculture 21, 30; barkcloth 70, 76; currencies 145; hunting 60, 61-2; ivory 170; markets 136; mining 77, 78; pastoralism 40, 45, 53, 54; pottery 86, 87, 88; slaves 117-18, 126, 161, 168, 169; trade 138, 139, 140, 153, 159; war 3, 169, 180, 181, 182, 183-4, 185-8, 191, 192-4, 196, 198, 203-5, 218, 219, 224; wood 228; *see also* Nyoro

Burton, R.F. 56-7, 87, 118, 123, 125, 152, 153, 154, 155, 156, 160-1, 180-1, 207, 214, 218, 234

Buruli 63, 138, 193, 198

Burundi 41

Busagala 195, 198

Busiro 4, 20-1, 22, 30, 44, 45, 49, 75, 80, 184, 243

Busoga 30, 52, 53, 60, 70, 71, 77, 109, 117, 126, 145, 166-7, 170-1, 181-2, 190, 192, 193, 194, 198, 199, 200, 201, 228, 245; *see also* Soga

Busongora 40, 47, 187, 191, 194, 195, 197

Busujju 4, 22, 44, 45

Buvuma 87, 117, 141, 199, 200, 207, 208, 209, 231, 233, 236-7, 246-7, 248

Buwekula 63, 194

Buzinza 198, 200

canoes 227-31: ceremonies 65; construction 234, 238-9, 241, 244; for *kabaka* 242, 246; for pleasure 242; role of 237; and slaves 167-8; and trade 140, 159, 164, 234-5; 237; travel 64, 109, 164, 235, 243; for wars 187, 193, 231, 232-3, 235, 236-8, 243, 244-5, 246

capital: food 33-4, 36-8; livestock 44; markets 141, 142, 143-4; roads 107, 108; slaves 123; state labour 111; trade 156-7, 158-9; *see also kabaka*

Casati, Gaetano 128

cattle 21, 22, 44: diseases of 43, 51, 119, 163, 164; as gifts 49-50; and Hima 41-3 importance 40, 45-6, 47, 48; killing of 51; trade in 51, 139, 163, 164; as tribute 52; and war 178, 200; as wealth 50

ceremonies 30, 33, 59, 65, 72, 128, 146-7, 158, 180-1, 186

Chaillé-Long, C. 30, 59, 108, 140, 208, 229-30

chiefs: 3, 4: and armies 207, 208-9, 217; and copper 85; and currencies 147, 149-50; and food 33, 37; and livestock 42, 43; and market fees 141-2; *mujasi* 216, 217; and navies 243-7; and politics 47-8; power of 80; and slaves 120, 121, 122, 125, 167; and state labour 105-7; and taxation 100-2; and trade 157-8; and weapons 221, 222, 224, 225; and women 41, 120, 121, 122, 123; *see also batongole*

children 117, 118-19, 121, 122, 126, 129, 164, 166-7, 193, 194, 221

Church Missionary Society 6

Chwa, Kabaka 4, 47, 79, 80, 81, 85, 218

Chwezi 72, 76, 78

clans 3-5: *diga* 187; 'fox' 244; *kasimba* 73, 218, 244; *kisimba* 82; *kkobe* 80, 218; *mamba* 48, 49, 80, 190, 238, 244; *mbogo* 62; *mbwa* 129; *mpindi* 73; *ngabi* 45, 78, 82, 129; *ngeye* 46, 79, 80, 105; *ngo* 24; *ngonge* 59, 72-3, 105, 125, 195; *njaza* 62; *njovu* 48; *nkejje* 244-5; *nkerebwe* 60; *nkima* 244, 245; *nnamunnoona* 73; *nnyonyi* 49; *nsenene* 46-7, 48, 84-5; *nte* 82; *nvuma* 49-50, 244; *nvubu* 244; *pangolin* 49; power of 80; and professions 96, 244-6; and totems 55-6; *see also batongole*; chiefs

class 95-7, 210-11; *see also* slavery

climate 235; *see also* drought; rainfall

cloth 74, 75, 137, 145-6: cotton 74, 150, 151, 152, 156, 158, 164, 165, 167; *see also* barkcloth; textiles; weaving

clothing 58-60, 70, 71, 72, 73, 74, 75, 136-7: bracelets 79, 84, 139; shoes 59

coffee 21, 27, 29-30, 37

colonial rule 7, 39, 99-102, 226

Colvile, Colonel H. 38, 118

Cook, A.R. 106

copper 79-80, 84-5, 139, 150, 156, 197, 245

cotton 28: cloth 74, 150, 151, 152, 156, 158, 164, 165, 167

cowries 140, 144, 145, 146-7, 149-50, 156

crime 166, 167

criminals 119

crops: 2, 21-2, 27-30, 32-3, 119, 155, 156; *see also* bananas; coffee; sweet potatoes; tobacco

cultural environment 31-2, 218

Cunningham, J.F. 98, 99

currencies 144-8, 150; *see also* beads; cowries

de Bellefonds, Colonel 57

death 122, 124, 126, 127, 146-7, 154, 155, 167-8, 180, 208

'Debatu' 24

Decle, L. 61, 107

diseases 35-6, 37, 39, 53, 55, 164, 197; *see also* livestock: diseases

dogs 56-7, 58

droughts 22, 31, 34, 35, 52, 63, 68

economy 15-16, 19-20, 25, 46, 77, 79, 90-2, 188, 251

elephants 58, 60-3, 150, 170; *see also* ivory

employment *see* labour

Entebbe 143, 241, 242-3

entertainment 128, 242

ethnic superiority 115, 117, 239-40

Europeans 6, 15-6, 158, 162, 221, 222; *see also* British; White Fathers

Fallers, L.A. 9, 96

famines 22, 32-3, 34-5, 39, 42, 197

Feierman, S. 23

Felkin, Robert 41, 43, 85, 87-8, 110, 124, 164, 165, 170

Fisher, A.B. 50, 96

fishing 64-8, 138, 227, 228, 237-8, 240-1, 244-5

flooding 241

food 27: and armies 198, 211, 212; blockades 233; diet 42, 48, 50; fish 64, 138; meat 50, 55-6; supply 32-5, 36-7,

38-9, 52, 53, 155, 198, 211, 212, 233;
trade in 138, 143-4, 156, 157, 158, 159;
and women 24, 26, 31, 123; *see also*
bananas; beer; coffee; crops; famines;
sweet potatoes
foreign relations 5-7, 47
foreigners 115-17, 126, 158, 161, 162, 207-
8, 214
Frazer, Sir James 184
fruits 22, 28, 155

Gambalagala 194
geography 1-2, 15, 20, 108-9
Girault 50, 60, 66, 72, 143, 163, 222-3, 243
gods 6, 31-2, 65, 68, 123, 164, 181-4, 185,
228, 239; *see also* religion
Gomba 4, 22, 44, 47, 50, 84
Gordon, General 6, 216-7
Gorju, J. 120
government 98-112
grains 21, 27-8, 155
Grant, James 6, 7, 50, 67, 68, 104, 105,
116, 117, 137, 139-40, 142, 158, 162,
163, 164, 208
groundnuts 29
guns: and bodyguards 216-7; bullets 77, 85,
165, 222, 223; condition of 221-2; for
hunting; 56, 61; repair 85-6, 138-9, 223;
skill in use of 214-5, 223; trade in 136,
150, 152, 165, 166, 167, 168, 171, 220-
3, 225; and war 178, 196, 201-2, 213,
219-20, 224-5, 226; *see also* blacksmiths

harems 41, 120, 121, 123, 125, 161, 164
Hattersley, C.W. 105, 120
Henige, David 5, 10-11
herdsmen 45-50, 55
highways *see* roads
Hima 40-3, 46-7, 48, 55, 97, 115, 161, 162,
163
historiography 7-12, 15-6, 19-20
Hopkins, A.G. 227
house-building 105
hunting 55-6, 57-8, 60-3, 66, 150

IBEAC (Imperial British East Africa
Company) 7, 38, 53, 157
Iliffe, J. 38, 75, 146
indentureship 129-30
inheritance 126, 127
international relations 5-7, 47

iron 77-9, 187, 218
iron-working 22, 76-84, 138, 139; *see also*
blacksmiths; guns; tools; weapons
Iru 41
ivory 58, 60, 62, 63, 85, 138, 139, 147-8,
150, 152, 153, 154, 156, 157, 160, 165,
167, 168, 170-1, 225, 234; *see also*:
elephants

Johnston, Harry 99, 108, 142
Junju, Kabaka 5, 73, 74, 82, 187-8, 189

kabaka ('head of clan heads'): abuse of state
112; and armies 206-17; and barkcloth
72, 73-4; bodyguard of 207, 214-17,
223; and canoes 242, 246; and
ceremonies 180; and currencies 147,
148; food supply 33-4, 37; and IBEAC;
38; and indentureship 129-30; and
livestock 41, 42, 43, 44; loyalty to 15,
190-1, 194-5, 202, 203, 207, 210, 216,
217; power of 3-4, 6, 80, 98-9, 120,
151, 217; and skins 59; and slaves 116-
17, 118, 119-20, 121, 123; and state
labour 103-4; and taxation 98-102; and
trade 141-2, 143, 158; and war 181;
and weapons 158; and women 41, 120,
121, 122, 123; *see also* individual *kabaka*
Kabarega 117, 136, 138, 160, 198, 204,
212, 220, 224
Kagehyi 164, 167
Kagera, river 150, 187, 189, 197
Kagwa, Apolo: on agriculture 21-2, 26; on
armies 215; on barkcloth 73; on
bodyguards 216; on canoes 228, 229,
230, 232-3, 244; on copper 84-5; on
currencies 146-7; on Entebbe 242; on
fishing 64, 65; on food 33; on Hima 40;
historiography 5, 8; on hunting 56, 57,
62, 63; indentutureship of 129-30; on
iron-working 78, 79, 80-1, 82, 83; on
navies 246; pastoralism 42, 44, 45, 46,
47, 48, 49, 51; on peace 193; on roads
111; on slaves 119; on state labour 103,
105; on tanning 60; on taxation 100,
101, 102; on trade 150; on treasury 99;
on war 183, 185, 190, 192, 193-4, 196,
197, 203, 208
Kakungulu 45, 188, 190, 191, 192-3, 194
Kamanya, Kabaka 5, 34, 45, 86, 103, 189,
190-5, 232-3, 244

Kamba 157
Kamurasi 159, 160
Karagwe 52, 70, 74, 136, 140, 150, 152,
    159, 161, 164, 198, 201, 220
'Kari' 43
Kasai 21
Katanga 79-80
Kateregga, Kabaka 146-7
Katonda 31, 32
Katonga, river 109, 228, 241-2, 245
Katwe 141
Kavirondo 77, 139
Kayemba, Kabaka 244
Kedi 203, 224, 232-3
Kenny, M. 9, 141, 230, 239
Kenya 157
Khartoum 28
Kibiro 140, 144, 160
Kibuga 154
Kibuka 181, 185, 186, 210, 219, 239
Kiggala, Kabaka 242
Kimbugwe, Kabaka 59
Kimera, Kabaka 48, 62, 72-3, 78-9
kinglists 4-5
kings *see* individual *kabaka; kabaka*
Kintu 4-5: and agriculture 23-4, 30, 31; and
    barkcloth 72; and canoes 238, 244; and
    currencies 145; and hunting 55-6; and
    iron-working 80; and livestock 31, 45-6,
    47, 48; as mythology 79, 80; and
    pottery 86; and state labour 103, 105;
    and weapons 218
Kisawo 79, 80
Kisubi 46
Kisule 85, 86
kitawi (clan heads) 101-2; *see also* chiefs
Kitching, A.L. 39
Kitesa 44, 45
Kiwanuka, M.S.M. 5, 9, 10, 11, 112, 186,
    213, 215, 223, 238
Kiwewa, Kabaka 7, 37, 168
Kiziba 53, 81, 104, 150, 159, 187, 189, 197
Koki 76, 82, 83, 109, 138, 197, 198
Kollmann, P. 105
Kottak, C.P. 9-10, 215
Kufro 154, 159
Kyabaggu, Kabaka 150, 151
Kyadondo 4, 20-1, 22, 102, 184
Kyagwe 3, 4, 20-1, 24, 44, 62, 66, 77, 78,
    82, 107, 125, 141, 182, 184, 187, 229,
    232, 240-1

Kyanamugera 44, 45
Kyoga, Lake 138, 193, 238
Kytawa 81, 197

labour 25, 39: *kasanvu* ('forced') 104; pay
    83-4, 240; private 105; state 95, 97, 98,
    103-6, 111, 239-40; work ethic 25, 39,
    124; *see also* slavery
lakes 64-6, 68-9, 76, 77; *see also* individual
    lakes
landscape 20, 40
lawlessness 166, 167
lions 56
livestock 2: diseases 43, 51, 52-5, 119, 163,
    164; goats 40, 42, 44, 46, 50, 52, 137;
    importance 47; plundering 36, 43, 45,
    53; sheep 44, 47; and taxation 42, 52;
    and trade 42, 45, 50, 51-2, 139; and war
    45, 197; and wealth 31, 40, 50, 51; *see
    also* cattle; food: meat; herdsmen;
    hunting
Livingstone, David 159, 202
Livinhac, W.F. 32, 35, 83, 104, 116, 126,
    127, 166, 171, 200, 212, 226, 236, 239
Lloyd, A.B. 87, 118
Lourdel, Pere 35, 42, 44, 49, 52, 75, 118,
    119, 125, 127-8, 166, 167-8, 204, 216,
    217, 221
Lovejoy, Paul 161, 163
Low, D.A. 9, 24, 154, 215
Lugard, F.D. 30, 43, 51, 53, 54, 55, 75, 85,
    86, 111, 124, 137, 141, 143-4, 145-6,
    212, 222, 225
luxury commodities 150, 151, 152

Macdonald, J.R. 63, 100-1, 104-5, 117-18,
    162, 213
Mackay, A.M.: on bodyguards 216, 217; on
    canoes 231; on cotton 28; on food 35;
    and guns 85, 86; on iron 77, 82; on
    livestock 43, 52; on Sesse 240; on slaves
    116, 122, 123, 124, 128, 163-4; on
    trade 156, 167, 170-1; on war 202, 236,
    248; on weapons 218, 221
Magere 80, 218
Mair, Lucy 75
maize 21, 28-9
markets 136, 138, 139, 140, 141-4, 156,
    240-1
marriage 121, 122, 124, 126
marrows 29

Masai 157

Mawanda, Kabaka 5, 45, 82, 103, 112, 187, 231, 232, 244-5

Mawogola 63, 187

Mawokota 20-1, 22, 45, 47, 60, 65, 73, 75, 76, 106, 228

men: and agriculture 26; and pottery 87; role of 97-8, 122; slaves 118, 162, 164; and war 24, 179, 210; *see also* soldiers

Mengo 38, 87

metals 139: brass 84, 139, 150, 156; copper 79-80, 84-5, 139, 150, 156, 197, 245; iron 77-9, 187, 218; *see also* blacksmiths; guns; iron-working; weapons

milk 42, 46

millet 26, 27, 29

mining 77-9; *see also* metals

Mirambo 200, 202-3, 221, 234, 235

Mirim 183

missionaries 6, 8, 38, 41, 43, 99, 123, 158, 166, 171, 184, 201, 216, 225, 235-6; *see also* individual missionaries; White Fathers

Miti, J. 145, 155, 203

Mounteney-Jephson, A.J. 117

Mpoma 21

Mukasa 65, 164, 181, 183, 228

Mulira, E.M.K. 114

Mulondo, Kabaka 218

Munyonyo 242

Mutebi, Kabaka 49, 180

Mutebi II, Kabaka 181

Mutesa, Kabaka 5, 7: and armies 207, 209, 215, 221; and bodyguards 207, 214, 216; and canoes 242; coffin of 82; and copper 84-5; and currencies 145; and diseases 35; and dogs 57; and hunting 57, 66; and ivory 143, 170; and Kagwa, Apolo 129-30; and livestock 45; and loyalty 217; and navies 228, 236-7; omnipotence 11, 15; and pastoralism 43, 51, 53; personality 155; and ports 242, 243; and religion 6, 130, 201, 224; and Sesse 238, 239-40; and slavery 117, 118, 123, 125, 143, 164, 166-7, 169; and state labour 104, 239-40; and state power 236; and taxation 100; and trade 143, 153, 155, 157, 158-9, 160, 234; and war 181, 182-3, 187, 190, 198-204, 220, 236-7; and weapons 77, 85, 219, 220, 221, 222, 223, 224, 226; and wild

animals 56, 59; and women 123

Mwanga, Kabaka 5: accession 186, 219; and armies 224; deposition 37, 53, 112, 248; and famine 35, 38, 39; and ivory 61, 170-1; and livestock 43, 45, 52; and loyalty 217; and religion 6-7, 37, 61, 85-6, 112, 130, 204, 217, 224; and royal army 216; and slavery 118, 169; and state labour 111, 112; and taxation 99, 111, 112; and trade 153, 155-6; and war 181, 186, 204-5; and weapons 85-6, 186, 219, 224, 226

Mwanga I, Kabaka 49

mythology 79, 80

Nakibinge, Kabaka 5, 26, 49-50, 81, 119, 185-6, 218, 219, 244

Nambi 97

Namenyeka 48, 49

Namugala 103

navies 157, 159, 197, 227, 232-3, 235, 236-9, 243-50

Nende 181-3

Ngandu 154, 159

Nile, river 66-7, 138, 157, 160, 192

Ntusi 144, 146, 149

Nyamwezi 80, 117, 152, 161, 200, 202, 220

Nyoro: and barkcloth 72; and iron-working 82; and plundering 45; and pottery 86, 87; slaves 116, 117, 118, 121-2, 168; trade with 138, 139, 159, 160, 168; and war 186, 191, 196, 224-5; *see also* Bunyoro

O'Flaherty 35, 52, 53, 143, 169, 170, 203, 247

Ogot, Bethwell 178

onions 29, 155

Pasha, Emin 6: and agriculture 20-1, 24, 26, 30, 31; on barkcloth 71; on currencies 145; on highways 107, 108; on iron-working 77-8; on pastoralism 21, 41-3, 44; on ports 241; on pottery 87, 88; rescue of 204; on slavery 117, 120, 164; on trade 136-7, 138-9, 140, 155

pastoralism 21, 40, 44-5, 47-8, 97; *see also* cattle, livestock

pasture 43-5

peace 196-7

Pearson 35, 118-19, 200, 202
peas 27, 29
Pemba 161
Pilkington 122
plantains *see* bananas
plantations 21, 25-7, 37, 38, 39, 43, 48, 60, 63, 71
plundering 36, 43, 45, 53, 97, 111, 112, 118, 119, 189, 191, 196, 211, 212, 218
political kingdom 3-7
politics 24-5, 79, 80, 188, 189-90: and pastoralism 47-8; upheavals 10, 36-9, 53, 63, 168; *see also* foreign relations; war
population 2, 36, 38, 41, 43-4, 48, 63, 111, 116, 123, 128, 164, 165
Portal (brother of Gerald) 98
Portal, Sir Gerald 7, 99-100, 101-2, 104, 107, 109
ports 240-3
pottery 86-9
poverty 38-9, 89, 114
professions 96-7, 124; *see also* individual crafts and professions
public works, construction of 95, 103, 105, 106, 125, 139

rainfall 20, 21, 22-3, 31, 36, 69, 109, 212; *see also* droughts; flooding
religion 6-7, 23, 24, 31-2, 50, 61, 85-6, 123, 130, 201, 217, 224; *see also* gods
'religious wars' 5-7, 37, 111, 112, 204, 226
rice 28, 155
Richards, A.I. 9, 23
rivers 66-9, 108-9, 138, 212; *see also* individual rivers
roads 105, 106, 107-11, 139, 211
roots 27, 32-3; *see also* sweet potatoes
Roscoe, John: on barkcloth 71-2, 73; on basketwork 89; on canoes 228, 229, 231, 238, 242; on crops 26, 28; on currencies 145, 146, 147, 148; on death 124; on fishing 65, 67-8; on food 36, 64; historiography 8; on livestock 48, 49; on metals 76, 78, 84, 85, 139; on navies 243; on pottery 87, 88; on Sesse 238-9; on slaves 116, 123, 126, 162; on state labour 104; on taxation 101; on trade 141, 142; on war 184, 209, 210-11, 212
Rowe, J.A. 9, 154
Rumanika 154, 159, 198, 220
Rusch, Walter 10-11, 55, 97

Rwanda 41, 45, 146, 200

salt 138, 139, 140-1, 160, 231
Sanga 146
Sango 72, 74
Schiller, L. 120, 121
Scott, R. 78, 87
Semakokiro, Kabaka 5, 28, 63, 73-4, 146, 150, 151, 188-9
Sensalire 48
services 138-9
sesame 26, 27, 29
Sesse 37, 49, 65, 70, 78, 119, 197, 228, 238-40, 246, 247, 248
Sewankambo 190-1, 192, 193, 232-3
Singo 4: crops 30, 37; fishing 66; hunting 57, 63; mining 77, 78; pastoralism 21, 43, 44, 45, 46, 68; roads 107, 108; shrines 183; slaves 117; war 188, 190, 209, 212
skins 58-60, 73, 137, 138
slaves 37, 38-9, 51, 75, 95, 113-132, 150, 152-3, 156, 157, 158, 159: anti-slave treaty 161; trade in 160-170, 221, 234-5; and war 178, 200
Smith, Robert 12, 177-8, 219, 228
Snay bin Amir 152, 153, 214
Soga 47, 52, 66, 70; 117, 128, 138, 140-1, 144, 157, 160, 166-7, 190, 225, 230, 233; *see also* Busoga
soldiers 36, 43, 159, 160, 180, 182-3, 184, 196, 198, 200, 202, 209-11, 213; *see also* armies; navies; war
sorghum 21
Southwold, Martin 9, 215
Speke, John 6, 7: on barkcloth 72; on canoes 230-1; on copper 85; on crops 29; on currencies 146; on fishing 64, 65, 67, 138; on flooding 241; on food 33; on hunting 57-8; on iron-working 85; on livestock 43, 50, 51; on lions 56; on navies 245; on ports 242; on rivers 109; on roads 107; on skins 59; on slaves 114, 121, 126-7; on trade 138, 139, 140, 153-5, 156, 157, 158, 159-60; on war 208; on weapons 219, 220
sports 57, 60, 66, 219
ssazas ('counties') 4, 21, 22, 82, 186, 206-7, 208, 209
Stanley, H.M.: on animals 56, 57, 60; on bodyguards 214; on canoes 231, 232,

236-7, 242; on chiefs 225; on crops 23-4, 26, 28; on fishing 64, 67; on navies 233, 245-7; on ports 241, 242; on roads 107; on Sesse 239; on slaves 116, 117, 123, 125; on trade 234; on war 81, 197, 199, 200, 202, 204, 207-8, 209, 210, 232, 233, 246-7

Sudan 6, 159, 160, 204, 223

sugar cane 22, 27, 29

Suna, Kabaka 5, 6: and animals 56-7; bodyguard of 214, 215; death of 154, 155; and famine 34, 42; harem of 123; and human sacrifice 128; and navies 233, 234; and roads 110; and slaves 118, 123, 153, 160; and state labour 103; and taxation 99, 100; and trade 149, 152, 153, 156, 157, 159, 197-8, 233; and war 81, 192, 194-8, 210, 220; and weapons 218

Swahili 29, 157

sweet potatoes 21, 22, 24, 26-7, 28, 29, 31, 37, 38, 48, 50

Tabora 28, 135, 152, 157, 159, 171, 202

Tanzania 195

taxation 95, 98-102, 111, 112, 239-40: currencies 75, 147; exemption 97, 136; hut tax 137; of livestock 42, 52; market fees 21, 141-2, 143, 144; of *ssazas* 21; trade duties 136, 235; and war 210; *see also* labour: state; tribute

Tebandeke, Kabaka 147

Ternan, T. 118, 242

territorial expansion 1, 3, 5, 44-5, 47, 72, 74, 162, 185, 187-8, 189-94; *see also* war

textiles 70, 74, 75; *see also* barkcloth; cloth; clothing; cotton; weaving

Thomas, H.B. 78, 87

Thruston, A.B. 107-8, 118

tobacco 27, 30, 138, 139

tomatoes 27, 29

tools 30, 71, 76, 77, 78-9, 81, 83, 84, 86, 138, 139, 150, 230

Toro 30, 40, 78, 118, 141, 201

Tosh , J. 9, 136, 146

Toussaint-Samat, M. 25

trade 135-6, 189: in bananas 77; in barkcloth 52, 70, 74, 75, 136-8; coastal 6, 149-73, 197-8, 227-34; in cloth 150, 151, 152, 156, 158; in crops 27-8; duties 136, 235; in fish 138; in ivory 60, 138,

139, 150, 152, 156; in livestock 42, 45, 50, 51-2, 139; in luxury commodities 150, 151, 152; in metals 77, 79-80, 138, 139, 156, 197; regulations 141-2, 156, 158; and roads 109-111; in salt 138, 139, 140-1, 231; in tobacco 138, 139; in tools 138, 139, 150; and war 197-9, 202, 249; in weapons 139, 150, 152, 155, 220-3 *see also* beads; cowries; currencies; food; markets; slaves;

Trevor-Roper, Hugh 179

tribute 95, 139, 170, 192, 199, 238 *see also* taxation

Trowell, M. 71, 144

Tucker, A.R. 156

Tutsi 41

Twaddle, Michael 10, 11, 113, 114, 162, 216, 219-20, 226

Uganda Agreement (1900) 7

Unyanyembe 135, 156, 160-1, 202, 221

Victoria, Queen of Great Britain 59

Victoria, Lake 20-1, 23, 37, 64, 65, 76, 77, 78, 95, 114, 138, 140-1, 157, 159, 161, 163-4, 167-8, 189, 196, 198, 227-50

Wakoli 170-1

Walker 36, 37

Waller, R.D. 10, 41, 158

Walukaga 82, 83, 85-6, 218

Walumbe 97

Wamala, Kabaka 46

Wamala, Lake 44, 46, 229

Wanema 49, 119, 243

war: with Bukedi 194, 201, 244; with Bunyoro *see* Bunyoro: war; with Busoga 181-2, 190, 192, 193, 194, 245; with Buvuma 117, 199, 200, 207, 208, 209, 231, 236-7, 246-7, 248; ceremonies 180-1; civil war 190, 198; 'copper war' 197-8; and economic gain 162, 178, 184-5, 187, 189, 210, 247-50; exemption from 97; failure 198-204, 248; and iron-working 81-2, 187; and livestock 45, 197; and loyalty 190-1, 194-5, 201, 203, 239, 248; motivation for 178-9, 184-5, 210; and regional strategy 162, 248-9; and religion 181-4; 'religious wars' 5-7, 37, 111, 112, 204, 226; and slaves 115, 120-1, 126, 161-2, 168, 178; and state power 178-9, 185, 197-8; tactics 177-8, 199-200, 211-13, 236-7; terminology 178; and trade 197-9, 202, 249; *see also* armies; canoes; guns; navies; territory; weapons

water 68-9

wealth 50, 84, 99, 123, 135, 136, 147, 151

weapons 79, 150, 155, 185: bows and arrows 186, 218-19; clubs 212; daggers 218; shields 187, 201, 218, 219, 226; spears 80-1, 83, 84, 85, 139-40, 187, 195, 201, 208, 211, 213, 218, 219, 226; sticks 224; swords 223; *see also* guns; trade: in weapons

weaving 89

Were, Gideon 72

wheat 28, 155

White Fathers 36, 42, 49, 58, 61, 72, 77, 83, 104, 116, 118, 119, 125, 127-8, 130, 236, 243

Wilks, I. 12, 19-20, 109

Wilson , C.T. 39, 108, 125-6, 130, 160, 222, 228, 235, 239

women: and agriculture 21, 24, 26, 32; and barkcloth 73; and basketwork 89; and economic independence 89; Hima 41, 120, 161, 162, 163; and pastoralism 42; and pottery 87; role of 97-8, 122, 165; as slaves 97, 116, 117, 118, 119, 120-3, 124, 126, 161, 162, 163, 164-5, 166-7; and war 178, 179

wood 187, 218, 228

Wright, Michael 9, 215, 222

Wrigley, Christopher 5, 9, 11, 19, 20, 23, 24, 26-7, 31, 32, 35, 40, 114, 150

yams 22, 27, 29, 33, 37

Zanzibar 6, 153, 154, 155, 159, 161, 163, 234

Zimbe, B.M. 45, 46, 83, 111, 112, 115, 125, 129, 153, 157, 181, 182-3, 186, 201, 203, 216, 217, 221, 223, 224, 225-6

Zulu 177, 188, 195